T0181225

Lecture Notes in Computer Science   14354

FoLLI Publications on Logic, Language and Information

Subline of Lecture Notes in Computer Science

More information about this series at https://link.springer.com/bookseries/558

Alexandra Pavlova · Mina Young Pedersen ·
Raffaella Bernardi
Editors

Selected Reflections in Language, Logic, and Information

ESSLLI 2019, ESSLLI 2020 and ESSLLI 2021
Student Sessions
Selected Papers

 Springer

Editors
Alexandra Pavlova 🆔
Institute of Logic and Computation
TU Wien
Vienna, Austria

Mina Young Pedersen 🆔
Department of Information Science
and Media Studies
University of Bergen
Bergen, Norway

Raffaella Bernardi 🆔
University of Trento
Rovereto, Italy

ISSN 0302-9743   ISSN 1611-3349 (electronic)
Lecture Notes in Computer Science
ISBN 978-3-031-50627-7   ISBN 978-3-031-50628-4 (eBook)
https://doi.org/10.1007/978-3-031-50628-4

This Springer imprint is published by the registered company Springer Nature Switzerland AG
The registered company address is: Gewerbestrasse 11, 6330 Cham, Switzerland

Paper in this product is recyclable.

Preface

We are very happy to present the proceedings volume containing selected papers from the Student Session of the European Summer School in Logic, Language and Information (ESSLLI) from the years 2019, 2020, and 2021. ESSLLI has been a yearly event since 1989, held under the auspices of the Association for Logic, Language and Information (FoLLI). In 2019, ESSLLI was held at the University of Latvia, Riga. Due to COVID-19, ESSLLI could not be held as a physical summer school in 2020 and 2021. But even a global pandemic could not stop the Student Session, which was organized virtually for these two summers. In 2020, the ESSLLI Student Session was held together with WeSSLLI, the online version of the North American Summer School in Logic, Language and Information (NASSLLI) at Brandeis University. In 2021, the Student Session was part of the virtual ESSLLI hosted by the Free University of Bozen-Bolzano.

The ESSLLI Student Session is an excellent venue for students to present their work and receive valuable feedback from renowned experts in their respective fields. The Student Session accepts submissions for three different tracks: Language and Computation (LaCo), Logic and Computation (LoCo), and Logic and Language (LoLa). The total number of submissions over the years 2019, 2020, and 2021 was 81. These papers went through a double-blind reviewing process. Out of these, a total of 54 were accepted as either long or short talks, or poster presentations during the summer school. After each year of the Student Session, authors of selected papers were invited to submit an extended and revised version, which went through another round of single-blind peer review. Of these papers, 13 made it into this volume. As a result, the volume displays an impressive and varied assortment of topics: ranging from exploring conversational reasoning without quantity to dissecting the pragmatic role of silence and dissent, investigating the sentence-final particle *de* in Mandarin, and proving completeness using an automated theorem prover, as well as addressing issues in formal logic and epistemic reasoning. Together, these papers offer a diverse perspective on the complex interactions between studies in logic, language, and information.

A great number of people contributed to making this volume possible. We would like to thank the ESSLLI and WeSSLLI Organizing Committees for helping us navigate the online format and for organizing the entirety of the offline and online summer schools. Thank you also to the program committee chairs for their invaluable help and support. In particular, we want to thank Darja Fišer of the ESSLLI Standing Committee and the president of FoLLI, Larry Moss. Another great thank you goes to the Student Session chairs and track co-chairs, Merijn Beeksma, Jeremie Dauphin, Asta Halkjær From, Rafael Kiesel, Matteo Manighetti, Alexandra Mayn, Dean McHugh, Jonathan Pesetsky, Vinit Ravishankar, Eugénio Ribeiro, Merel Semeijn, Dage Särg, Anna Wegmann, and Zhuoye Zhao, for their expert opinion and efficient work in the reviewing process and organization of the Student Session. We especially want to thank the chair of 2019 Matteo Manighetti for his help in the editing work of this volume. Thank you to the editors-in-chief of FoLLI, Michael Moortgat and Valentin Goranko, for assistance in the process of going from a bundle of papers to a published book. We would also like to thank the excellent reviewers in both rounds of peer review. A considerable part of the research community around ESSLLI has taken part in reviewing for this volume, as can be seen in the impressive list of program committees and reviewers below. Thank you also area experts, for the support of the co-chairs and valuable feedback during the sessions. Thank you to the previous chairs of the Student Sessions for their experienced advice and for providing us with materials from the previous years. Our most important acknowledgment goes to the authors who submitted their work to the Student Session: Thank you for making the event such an exciting experience to organize and attend.

September 2023

Alexandra Pavlova
Mina Young Pedersen
Raffaella Bernardi

Organization

Editors

Alexandra Pavlova   Technische Universität Wien, Austria
Mina Young Pedersen   University of Bergen, Norway
Raffaella Bernardi   University of Trento, Italy

Program Committee Chairs

Louise McNally   Universitat Pompeu Fabra, Spain
Jurģis Šķilters   University of Latvia, Latvia
Sophia Malamud   Brandeis University, USA
James Pustejovsky   Brandeis University, USA
Raffaella Bernardi   University of Trento, Italy
Michael Moortgat   Utrecht University, The Netherlands

Local Organizing Committee Chairs

Juris Borzovs   University of Latvia, Latvia
Līga Zariņa   University of Latvia, Latvia
Diego Calvanese   Free University of Bozen-Bolzano, Italy

FoLLI Management Board

Larry Moss   Indiana University, USA
Sonja Smets   University of Amsterdam, The Netherlands
Louise McNally   Universitat Pompeu Fabra, Spain
Nina Gierasimczuk   Technical University of Denmark, Denmark
Jakub Szymanik   University of Trento, Italy
Benedikt Löwe   University of Amsterdam, The Netherlands
Pritty Patel-Grosz   University of Oslo, Norway
Philippe Schlenker   École Normale Supérieure, France
Valentin Goranko   Stockholm University, Sweden

Program Committees

Eleri Aedmaa   Institute of the Estonian Language, Estonia
Bahareh Afshari   University of Amsterdam, The Netherlands
Omar Agha   New York University, USA
Dorothy Ahn   Rutgers University, USA
Natasha Alechina   Utrecht University, The Netherlands
Maria Aloni   University of Amsterdam, The Netherlands

Alexander Göbel	Princeton University, USA
Mira Grubic	University of Potsdam, Germany
Ronald de Haan	University of Amsterdam, The Netherlands
Markus Hecher	Technische Universität Wien, Austria
Robert Henderson	University of Arizona, USA
Daniel Hoek	Virginia Polytechnic Institute and State University, USA
Lisa Hofmann	University of Stuttgart, Germany
Vincent Homer	University of Massachusetts Amherst, USA
Andrea Horbach	FernUniversität in Hagen, Germany
Shay Hucklebridge	University of Massachusetts Amherst, USA
Maria Hämeen-Anttila	University of Helsinki, Finland
Paloma Jeretič	New York University, USA
Kimberly Johnson	University of Massachusetts Amherst, USA
Hana Möller Kalpak	Stockholm University, Sweden
Ezra Keshet	University of Michigan, USA
Rafael Kiesel	Technische Universität Wien, Austria
Natasha Korotkova	Utrecht University, The Netherlands
Yusuke Kubota	National Institute for Japanese Language and Linguistics, Japan
Ekaterina Kubyshkina	Università degli Studi di Milano, Italy
Louwe B. Kuijer	University of Liverpool, UK
Florian Kunneman	Vrije Universiteit Amsterdam, The Netherlands
Stepan Kuznetsov	Russian Academy of Sciences, Russia
Andrew Lamont	University College London, UK
Gabriella Lapesa	University of Stuttgart, Germany
Pierre Larrivée	Université de Caen Normandie, France
Daniel Lassiter	University of Edinburgh, UK
Sven Laur	University of Tartu, Estonia
Kristina Liefke	Ruhr Universität Bochum, Germany
Matthias Lindemann	University of Edinburgh, UK
Fenrong Liu	Tsinghua University, China
Gunnar Lund	Harvard University, USA
Andy Lücking	Goethe-Universität Frankfurt am Main, Germany
Emar Maier	University of Groningen, The Netherlands
Didier Maillat	University of Fribourg, Switzerland
Mora Maldonado	Université de Nantes, France
Sonia Marin	University of Birmingham, UK
Laia Mayol	Universitat Pompeu Fabra, Spain
Elin McCready	Aoyama Gakuin University, Japan
Paula Menéndez-Benito	University of Göttingen, Germany
Zahra Mirrazi	University of Massachusetts Amherst, USA
Maša Močnik	Massachusetts Institute of Technology, USA
Jacques Moeschler	Université de Genève, Switzerland
Kadri Muischnek	University of Tartu, Estonia

Roland Mühlenbernd	Leibniz-Zentrum Allgemeine Sprachwissenschaft, Germany
Kaili Müürisep	University of Tartu, Estonia
Alberto Naibo	Université Paris 1 Panthéon-Sorbonne, France
Arianna Novaro	Toulouse University, France
Andrés Occhipinti Liberman	Universitat Pompeu Fabra, Spain
Tiago Oliveira	Tokyo Medical and Dental University, Japan
Edgar Onea	University of Graz, Austria
Siim Orasmaa	University of Tartu, Estonia
Magdalena Ortiz	Technische Universität Wien, Austria
Rainer Osswald	Heinrich Heine University Düsseldorf, Germany
Aybüke Özgün	University of Amsterdam, The Netherlands
Deniz Özyıldız	Universität Konstanz, Germany
Carlo Proietti	CNR, Italy
Tudor Protopopescu	City University of New York, USA
Carlos Ramisch	Aix-Marseille University, France
Louise Raynaud	University of Göttingen, Germany
Rasmus K. Rendsvig	University of Copenhagen, Denmark
Eugénio Ribeiro	Universidade de Lisboa, Portugal
Ricardo Ribeiro	Instituto Universitário de Lisboa, Portugal
Tom Roberts	University of California Santa Cruz, USA
Floris Roelofsen	University of Amsterdam, The Netherlands
Jacopo Romoli	Heinrich Heine University Düsseldorf, Germany
Eszter Ronai	Northwestern University, USA
Konstantin Sachs	Eberhard Karls Universität Tübingen, Germany
Agata Savary	François-Rabelais University of Tours, France
Anders Schlichtkrull	Aalborg University, Denmark
Fabian Schlotterbeck	Eberhard Karls Universität Tübingen, Germany
Helmut Schmid	Ludwig-Maximilians-Universität München, Germany
Jeremy Seligman	University of Auckland, New Zealand
David Shanks	McGill University, Canada
Ian Shillito	Australian National University, Australia
Kairit Sirts	University of Tartu, Estonia
Marija Slavkovik	University of Bergen, Norway
Sonja Smets	University of Amsterdam, The Netherlands
Pia Sommerauer	Vrije Universiteit Amsterdam, The Netherlands
Alexander Steen	University of Greifswald, Germany
Lutz Straß burger	Inria Research Centre Saclay - Île-de-France, France
Yasutada Sudo	University College London, UK
Peter Sutton	Universitat Pompeu Fabra, Spain
Jakub Szymanik	University of Trento, Italy
Radek Šimík	Charles University, Czechia
Mike Tabatowski	Northwestern University, USA
Eri Tanaka	Osaka University, Japan
Nadine Theiler	University of Amsterdam, The Netherlands
Leon van der Torre	University of Luxembourg, Luxembourg

Lucas Tual	Université de Genève, Switzerland
Wataru Uegaki	University of Edinburgh, UK
Carla Umbach	Leibniz-Zentrum für Allgemeine Sprachwissenschaft, Germany
Fernando Velázquez-Quesada	University of Amsterdam, The Netherlands
Hennie van der Vliet	Vrije Universiteit Amsterdam, The Netherlands
Jørgen Villadsen	Technical University of Denmark, Denmark
Ivan Vulić	University of Cambridge, UK
Johannes Wahle	German Center for Neurodegenerative Diseases, Germany
Yanjing Wang	Peking University, China
Yì N. Wáng	Sun Yat-sen University, China
Alex Warstadt	ETH Zürich, Switzerland
Matthijs Westera	Universiteit Leiden, The Netherlands
Emil Weydert	University of Luxembourg, Luxembourg
Sophie von Wietersheim	Eberhard Karls Universität Tübingen, Germany
Malte Willer	University of Chicago, USA
Yoad Winter	Utrecht University, The Netherlands
Yimei Xiang	Rutgers University, USA
Fan Yang	University of Helsinki, Finland
Wenpeng Yin	Pennsylvania State University, USA
Hedde Zeijlstra	University of Göttingen, Germany
Zhuoye Zhao	New York University, USA
Sarah Zobel	Humboldt Universität zu Berlin, Germany
Giorgia Zorzi	Western Norway University of Applied Sciences, Norway
Thomas Ågotnes	University of Bergen, Norway

Additional Reviewers

Chris Barker
Moshe E. Bar-Lev
Francesco Belardinelli
Keny Chatain
Ivano Ciardelli
Cornelia Ebert
Patrick Elliott
Peter van Elswyk
Thorsten Engesser
Rustam Galimullin
Berit Gehrke
Sanford Goldberg
Umberto Grandi

Jens Ulrik Hansen
Andreas Herzig
Justin Khoo
Manuel Križ
Jérémy Ledent
Haoze Li
Mingming Liu
Teresa Marques
Olav Mueller-Reichau
Michael Moortgat
Sergio Rajsbaum
Agata Renans
Christian Retore

Robert van Rooij

Paolo Santorio

Merel Scholman

Todd Snider

Benjamin Spector

Thomas Studer

Alessandra Tanesini

Zoi Terzopoulou

Contents

Conversational Reasoning in the Absence of Quantity

Cathy Agyemang[✉]

Department of Cognitive Science, Carleton University, Ottawa K1S 5B6, Canada
cathyagyemang@cmail.carleton.ca

Abstract. Fox (2014) argues that cancelling the Maxim of Quantity can minimally dissociate between the pragmatic (primarily neo-Gricean) and grammatical approaches to scalar implicature. Under the pragmatic approach, scalar implicatures only arise as a result of adherence to the maxim of Quantity. The grammatical approach can predict that scalar implicatures remain available, in principle, when Quantity is not a conversational requirement as they arise from mechanisms independent of the maxim of Quantity. The present study operationalizes Fox's game-show scenario into an experiment in which participants are tasked with determining which items are associated with money. The host, who is reticent about their knowledge, provides partial information (disjunctions and numerals) as hints to help the contestants. Experimental results demonstrated that participants can strengthen the meaning of disjunctions and numerals to help them make judgments about the relevant alternatives. The present work provides experimental evidence for the availability of scalar implicatures in a conversational context where the speaker does not obey the maxim of Quantity.

Keywords: Maxim of Quantity · Scalar Implicature · Exhaustification · Probability Judgments · Experiment

1 Introduction

Scalar implicatures strengthen the basic meaning of a sentence by maximizing the quantity of information communicated to a listener. For example, the disjunction *Susie ate cake or ice-cream* can be strengthened from its basic (literal) meaning *Susie ate cake or ice-cream*, **or both** to an exclusive disjunction, *Susie ate cake **or** ice-cream, **but not both**.* [15,16]. The mechanism by which scalar implicatures arise is the subject of debate. The derivation of scalar implicatures has been described by two approaches: the pragmatic approach, specifically, neo-Gricean [16,18] and the grammatical approach [7,11]. These approaches differ primarily in whether the conceptual burden of generating scalar implicatures rests with post-compositional mechanisms based on conversational reasoning or if they are the result of language-specific operations and parsing preferences [6,7,11]. Under this pragmatic approach, scalar implicatures are the results of the adherence the conversational maxim of Quantity. Quantity stipulates that

A. Pavlova et al. (Eds.): ESSLLI 2019/2020/2021, LNCS 14354, pp. 1–13, 2024.
https://doi.org/10.1007/978-3-031-50628-4_1

a conversational contribution is required to be maximally informative to the current purposes of the exchange and is based on the presumption that the speaker aims to participate cooperatively towards the conversational goals. Alternatively, the grammatical approach (also known as the hybrid approach; [33]) establishes that scalar implicatures do not arise from the maxim of Quantity and are instead computed as a result of a linguistic operator akin to *only* being optionally applied to a sentence that is ambiguous between a basic and strengthened meaning [6,7].

Noting that the neo-Gricean pragmatic approach affirms that the maxim of Quantity is necessary to generate scalar implicatures, while the grammatical approach does not, Fox indicates that cancelling the maxim of Quantity as a conversational requirement would lead to contrasting predictions about the availability of scalar implicatures. Fox motivates this further using the example of a game-show scenario where the host, as the conversational speaker, is not required to be maximally informative to a contestant [12]. The current study constructs an experimental design based on Fox's game show to investigate the availability of scalar implicatures when the maxim of Quantity is cancelled.[1]

1.1   Scalar Implicature Through Pragmatic Strengthening

Traditional Gricean pragmatics and neo-Gricean pragmatics establishes that scalar implicatures are the result of the maxim of Quantity [16]. Specifically, Quantity leads to the derivation of the so-called primary scalar implicature [27]. The primary scalar implicature is derived from the listener presuming that the speaker would be maximally informative for the purposes of the conversation and as such inferring that the basic meaning of the sentence is false. In the aforementioned example, the listener reasons that it is not the case that speaker believes Susie had both cake *and* ice-cream, otherwise the speaker would simply state this. This interpretation is further strengthened by the secondary scalar implicature which denies the stronger scalar alternative. Using the opinionatedness criterion, listeners adopt the reasoning that a speaker is opinionated on the falsehood of a claim that is stronger than what is asserted (e.g., denying the conjunction in the case of disjunction). This also known as the competence assumption, [31]; experthood assumption [28]; and authority assumption [13]). Following the example once again, the listener reasons that the speaker believes that Susie had cake *or* ice-cream, *but not both*.

In the neo-Gricean pragmatic view, the secondary scalar implicature follows necessarily from the primary scalar implicature through the epistemic step, which is the presumptive belief about a speaker's knowledge states [9,27,28] based on the opinionatedness criterion. Therefore, under Quantity, the conversational contribution is presumed to represent all of the speaker's knowledge, which ultimately strengthens the asserted statement by denying an even stronger claim.

---

[1] As noted by an anonymous reviewer, it should be emphasized that the cancellation of Quantity is a theoretical move proposed by Fox and not a guaranteed fact of the game show scenario. The status of the cooperation in strategic conversations, such as the one presented in this paper, is briefly discussed in the conclusion.

1.2   Scalar Implicature Through Grammatical Exhaustification

Grammatical exhaustification is the application of a covert operator *exh*, analogous to the term *only*, which can parse the sentence to a strengthened meaning. Similar to the neo-Gricean pragmatic account, the grammatical approach derives inferences by defining relevant alternatives to what could have been said. Instead of denying the scalar alternatives using pragmatic reasoning, a exhaustification operator (*exh*) is applied to the sentence's meaning. Grammatical exhaustification is marked by optionality, as there is no specification on when the strengthened meaning should be the preferred interpretation in comparison to the basic meaning. Grammatical exhaustification allows both the basic and the strengthened meaning to be available to a listener but does not provide any influence as to how the ambiguity in interpretation is resolved. How a listener decides between the candidate interpretations has been argued to occur through pragmatic mechanisms (see strongest meaning hypothesis, originally in [8]). In this formulation, the use of *exh* is justified by contextual information that suggests that the strengthened meaning is more likely.

2   Background

The objective of Fox's thought experiment on cancelling Quantity is to demonstrate the difference in how the neo-Gricean pragmatic approach and grammatical exhaustification account for circumstances when a speaker does not need to communicate all the information relevant to the conversational goals. This pragmatic approach predicts that if the maxim of Quantity is no longer a conversational requirement, then scalar implicatures should not be available. The grammatical approach under exhaustification predicts that scalar implicatures should *in principle* be available as an interpretation despite Quantity being cancelled as part of the conversation.

Fox presents a hypothetical game show scenario, where there are five boxes out of a hundred that have a million dollars inside. The game show host knows which boxes have money inside of them but mentions that she will not explicitly tell the contestants this information, deactivating the maxim of Quantity. The host will provide the contestant with some partial information to help them make a choice. Fox illustrates one potential round of the game show (p. 12):

(1)   There is money in box 20 or 25.

The scalar implicature that could be computed from (1) is that there is money either in box 20 or there is money in box 25, but not both. An inclusive interpretation where the implicature is not generated could possibly arise given the parameters of the game (cancellation of Quantity)[2], such as in (2):

(2)   There is money in box 20 or 25 or both.

To reiterate, under the neo-Gricean pragmatic approach, implicatures are derived from conversational maxims. Since the maxim of Quantity is deactivated in the context of a game show, under this view the listener should not be able generate the scalar implicature from (1). Under the neo-Gricean pragmatic approach, both (1) and (2) represent an inclusive disjunction. Since Quantity is suspended, a listener operating under this approach cannot derive the scalar implicature that the speaker believes it is false that there is money in both box 20 or 25.

Fox further demonstrates that it is acceptable for a contestant to refute that there is money in both box 20 and 25 when given (1) as a hint, where exclusivity is available and it is odd to refute this when given (2) as a hint where it is not [12].

The grammatical approach predicts that scalar implicatures should be available despite Quantity being deactivated as they arise through grammatical processes rather than pragmatic strengthening. Specifically, through grammatical exhaustification exh[3]

(3) $p \vee q$
        $exh(p \vee q)$
        $(p \vee q) \wedge \neg(p \wedge q)$

While Fox's original characterization only includes disjunctive statements, this study extends this line of reasoning to numerals. This is of particular interest since the scalar implicatures that arise from numerals are demonstrably salient and often preferred in certain contexts [19,22][4] Consider (4)

(4)   a. There is money in one box.
        b. There is money in *exactly* one box.
        c. There is money in *at least* one box.

---

[2] Note that there is both an implicit and explicit cancellation of Quantity. The maxim of Quantity is contextually cancelled under the presumption that the purpose of the game show is not to simply tell the contestant where the money is, whether the host is aware or not. This is reinforced through explicit cancellation as the host is specifically described to be aware of where the money is and is unwilling to let the contestant know.

[3] The exhaustification operator represents the conjunction of two propositions. The first being that what is asserted is true, and the other is that the relevant alternatives that are not entailed by this assertion is false [29,33]. Note that this is a similar formulation to the strongest meaning hypothesis [8].

[4] It should also be noted that some pragmatic theoretical frameworks consider scalar implicatures in numerals to be the result of semantic (grammatical) mechanisms, when they do not otherwise endorse the grammatical exhaustification approach for scalar implicatures. See Geurts and Breheny, respectively, [5,14] for discussion on the "ambiguity" view and "exactly-one" view.

The availability of scalar implicatures in this case is particularly relevant to addressing a Question Under Discussion (QUD). A QUD is indicates the topic of discourse at a given moment in the conversation. The QUD is representative of a speaker's beliefs, goals and intentions [24,25]. A strengthened reading as in (4-b) would be a precise answer to the QUD of the number of boxes contain a million dollars. This should be greatly preferred to a basic reading as in (4-c). Answering of a Question Under Discussion (QUD) requires the determination of the truth value of relevant alternatives and is further specified by the number of alternatives that can answer the question. Thus, an answer will fully or partially satisfy a question by asserting or denying at least one of the specified alternatives [17,26]. Scalar implicatures reduces the set of alternatives that could sufficiently provide an answer to the QUD.

Going further, it is likely that a strengthened meaning derived from a scalar numeral as in (4) compared a disjunctive sentence (1) is more useful to a contestant in this scenario. It would be more informative to know that there is *exactly* one box that contains a million dollars than to know that either box 20 or box 25 *but not both* have a million dollars. It is of interest to determine there are any significant empirical differences in how participants reason with disjunctions and numerals.

Related investigations into the availability and computation of scalar implicatures outside of fully cooperative contexts have demonstrated scalar implicatures are still available. For example, scalar implicatures were demonstrably generated when the speaker is portrayed to not be well-informed [9]. However, it has also been shown that scalar implicatures are often generated in lower quantities (e.g., Dulcinati et al., [10]), and when they are generated they are more likely be cancelled upon revision [23]. The general rationale given for this is that the scalar implicature are cancelled based on the unreliability of the information conveyed and the listener's intuitions of the speaker's belief states.

3   Experiment

3.1   Research Question

The current study aims to empirically answer the fundamental question of the extent that scalar implicatures remain available when Quantity is cancelled. This study compares the neo-Gricean pragmatic approach, which predicts that scalar implicatures are not available in Fox's game show scenario to the grammatical approach which makes the opposite prediction.

3.2   Methods

Participants. 210 participants were recruited either as volunteers from a community sample or as students from the Carleton University undergraduate research pool. Volunteers received an invitation to the study shared via social media and did not receive any compensation for their participation. Undergraduate participants received partial course credit (0.25%) in an introductory Cognitive Science course. The study was approved by the Carleton University Research Ethics Board.

3.3   Design and Materials

The present study adapted Fox's game scenario paradigm, using a 2(Implicature Availability) X 2(Previous Outcome) X 2(Scalar Item) within-subjects design, where the participant saw a disjunction or a numeral that either licenses or cancels a scalar implicature. Participants saw four disjunctive sentences and four numerals. Additionally, the participants were informed of the approximate likelihood associated with a particular answer based on the host's hint and the outcome (winning or losing) from a previous contestant. Response choices and response time data (in seconds) were collected. See Tables 1 and 2 for item design. Response time data was comprised of the time to fully read the scenario and make a decision about which alternative is more likely.

Table 1. Disjunction experimental item design.

Your task is to choose a numbered box. There are 100 numbered boxes in total and five of them contain a million dollar prize. The host tells the first contestant that there is money in [**box 20 or box 25/box 20 or box 25 both**]. This contestant picks box 20 and [**finds a million dollars there/ discovers that the box is empty**]. Imagine you are the next contestant in this game.
The host does not give you any new hints. Which action are you most likely to take?
a.) Choose box 25
b.) Choose another box

Table 2. Numerals experimental item design.

Your task is to choose a numbered door. There are eight numbered doors and four of them are associated with a million dollar prize. The host tells the first contestant that there is money associated with [**one/at least one**] door with a number less than 3. The contestant before you picks Door 1 and [**wins a million dollars /does not win any money**]. Imagine you are the next contestant in this game. The host does not give you any new hints. Which action are you most likely to take?
a.) Choose Door 2
b.) Choose another door

Predictions. Under the neo-Gricean pragmatic approach, there should be no difference between disjunctions as scalar implicatures are conceptually unavailable. Both disjunctions ought to be interpreted inclusively (e.g., there is money in box 20 or 25 or both). Therefore, participants should base their judgments solely on whether the previous contestant who chose one of the specified disjuncts had won or lost. If the previous contestant had won, the listener can reason that it is possible that the other disjunct is also associated with money (box 25). As there was already money associated with one of the disjuncts, the likelihood of the other disjunct is not higher than another option. Thus, participants should be relatively equally likely to choose between the specific disjunct and another option. If the previous contestant had lost, the participant should reason that the likelihood of there being money in the other disjunct is higher than another non-specific option.

As scalar implicatures remain accessible to a listener in the grammatical approach, this account predicts is that there should be an interaction between the implicature (whether it is available or unavailable) and the previous outcome (winning or losing). Specifically, when the previous contestant does win money, participants under the condition where the implicature is available (e.g., box 20 or box 25 ⇒ but not both) should reason that there was money associated with *only* one of the disjuncts. They should then find it more likely that there is money in another option as opposed to the other disjunct. When the implicature is unavailable (box 20 or box 25 **or both**) and the previous contestant had won, participants should be equally likely to choose the other disjunct (box 25) and another box. In this case, having money associated with one disjunct does not negate that there is also money associated with the other. Consistent with the neo-Gricean pragmatic approach, when the previous contestant lost, participants ought to choose the specified alternative (e.g., box 25) regardless of whether the implicature is available or unavailable. Table 3 outlines the experimental conditions and their predicted outcomes under the competing approaches.

Table 3. Predicted outcomes from neo-Gricean pragmatic and grammatical approaches for disjunctions.

Approach	Disjunction	Previous Outcome	Predicted Choices
Pragmatic	**box 20 or 25**	**won**	**another box ≈ box 25**
	box 20 or 25 or both	won	another box ≈ box 25
	box 20 or 25 or both	lost	box 25 > another box
	box 20 or 25	lost	box 25 > another box
Grammatical	**box or 25**	**won**	**another box > box 25**
	box 20 or 25 or both	won	another box ≈ box 25
	box 20 or 25 or both	lost	box 25 > another box
	box 20 or 25	lost	box 25 > another box

For the condition in bold, the neo-Gricean pragmatic and grammatical approaches differ in their predicted choices, due to the debate on the availability of the implicature. While only the predictions for the disjunctions are presented here, the same logic applies for numerals. Specifically, when there is money in one of two options (e.g., door 1, door 2) and the previous contestant won, the neo-Gricean pragmatic approach predicts that a specified alternative (e.g., door 2) and the choice for "another option" should be equally likely. The grammatical approach instead predicts a preference for another option over the specified alternative, due to the availability of the implicature *exactly* one.

8   C. Agyemang

For the response times, the results may be consistent with the respective literature on numerals and disjunctions. Namely, the basic interpretation in disjunctions will be faster to process compared to its strengthened counterpart [21, 30]. For numerals, the opposite finding could arise, where the strengthened meaning would be more easily accessed to the basic counterpart [19, 22]. That said, empirical data is lacking on the time course of scalar implicature when conversational maxims do not apply. Similarly, there may be emergent patterns resulting of one of the alternatives being asserted or negated (e.g., faster responses times when the previous contestant won after picking a given box), although what they might be is unclear.

3.4   Results

Descriptive Statistics. Extreme outliers were identified using the boxplot method and further corroborated using the interquartile range. Outliers were trimmed from the dataset before subsequent analysis. Table 4 denotes the mean proportions of responses for the alternative given in the experimental item (e.g., box 25) and the mean response times per experimental condition. The greater the numerical value, the more choices were made for the specified alternative. Conversely, the smaller the numerical value, the more choice were made for "another option".

Table 4. Response proportions and response times (s) and standard errors for each experimental condition.

Item	Implicature	Prev. Outcome	Response Prop'n (SE)	RT (SE)
Disjunctions	Available	Won	0.22 (0.05)	32.1 (1.6)
	Available	Lost	0.82 (0.05)	27.4 (1.5)
	Unavailable	Lost	0.86 (0.04)	29.2 (1.5)
	Unavailable	Won	0.39 (0.06)	33.6 (2.0)
Numerals	Available	Won	0.26 (0.06)	31.0 (1.8)
	Available	Lost	0.86 (0.04)	28.5 (1.8)
	Unavailable	Lost	0.81 (0.05)	27.8 (1.4)
	Unavailable	Won	0.44 (0.07)	33.1 (1.7)

Response Times. Response times were collected as the total time for the participant to read the context and make a response to the question of interest. Response times were transformed to a logarithmic scale to approximate normality and were subsequently analyzed[5] using a linear mixed model with the "lmer" function from the "lme4" package in R [4]. Implicature availability and prior outcome were coded as fixed effects. Based on recommendations by Barr et al.

---

[5] Please note that the analyses presented in this paper were planned in advance as part of the author's thesis prospectus meeting.

(2013) [3], a maximal random effects structure was used, namely one that would not fail to converge. The random structure adopted a per-participant random adjustment to the fixed outcome intercept ($SD = 0.13$, $r = -0.21$). Additionally, the fixed effect of outcome was included to the random slope term. Item as a random effect was not included in the structure as it had a low variance and would fail to converge or overfit the data when added to the formula. A likelihood ratio test determined that there was significant main effect of prior outcome ($\chi^2(1) = 16.06$, $p < 0.0001$). If previous contestant won, participants were on average four seconds slower to respond (32.1 s) than if the previous contestant lost (28.1 s; $\beta = -0.13$, $t = -4.04$, $p < 0.0001$). The p-value was adjusted using the Tukey method to correct for multiple comparisons. There was no influence of the type of scalar item (disjunction or numeral) on the response time ($\chi^2(1) = 2.62$, $p = 0.11$). Likewise, there was no main effect of implicature ($\chi^2(1) = 0.76$, $p = 0.38$). Looking at the relationship between response times and response choices, while not significant, a linear regression suggests a general trend ($\beta = 0.22$, $t = 0.82$ $p = 0.41$)[6]. Participants were slightly faster to choose the given alternative (29.1 s) compared to choosing another option (31.4 s). This effect arose independently of the effects prior outcome, type of scalar item or the availability of the implicature.

Response Choices. Response choices for both disjunctions and numerals were analyzed using a logistic mixed model with the "glmer" function from the "lme4" package in R [4]. Implicature availability, type of scalar implicature and previous outcome were coded as fixed effects. Similarly for the random effects structure used for the response times, the model used a per-participant random adjustment to the fixed outcome intercept and outcome was added as a fixed effect to the random slopes ($SD = 1.73$, $r = -0.98$). Overall, there was a significant two-way interaction between previous outcome and implicature availability, as determined by a likelihood ratio test ($\chi^2(1) = 5.93$, $p < 0.015$). When the previous contestant won and the implicature was unavailable (e.g., box 20 or 25 or both) participants were more likely to choose the specified alternative (box 25) than when the implicature was available (box 20 or 25, but not both; $\beta = 0.84$, $z = 2.88$, $p = 0.021$; Tukey adjusted). When the previous contestant did not win money, participants strongly preferred the specified alternative regardless of whether the implicature was available or blocked ($\beta = -0.38$, $z = -0.93$, $p = 0.79$; Tukey adjusted). Again, there was no influence of the type of scalar item (disjunction or numeral) on the response choices ($\chi^2(1) = 1.53$, $p = 0.22$). This is the pattern of results that was predicted by the grammatical approach. The neo-Gricean pragmatic approach would have predicted a main effect of outcome with no interactions (two parallel lines with greater values when the previous contestant lost and smaller values when the previous contestant won). Figures 1a & 1b illustrate the proportions of response choices for the given alternative (e.g., box 25) as they are described in Table 4.

---

[6] Random effects were not included in this analysis to avoid overfitting the data.

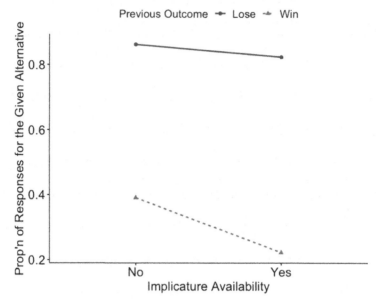

(a) Proportion of response choices for disjunctions as function of implicature availability and outcome.

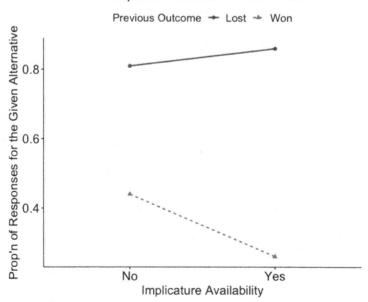

(b) Proportion of response choices for numerals as function of implicature availability and outcome.

Fig. 1. Response choices for disjunctions and numerals

4 Conclusion

4.1 Discussion of Results

The results of this study are consistent with the predictions of Fox (2014) under the grammatical exhaustification approach to scalar implicature, where, scalar implicatures remain available when Quantity is not active [12]. This current study demonstrate a listener can make use of an available scalar implicature to strengthen the meaning of a sentence. As a manipulation check, when the previous contestant lost, the predictions from either theoretical approach state that participants ought to choose the specified alternative, regardless of whether the implicature is available or not. Generally, participants chose responses consistent with this prediction, with higher proportions of choices for the specified alternative compared to the choice of another option.

Response times also support this, such that, participants were quicker to respond to an item when they are told that the participant previously lost than when they won. These results for response choice were not influenced by the type of scalar implicature (disjunction/numeral). There were no difference in response times for the specified alternative compared to another option. This result does not support the prediction that response times would be faster for those who did not generate the scalar implicature in disjunctions and faster for those who did generate them in numerals. This effect is partially attributable to the experimental design, as the response time included the time to read the scenario and then respond to the question. This metric is likely to not be precise enough to capture the respective processing mechanisms of disjunctions and numerals.

Another limitation of the study is that it was administered as a within-subjects design, where participants saw conditions in which the implicature was available and in which the implicature was not. A potential consequence of this could be that participants were comparing the difference between the plain disjunction or numeral (e.g., box 20 or 25) with such items that cancelled the implicature (e.g., box 20 or 25 or both). This comparison may have prompted individuals to generate the scalar implicature independently of Quantity being cancelled. Thus a between-subjects design should be conducted to provide additional support for the current findings. Additionally, the use of Hurford's disjunctions ("box 20 or 25 or both") to cancel the implicature presents an additional challenge to neo-Gricean pragmatics. Here, the disjunction "box 20 or 25 or both" is presumed to be equivalent to "box 20 or 25", irrespective of cancelling the maxim of Quantity ([1] and see [20] for further discussion)[7]. This observation presents added considerations for the feasibility of the neo-Gricean views of scalar implicature outside of ideal contexts.

---

[7] Note that Attentional pragmatics argues for a similar solution to Hurford's Constraint as it does for implicature availability when Quantity is cancelled, by considering semantics where "A or B" is not equivalent to "A or B or both" (see Westera [32]).

One aspect of the game show scenario that remains unclear is the extent to which this context exists outside the realm of cooperative conversation. While the context is set up such that it is understood that the host will not be fully cooperative for the contestant's goals (to win the money), the host's use of hints to guide the contestant suggest some level of cooperation towards the contestant's goals. This is of course reliant on the assumption that the host is not deceiving the contestant with her hints. Further to this, it has been argued that for non-cooperative contexts, the question is not whether scalar implicatures are available at all, but rather the "safety" of the implicature and how reliable the information is that the speaker conveys to a listener given the supporting contextual information [2]. Future studies should probe both into participants' belief about the speaker's intentions, belief and knowledge states outside of cooperative conversation, as well as level of cooperation. For example, either emphasizing that the host's hints are completely truthful despite not being maximally informative, or mentioning that the host can potentially lie in hints to deceive a contestant.

Generally, this investigation points to further insights into the conventions that persist in non-cooperative contexts. The present study demonstrate one such phenomenon, where scalar implicatures can arise in contexts were the speaker is not maximally cooperative with the listener.

Acknowledgments. I would like to express my immense gratitude to my supervisor, Dr. Raj Singh, for his fruitful conversations and astute feedback that greatly contributed in developing this work. I would also like to thank the ESSLLI reviewers for their patient and detailed feedback that was instrumental in significantly improving the quality of this research article. All remaining errors are my own.

References

1. Alonso-Ovalle, L.: Disjunction in Alternative Semantics. Ph.D. thesis, University of Massachusetst, Amherst (2006)
2. Asher, N., Lascarides, A.: Strategic conversation. Semant. Pragmat. **6**, 1–2 (2013)
3. Barr, D.J., Levy, R., Scheepers, C., Tily, H.J.: Random effects structure for confirmatory hypothesis testing: keep it maximal. J. Mem. Lang. **68**(3), 255–278 (2013)
4. Bates, D., Mächler, M., Bolker, B., Walker, S.: Fitting linear mixed-effects models using lme4. J. Stat. Softw. **67**(1), 1–48 (2015). https://doi.org/10.18637/jss.v067.i01
5. Breheny, R.: A new look at the semantics and pragmatics of numerically quantified noun phrases. J. Semant. **25**(2), 93–139 (2008)
6. Chierchia, G., Fox, D., Spector, B.: The grammatical view of scalar implicatures and the relationship between semantics and pragmatics (2008)
7. Chierchia, G., et al.: Scalar implicatures, polarity phenomena, and the syntax/pragmatics interface. Struct. Beyond **3**, 39–103 (2004)
8. Dalrymple, M., Kanazawa, M., Mchombo, S., Peters, S.: What do reciprocals mean? In: Semantics and Linguistic Theory, vol. 4, pp. 61–78 (1994)
9. Dieuleveut, A., Chemla, E., Spector, B.: Weak and strong quantity implicatures-an experimental investigation. Ms. LSCP & IJN (2016)

10. Dulcinati, G., Pouscoulous, N.: Cooperation and exhaustification. In: Pre-proceedings of Trends in Experimental Pragmatics, pp. 39–45 (2016)
11. Fox, D.: Free choice and the theory of scalar implicatures. In: Presupposition and Implicature in Compositional Semantics, pp. 71–120. Springer, Heidelberg (2007). https://doi.org/10.1057/9780230210752_4
12. Fox, D.: Cancelling the maxim of quantity: another challenge for a gricean theory of scalar implicatures. Semant. Pragmat. **7**, 1–20 (2014)
13. Geurts, B.: Quantity Implicatures. Cambridge University Press, Cambridge (2010)
14. Geurts, B., Steingarten, J.: Take 'five': the meaning and use of a number word. In: Non-Definiteness and Plurality, Benjamins, Amsterdam/Philadelphia, pp. 311–329 (2006)
15. Grice, H.P.: Studies in the Way of Words. Harvard University Press, Harvard (1989)
16. Grice, H.P.: Logic and conversation. In: Speech Acts, pp. 41–58. Brill (1975)
17. Groenendijk, J.A.G., Stokhof, M.J.B.: Studies on the Semantics of Questions and the Pragmatics of Answers. Ph.D. thesis, Univ. Amsterdam (1984)
18. Horn, L.R.: On The Semantic Properties Of Logical Operators in English. Ph.D. thesis, University of California (1972)
19. Marty, P., Chemla, E., Spector, B.: Interpreting numerals and scalar items under memory load. Lingua **133**, 152–163 (2013)
20. Meyer, M.C.: Deriving hurford's constraint. In: Semantics and Linguistic Theory, vol. 24, pp. 577–596 (2014)
21. Noveck, I.A.: When children are more logical than adults: experimental investigations of scalar implicature. Cognition **78**(2), 165–188 (2001)
22. Papafragou, A., Musolino, J.: Scalar implicatures: experiments at the semantics-pragmatics interface. Cognition **86**(3), 253–282 (2003)
23. Pryslopska, A.: Implicature in uncooperative contexts. Master's thesis, University of Tubingen (2013)
24. Roberts, C.: Information structure: Towards an integrated theory of formal pragmatics, volume 49 of. Technical report, OSU Working Papers in Linguistics (1996)
25. Roberts, C.: Context in dynamic interpretation. Handb. Pragmat. **197**, 220 (2004)
26. van Rooy, R.: Conversational implicatures and communication theory. In: Current and New Directions in Discourse and Dialogue, pp. 283–303. Springer, Heidelberg (2003). https://doi.org/10.1007/978-94-010-0019-2_13
27. Sauerland, U.: Scalar implicatures in complex sentences. Linguist. Philos. **27**(3), 367–391 (2004)
28. Sauerland, U.: The epistemic step. Exp.Pragmat. **10** (2005)
29. Singh, R.: Context, content, and the occasional costs of implicature computation. Front. Psychol. **10**, 2214 (2019)
30. Tieu, L., Romoli, J., Zhou, P., Crain, S.: Children's knowledge of free choice inferences and scalar implicatures. J. Semant. **33**(2), 269–298 (2015)
31. Van Rooij, R., Schulz, K.: Exhaustive interpretation of complex sentences. J. Logic Lang. Inform. **13**(4), 491–519 (2004)
32. Westera, M.: Hurford disjunctions: an in-depth comparison of the grammatical and the pragmatic approach. Under review (2020)
33. Zhan, L.: Scalar and ignorance inferences are both computed immediately upon encountering the sentential connective: the online processing of sentences with disjunction using the visual world paradigm. Front. Psychol. **9**, 61 (2018)

Silence, Dissent, and Common Ground

Lwenn Bussière-Caraes[✉][iD]

Institute for Logic, Language and Computation (ILLC), University of Amsterdam,
Amsterda, The Netherlands
bussiere@sequitur.eu

Abstract. In a certain picture of cooperative conversation, 'silence gives assent'. However, in adversarial contexts, structured by power dynamics, silence may be a powerful expression of dissent. To reconcile these opposite interpretations, I propose an analysis of silence as the expression of a default attitude. Given pragmatic cues, participants infer the cooperativeness of conversational settings. Depending on cooperativeness, they assign a default attitude (of assent, of suspension of judgment, of dissent) to other participants, that they take intentional silence to express. This analysis takes the main effect of speech acts to be *proposals* to update the conversational Common Ground, and highlights the necessity of assent in conversational updates.

Keywords: speech acts · silencing · Pragmatics · update semantics

1 Introduction

In the Common Ground picture (Stalnaker 1999; 2002) speech acts are proposals to update a Common Ground of information. For example, an assertion that *it is raining* is a proposal to add information to the common ground. If the proposal is accepted, the participants add the proposition that *it is raining* to the set of propositions they agree upon. Stalnaker himself does not emphasize the notion of proposal. To him, it is enough that participants voice no objection for an update to take place. In this sense, 'silence gives assent' (Sect. 2). But silence does not guarantee acceptance. In fact, 'eloquent silences' Tanesini (2018) may convey dissent (Sect. 3). I argue that context, depending on how cooperative it is, supplies an interpretation for the silence of an audience (Sect. 4). Based on pragmatic cues (I identify some), a speaker ascribes a default attitude to the audience. Then, she takes silence to express this default attitude. With this picture of silence, one can analyse non-cooperative contexts in a Common Ground perspective (Sect. 5). In turn, this gives full weight to an analysis of speech acts as update proposals: in non-cooperative contexts, the update may require more than an absence of objection to go through.

This work has received funding from from the European Research Council (ERC) under the European Union's Horizon 2020 research and innovation programme (grant agreement number 758540) within Luca Incurvatis project EXPRESS, *From the Expression of Disagreement to New Foundations for Expressivist Semantics.*

A. Pavlova et al. (Eds.): ESSLLI 2019/2020/2021, LNCS 14354, pp. 14–23, 2024.
https://doi.org/10.1007/978-3-031-50628-4_2

2   Silence and Common Ground

The Common Ground picture of conversation, developed by Stalnaker (1970; 1973; 1974; 1999; 2002), characterizes speech acts as update proposals on a Common Ground shared by the participants. The Common Ground, as a conversational backdrop, keeps track of commitments that the participants undertake. The *context set* is the intersection of such commitments, i.e. what the participants jointly commit to. If we represent commitments as propositions (i.e. sets of possible worlds), the common ground consists of possible worlds compatible with beliefs that the participants have publicized, and the context set is the intersection of such possible worlds, which is possible worlds that are compatible with what the participants have jointly committed to.

Against this backdrop, speech acts perform updates. When they are accepted, they modify the context set in such and such way. In fact, what uniquely characterizes distinct speech acts is the type of update they perform if they are accepted by the participants in conversation. The structure of the Common Ground can be more or less complex to account for the update behaviour of different speech acts. Farkas and Bruce (2010) show how to implement the effect of polar questions in a common ground like model, while Portner (2004; 2007) analyzes imperatives as proposals to update participants to-do lists. For the paradigmatic example, an assertion that p has the unique effect of adding the information that p to the context set. It does so removing all non-p worlds from the context set. Of course, this update on the context set only goes through if all the participants agree to add p to their joint commitments.

One key point to determine acceptance is that, according to Stalnaker, an update is accepted *unless it is rejected*:

> To make an assertion is to reduce the context set in a particular way, *provided that there are no objections from the other participants in the conversation* ... This effect is avoided only if the assertion is rejected. (Stalnaker 1999, p86, emphasis mine)

Stalnaker does not give much importance to the notion of proposal. He focuses on the update behaviour of speech acts. So it is enough for him to consider a weak notion of acceptance, closer to 'illocutionary uptake' (Austin 1975; Searle 1969), and to assume that acceptance is granted unless the participants state otherwise.

This goes hand in hand an idealized picture of conversation at stake in Common Ground models. Participants are assumed to be competent speakers, free to speak, and cooperative, in a Gricean manner (Grice 1967). So they share a common goal to harmonize and maximize the shared information. In this scenario, the audience has a responsibility to reject updates they do not agree with (Pettit 2002; Tanesini 2018). They are not prevented from speaking in any way, and the cooperative thing to do is to clearly indicate their assent – or dissent – with the speaker's utterances. If it is further idealized that power dynamics do not muddy the picture, or that the audience is somehow biased against accepting the discourse moves of the speaker, then acceptance arises as a default. Pettit

2002, Goldberg 2016; 2018; 1967 argue that in the absence of defeaters (power dynamics, silencing, inability of the audience to speak) silence conveys assent.

Throughout, I consider cases where silence is an intentional absence of communication. So the notion of silence at stake does not cover cases of non-verbal communication or non-communicative silences (Saville-Troike 1995). Non-verbal communications, such as writing or gestures, still deploy devices of communication (and thus separately indicate assent or dissent). Non-communicative silences, like pauses to take a breath or process speakers contributions, do not translate to an audience intention. By contrast, an intentional silence marks a conscious decision not to speak.

The stalnakerian framework interpret intentional silence as assent: the audience does not oppose what the speaker is adding to the Common Ground. While fully understanding how assent emerges as a default is complex, the assertion example provides telling clues:

> Assertions project confirmation, and therefore the move of confirming an assertion is the least marked next discourse move. (Farkas and Bruce 2010, p93)

When silence is intentional, it signifies that the participant opts out of performing an utterance. Thus, the least marked discourse move can be attributed to them. In the example, confirming an assertion. Similarly, when a speaker has authority to give orders, or make promises, a default assent arises from silence.

Goldberg (1967) likens this presumption of assent to a 'tacit acceptance procedure'.

Example 1. A committee sets a report to be tacitly accepted unless an objection is raised by May 3rd.

Example 2. The officiant instructs the audience to 'speak now or forever hold your peace'. If they remain silent, the marriage takes effect.

Example 3. The teacher tells her students to interrupt her whenever they have a question or objection.

In 'tacit acceptance procedures', the conversational setting is explicitly structured so that silence expresses assent. Similarly, the idealized common ground picture attributes to the audience a default attitude of assent (they will voice their dissent). So intentional silences are taken to convey that the least marked an absence of rejection to a proposal. Silence, being an absence of rejection, stands for assent.

3   Silent Dissent

The stalnakerian picture is rather idealistic; in real life, the situation is more complicated, and silence does not automatically mean assenting to an update. In fact, Tanesini (2018) collates examples of *eloquent silences*: silences whereby the audience expresses something distinct from assent. She follows Saville-Troike 1995 in distinguishing 'eloquent silences' both from non-verbal communication and from non-communicative silences. Non-verbal communications, such as writing, or gestures, are not silences, as they still deploy devices of communications. On the opposite end of the spectrum, pauses to take a breath, process what the speaker just said, are silences that enable communication, but don't have themselves communicative functions. In both these cases, the silent participant does not make clear an intention to convey something by their silence. Thus, in a Gricean sense, they do not communicate anything by their silence.

By contrast, eloquent silences have a communicative intention. Examples of eloquent silences abound: the politically loaded silence of white audiences when confronted to discrimination stories from persons of colour (DiAngelo 2012); the pointed silence that follows an offensive remark at a dinner party, followed by a topic change; defiant silence faced with a question, or an order, ... Far from being cooperative silences, these eloquent silences signal that the audience refuses to cooperate in the conversation (Tanesini 2018).

DiAngelo (2012) analyzes the case of 'white silence' as enmeshed with power dynamics. Its effects, during antiracist discussions, differ:

> Silence has different effects depending on what move it follows. For example, if white silence follows a story shared by a person of color about the impact of racism on their lives, that silence serves to invalidate the story. People of color who take the social risk of revealing the impact of racism only to be met by white silence are left with their vulnerability unreciprocated. [...] Conversely, when white silence follows a particularly problematic move made by a white participant, that silence supports the move by offering no interruption; in essence, white silence operates as a normative mechanism for these tactics. When white silence follows a white, antiracist stand (such as challenging one's fellow whites to racialize their perspectives), it serves to isolate the person who took that stand. This isolation is a powerful social penalty and an enticement to return to the comfort of white solidarity. In this context, white silence denies the support that is critical to other whites working to develop antiracist practice. (DiAngelo 2012, p5)

However, the crucial point is that silences from a person in power who is expected to participate and contribute in a conversation convey a refusal to engage, and thus an implicit agreement to a statu quo.

The converse also stands: in imbalanced power dynamics, silence from an inferior party can convey their disagreement in a form that is less susceptible to punishment.

Example 4. Your boss makes a sexist joke. You are not in a position to call them out on their behaviour. You remain silent, exchanging loaded glances with sympathetic coworkers

Both of these examples are cases of 'eloquent silences', according to Tanesini (2018). In a situation where the audience is expected to continue the conversation, but instead elects to remain silent, they signal that something is awry. Eloquent silences have a specific illocutionary force, that of blocking a conversation (or attempting to). Occurring after assertions, they can evoke disinterest, refusal to share the commitment the assertion seeks to introduce. After questions, they convey a refusal to answer, or engage with a certain topic. In general, they express a refusal of the audience to engage with a certain content.

> The person who is deliberately keeping silent, instead, indicates that something is amiss with the conversation which, therefore, cannot continue as normal. It may be worth noting in this regard how awkward silence often is in conversation. Silence is uncomfortable because it often marks the fact that things are not going well with the conversational exchange. (Tanesini 2018, p16)

Eloquent silences are distinct from the kind of silence at stake in the idealized stalnakerian picture. They are also extremely common, which makes clear that non-cooperative contexts, where the audience is not assumed to agree with the speaker until they explicitly claim their agreement, are far from being exceptional. And that in such contexts, silence means dissent.

What this paper aims to show is that different readings on silence, that distinguish an absence of objection from an assent, can be incorporated in a stalnakerian framework.

4   Silence and Default Attitudes

My stance is that silence is not, *per se*, an expression of assent or dissent. Instead, a conversational context supplies a *default attitude* of the audience with respect to the speaker's utterances. When the audience remains silent, they are assigned this default attitude. In an idealized context, *à la* Stalnaker, the audience is assigned a default attitude of assent when they remain silent. And, in non-cooperative contexts, silence of the audience can supply a default attitude of defiance, or dissent, with respect to the speaker's updates.

4.1   Dialogue Cooperativeness

To categorize the adversarial, or cooperative, levels of contexts, I help myself to the four scenarios of dialogue that Dutilh Novaes identifies for Prover-Skeptic argumentation games:

(1) Prover and Skeptic have a common goal, that of establishing the validity or invalidity of proofs, and no (conflicting) individual goals (they either win or lose together). They each perform a different task, but in view of a common interest (or converging individual interests). This is a purely cooperative, division-of-labor game, where neither player can 'win' alone; both players will benefit from achieving the overall goal of correctly identifying (in)validity.

(2) Prover wants her proof to go through no matter what (as this counts as a win for her), regardless of whether it is a valid proof or not. Skeptic, by contrast, wants valid proofs to go through and invalid ones to be refuted, and is neutral with respect to 'pay-offs' of the game for him (no win or loss). Here, Prover can win or lose the game, and Skeptic can neither win nor lose (the outcome is neutral for him).

(3) Skeptic wants to block (refute) the proof no matter what (as this counts as a win for him), regardless of whether it is a valid proof or not. Prover, by contrast, wants valid proofs to go through and invalid ones to be refuted, and is neutral with respect to 'pay-offs' of the game for her (no win or loss). Here, Skeptic can win or lose the game, and Prover can neither win nor lose (the outcome is neutral for her).

(4) At a lower level, the game is a classical adversarial, zero-sum game: Prover wins if the proof goes through, Skeptic wins if the proof is refuted or otherwise blocked. But, at a higher level, they are in fact cooperating to establish whether a proof is valid or not.

(Dutilh Novaes 2020, p55sq)

Dutilh Novaes applies these different scenarii to particular dialogues, whose practice is exemplified in mathematical proofs. However, the taxonomy is useful when extended to casual, or normal conversations to gauge their level of cooperativeness or adversariality:

1. **Fully cooperative dialogue:** Speaker and Audience have a common conversational goal. For example, to establish the truth or falsity of a claim; to settle on a movie to watch; to maximise the number of sailing-related puns in their dialogue. They have no conflicting individual goals.

2. **Semi-cooperative dialogues:**[1] Speaker and Audience conversational goals partially align. Speaker wishes to convince an agnostic Audience to have a church wedding; Speaker presents her paper to an audience of her peers; Speaker questions an Audience decision.

3. **Adversarial dialogues:** Speaker and Audience conversational goals do not align. Speaker debates an hostile Audience; a black Speaker wishes to challenge discrimination to a white Audience; Speaker orders her teenage child to clean their room.

Whether the dialogue is cooperative or adversarial, in turns, impacts how the Speaker perceives the silence of her audience. In a cooperative setting, Speaker is likely to interpret her audience's silence as assent. Her conversational move went through. She suggests an action movie, her Audience stayed silent and followed her to the DVD shelf. On the other hand, adversarial settings introduce dissent as a default attitude. When the teenage child stays silent after being asked

---

[1] This is in correspondence with Dutilh Novaes' (2) and (3) scenarii of Prover-Skeptic dialogues, where Prover and Skeptic individual goals conflict in some respect. These scenarii are semi-cooperative in that one of the participants is neutral with respect to the conversational outcome.

to clean their room, they express their rebuttal of the imperative. Finally, semi-cooperative settings introduce an interesting read on silence. Speaker answers an Audience question about her paper. Her Audience remains silent, not expressing assent or dissent. Speaker deduces that she has to provide more information to ground her claim.

4.2   Identifying Dialogue Situations

How the speaker perceives the dialogue situation, whether it is more or less adversarial, influences the default attitude she attributes to her audience. In a fully cooperative situation, the 'tacit acceptance procedure' of idealized stalnakerian models applies. By contrast, in adversarial situations, silence is perceived as hostile, a refusal to let a speech act go through. The perceived cooperativeness is influenced by the explicit discourse moves that the participants make in the conversation, and by various pragmatic factors. Discourse moves can convey cooperation or adversariality in a more or less overt manner: enthusiastic assent, explicit rejections, etc. If an audience rejects every move that the speaker attempts, the speaker will identify an adversarial situation. But speakers and audience also use pragmatic cues to assess cooperation, and thus attribute default attitudes. I identify some of these pragmatic cues.

Priors. A speaker goes in a conversation with certain beliefs concerning the other participants and whether the conversation is cooperative. When she tells her teenage child to clean their room, she expects some resistance. When she discusses which movie to watch with her friend, she assumes that their conversational goals align: find a movie that they will both enjoy.

These priors are of course defeasible. At any point, the speaker may reassess the situation, and discover that a setting is more, or less cooperative than she previously thought. She can also investigate whether her audience actually holds the default attitude she attributes them.

Example 5. After asking her child to clean their room, and meeting only silence, the speaker checks in. 'Did you hear me? Does that mean you will clean up?'

These priors are influenced by what the speaker knows of the audience beliefs and attitude, but also by the sociological factors at stake, such as power dynamics, epistemic authority, politeness, etc.

Power Dynamics and Adversariality. Sociological factors also influence the perceived cooperativeness of a situation. When a speaker is an authority in a conversation (be it because she has more socio-political power, or more knowledge), it is likely that silence indicates audience assent (6). If the audience is an authority, then the speaker can interpret silence as unconvinced, or hostile.

Example 6. A teacher is giving a history lesson in front of her class. She is confident that she knows more on the lesson topic than her students.

Example 7. A student has claimed that dolphins are mammals. Her professor asks her to justify her claim. The student goes through her evidence.

In (6), as long as there are no objections to clear up, the teacher can safely assumes that her students' silence stands for an assent to update the common ground with the contents of her lesson. In a context such as (7), the student assumes that, when her teacher keeps silent, she needs to provide more evidence. The update is not going through unless her audience explicitly allows it.

Paralinguistic Cues. A third type of pragmatic factors to consider are paralinguistic cues. It is very rare that an audience is entirely 'silent', in the sense delineated by Tanesini. Instead, audiences nod, look skeptical, smile, frown, hum with interest, etc. These para-linguistic cues come into play for the speaker to distinguish between an audience that is silent because they assent to the update proposals, and an audience keeping silence out of disinterest, or boredom.

Example 8. A teacher is giving a history lesson in front of her class. Upon seeing perplexed frowns, she realizes that she needs to provide more details on the changes in U.S. foreign policy following the Cuba missile crisis.

Example 9. I advise my friend to read *The Last Girl Scout.* He seems unsure, so I make a case for the book, until he hums with interest.

The paralinguistic cues allow the speaker to interpret in a more fine-grained manner attitude her audience holds towards her discourse. She can change her perception of the cooperativeness degree of a conversation.

4.3   From Cooperativeness to Interpretation of Silence

Following different pragmatic cues, more or less overt, a speaker determines whether a dialogue is cooperative or adversarial. From this, she attributes a default attitude to her audience. If the conversational situation is cooperative, she assumes that her audience shares her conversational goals, and thus that the less marked attitude is assent. In cooperative settings, silence is interpreted as an assent. If the conversational situation is adversarial, she assumes that her discourse move is not accepted until an explicit confirmation is reached. In adversarial setting, silence is interpreted as dissent. If the situation is semi-cooperative, the speaker may be unsure whether her discourse move is accepted or rejected, unless there is an explicit confirmation or rejection from the audience. The semi-cooperative setting makes it likely that a silence is an invitation to ground her assertion with evidence, explain her question, show that her request makes sense. The speaker attributes these default attitudes to an audience until proven otherwise; either by an explicit discourse move (confirmation, rejection), or by pragmatic cues that indicate changes in the cooperativeness.

5   Silence and Updates

The perceived cooperativeness of a conversation provides three interpretations of silence:

1. Fully cooperative conversation: silence means assent
2. Semi-cooperative conversation: silence means 'tell me more!'
3. Adversarial conversation: silence means dissent

This allows us to define distinct behaviours of conversational updates depending on conversational cooperativeness. Speech acts can be taken, for simplicity sake, to be proposals to update a (more or less complex) conversational common ground in certain ways (Sect. 2). These proposals may be accepted or rejected by the participants in a conversation. Or the audience may suspend their judgment, leaving the common ground undecided on the speech act, and keeping both worlds compatible and incompatible with the update in the context set.

The perceived cooperativeness of a conversation determines the default result of a proposal:

1. Fully cooperative conversation: The update goes through *unless explicitly rejected by the participants*.
2. Semi-cooperative conversation: The update remains undecided *until the participants assent or dissent*.
3. Adversarial conversation: The update is rejected *unless explicitly accepted by the participants*.

In turn, this requires us to separate two essential effects of speech acts. First, the effect of adding to the conversational record that a proposal to update the common ground in a certain way was made. Second, the effect of updating the common ground *only if* the proposal is accepted. The requirements for acceptance can be determined depending on the cooperativeness of the dialogue. In some cases, acceptance only requires an absence of rejection. In others, acceptance needs to be made explicit, or even enthusiastic.

6   Conclusions

Taking silence to express a default attitude, not necessarily an assent, complicates the Stalnakerian picture. But it also shows how we can model, and even make use of non-cooperative contexts when analyzing the effects of speech acts on a less idealized picture of conversation. Moreover, taking seriously silence emphasizes the talk of 'proposals' when considering the effect of speech acts on common ground. While the full update effect of a speech act can only occur if the participants assent to the update, the first and main effect of most speech acts is to issue a *proposal* to update. No matter the reaction of the participants, the proposal goes on the conversational record. And considering that silence might not mean immediate assent also highlights the part that pragmatic cues play into determining uptake from the participants in a conversation.

References

Austin, J.L.: How to do things with words. In: Sbisà, J.O. (ed.) Urmson Marina, 2nd edn. (1975)

DiAngelo, R.: Nothing to add: a challenge to white silence in racial discussions. Understand. Dismantling Privil. **2**, 1–17 (2012)

Novaes, C.D.: The Dialogical Roots of Deduction: Historical, Cognitive, and Philosophical Perspectives on Reasoning. Cambridge University Press, Cambridge (2020)

Farkas, D.F., Bruce, K.B.: On reacting to assertions and polar questions. J. Semant. **27**(1), 81–118 (2010)

Goldberg, S.: Arrogance silence and silencing. Proc. Aristot. Soc. **90**, 93–112 (2016)

Goldberg, S.: Dissent: Ethics and epistemology. In: Johnson, C.R. (ed.) Voicing Dissent. Routledge (2018)

Goldberg, S.: Assertion, Silence, and the Norms of Public Reaction. Manuscript. Grice, Herbert Paul. Studies in the Way of Words. Harvard University Press, Cambridge (1967)

Grice, H.P.: Studies in the Way of Words. Harvard University Press, Cambridge (1967)

Pettit, P.: Enfranchising Silence. In: Rules, Reasons, Norms, pp. 367–78. Clarendon Press (2002)

Portner, P.: The semantics of imperatives within a theory of clause types. In: Proceedings of Semantics and Linguistic Theory, vol. 14. CLC Publications (2004)

Portner, P.: Imperatives and modals. Nat. Lang. Seman. **15**, 351–383 (2007)

Saville-Troike, M.: The place of silence in an integrated theory of communication. In: Tannen, D., Saville-Troike, M. (eds.) Perspective on Silence, 2nd edn, pp. 3–18. Ablex Publishing Corporation (1995)

Searle, J.R.: Speech Acts. Cambridge University Press, Cambridge (1969)

Stalnaker, R.C.: Pragmatics. In: Synthese, vol. 22 (1970)

Stalnaker, R.C.: Presuppositions. J. Philos. Log. **2**, 447–57 (1973)

Stalnaker, R.C.: Pragmatic presuppositions. In: Munitz, M., Under P. Reprinted in Stalnaker (eds.) Semantics and Philosophy, pp. 197–213. New York University Press, New York (1974)

Stalnaker, R.C.: Context and Content. Oxford University Press, Oxford (1999)

Stalnaker, R.C.: Common ground. Linguist. Philos. **25**, 701–21 (2002)

Tanesini, A.: Eloquent silences: Silence and dissent (2018)

Sentence-Final Particle *de* in Mandarin as an Informativity Maximizer

Jun Chen[1]([✉]) and Sean Papay[2]

[1] Institute of Linguistics, University of Stuttgart, Stuttgart, Germany
jun.chen@ling.uni-stuttgart.de
[2] Institute for Natural Language Processing, University of Stuttgart, Stuttgart, Germany
sean.papay@ims.uni-stuttgart.de
https://www.ling.uni-stuttgart.de/institut/team/Chen/,
https://www.ims.uni-stuttgart.de/institut/team/Papay/

Abstract. In this study, we provide a new empirical generalization of the meaning contribution of the Mandarin sentence-final particle *de* from an information maximizer perspective. Based on the cross-entropy model, we quantify the informativity associated with the prejacent that *de* attaches to. We further explore the plausibility of applying cross-entropy methods (as well as related Kullback-Leibler divergence-based methods) across languages, as a precise model of understanding the subtle pragmatic meanings of sentence-final particles in general.

Keywords: Game-theoretic Pragmatics · Sentence-final Particle · Speaker-oriented Meaning · Cross-entropy · Rational Speech Act Model

1 Introduction

East Asian sentence-final particles (SFPs) express a range of subtle, speaker-oriented meanings that pertain to the way the speaker conveys her belief states to the listener (e.g. Kuno 1973, Chu 1998, Simpson 2014, Constant 2014). The aim of this study is to motivate employing information-theoretic methods as a way to obtain a fine-grained understanding of the non-literal meaning expressed by these particles. Specifically, we present a formal characterization of the Mandarin Chinese sentence-final particle *de*, based on cross-entropy as a part of the Rational Speech Act model (Shannon 1948, Jäger 2007, Goodman and Stuhlmüller 2013). In a nutshell, we entertain the novel idea that there is a sentence-final use of *de*, with which the speaker signals that an answer is the most informative given all the alternatives, in response to the question under discussion in the immediate discourse.

The remainder of the paper is structured as follows. We first present data demonstrating the constraints that *de*-answers are subject to in comparison against answers without the *de* particle. We then motivate an informal idea according to which the pragmatic constraint established above is captured by the intuition that *de*-answers must be the most informative in the context. This is followed by a formal implementation of information load in terms of negated cross-entropy. Afterwards we discuss potential alternatives to the RSA approach and discuss applications of the information-theoretic approach to other particles.

ⓒ The Author(s), under exclusive license to Springer Nature Switzerland AG 2024
A. Pavlova et al. (Eds.): ESSLLI 2019/2020/2021, LNCS 14354, pp. 24–43, 2024.
https://doi.org/10.1007/978-3-031-50628-4_3

2   Data

Our central empirical claim is that in a cooperative game (assuming the conversational principle of cooperativity translates into the assumption that communication is a cooperative game, cf. Merin 2011, van Rooij 2004, Jäger 2007), the speaker may add the particle *de* to a propositional answer to signal that she conveys the most informative answer to her knowledge. As far as we are concerned, this observation has not been made in the literature. Note our observation concerns a very specific case of the use of *de*. By focusing on only one novel function, we did not do justice to the rich body of research on the many independent functions of the sentence-final particle *de* in Mandarin. See Simpson and Wu (2002), Paul and Whitman (2008), Cheng (2008), Hole (2011), among others, for detailed discussions.[1]

We will limit our discussion to contrastive topic-marked answers that address an immediate prior question under discussion (QuD). We first consider the case where the QuD established in prior context is addressed via partial answers. Imagine it is in the knowledge of B that teacher Cai takes charge of reimbursement on Monday, and teacher Wang takes charge of reimbursement on the other weekdays (Tuesday till Friday).[2] Now this information is not part of mutual knowledge, i.e. it is not already known by A. Given this, B may offer a partial answer providing information about teacher Cai, together with another partial answer with B's information about teacher Wang, as shown in (1).

(1)   QuD (Speaker A): Who should I find if I want to get reimbursement? B answers:

Zhouyi shi cai laoshi fuze   baoxiao.   Cong zhouer dao zhouwu
Monday COP Cai teacher in.charge reimbursement from Tuesday till Friday
dou shi   wang laoshi fuze   baoxiao.
PRT COP Wang teacher in.charge reimbursement

'On Monday, [teacher Cai]_F is in charge of reimbursement. From Tuesday until Friday, [teacher Wang]_F is in charge of reimbursement.'

Narrow focus answers to a *wh*-question may also be formed by appending the *de* particle to the end of the sentence (Hole 2011). Crucially, however, the two partial answers in the above context do not equally lend themselves to *de*-attachment. As the contrast in (2a)–(2b) illustrates, we find that *de* felicitously attaches to the partial answer about teacher Wang. In comparison, attaching *de* to the partial answer about teacher Cai

---

[1] *De* relates to a number of focus-marking construction types, with a much broader distribution than the current scope delineated by contrastive topics. The previous characterizations of *de*'s meaning appear to be distinct from our upcoming proposal, although we consider it likely that the contribution of *de* in some or all of these environments could be unified. In the future we hope to pursue if our information optimizer meaning can be reconciled with previous proposals. We briefly point out some potential connections in footnote 7 and Sect. 3.3.

[2] We assume here that *Monday* and *Tuesday to Friday* are contrastive topics, each indexing a subquestion that is part of the prior *overall* question (Büring 2003). The subquestion corresponding to *Monday* is resolved by a contrastive focus (*teacher Cai*), which is part of the comment to the contrastive topic. Similarly, the topic *Tuesday to Friday* pairs up with the contrastive focus *teacher Wang*.

gives rise to degraded judgment.[3] Intuitively speaking, B's knowledge about teacher Wang is *more informative* given the context.[4]

(2)   QuD (Speaker A): Who should I find if I want to get reimbursement? B answers:

   a. Zhouyi shi cai laoshi fuze   baoxiao.   Cong zhouer dao
      Monday COP Cai teacher in.charge reimbursement from Tuesday until
      zhouwu dou shi Wang laoshi fuze   baoxiao   **de**.
      Friday DOU COP Wang teacher in.charge reimbursement DE
      'On Monday, [teacher Cai]$_F$ is in charge of reimbursement. From Tuesday until Friday, [teacher Wang]$_F$ is in charge of reimbursement.'

   b. ??Zhouyi shi cai laoshi fuze   baoxiao   **de**. Cong zhouer
      Monday COP Cai teacher in.charge reimbursement DE from Tuesday
      dao zhouwu dou shi Wang laoshi fuze   baoxiao.
      until Friday PRT COP Wang teacher in.charge reimbursement
      'On Monday, [teacher Cai]$_F$ is in charge of reimbursement. From Tuesday until Friday, [teacher Wang]$_F$ is in charge of reimbursement.'

The same QuD may be addressed with the *Tuesday-to-Friday* answer preceding the *Monday* answer, in which case there are two more permutational possibilities, given in (3). Still, the pattern is that *de* prefers the more informative answer about teacher Wang to the less informative answer about teacher Cai: (3a) is judged better than (3b).

(3)   QuD (Speaker A): Who should I find if I want to get reimbursement? B answers:

   a. Cong zhouer   dao zhouwu dou shi Wang laoshi fuze
      from Tuesday until Friday   PRT COP Wang teacher in.charge
      baoxiao   **de**. Zhouyi shi cai laoshi fuze   baoxiao.
      reimbursement DE Monday COP Cai teacher in.charge reimbursement
      'From Tuesday until Friday, [teacher Wang]$_F$ is in charge of reimbursement. On Monday, [teacher Cai]$_F$ is in charge of reimbursement. '

   b. ??Cong zhouer   dao zhouwu dou shi Wang laoshi fuze
      from Tuesday until Friday   PRT COP Wang teacher in.charge
      baoxiao.   Zhouyi shi cai laoshi fuze   baoxiao   **de**.
      reimbursement Monday COP Cai teacher in.charge reimbursement DE
      'From Tuesday until Friday, [teacher Wang]$_F$ is in charge of reimbursement. On Monday, [teacher Cai]$_F$ is in charge of reimbursement.'

The acceptability pattern holds for other ways to partition partial answers, as far as the contrasting partial answers differ in informativity. Thus, in (4a)–(4b), *de* cannot attach to a proposition expressing quantification over a small number of events, when

---

[3] Here the judgment has to be elicited based on the *particular* prior context. An *out-of-the-blue* utterance does not yield a similar contrast of acceptability. The same applies to subsequent reported judgments.

[4] The acceptability of (2b) is improved when the speaker wants to emphasize Monday as particularly relevant to the question under discussion under a different belief state. We return to this issue shortly.

this partial answer is contrasted against another answer expressing quantification over a majority of events. The infelicity disappears if *de* is attached to the 'majority-event' answer.

(4) QuD (Speaker A): Who should I find if I want to get reimbursement? B answers:

    a. Ou'er   shi cai laoshi fuze   baoxiao   (??**de**). Yiban
        occasionally COP Cai teacher in.charge reimbursement (DE)   usually
        shi wang laoshi fuze   baoxiao   (**de**).
        COP Wang teacher in.charge reimbursement (DE)
        'Occasionally, [teacher Cai]$_F$ is in charge of reimbursement. Usually, [teacher Wang]$_F$ is in charge of reimbursement.'

    b. Youshihou shi cai laoshi fuze   baoxiao   (??**de**). Daduoshu
        sometimes COP Cai teacher in.charge reimbursement (DE)   most
        shihou shi wang laoshi fuze   baoxiao   (**de**).
        time   COP Wang teacher in.charge reimbursement (DE)
        'Sometimes, [teacher Cai]$_F$ is in charge of reimbursement. Most of the time, [teacher Wang]$_F$ is in charge of reimbursement.'

Again, bare, *de*-less narrow focus answers receive no degraded judgment in either order, evidenced in (5).

(5) a. Ou'er   shi cai laoshi fuze   baoxiao,   yiban dou shi
        occasionally COP Cai teacher in.charge reimbursement usually PRT COP
        wang laoshi fuze   baoxiao.
        Wang teacher in.charge reimbursement
        'Occasionally, [teacher Cai]$_F$ is in charge of reimbursement. Usually, [teacher Wang]$_F$ is in charge of reimbursement.'

    b. yiban dou shi wang laoshi fuze   baoxiao,   ou'er
        usually PRT COP Wang teacher in.charge reimbursement occasionally
        shi cai laoshi fuze   baoxiao.
        COP Cai teacher in.charge reimbursement
        'Usually, [teacher Wang]$_F$ is in charge of reimbursement. Occasionally, [teacher Cai]$_F$ is in charge of reimbursement.'

The observed pattern is supported by a pilot judgment survey we conducted (20 participants, see our details in the appendix). As Fig. 1 shows, our findings reveal that when two partial answers are juxtaposed, judgments are significantly better with *de* attached to the 'more-situation' partial answer than the 'fewer-situation' one.[5] In addition, the

---

[5] An anonymous reviewer wonders if *de* can attach to both partial answers (of varying informativity) at the same time. To test this, we consulted five native speakers about the following *de*-answers in (i).

(i) QuD (Speaker A): Who should I find if I want to get reimbursement? B answers:

order of the two answers is not significant, excluding the possibility that the contrast is due to the preference for uttering the more informative partial answer earlier.[6]

Condition	Position of *de*	mean values
a.	Tue--Fri/usually *de* < Mon/occasionally	6.331
b.	Mon/occasionally < Tue--Fri/usually *de*	5.797
c.	Tue--Fri/usually < Mon/occasionally *de*	4.631
d.	Mon/occasionally *de* < Tue--Fri/usually	4.422

Fig. 1. Pattern of judgment based on permutations of partial answers with placement of *de*. Only English translation is provided. '<' represents linear precedence. Condition (a) thus reads as: *"From Tuesday until Friday/usually, Wang handles refunds de. On Monday/occasionally, Cai handles refunds."*('***': $p <0.001$; '**': $p <0.01$; 'n.s.': not significant).

Apart from partial answers, (6) shows that *de* can appear with answers that completely address a prior *wh*-question.

a. ??Cong zhouer dao zhouwu dou shi Wang laoshi fuze   baoxiao   **de**.
   from Tuesday until Friday PRT COP Wang teacher in.charge reimbursement DE
   Zhouyi shi cai laoshi fuze   baoxiao   **de**.
   Monday COP Cai teacher in.charge reimbursement DE
   'From Tuesday until Friday, [teacher Wang]_F is in charge of reimbursement. On Monday, [teacher Cai]_F is in charge of reimbursement.'

b. ??Ou'er   shi cai laoshi fuze   baoxiao   **de**. Yiban shi wang
   occasionally COP Cai teacher in.charge reimbursement DE usually COP Wang
   laoshi fuze   baoxiao   **de**.
   teacher in.charge reimbursement DE
   'Occasionally, [teacher Cai]_F is in charge of reimbursement. Usually, [teacher Wang]_F is in charge of reimbursement.'

The speakers either found the examples to be less natural compared to the sentences with one *de* as in (4), or were not sure what role *de* was playing here (note again the judgments crucially depend on the particular context here). The data are obviously very subtle. As the pilot judgment survey in Fig. 1 shows, the rating difference associated with different *de*-placement is statistically significant, but not very far apart. This would be typical if the meaning contribution of the *de* particle is derived from pragmatics (game-theoretic pragmatic meaning), instead of from grammar. A more general pattern of the placement of *de* will have to await formal experiments in the future.

---

[6] The mild differences between the (a)-sentences and the (b)-sentences could be a factor of the linear order between partial answers. With a partition into two information chunks/units in place, holding back the more informative chunk (and uttering first the less informative chunk) could lead to a violation of the maxim of Quantity. The maxim is maintained if the more informative partial answer precedes the less informative one (afterwards, what's left is now the most informative chunk available, so that no violation is incurred). In this way, our finding that it is more natural to utter first the more informative partial answer follows from independent Gricean grounds. Crucially, since both (a) and (b) sentences are rated better than (c), the constraint of *de*-placement cannot be reduced to linear precedence alone.

(6)   Context: A: Who should I find if I want to get reimbursement? B answers:

Shi   cai laoshi fuze   baoxiao   **de**.
COP Cai teacher in.charge reimbursement DE
'[Teacher Cai]$_F$ is in charge of reimbursement (there are no others).'

The fact that *de* can attach to complete answers accords well with the information maximizer characterization of *de*. If we consider a *de*-answer as providing the most informative answer to the speaker's knowledge, then the complete answer is (vacuously) the most informative answer a speaker can provide, as other alternatives than the one that corresponds to the focus value denoted by the prior question's *wh*-part are excluded.[7]

---

[7] An anonymous reviewer points out the following case where *de* cannot attach to a complete answer to a *wh*-question:

(ii)   Context: Who did John invite?
Yuehan qing-le   mali (#de).
John   invite-ASP Mali DE
'John invited Mary. '

From this we see the above pattern in contrastive partial answers does not directly generalize to all exhaustive answers. We do not have a story of the unacceptability here. We would like to point out that in some cases where a complete answer is presented via the explicit enumeration of all members that correspond to a true answer, attaching *de* to the end appears to be much better. According to our consultation, in the scenario where the following three slopes in the (a) answer are all there are that allow for skiing, adding *de* sentence-finally is quite natural, compared to the degraded (b)-answer with no enumeration. Importantly, using *de* here is better than using it with an utterance that the speaker knows is not a complete answer. For example, given the same scenario, adding *de* to a non-exhaustive answer as in (c) is less natural (to the extent that some speakers accepted it as fine, the meaning they obtained conveyed a separate dimension of speaker attitude implied by *de*, unrelated to focus marking).

(iii)   a. Context: Which slope is open to skiing?
Wangjiapo, Zhangjiapo he Zhaojiapo zhei san-chu   shi keyi huaxue de.
Wang.slope, Zhang.slope and Zhao.slope these three-place COP can ski   DE
'The three slopes, Wang's slope, Zhang's slope as well as Zhao's slope, are allowed for skiing.'

   b. Context: Which slope is open to skiing?
You san-chu   po   keyi huaxue ($^?$de).
have three-place slope can ski   DE
'Three slopes are allowed for skiing.'

   c. Context: Which slope is open to skiing?
Wangjiapo keyi huaxue ($^?$de).
Wang.slope can ski   DE
'Wang's slope is allowed for skiing.'

The pattern seems to suggest with all else controlled, *de* favors more informative answers. Also, we suggest whether explicit alternatives are offered, or contrasted, might influence the acceptability of *de*-attachment. There are other confounding factors that impact the use of the information optimizer *de* in complete answers: We find that adding the copula *shi* improves the judgment significantly in many cases, and there is also a subject-object asymmetry at play (an object focus resists *de* more than a subject focus).

Finally, under the different context in (7), *de* shifts to the 'Monday-teacher Cai' answer. Here the situation is such that teacher Wang handles reimbursement by default, hence Wang is expected by both the speaker and the listener for the purpose. The knowledge about Cai's handling of reimbursement is exceptional and not previously expected, hence it carries the higher information load. We return to the case with (7) in Sect. 4.1.

(7)   Context: There is prior knowledge that teacher Wang is much more likely than teacher Cai to handle refunds (e.g. Cai only handles refunds when Wang is on sick leave)

Zhouyi shi cai laoshi fuze   baoxiao   **de**. Cong zhouer   dao
Monday COP Cai teacher in.charge reimbursement DE from Tuesday until
zhouwu dou shi Wang laoshi fuze   baoxiao.
Friday   PRT COP Wang teacher in.charge reimbursement

'On Monday, [teacher Cai]$_F$ is in charge of reimbursement. From Tuesday until Friday, [teacher Wang]$_F$ is in charge of reimbursement.'

3   Analysis

3.1   Background

In the above we have argued that the *de* particle encodes an informativity optimizer, to the effect that the answer it attaches to is the most informative the speaker can convey to the listener. Our goal now is to provide a precise characterization of the notion of informativity that underpins our analysis. To achieve this goal we adopt a framework coupling information theory with Bayesian statistics. Specifically, we build our analysis upon the Rational Speech Act (RSA) model (Frank and Goodman, 2012, Goodman and Stuhlmüller 2013, Franke and Jäger 2012, Spector 2017), with which we measure the amount of information contained in a given proposition and compare it with that of minimally different propositions. We define informativity as the bits of information that remain missing for the hearer to figure out with certainty what the real world is like. Further assuming that the number of bits of information still missing to the hearer is finite (as long as the speaker is not lying) and calculable, we are thus able to quantify the relative informativity of competing partial answers.

Our modeling of informativity in comparing partial answers finds a predecessor in the analyses of mention-some answers. It is well known that *wh*-questions can be addressed by partial answers that only mention *some* positive instances (e.g. Hamblin 1973). The question in (8), in a context where a tourist is new to the town, is more appropriately answered by mentioning just one place where he can successfully get newspaper (a partial answer), instead of mentioning all the relevant places exhaustively (a complete answer). That is, mentioning just one element of the set of alternative, 'equally best' places suffices to resolve the question.

(8)   Where can I buy newspaper?

A more recent work from van Rooij (2004) argues that whether the mention-some reading suffices to resolve the question depends on the expected utility of the answers. Assuming asking the question is cost free, together with an 'empty' context and a set of answer rules that determine which answer will be given in which worlds, van Rooij shows that it is possible to calculate the expected utility of the *wh*-question in both mention-some and mention-all readings. Due to the property of mention-some and mention-all questions denoting two partitions that have subset relations, s.t. $Q_{\text{some}} \sqsubseteq Q_{\text{all}}$, the average utility of the mention-some reading of the question can never be higher than the utility of the corresponding mention-all reading. Importantly, there are cases where the expected utility of the two coincides: If the mention-some answer is known to be equally useful as the mention-all answer, and needs less effort or is shorter, then the *wh*-question receives the mention-some interpretation.[8]

Note the current paper will approach informativity using a system similar to van Rooij's, but a lot more specific (i.e. based on cross-entropy). van Rooij's notion of expected utility coincides exactly with cross-entropy when informativity is used as a utility function. However, the formalism in van Rooij (2004) encompasses a broad array of arbitrary utility functions in an arbitrary game, whereas our proposal only involves informativity (identifying the most informative answers, without considering other most useful answers). In this sense, van Rooij's powerful system might have been overkill, when simple information theory is sufficient.

It is also worth pointing out that the notion of expected utility that captures mention-some answers does not extend directly to the condition governing the use of a *de*-answer. The two environments differ in that *de* only requires that its prejacent have the highest informativity compared to its alternatives. This way, *de* may attach to a partial answer even if it is not as useful as the mention-all answer: It just needs to be more useful than its potential sister partial answers (e.g. *Tuesday to Friday* versus *Monday*). In addition, capturing mention-some answers heavily relies on the cost of each utterance, i.e. a mention-some answer in most cases is significantly shorter than the mention-all

---

[8] The RSA model predicts an interaction between (shared) knowledge and captures how detailed the speaker's belief states could influence a listener's interpretation. As such, it is particularly suitable for characterizing expected utility, as the latter is a quantity that depends on the speaker's belief distribution (Frank and Goodman 2012, Goodman and Stuhlmüller 2012). This advantage also makes RSA modeling a powerful tool in capturing incremental cancellation within the classic scalar implicature, e.g. uttering *some P* invites the inference that *not all P* (Horn 2005). The ability to cancel such *not-all* inference is subject to the increasing knowledge given a situation. In general, the extent to which an implicature can be cancelled depends on what the listener knows about the speaker's knowledge state. Consider a scenario with three apples in total. The speaker and the listener have the conversational goal of conveying the information about the number of red apples in the simplest way. In the case where the speaker has complete knowledge of the number of red apples, and the listener knows that the speaker has complete knowledge, then the listener is very likely to infer 'not all apples are red', upon hearing the speaker's utterance 'some apples are red'. Consider now an alternative scenario where the speaker has partial access to information about the apples, e.g. he only knows if one apple is red, and the listener knows the speaker does not have complete knowledge. Then the listener is less likely to draw a *not-all* inference upon hearing 'some apples are red', compared to the previous scenario. Thus, the implicature is 'canceled.'.

answer. Unlike the contrast between mention-some and mention-all answers, the contrasting partial answers *de* potentially attaches to does not differ much in terms of cost.

3.2 Formal Implementation

We now propose an analysis of the *de*-particle in an RSA-based Bayesian framework, in which the knowledge states of the speaker and the listener are represented probabilistically. We start with a description of our model and how it characterizes the *de* particle. We then demonstrate that alternative characterizations of informativity based on entailment faces challenges to capture the same data, offering additional motivation for our use of the probabilistic machinery. We will see later in Sect. 4 that such setting additionally allows us to represent phenomena such as imperfect speaker knowledge, or arbitrary common-knowledge priors.

In our model, *de* is characterized as an informativity maximizer in information-theoretic terms, by measuring the **cross-entropy** encoded in the prejacent of the particle. To do so, the following components are required:

- a set T of all possible worlds (or equivalence classes of worlds, where two worlds are equivalent if they address the QuD in the same way);
- a speaker, who holds a belief state $S(t)$ over the worlds $t \in T$ that she would like to convey;
- a listener, who forms a belief state $L(t|m)$ over worlds $t \in T$, dependent on some message m.

Informativity thus can be measured as the amount of information provided about the speaker's belief state, representable as the negation of the cross entropy H (Shannon 1948) between the speaker's and listener's belief states after the speaker communicates message m, i.e.

(9) $-H(S(\cdot), L(\cdot|m)) = \sum_{t \in T} S(t) \log L(t|m)$.

Utterances which bring the listener's belief state closer to the speaker's have a higher informativity, while utterances which contradict worlds deemed possible by the speaker have a negative infinite informativity.

Consider now the following example for illustration.

(10) QuD: Who should I find if I want to get a refund this week?

{Zhouer yizhi   dao zhouwu}/ {yiban}, dou shi Wang laoshi fuze
{Tuesday all.the.way until Friday}/ {usually} PRT COP Wang teacher handle
baoxiao (**de**); {zhouyi}/{ou'er},   shi cai laoshi fuze   baoxiao (??**de**).
refund (DE); Monday/occasionally COP Cai teacher handle refund   (DE)

'From Tuesday until Friday/Usually, teacher Wang handles refunds; On Monday/Occasionally, teacher Cai handles refunds.'

Let T be the set of all who's-in-charge assignments, each such assignment mapping one day of the workweek to one of two people who handle refunds. Let $S(t) = \delta_{t,s}$, where $s \in T$ is the unique world described in example (10), i.e. the speaker has perfect knowledge of world s. Finally, let $L(t|m)$ be the uniform distribution over all worlds consistent with the literal meaning of m, i.e. a literal listener with a uniform prior over worlds. From this, the informativity of a message m is $\log L(s|m)$. If m is compatible with s, this is the negative logarithm of the number of sets of worlds compatible with m. As logarithms are monotonic, informativity can be measured by counting sets of worlds: utterances with more compatible worlds are less informative.

The response featuring *from Tuesday to Friday* is compatible with 2 sets of worlds, and *on Monday* with 16 sets of worlds (thus more uncertain and less informative). In the case of quantifier *usually*, assuming it represents *more than half of the weekdays*, the proposition is compatible with 16 sets of worlds. As for *occasionally*, assuming a meaning of *at least one weekday*, the second proposition is compatible with 31 sets of worlds, and is thus less informative (as it only excludes one possibility). Hence we can formally capture the intuition that example (10)'s first proposition is more informative than the second.

Now the constraint for the *de* particle to attach to the more informative proposition can be formulated accordingly. We postulate the following pragmatic constraint of *de*, in which the usefulness of an utterance is characterized in terms of informativity. Here we use the notion 'maximal' to mean the largest value given a set of numeric data: *De* attaches to the chunk that is *more* informative than alternative chunks, hence maximally informative (i.e. the most informative among all the alternatives).

1. Maximal informativity condition
   de $(p)(w)$ is felicitous iff the informativity $I_{max}(u|w)$, given the utterance u at w that corresponds to the proposition containing *de* and its prejacent p.
2. Definition of I_{max}
   Given alternatives to u at w, where $Alt(u) = \{u_1, u_2,... u_i\}$ and $Alt(u)$ is triggered by contrastive topic marking, $I_{max}(u|w)$ iff $\forall_j : I(u|w) > I(u_j|w)$.

3.3 Comparison with Other Proposals

Our above notion of utterance informativity differs from the understanding of informative answers in terms of the entailment relation. The entailment-based characterizations have been employed to capture exhaustive answers. A standard treatment of exhaustive answers based on entailment relations makes use of Dayal (1996)'s answerhood operator, which takes a question meaning as its input and outputs the *conjunction* of all true propositions (assuming answers are propositions). In what follows, we illustrate with a slightly different approach that treats partial answers as elements of partially ordered domain (Szabolcsi and Zwart 1993, Champollion 2017), which makes it straightforward to rank partial answers. That is, partial answers encoded in the proposition could be mapped to the join semilattice.

A partial ordering is a reflexive, transitive, antisymmetric relation, defined in (11).

(11)   a. Reflexivity: Everything is part of itself.

b. Transitivity: Any part of any part of a thing is itself part of that thing.

c. Antisymmetry: Two distinct things cannot both be part of each other.

d. Unique sum: Every nonempty set has a unique sum.

A free join semilattice could be described by its property of reflexivity, transitivity, antisymmetry, taken together with the uniqueness of sum.[9] A typical model is shown in Fig. 2.

(12)   A binary sum $x \oplus y$ is defined as:
The sum of two things is the thing which contains both of them and whose parts each overlap with one of them.

Suppose the relevant context contains a QuD *who will come?* and a domain consisting of individuals {Zhangsan, Lisi, Wangwu}, we arrive at a set of propositions based on atomic individuals: {$^\wedge$Zhangsan will come, $^\wedge$Lisi will come, $^\wedge$Wangwu will come}. These propositions form a free join semi-lattice based on the entailment relation, from which we have all the possible Hamblin answers. Using a, b, c to stand for Zhangsan, Lisi and Wangwu, respectively, and using K to refer to the extension of *will come*, the set of Hamblin answers are then represented as {$K(a)$, $K(b)$, $K(c)$, $K(a+b)$, $K(a+c)$, $K(b+c)$, $K(a+b+c)$}. The exhaustive (actual) answer then corresponds to the highest level of summation, based on the mapping of the summations given the partial answers. The answer at the highest level asymmetrically entails the other Hamblin answers. In this sense, the exhaustive answer is the most informative among alternative answers.

However, the entailment-based characterizations are ill-suited for informative answers under our definition of expected utility. We illustrate with the example (13).

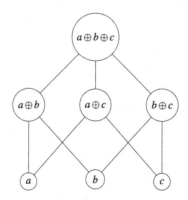

Fig. 2. An example for a free join semilattice with binary sums

(13)   QuD (Speaker A): When can I get reimbursement? B answers:

---

[9] The freedom property means that whenever two pairs of elements are distinct, their unions are distinct (Szabolcsi and Zwarts 1993).

??Zhouyi shi cai laoshi fuze   baoxiao   **de**. Cong zhouer dao
Monday COP Cai teacher in.charge reimbursement DE from Tuesday until
zhousan   dou shi Wang laoshi fuze   baoxiao.
Wednesday PRT COP Wang teacher in.charge reimbursement

'On Monday, [teacher Cai]$_F$ is in charge of reimbursement. From Tuesday until
Wednesday, [teacher Wang]$_F$ is in charge of reimbursement.'

In the current example, the information that varies in the two partial answers (*Tuesday until Wednesday* versus *Monday*) could be recognized as two elements on the join semilattice.[10] One may propose that the information maximizer *de* is attached to the highest level of summation. However, the solution faces the problem that the information conveyed by contrasting partial answers is not comparable on a join semilattice. *Monday* is a basic element at the bottom level of the semilattice (e.g. *a* in Fig. 2). It is considered as an atom of the lattice, since it has no further proper part in the current context. On the other hand, *Tuesday until Wednesday* corresponds to a join of the atom *Tuesday* (*b*) and the atom *Wednesday* (*c*). This join could be represented by $b \oplus c$ in Fig. 2. Though it seems that *Tuesday until Wednesday* (i.e. $b \oplus c$) is positioned higher than the atom *Monday* (*a*) on the semilattice, they are incomparable since *a* is not a proper part of $b \oplus c$ and vice versa. In other words, *Monday* is not a part of *Tuesday until Wednesday* that is distinct from *Tuesday until Wednesday* and vice versa. (*Tuesday* would be a proper part of *Tuesday until Wednesday*). Thus, in the current case, a lattice-theoretic formulation cannot predict that *Tuesday until Wednesday* is more informative than *Monday*.

Aside from the incomparability problem with elements that do not stand in a part-of relation, the entailment-based approach also fails to cover cases where the dynamic update during the speaker-listener interaction leads to the change in the relative informativity of individual messages. For example, an atomic answer that encodes an unlikely event (represented in the prior knowledge states) may receive a higher expected utility, which cannot be reflected in terms of the entailment relation (see Sect. 4.1 in the following for details). As another example, the presentational order of information affects the epistemic knowledge about the speaker belief state: The information presented at the beginning would imply the current knowledge state of the speaker. Consider a setting where the listener expects a conventional temporal/numeral order. If the speaker starts with a partial answer about Tuesday (instead of Monday), the listener may realize that information about Monday is unexpectedly not provided. This could be accounted for by the first-level recursive RSA model. The first-level listener, upon hearing the partial answers presented in an unconventional temporal ordering, now assigns a lower utility value (or a higher cost, depending on the details of the setting) to the partial answer with Monday. Intuitively, the listener would infer that either the speaker does not know about Monday, or anticipates more important information about Monday in the later conversation.

---

[10] We are simplifying our discussions here. In our example, the actual QuD is broken down into pair-list questions where the atomic answers take the form of weekday-teacher pairs. We want to avoid such complication.

To sum up, the entailment-based account faces problems in two aspects: 1) the case where two partial answers are not in a part-of relation (e.g. *Monday* vs. *Tuesday until Wednesday*); 2) the case involving backward inference and the update over speaker's prior knowledge state. Our account thus enjoys the advantage of measuring differences in expected utility in mutually non-entailing propositions, as well as keeping track of the dynamic update of (shared) knowledge.

As an anonymous reviewer points out, there are many versions of characterizations of *de* that may relate to our analysis. As argued by Soh (2018), *de* marks private evidence, where 'private' is defined in terms of an accessibility relation: The speaker uses *de*, when she has access to an evidential source, yet the listener cannot access it. While the environment of use in Soh (2018), particularly the case with the *shi...de* cleft, is not identical to ours, we want to suggest these two uses of *de* might be facets of an overarching meaning. In proposing that *de* attaches to the most informative answer, we rely on the intuition that the utterance brings the listener's belief closer to the speaker's than other alternatives. In a similar vein, an utterance based on evidence that the listener cannot otherwise access eliminates more uncertain worlds on the part of the listener and therefore brings the listener's belief closer to the speaker's than alternative utterances that the listener could independently access. If this intuition is on the right track, it is possible that the characterization in Soh (2018) could be analyzed in a cross-entropy framework. We leave this question open.

4   Extensions

As the RSA literature has argued, entailment-based semantics is not particularly suitable at dealing with various kinds of sentence-final particles that interact with the ever-updating speakers/listener belief states, yet Bayesian based frameworks can overcome such issues. Such Bayesian approaches are particularly suitable when we wish to account for uncertainty from different perspectives, such as when modeling the pragmatic reasoning of two interlocutors with differing access to information. For example, if a listener would like to infer what a speaker meant under a specific context, it is also necessary for her to reason about the epistemic states of that speaker (Goodman and Stuhlmüller 2013, Herbstritt and Franke 2019, Scontras et al. 2021).

Nevertheless, the current framework is not detached from possible world semantics. As we have addressed in the formal implementation section, the informativity can be reduced to counting the possible worlds under certain assumptions. Our model promises to expand beyond the use of the *de* particle and apply to more cases involving speaker-listener interaction. Specifically, we show that the current model is able to capture the case where the speaker and the listener have an arbitrary common knowledge prior (Sect. 4.1). Additionally, we show that with minimal changes, the model could be expanded to capture other sentence-final particles (Sect. 4.2).

4.1   Cases with Enriched Prior Knowledge

We have so far assumed a uniform common knowledge prior for the listener and the speaker. However, the setting of our model could be changed to accommodate more data. We have already seen in example (7) that *de* can switch to a 'fewer-situation' partial answer when the speaker and the listener both share a common knowledge that those situations are unlikely. A similar example is in (14), in which *de* attaches to the more exceptional *Cai-Monday* pair, given that teacher Cai only handles refunds when teacher Wang is on vacation.

(14)   Context: Everyone knows that teacher Wang is usually in charge for refunds, and teacher Cai is in charge when teacher Wang is on vacation. A asked: 'Who should I find if I want to get a refund this week?' B:

zhouyi shi Cai laoshi fuze   baoxiao   **de**. zhouer yizhi
Monday COP Cai teacher in.charge reimbursement **DE** Tuesday all.the.way
dao zhouwu, hai shi   Wang laoshi fuze   baoxiao.
until Friday   still COP Wang teacher in.charge reimbursement
'On Monday, teacher Cai is in charge of reimbursement. From Tuesday until Friday, it is still that teacher Wang is in charge of reimbursement.'

In other words, the speaker and the listener both hold non-uniform priors, with higher probabilities assigned to worlds in which teacher Wang is in charge the majority of days except for the days when she is on vacation. In addition, the speaker knows that the listener doesn't know when teacher Cai is on vacation. If we further assume that teacher Cai has a 1% probability of taking vacation any given day, and that each day is independent, we can use our proposal to calculate informativities explicitly.[11]

Assume a situation where teacher Wang is out for vacation on Monday, and is back to work starting Tuesday. This yields a work schedule with teacher Cai in charge on Monday, and teacher Wang on charge from Tuesday to Friday – we notate this world state s. By our priors, the probability of s is $0.01*(1-0.01)^4$ (given that the probability that teacher Wang is on vacation is 0.01, and there are five working days in a week). After hearing the utterance m_1 'On Monday, teacher Cai is in charge of reimbursement,' the conditional probability of s given the utterance ($L(w|u)$) is 0.99^4. Similarly, given the proposition m_2 'from Tuesday until Friday, teacher Wang handles refund', the corresponding conditional probability is 0.01. From this, the informativity of the corresponding proposition could be calculated by $\log L(s|m)$. This yields an informativity of approximately -0.0174 for m_1, and exactly -2 for m_2. Therefore, we predict that *de* prefers the *Monday-Cai* utterance, since it is more informative in this situation.

In sum, the informativity of our utterances is affected by both the number of events addressed, and the probabilities of those events. As we see in our example, an utterance addressing a single unlikely event can be more informative than one addressing many likely events.

4.2 Other Particles

The information-theoretic approach developed for *de* promises to be expanded to capture a broad range of particles that are shown to compare the interlocutors' belief states.

---

[11] We acknowledge that here the example setting is unrealistic. The purpose of using oversimplified assumptions is to enable a demonstration of the way informativity is calculated in nonuniform prior cases by feeding concrete numbers into the model.

The Mandarin Sentence-Final Particle. *ne* We illustrate with the so-called declarative-final use of the particle *ne* in Mandarin, where *ne* is confined to the sentence-final position in the declarative clause type.[12] The following set of data establish the core function of declarative-final *ne* (Lin 1984, Guo 2005, Constant 2014). The context in (15) involves a new belief on the part of the speaker and an acknowledgement of a previous false belief: At the time A utters the sentence, speaker B's belief state must be updated in a way that contradicts B's pre-utterance belief that A would have time today (*ne*'s prejacent *p*).

(15)   A: I have to go now.

      B: zheme kuai? wo yiwei   ni jintian you shijian **ne**.
          this   fast   I   falsely.believe you today have time   NE
          'This fast! I thought you have time today.'

The empirical generalization appears to be that *ne* indicates a drastic difference between the speaker's belief state at the utterance time and her previous belief states. The particle can attach to a prejacent that is being updated to the current belief state, or to a prejacent that represents the pre-utterance belief state, e.g. by collocating with the attitudinal verb *yiwei* 'falsely believe'. If a third party overheard the conversation, they obtain this prior-posterior shift immediately signaled by the particle. In other words, the third party listener can deduce what was and is the speaker's belief state because of the existence of the particle.

We can capture this generalization under an information-theoretic approach. The difference between the speaker's prior and posterior belief state could be measured by Kullback-Leibler (KL) divergence, (Baldi 2002), i.e. for given a message m, $H(L(\cdot|m), L(\cdot)) - H(L(\cdot|m))$. This treatment could be seen as a different type of extension of our account of informativity used earlier: KL divergence differs from cross-entropy only by the posterior entropy $H(L(\cdot|m))$. While the informativity of an utterance measures how much it brings a listener's belief state towards the speaker's, here we measure how much the speaker's belief state has changed before and after she obtained the information from the addressee or the context.

Take example (15) for an illustration. Prior to A's utterance, the speaker B assigned a high probability towards the event that *A has time today*. Again using oversimplified assumption, Speaker B believes that either A has time or A does not have time, i.e. a binary choice. Upon hearing A's utterance, the posterior belief state of B is flipped to the side where A does not have time, to which B consequently assigns a high probability. The drastic change of belief states of the speaker B (i.e. the difference between low and high probability assignments) predicts a **high** KL divergence. In this way, it is possible to quantify the difference between the speaker B's prior and posterior belief states by $S(m) = -\log(L(\text{does not have time}))$, where L is the speaker's prior.

---

[12] *Ne* has elsewhere been shown to assume the function of a contrastive topic marker (when selecting for a noun phrase in the sentence-medial position) as well as a fragment question marker (Constant 2014). East Asian particles are known for their multifunctionality. For instance, the particle *de* additionally assumes the function of a relativizer, a nominalizer and a possessive marker (Chao 1968).

The Japanese Sentence-Final Particle. *no* The KL divergence modeling also carries over to other sentence-final particles encoding a speaker meaning. We take the Japanese SFP *no* for illustration. Of interest to us is the use given in (16) and (17). Both contexts involve a lack of shared knowledge (Kuroda 1973; Inoue 1982; Iwasaki 1985; Aoki 1986; Cook 1990), in which the proposition ascribed to the speaker is not compatible with the belief held by the listener up to the point of utterance. By using *no*, the speaker thus signals that her proposed update of *no*'s prejacent to the common ground requires a drastic change to the listener's prior belief.[13]

(16) Context: Speaker A saw a butter on the table and complained that she doesn't like the salted butter. B answers:

    B: kore-ga oshio-o haitte   nai batta na **no**.
        this-SBJ salt-ACC add-PROG NEG butter PRT NO
        'This is the butter without salt inside.'

(17) A: The plate is broken. Do you think Dora-chan broke it?

    B: Dora-chan wa sakki   wotasi to   issyoni ita   **no**.
        Dora.DIM TOP just.now I   CONJ together COP.PST NO
        'Dora-chan was together with me just now (so he could not have done it).'

Information theoretically, the difference between the **listener's** prior and posterior belief state could also be measured by KL divergence.[14] Consider example (16). The context indicates a low-entropy prior belief state, where A believes with high probability that the butter is salted. For simplicity, we assume butter-saltedness to be a binary variable, with the prior belief distribution highly skewed in the direction of it *being salted*. Since the utterance m contradicts the listener's expectation, after the utterance the listener's posterior belief state is flipped towards certain belief in *unsalted* butter. This drastic difference between prior and posterior belief states should be reflected by a high KL divergence. More explicitly, we could quantify how 'far' the listener's belief state has shifted upon hearing this utterance, based on $S(m) = -\log(L(unsalted))$, where L is the listener's prior. In sum, our treatment of *ne* can be modified to provide a characterization of the *no* particle. Such treatment is theoretically desirable, as the distance between the prior and posterior belief states of the speaker can be directly measured by interpretable units such as bits, if concrete numbers are given to the speaker's prior and posterior probability.

Part of the motivation of using a Bayesian framework lies in that it is probability-based, i.e. non-truth conditional. With a probability-based framework, the speaker's attitude can be intrinsically modeled as a hint to her prior belief state. We can demonstrate that with a given belief state, the speaker uses a specific particle to address the

---

[13] *No* is further claimed to convey a sense of authority on the part of the speaker (i.e. a reliable evidential source) (e.g. Cook 1990). We will leave this layer out of our discussion.

[14] We are not strictly interested in the listener's actual belief state, but the speaker's belief about the listener's belief state, since the speaker is of course the one who must decide whether she wants to use the particle.

distance between the prior and posterior belief state, which is directly linked to her surprised attitude.

One difficulty with such proposals is their reliance on explicit probabilities for belief states, which are usually not available in naturalistic settings. However, contexts involving observations from known random processes can be constructed to ensure that rational actors would hold specific belief states. For instance, our proposals could be tested using a ball-in-urn setting such as that used in Herbstritt and Franke (2019). Contexts could describe rational actors' partial observations of some of the balls, and their probabilistic beliefs about the unobserved balls could be quantified exactly. Explicit probabilities from varying perspectives could be calculated for propositions about the colors of the balls, and these could be used to calculate KL-divergences to determine the applicability of different sentence final particles on different utterances. For example, to test the applicability of the particle *ne* on an utterance describing the color of the balls in an urn (e.g. "Most of the balls are red."), we could explicitly compute a rational speaker's belief states before (i.e. prior) and after observing the color of a subset the balls (i.e. posterior), and calculate the KL-divergence between these belief states. In addition, while reliance on probabilities does make our proposals more difficult to validate, it does not detract from their utility. Once there is proper experimental validation, such a probabilistic formalism could even be used with Bayesian reasoning to glean insight into interlocutors' priors about more naturalistic settings based on their use of such particles.

5   Conclusion

In this study, we claim that the Mandarin sentence-final particle *de* is used to indicate that the speaker signals that an answer is the most informative, in response to the question under discussion in the immediate discourse. We then show that cross-entropy allows for a formally precise modeling of the pragmatic notion of informativity. Our case study opens the way for the wider applicability of the cross-entropy method (as well as related KL divergence-based methods as part of the RSA-based approach), which we argue is a natural apparatus for capturing the speaker meanings of discourse particles across languages.

We end by noting that the probabilistic reasoning we have assumed is encoded in the meaning of the discourse particles. In doing so we deviate from the more traditional view where truth-conditional denotations are fed to a probabilistic/Bayesian pragmatics. The current approach thus is in line with recent developments towards a complex interface approach to meaning, encompassing the realm of probabilistic semantics/pragmatics (e.g. Champollion et al. 2019), as well as other facets such as the speech act theory (e.g. Krifka 2017, 2019).

Acknowledgements. We appreciated to the anonymous reviewers for the ESSLLI Student Session 2021 for their valuable comments and suggestions. We would also like to thank the editors who put the *Best Student Session Papers 2019–2021 Springer Volume* together. We have also benefited from discussions with Daniel Hole, Judith Tonhauser, Fabian Bross, Sebastian Padó and Swantje Tönnis, as well as audiences at the student session and the linguistic colloquium at University of Stuttgart. All the remaining errors are our own.

Appendix

We conducted a pilot acceptability judgement task, with the aim of addressing the question of whether the placement of *de*-particle is subject to the type of partial answer and subject to the relative order of partial answers.

Participants.   A total of 20 participants were recruited (11 male, 9 female, average age: 23.7 ± 1.13). All participants were Mandarin native speakers currently enrolled in non-linguistics undergraduate programs from a college in China.

Material.   A total of 32 target sentences were distributed across 4 lists, randomised across participants, with 8 items apiece. Each list follows a Latin square design. One variable is the placement of the particle *de* (first vs. second prejacent). The other is the numbers of situations (i.e. informativity). All combinations of the ordered partial answers are summarized in Table 1. Each individual rates 8 target sentences and 24 fillers on a Likert scale from 1 to 7 (ascending order, 1 being the least natural/least acceptable). All items follow a prior *wh*-question indicating the immediate QuD.

Table 1. Only English translation is provided. '$<$' represents linear precedence. Condition (a) thus reads as: *"From Tuesday until Friday/usually, Wang handles refunds de. On Monday/occasionally, Cai handles refunds."*

Condition	Position of **de**
a.	Tue–Fri/usually **de** $<$ Mon/occasionally
b.	Mon/occasionally $<$ Tue–Fri/usually **de**
c.	Tue–Fri/usually $<$ Mon/occasionally **de**
d	Mon/occasionally **de** $<$ Tue–Fri/usually

Procedure.   The task is conducted online on Qualtrics. A target sentence's *wh*-context is displayed on the same page as the target, with scores (1–7) horizontally aligned at the lower half of the page. A radio button is present underneath each score. After choosing a score by mouse-clicking on a radio button, the participant clicks on the CONTINUE button to proceed to the next sentence.

Results. An ordinal mixed effect model (Christensen 2019) is adopted: *a*, *b*, *c* conditions are contrast-coded against the reference level of the condition *d*. No significant effect is observed between condition *c* and *d* by an ordinal mixed model (Christensen 2019, Tukey α-adjustment), with a random intercept for participant and item and a random by-participant slope. However, a significant difference is observed between condition *a* and *d*, where the *de*-particle attached to a 'more-situation' prejacent is preferred over the 'fewer-situation' prejacent (see Fig. 3).

Our preliminary acceptability judgment task reveals that when partial answers (i.e. two partial sentences) are juxtaposed, judgments are significantly better with *de* attached to the 'more-situation' partial answer than the 'fewer-situation' one. The order of the two answers is not significant, excluding the possibility that the contrast is due to the preference for uttering the more informative partial answer earlier.

Condition	Position of *de*	mean values
a.	Tue--Fri/usually *de* < Mon/occasionally	6.331
b.	Mon/occasionally < Tue--Fri/usually *de*	5.797
c.	Tue--Fri/usually < Mon/occasionally *de*	4.631
d.	Mon/occasionally *de* < Tue--Fri/usually	4.422

Fig. 3. Pattern of judgment based on permutations of partial answers with placement of *de*. Only English translation is provided.('***': $p < 0.001$; '**': $p < 0.01$; 'n.s.': not significant).

References

Baldi, P.: A computational theory of surprise. In: Farrell, B., van Tilborg, H. (eds.) Information, Coding, and Mathematics, pp. 1–25. Norwell, Norwell (2002)

Büring, D.: On D-trees, beans, and B-accents. Linguist. Philos. **26**(5), 511–545 (2003). https://doi.org/10.1023/A:1025887707652

Champollion, L.: Parts of a Whole: Distributivity as a Bridge Between Aspect and Measurement. Oxford University Press, Oxford (2017)

Champollion, L., Alsop, A., Grosu, I.: Free choice disjunction as a rational speech act. In: Proceedings of SALT, vol. 29, pp. 238–257 (2019)

Chao, Y.R.: A Grammar of Spoken Chinese. University of California Press, Berkeley (1968)

Cheng, L.L.-S.: Deconstructing the shi...de construction. Linguist. Rev. **25**, 235–266 (2008)

Chu, C.: A Discourse Grammar of Mandarin Chinese. Peter Lang, Berlin (1998)

Constant, N.: Contrastive topic: Meanings and Realizations. Ph.D. thesis, University of Massachusetts at Amherst (2014)

Cook, H.M.: An indexical account of the Japanese sentence-final particle No. Discourse Process. **13**, 401–439 (1990)

Dayal, V.: Locality in wh-quantification: Questions and relative clauses in Hindi. Kluwer Academic Publishers, Dordrecht (1996)

Frank, M., Goodman, N.: Predicting pragmatic reasoning in language games. Science **336**(6084), 998–1008 (2012)

Franke, M., Jäger, G.: Probabilistic pragmatics, or why Bayes' rule is probably important for pragmatics. Z. Sprachwiss. **35**(1), 3–44 (2012)

Goodman, N., Stuhlmüller, A.: Knowledge and implicature: modeling language understanding as social cognition. Top. Cogn. Sci. **5**(1), 173–184 (2013)

Guo, W.: The discourse function of the Chinese particle ne in statements. J. Chin. Lang. Teach. Assoc. **40**(1), 47–82 (2005)

Hamblin, L.: Questions in Montague English. Found. Lang. **10**, 41–53 (1973)

Herbstritt, M., Franke, M.: Complex probability expressions & higher-order uncertainty: Compositional semantics, probabilistic pragmatics & experimental data. Cognition **186**, 50–71 (2019)

Hole, D.: The deconstruction of Chinese shi...de clefts revisited. Lingua **121**(11), 1707–1733 (2011)

Horn, L.: The border wars: a neo-gricean perspective. In: von Heusinger, K., Turner, K. (eds.) Where Semantics Meets Pragmatics, pp. 21–48. Oxford University Press, Oxford (2005)

Jäger, G.: Game dynamics connects semantics and pragmatics. In: Pietarinen, A.-V. (ed.) Game Theory and Linguistic Meaning, pp. 89–102. Elsevier, Amsterdam/New York (2007)

Krifka, M.: Epistemic, evidential and discourse modalities in commitment space semantics. In: Not-At-Issue-Meaning and Information Structure Workshop **1**, 1–13 (2017)

Krifka, M.: Layers of assertive clauses: propositions, judgements, commitments, acts. In: Hartmann, J., Wöllstein, A. (eds.) Propositional Arguments in Cross-Linguistic Research: Theoretical and Empirical Issues, pp. 1–45. Gunter Narr Verlag, Tuebingen (2019)

Kuno, S.: Nihon-Bunpoo Kenkyuu. Taisyukan, Tokyo (1973)

Lin, W.: What does the Mandarin particle NE communicate? Cahiers de Linguistique - Asie Orientale 13(2), 217–240 (1984)

Merin, A.: Information, relevance, and social decision making: some principles and results of decision-theoretic semantics. In: Ginzburg, J., Moss, L., de Rijke, M. (eds.) Logic. Language, and Information, pp. 179–221. CSLI Publications, Standford (2011)

Paul, W., Whitman, J.: Shi...de focus clefts in Mandarin Chinese. Linguist. Rev. 25(3–4), 413–451 (2008)

Scontras, G., Tessler, M.H., Franke, M.: A practical introduction to the rational speech act modeling framework. arXiv preprint arXiv:2105.09867 (2021)

Shannon, C.: A mathematical theory of communication. Bell Syst. Technical J. 27(3), 379–423 (1948)

Simpson, A.: Sentence-final particles. In: The Handbook of Chinese Linguistics, pp. 156–179, 2014

Simpson, A., Zoe, W.: From D to T-determiner incorporation and the creation of tense. J. East Asian Linguis. 11(2), 169–209 (2002)

Soh, H.L.: Mandarin Chinese sentence final de as a marker of private evidence. In: Proceedings of the Linguistic Society of America, vol. 3, no. 22, pp. 1–14 (2018)

Spector, B.: The pragmatics of plural predication: homogeneity and non-maximality within the rational speech act model. In: Proceedings of the 21st Amsterdam Colloquium, pp. 435–444 (2017)

Szabolcsi, A., Zwart, F.: Weak islands and an algebraic semantics for scope taking. Nat. Lang. Seman. 1(3), 235–284 (1993)

van Rooij, R.: Utility of mention-some questions. Res. Lang. Comput. 2(3), 401–416 (2004)

The Impact of Propositional Messages on Termination of Declarative Distributed Systems

Francesco Di Cosmo$^{(\boxtimes)}$ [ID]

Free University of Bozen-Bolzano, Bolzano, Italy
`fdicosmo@unibz.it`

Abstract. Declarative Distributed Systems (DDSs) are data-centric distributed systems grounded in logic programming. Enjoying a close correspondence between the distributed programs and their formal semantics, they configure as an interesting model for studying formal verification of distributed systems. Unfortunately, recent studies proved that the DDS model-checking problem is undecidable, unless boundedness conditions are imposed on the various DDS data-sources. Nevertheless, to check boundedness is, again, undecidable. Thus, we investigate whether it is possible to lift it in favor of syntactic, decidable conditions on the expressiveness of the data-sources. Considering the available decidability results, in this paper we study the impact of weak message expressiveness in place of channel-boundedness and obtain flexible decidability results on DDS verification. Those indicate that boundedness can sometimes be lifted in favor of decidable constraints, while retaining the decidability of the verification problem.

Keywords: Logic-Programming · Distributed-Systems · Model-Checking

1 Introduction

Declarative Distributed Systems (DDSs) are a model of distributed computing grounded in logic programming motivated by Declarative Networking [21] and Business Process Analysis [8]. A number of similar models were considered in the literature, indicating that the declarative paradigm allows for concise and intuitive implementations of the distributed behavior [24]. For example, DDS-like systems were used for security and provenance in distributed query processing [28,29], in the analysis of asynchronous event systems [1], and as the core of the Webdam language for distributed Web applications [2]. A common trait of these models is data-centricity, i.e., local node computations consist of queries over relational databases (DBs), which provide a close relationship between the programs and their formal semantics. In turn, this feature simplifies the development of analysis tools and techniques [22,26]. Those were exploited in various settings, but providing only empirical and experimental assessments [13,14,22,26], or formal models to study distributed query computation strategies [5–7], disregarding their temporal evolution. Our broad research objective is to fill that gap. Specifically we aim at a comprehensive, rigorous study of DDS verification through model-checking techniques.

Unfortunately, by elaborating on the infinite variety of data DDSs have, in principle, to handle, Calvanese et al. [10,11] showed that the problem of DDS model-checking is undecidable unless constraints are placed on the DDS specification. In fact, decidability can sometimes be gained by placing boundedness conditions on the various system data-sources. For example, by bounding all data-sources, even if the DDS transition system remains, in general, infinite-state, it can be finitely abstracted and it is possible to exploit mature model-checking techniques over that abstraction. Thus, it is possible to verify bounded DDSs against sophisticated temporal logics. However, Babak et al. [9] showed that boundedness properties are themselves undecidable, in general. This means that, while we can verify bounded DDSs, we cannot recognize whether a given arbitrary DDS is bounded or not. Thus, actually, the decidability results enabled by boundedness cannot be directly exploited in the development of tools for DDS verification.

Notwithstanding, it could still be possible to mitigate that negative result. In fact, some of the currently available undecidability proofs about the verification of unbounded DDSs crucially exploit the full expressive power of DDS data-centric messages. It is currently not known whether tweaking that power would lead to decidable cases even in absence of boundedness conditions. Since the message expressiveness can be weakened by enforcing syntactical (thus decidable) constraints on the message structure, a positive decidability result of this kind would definitively pave the way for the implementation of verification tools for a limited, but recognizable, class of DDSs.

The verification of distributed systems has traditionally been studied over data-unaware models. A classic example is that of Communicating Finite State Machines (CFSMs), whose reachability problem has been extensively studied considering various semantics for the communication mechanism, e.g., exploiting point-to-point communication channels that are perfect (all sent messages are received in the right order), lossy (some message could be lost), or unordered (all messages are received, but the reception order is unknown). It turned out that establishing reachability of a finite set of target CFSM states is undecidable over perfect channels, already over single node networks and with empty channels in the target [12], while it is decidable over lossy and unordered ones [4].

A notable, first difference between CFSMs and DDSs is that DDS messages not only carry information, as in the case of CFSMs, but are also responsible to trigger the node activation at their reception. For example, while a CFSM with empty channels can, in general, continue its computation, a DDS with empty channels cannot and, thus, terminates. Thus, the aforementioned formulation of CFSM reachability is reminiscent of termination of DDSs, i.e., whether there is at least one way to reach a state in which the computation stops. A second difference regards the data-centricity of messages: while CFSM messages are letters over a finite alphabet, DDS messages are single database tuples over a transport signature. Hence, DDSs seem powerful enough to capture CFSMs. In fact, a signature of zero-ary, i.e., propositional, symbols amounts to a finite alphabet. Moreover, since propositional DDS messages could not contain any tuple of data, we regard them as the least expressive DDS messages possible.

In light of this, in our previous work [16], we showed how these differences can be circumvented, allowing us to encode CFSMs into DDSs with propositional messages (for the undecidable cases) and vice-versa (for the decidable ones), indicating a close correspondence between the two models. However, that technique suffers of two issues: undecidability can be proved only over DDSs that enjoy some form of non-determinism (since CFSM nodes can choose non-deterministically to perform either a reading or a writing transition); the encoding for the decidable cases cannot be easily exploited to other verification problems. To solve these issues, in this paper, we exploit the same idea of [16], but providing reduction to and from alternative computation models. Specifically, undecidability is proved via a reduction from deterministic two-counter machines (2CMs), whose termination is undecidable, while decidability is proved via reductions to Petri-Nets (PNs), which enjoy several, widely studied decidable problems (see, e.g., [23]). By doing so, we obtain stronger and more flexible undecidability/decidability results.

To that end, in the next Sect. 2, we provide preliminaries about termination problems, 2CMs, PNs, and DBs. Then, in Sect. 3, we provide a fine-grained introduction and formalization of the DDS model. In Sect. 4, we define the problem studied in this paper, i.e., verification of termination of bounded DDSs with unbounded channels and propositional messages. Afterwards, in Sect. 5 and Sect. 6, we chart the decidability boundary of DDS termination over different types of communication channels. Finally, in Sect. 7, we discuss our results and highlight directions for future works.

2   Preliminaries

2.1   Configuration Graphs

Configuration graphs are used to formalize the computations of systems by describing their configurations and transitions.

Definition 1. *A* configuration graph *(CG)* Υ *is a triple* (Q, E, Q_0) *such that* Q *is called the* set of configurations, $E \subseteq Q \times Q$ *is called the* set of transitions, *and* $Q_0 \subseteq Q$ *is called the* set of initial configurations. *Given a configuration* $q \in Q$, *the set* $succ(q)$ *of* successors *of* q *is the set* $succ(q) = \{q' \mid (q, q') \in E\}$. *If* $succ(q)$ *is empty,* q *is called* terminal.

The computation runs of a system are formalized by the paths in its CG.

Definition 2. *Given a CG* $\Upsilon = (Q, E, Q_0)$, *a* run *in* Υ *is a maximal sequence* $(q_i)_{i \leq n}$, *for some* $n \in \mathbb{N} \cup \{|\mathbb{N}|\}$ *such that, for each* $i < n$ *and* $i > 0$, $q_i \in Q$,

$(q_{i-1}, q_i) \in E$ and $q_0 \in Q$. the run is finite (infinite) if $n \in \mathbb{N}$ $(n = |\mathbb{N}|)$. A configuration $q' \in Q$ is reachable from a configuration $q \in Q$ if there is a finite run $q, \ldots, q'$ in Υ.

In what follows, we interpret computation models as specifications of CGs. Thus, a model with a finite definition may specify an infinite-state CG. Several decision problems can be defined over CGs. In this paper, we are interested in the reachability and termination problems.

Reachability asks whether a target configuration is reachable from a given one.

Problem (Reachability)

Input. A specification of a CG $\Upsilon = (Q, E, Q_0)$ and $q_1, q_2 \in Q$.
Output. Whether q_2 is reachable from some q_1.

Termination problems ask whether it is possible to reach, from one or all initial configurations, a terminal configuration.

Problem (E- and A-termination)

Input. A specification of a CG $\Upsilon = (Q, E, Q_0)$.
Output of E-termination. Whether, for some $q_0 \in Q_0$, there is a terminal configuration $q \in Q$ reachable from q_0.
Output of A-termination. Whether, for each $q_0 \in Q_0$, there is a terminal configuration $q \in Q$ reachable from q_0.

Two CGs may be equivalent w.r.t. some property. This happens, e.g., when some form of mutual simulation is enforced. Different types of simulation capture equivalence for different properties. We introduce a type suitable to analyze E- and A-termination problems.

Definition 3. *Given two CGs $\Upsilon^1 = (Q^1, E^1, Q_0^1)$ and $\Upsilon^2 = (Q^2, E^2, Q_0^2)$, a bisimulation B between Υ^1 and Υ^2 is a relation $B \subseteq Q^1 \times Q^2$ such that:*

- *If $(q_1^1, q_2^1) \in E^1$ and $B(q_1^1, q_1^2)$ for some $q_1^2 \in Q^2$, then there is some $q_2^2 \in Q^2$ such that $(q_1^2, q_2^2) \in E^2$ and $B(q_2^1, q_2^2)$.*
- *If $(q_1^2, q_2^2) \in E^2$ and $B(q_1^1, q_1^2)$ for some $q_1^1 \in Q^1$, then there is some $q_2^1 \in Q^1$ such that $(q_1^1, q_2^1) \in E^1$ and $B(q_2^1, q_2^2)$.*

Υ^1 and Υ^2 are bisimilar if there is a bisimulation B such that:

- *For each $q_0^1 \in Q_0^1$ there is a $q_0^2 \in Q_0^2$ such that $B(q_0^1, q_0^2)$.*
- *For each $q_0^2 \in Q_0^2$ there is a $q_0^1 \in Q_0^1$ such that $B(q_0^1, q_0^2)$.*

Because of the requirements relating initial configurations, it is immediate to check that termination problems are invariant under bisimilarity.

Theorem 1. *Given two CGs $\Upsilon^1 = (Q^1, E^1, Q_0^1)$ and $\Upsilon^2 = (Q^2, E^2, Q_0^2)$, if they are bisimilar, then Υ^1 E-terminates (A-terminates) iff Υ^2 E-terminates (A-terminates).*

2.2   2 Counter Machines

2CM are a well known universal model of computation that extends finite state automata (FSA) with two counters ranging over $\mathbb{N}$. The 2CM rules, called *instructions*, execute FSA transitions according to and updating one of the counters.

Definition 4. *A 2CM K is a tuple $K = (Q, q_0, q_f, Inst)$ such that Q is a finite set of states, which includes the initial state q_0 and the* final *state q_f, $q_0 \neq q_f$, and Inst is a finite set of* increment *and* conditional decrement *(also simply called* decrement*) instructions where:*

- *An* increment instruction *is a tuple $(+, q, q', i)$, for some $q \in Q \setminus \{q_f\}$, $q' \in Q$ and $i \in \{1, 2\}$;*
- *A* decrement instruction *is a tuple $(-, q, q', q'', i)$ for some $q \in Q \setminus \{q_f\}$, $q', q'' \in Q$,and $i \in \{1, 2\}$.*

A state $q \in Q$ is related to an instruction $\delta \in Inst$ if q is the second component of δ. A 2CM is deterministic *if, for each $q \in Q \setminus \{q_f\}$, q is related to exactly one instruction.*

Notice that the final state is related to no instruction. Intuitively, instructions are executed only over their related state. Increment instructions $(+, q, q', i)$ substitute q with q' and increase counter i by 1. Decrement instructions $(-, q, q', q'', i)$ first check whether counter i is non-empty or empty. In the former case, q is substituted with q' and counter i is decreased by 1. In the latter case, q is substituted by q'' and the counters are not updated. This intuition is formalized as follows.

Definition 5. *Given a 2CM $K = (Q, q_0, q_f, Inst)$, a* configuration $\mathcal{K}$ *of K is a tuple $\mathcal{K} = (q, k_1, k_2)$ such that $q \in Q$ and $k_1, k_2 \in \mathbb{N}$. The configuration $\mathcal{K}' = (q', k_1', k_2')$ is a* successor *of $\mathcal{K}$ under an instruction $\delta \in Inst$, denoted by $\mathcal{K} \rightarrow^\delta \mathcal{K}'$, if one of the following holds, for some $i, j \in \{1, 2\}$ such that $i \neq j$:*

- *δ is an increment instruction $(+, q, q', i)$, $k_i' = k_i + 1$, and $k_j' = k_j$.*
- *δ is a decrement instruction $(-, q, q', q'', i)$, $k_i' = k_i - 1$ and $k_j' = k_j$.*
- *δ is a decrement instruction $(-, q, q'', q', i)$, $k_i' = k_i$ and $k_j' = k_j$.*

The CG $\Upsilon_K = (V, E, \mathcal{K}_0)$ of K is the CG such that V is the set of all configurations of K, $(\mathcal{K}_1, \mathcal{K}_2) \in E$ if $\mathcal{K}_1 \rightarrow^\delta \mathcal{K}_2$ for some $\delta \in Inst$, and $\mathcal{K}_0 = (q_0, 0, 0)$. A state $q \in Q$ is reachable *if there is a reachable configuration $\mathcal{K} = (q, k_1, k_2)$, for some $k_1, k_2 \in \mathbb{N}$.*

Since q_f is related to no instruction and each other $q \in Q \setminus \{q_f\}$ is related to exactly one instruction, each deterministic 2CM exhibits only one run. This run is finite iff q_f is reachable. The termination problems restricted to 2CMs are the termination problems for the CGs of 2CMs. Notice that, since there is only one initial configuration, E- and A-termination coincide. It is well known that termination of 2CMs is undecidable.

Theorem 2. *The (E- and A-) termination problem for 2CMs is undecidable.*

2.3   Multisets and Queues

Multisets generalize sets by allowing many occurrences of the same element. One way to formalize them is by viewing them as functions.

Definition 6. *A* multiset *M* over *a set U is a function $M : U \longrightarrow \mathbb{N}$. The set of multisets over U is denoted by $U^{\oplus}$.*

In what follows, the following notions on multisets are relevant.

Definition 7. *Given a set U and two multisets M_1 and M_2 over U:*

- $supp(M_1) = \{u \in U \mid M(u) \geq 1\}$.
- M_1 *is finite if $supp(M)$ is finite.*
- *For each $u \in U$, $u \in M$ if $u \in supp(M)$.*
- *The* size *$|M_1|$ of M_1 is $\sum_{u \in U} M_1(u)$, if $supp(M_1)$ is finite, or ∞, otherwise.*
- *$M_1 + M_2$ is the multiset M_3 over U such that, for each $u \in U$, $M_3(u) = M_1(u) + M_2(u)$.*
- *If, for each $u \in U$, $M_1(u) \geq M_2(u)$, $M_1 - M_2$ is the multiset M_3 over U such that, for each $u \in U$, $M_3(u) = M_1(u) - M_2(u)$.*
- *$M_1 \subseteq M_2$ if, for each $u \in U$, $M_1(u) \leq M_2(u)$.*

It is possible view sets as multisets by using their characteristic functions.

Definition 8. *Given a set U and a set $S \subseteq U$, the* characteristic function *of S over U is $\chi_S^U : U \longrightarrow \{0,1\}$ such that, for each $u \in U$, $\chi_S^U(u) = 1$ iff $u \in S$.*

Thus, we extend the notions in Definition 7 also to sets viewed as multisets. For example, Given a multiset M on U and a set $S \subseteq U$, $M + S$ denotes $M + \chi_S^U$.

A queue over a set X is a multisets with order.

Definition 9. *Given a set X, a* queue *σ over X is a finite sequence $[\sigma[1], \ldots, \sigma[n]]$, for some $n \in \mathbb{N}$ called* length *of σ (denoted $|\sigma|$), such that, for each $i \leq n$, $\sigma[i] \in X$. The* first *(last) element of σ is $\sigma[1]$ ($\sigma[n]$). The queue is* empty, *denoted by ε, if $n = 0$.*

As for multisets, we can define some operation on queues. Specifically, given $\sigma = [x_1, \ldots, x_n]$ and $\sigma' = [x_1', \ldots, x_{n'}']$, $\sigma - \{x_1\} = [x_2, \ldots, x_n]$ and $\sigma + \sigma' = [x_1, \ldots, x_n, x_1', \ldots, x_{n'}']$. Moreover, elements in queues have a multiplicity.

Definition 10. *Given $x \in X$ and a queue σ over X, the set $Occ(x)$ of occurrences of x is $\{i \mid x = \sigma[i]\}$. The* multiplicity *$\sigma(x)$ of x in σ is $|Occ(x)|$. The* support *of σ is $\{x \mid |Occ(x)| \geq 1\}$ We write $x \in X$ to mean that $x \in supp(\sigma)$.*

A multiset M can be used to induce the set of all queues whose element have the same multiplicity as in M. Only the case for queues induced by sets is relevant and, thus, formalized next.

Definition 11. *Given a set X, the set $Queues(X)$ of queues induced by X is the set of queues σ over X such that, for each $x \in X$, $\sigma(x) = 1$.*

2.4   Petri Nets

PNs [23] are a classic model of concurrent computation in which tokens markings places are consumed an produced by transitions.

Definition 12. *A PN is a tuple* (P, T, F) *where:*

1. P *is a finite set of places.*
2. T *is a finite set of transitions.*
3. P *and* T *are disjoint.*
4. $F : (P \times T) \cup (T \times P) \to \mathbb{N}$ *is called the flow function.*

The configurations of Petri Nets are called markings and, intuitively, mark each place with a finite number of tokens. These are consumed and produced by the transitions according to the flow function.

Definition 13. *Given a PN* $N = (P, T, F)$*, a* marking *for* N *is a multiset* $M : P \to \mathbb{N}$ *over the set of places. A transition* $t \in T$ *is* enabled *over a marking* M *if, for each place* $p \in P$*,* $M(p) \geq F(p, t)$*. A marking* M' *is* reachable by firing t *over* M*, denoted by* $M \to^t M'$*, if* t *is enabled over* M *and, for each* $p \in P$:

$$M'(p) = M(p) - F(p, t) + F(t, p)$$

We write $M \to M'$ *if there is some* $t \in T$ *such that* $M \to^t M'$.

It is natural to extend PNs with initial markings.

Definition 14. *A* marked PN *is a tuple* $N = (P, T, F, \mathcal{M}_0)$ *such that* $N' = (P, T, F)$ *is a PN and* $\mathcal{M}_0$ *is a set of markings for* N'*, called* initial marking set. N *is called* simply marked *if* $|\mathcal{M}_0| = 1$*. The* CG *of* N *is* $\Upsilon = (Q, E, \mathcal{M}_0)$ *such that* Q *is the set of all markings of* N *and* $(M_1, M_2) \in E$ *if* $M_1 \to M_2$.

A decision problem for marked PNs is the same problem restricted to CGs specified by multiply marked PNs.

Theorem 3. *Reachability for simply marked PNs is decidable [15].*

As long as the initial marking set is finite, the same holds also for non-simply marked PNs: termination[1] problems can be analyzed by checking reachability of at least one marking that does not enable any transition; these are in finite number.

Theorem 4. *Reachability and E- and A-termination for marked PNs with finite initial marking set is decidable.*

Petri nets have a standard graphical representation: places are represented by circles, transitions by rectangles, and, for each $p \in P$ and $t \in T$, the value $F(p, t)$ $(F(t, p))$ by an arrow from p to t (from t to p) labeled by $F(p, t)$ $(F(t, p))$; if the value is 0, the arrow is omitted; if the value is 1, the label is omitted; if

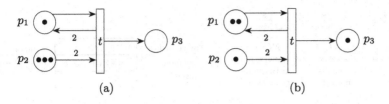

Fig. 1. The PN in Example 1 with markings M_0 (a) and M such that $M \to^t M$ (b).

$F(p,t) = F(t,p) \neq 0$, a single arrow with tips on both sides is depicted; for each $p \in P$ and marking M, the value $M(p)$ is represented by $M(p)$ tokens in $M(p)$.

Example 1. Figure 1a depicts the marked PN $N = (P, T, F, M_0)$ such that:

- $P = \{p_1, p_2, p_3\}$.
- $T = \{t\}$.
- $F(p_1, t) = 1$, $F(p_2, t) = 2$, $F(p_3, t) = 0$.
- $F(t, p_1) = 2$, $F(t, p_2) = 0$, $F(t, p_3) = 1$.
- $M_0(p_1) = 1$, $M_0(p_2) = 3$, $M_0(p_3) = 0$.

The transition t is enabled on M_0 and its firing reaches the marking M, depicted in Fig. 1b, such that $M(p_1) = 2$, $M(p_2) = 1$, $M(p_3) = 1$. Thus, $M_0 \to^t M$, $M_0 \rightsquigarrow M$, and M is reachable from M_0 in N. Since $M(p_2) < F(p_2, t)$, t is not enabled on M. Thus, M_0 and M are the only reachable markings in N.

2.5 Databases

We introduce DBs under the logic programming perspective (see [3]).

Definition 15. *A signature $\mathcal{S}$ is a finite set $\{S_1/a_1, \ldots, S_n/a_n\}$, for some $n \in \mathbb{N}$, where, for each $i \in \{1, \ldots, n\}$, S_i is a predicate symbol and $a_i \in \mathbb{N}$ is its arity. The domain Δ is a fixed, countably infinite set whose elements are called constants. A fact over $\mathcal{S}$ is a string $S(c_1, \ldots, c_a)$, for some $S/a \in \mathcal{S}$ and constants $c_1, \ldots, c_1 \in \Delta$.*

In this setting, DBs are interpretations of the predicates over the domain.

Definition 16. *Given a signature $\mathcal{S}$ and a subset $\Delta' \subseteq \Delta$, the Herbrand base $H(\mathcal{S}, \Delta')$ over $\mathcal{S}$ and Δ' is the set of all facts over $\mathcal{S}$ whose constants are in Δ'. A DB D over $\mathcal{S}$ is a subset $D \subseteq H(\mathcal{S}, \Delta)$. The active domain of D is the subset $\Delta' \subseteq \Delta$ of all constants occurring in the facts of D.*

---

[1] Note that this version of termination checks whether there is a terminating run and not whether there is a non-terminating run, whose complexity is known to be easier than reachability [20, 25].

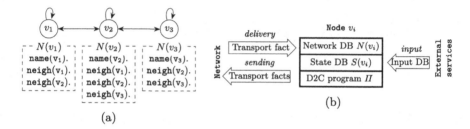

Fig. 2. Diagram of (a) a DDS network $\mathcal{N} = (V, E, N, type)$, where the node set V is $\{v_1, v_2, v_3\}$, the channel set E is the reflexive and symmetric closure of $\{(v_1, v_2), (v_2, v_3)\}$, N is depicted, and $type$ is either *perfect* or *unordered*, and of (b) an arbitrary data-centric DDS node v_i interacting in $\mathcal{N}$, with network DB $N(v_i)$, state $S(v_i)$, and D2C program Π.

Example 2. Directed graphs can be interpreted as DBs over a signature $\{V/1, E/2\}$. For example, assuming that $v_1, v_2 \in \Delta$, the complete digraph with self-loops over nodes v_1, v_2 is captured by the DB $\{V(v_1), V(v_2), E(v_1, v_2), E(v_2, v_1), E(v_1, v_1), E(v_2, v_2)\}$, whose active domain is $\{v_1, v_2\}$.

DB isomorphisms relate DBs that are equal up to constant renaming.

Definition 17. *Given a subset $\Delta' \subseteq \Delta$, a Δ'-isomorphism h is a permutation of Δ such that $h|_{\Delta'} = id_{\Delta'}$. Given a DB D, the DB $h(D)$ is the DB $\{S(h(c_1), \ldots, h(c_n)) \mid S(c_1, \ldots, c_n) \in D\}$. Two databases D_1 and D_2 are Δ'-isomorphic if there is a Δ'-isomorphism h such that $h(D_1) = D_2$.*

Example 3. The DB $D' = \{V(v_1), V(c_2), E(v_1, c_2), E(c_2, v_1), E(v_1, v_1), E(c_2, c_2)\}$ is $\{v_1\}$-isomorphic to the DB D in Example 2.

Query languages are used to extract information from DBs. The basic constructs of query languages based on Datalog [3] are atoms and literals.

Definition 18. *Let $\mathcal{V}$ be a countably infinite set of variables, disjoint from Δ. A term is either a constant or a variable. An atom, also called positive literal, over $\mathcal{S}$ is a formula $S(t_1, \ldots, t_n)$ for some $S_n \in \mathcal{S}$ and sequence of terms $t_1, \ldots, t_n$. A negative literal over $\mathcal{S}$ is a formula $\text{not} A$, for some atom A over $\mathcal{S}$. A literal over $\mathcal{S}$ is either a positive or a negative literal over $\mathcal{S}$.*

3   Declarative Distributed Systems

In this section we introduce DDSs, which are sets of asynchronously intercommunicating nodes over a network of point-point symmetric channels. Nodes are exposed to data from external services, and run declarative, logic programs.

3.1   Networks

DDS networks (see Fig. 2a) fix the topology and type of communication channels, and equip nodes with a relational representation of nodes neighborhood.s The topology amounts to a directed graph. We assume that this directed graph is symmetric and reflexive. The latter assumption is technically convenient and allows nodes to send messages to themselves.

Channels may be perfect, i.e., all sent messages are delivered in the same order they were sent, or imperfect. A common example of imperfection is lossyness: some message may lost, i.e., dropped from the channels; the others are delivered in the same order they were sent. However, as will be clear later, the termination problems of DDSs over lossy channels is trivial (unless further communication dynamics are enforced) and, thus, in this paper we do not study lossy channels. Instead, we consider another type of imperfection, i.e., unordered channels: all sent messages are delivered, but in a non-deterministic order. This type of imperfection is relevant, e.g., to model distributed applications communicating via protocols like UDP. Formally, the channel types boil down to a data-structure. For example, perfect channels are captured by queues, while unordered channels are captured by multisets.

In order, for nodes, to send messages to neighbors, networks provide nodes with a relational representation of the neighborhood (including the node itself). This is achieved by assigning to each node a network-DB, over the unary predicates **neighbor** (to list neighbor nodes) and **name** (which includes only the node name). For this to work, node names have to appear as constants in the network DBs, i.e., they are elements of the domain Δ on which DBs range. In this paper, we assume that networks do not evolve over time, i.e., nodes and channels are fixed and cannot be added or removed.

Definition 19. *A DDS network $\mathcal{N}$ is a tuple $\mathcal{N} = (V, E, N, type)$, where*

- (V, E) *is a (finite) direct3ed graph,*
- $V \subseteq \Delta$ *is a (finite) set of* nodes,
- $E \subseteq V \times V$ *is a (finite) symmetric and reflexive set of* channels,
- N *is a function that assigns to each node v a network DB $N(v)$ over the* network *signature* $\{\texttt{name}/1, \texttt{neighbor}/1\}$, *i.e.,* $N : V \longrightarrow \mathscr{P}(H(V, \{\texttt{name}/1, \texttt{neighbor}/1\}))$ *and* $N(v) = \{\texttt{name}(v)\} \cup \{\texttt{neighbor}(u) \mid (v, u) \in E\}$,
- *type* $\in \{queue, multiset\}$ *is called the* type *of the network.*

$\mathcal{N}$ *is* perfect *(*unordered*) if $\mathcal{N}$ is of type queue (multiset). The network $\mathcal{N}$ is a single-node network if it has only one node, i.e., $|V| = 1$.*

Since the results in this paper can be proved using single-node networks (and, afterwards, generalized to arbitrary networks - see Sect. 7), we formalize DDSs over single-node networks only (see [10] for an introduction of DDS over arbitrary unordered networks). Thus, unless explicitly stated otherwise, each DDS network is single-node over a fixed node v, i.e., it is either $(\{v\}, \{v, v\}, v \mapsto \{\texttt{name}(v), \texttt{neighbor}(v)\}, perfect)$ or $(\{v\}, \{v, v\}, v \mapsto \{\texttt{name}(v), \texttt{neighbor}(v)\}, unordered)$.

3.2   Data-Sources and Configurations

Given a, possibly non-single-node, DDS network, its nodes (see Fig. 2b) represent data-aware processes, dedicated to the manipulation of several data-sources in the form of relational DBs or facts. These are: state DBs, input DBs, and channel queues or multisets (according to the network type). Each of them ranges over a dedicated signature. A sequence of these signatures constitutes a DDS signature.

Definition 20. *A DDS signature Λ is a tuple $\Lambda = (\mathcal{S}, \mathcal{I}, \mathcal{T})$ of signatures called* state, input, *and* transport signature, *respectively, such that $\mathcal{S}$, $\mathcal{I}$, $\mathcal{T}$, and the network signature are pair-wise disjoint, and $\mathcal{T}$ contains the predicate* start$/0$. *A* message *is a fact over $\mathcal{T}$, i.e., an element of $H(\mathcal{T}, \Delta)$.*

The propositional message start is always part of $\mathcal{T}$ and it is used to enforce system start up (see Sect. 3.5 below). For each node, its state DB, over the state signature, represents the node memory. Its input DB, over the input signature, models currently available information provided by external services and/or users. Channels contain queues or multisets of transport facts. A combination of the content of all data-sources constitutes a DDS configuration.

Definition 21. *Given a single-node DDS network $\mathcal{N}$ (over node v), and a DDS signature $\Lambda = (\mathcal{S}, \mathcal{I}, \mathcal{T})$, a* configuration *is a tuple (S, I, C) such that $S \in \mathscr{P}(H(\mathcal{S}, \Delta))$ is a state DB for v, $I \in \mathscr{P}(H(\mathcal{I}, \Delta))$ is an input DB for v, and C is a queue, if $\mathcal{N}$ is perfect, or a multiset, if $\mathcal{N}$ is unordered, of messages for the channel (v, v).*

3.3   Computation Cycle

DDSs manipulate the information in the system, formalized as a DDS configuration, by performing computations as instructed by a declarative, logic program. Each computation step is an iteration of a computation cycle in which (on single-node networks):

1. Given the current configuration (S, I, C) of the system, a single message $m = C[1]$, if the network is perfect, or $m \in C$, if the network is unordered, is delivered from the channel to v;[2] the DB S is called *previous state DB*. If such a message m does not exist, the computation stops.
2. v is activated and runs a fixed program $\mathcal{P}$ over S, I, and m.
3. The program returns a new state DB S', denoted by $state(S, I, m)$, and a set of outgoing messages O', denoted by $out(S, I, m)$.
4. S is substituted by S', the messages in O' are cast, in a random order, on the channel, and I is substituted by an input DB J, according to an input policy.

We consider two input policies: interactive, i.e., the input DB I is updated into another input DB J, chosen non-deterministically at each step; autonomous, i.e., I is non-deterministically fixed at startup and never updated anymore, i.e., $J = I$.

---

[2] Notice that over non-single-node networks, this step is generalized so to deliver a single message from a single channel. This enforces asynchronous communication.

3.4 Programs

The program mentioned in Step 2 is written in the declarative language D2C [10], which is a specialization of the Datalog query language [3] to the distributed setting of DDSs. Specifically, an operator *prev* is used to query the previous state DB and a symbol @ is used to label messages with addresses. However, since we are working with single node networks, there is only one meaningful address (v itself) and, thus, we can avoid the usage of @ symbols. Since the results in this paper can be proved using a deterministic and non-recursive fragment of D2C (and, afterwards, generalized to full D2C - see Sect. 7), we formalize just that fragment.

Definition 22. *Given a a DDS network N and a DDS signature Λ, a DDS rule ρ is a formula of the form:*

$$ H \quad \textbf{if} \quad L_1, \ldots, L_n \ prev \ L_{n+1} \ldots, L_{n+m}, C_1 \ldots, C_k. $$

such that:

1. *H is either a state atom whose symbol does not occur in $L_1, \ldots, L_n$ or a transport atom distinct from* **start***.*
2. *$L_1, \ldots, L_n$ are state, input, network, and transport literals.*
3. *$L_{n+1}, \ldots, L_{n+m}$ are state literals.*
4. *$C_1, \ldots, C_k$ are inequality constraints of the form $t_1 \neq t_2$, where t_1 and t_2 are terms.*
5. *Each variable occurring in ρ occurs also in a positive literal in $L_1, \ldots, L_{n+m}$.*

H is called the head *of ρ, $L_1, \ldots, L_m, C_1, \ldots, C_k$ is called the* body *of ρ, and $L_{n+1}, \ldots, L_{n+m}$ is called the* scope of prev *of ρ. A DDS program is a finite set of rules.*

Roughly, when computing a program over a previous state DB S, input DB I, and incoming message m, the new state DB S' and set of outgoing messages O' are initialized to $\emptyset$. For each instantiation σ of the variables in the program into constants occurring in $S \cup I \cup N(v) \cup \{m\}$, each rule ρ is instantiated into a ground, i.e., variable-free, rule $\sigma(\rho)$. Now, until a fix-point is reached, choose such a ground rile and, if:

- the inequality constraints are satisfied,
- the literals in the scope of *prev* are true in the previous state DB S,
- the literals in the body, outside the scope of *prev*, are true in $S' \cup I \cup N(v) \cup \{m\}$,

then the variable-free head H is either added to S', if H is a state atom, or to O', if H is a transport atom. As for Datalog, the fix-point always exists and the computation terminates.

Example 4. Given a DDS network and the DDS signature $\Lambda(\{S/1\}, \{I/1\}, \{T/1\})$, an example of program is:

```
1 S(X) if T(Y), not I(Y) prev S(X), X≠ Y.
2 T(X) if S(X), name(N) prev not S(X), X≠ N.
```

Upon reception of a message $T(a)$ from the self-loop:

- Rule 1 states that, if a does not occur in the input DB and some value b occurs in the previous state DB, then $S(b)$ is added to the new state DB.
- Rule 2 states that, if some fact $S(a)$, with $a \neq v$, was already added in the new state DB (e.g., by rule 1), but it was not in the previous state DB, then, $T(a)$ is added to the set of outgoing messages, i.e., at the end of the computation, $T(a)$ is sent on the self-loop.[3]

Notation. For brevity, given heads $H_1, \ldots, H_n$, for some $n \in \mathbb{N}$, and a body B, $H_1; \ldots; H_n$ **if** B denotes the set of rules $\{H_1$ **if** $B., \ldots, H_n$ **if** $B.\}$.

Formally, the semantics of DDS programs is given via an encoding to Datalog with negation. Specifically, upon message reception:

- The state and transport signatures $\mathcal{S}$ and $\mathcal{T}$ are duplicated into a signature $\mathcal{S}' = \{S'/n \mid S/n \in \mathcal{S}\}$ and $\mathcal{T}' = \{T'/n + 1 \mid T/n \in \mathcal{T}'\}$, respectively.
- The program is rephrased over $\mathcal{S}'$ and $\mathcal{T}'$, i.e., each state atom (literal) $S(t_1, \ldots, t_n)$ occurring outside the scope of *prev* of some rule is substituted by $S'(t_1, \ldots, t_n)$ and each transport atom $T(t_1, \ldots, t_n)$ occurring in the head of some rule, is substituted by $T'(t_1, \ldots, t_n)$.

The result is a (non-recursive) Datalog program with negation, whose computation over $S \cup I \cup \{m\}$ returns a new state DB S'' over $\mathcal{S}'$ and set of outgoing messages O'' over $\mathcal{T}'$. The DDS program returns the rephrasing of S' and O' of S'' and O'' over $\mathcal{S}$ and $\mathcal{T}$, respectively.

Example 5. The Datalog encoding of the program in Example 4 is:

```
1 S'(X) if T(Y), not I(Y) prev S(X), X≠ Y.
2 T'(X) if S'(X), name(N) prev not S(X), X≠ N.
```

For example, rule 1 states that, upon reception of $T(a)$, if a does not occur in the input DB and some value b occurs in the previous state DB of v, then $S'(b)$, over the rephrased signature S', must be added to the new state DB. After rephrasing the new state DB to $\mathcal{S}$, we obtain a new state DB that contains $S(b)$.

Thanks to this encoding, the crucial property of genericity is transferred from Datalog to DDS programs, i.e., roughly, from isomorphic inputs, the program returns isomorphic outputs.

---

[3] Since we are working with single-node networks over the fixed node v, the usage of predicates **name** and **neighbor** can be avoided, since they are meaningful only if their tuples are instantiated to v itself. However, if we did not know the name of the single-node, the predicates would be, again, helpful.

Theorem 5. *Each DDS program $\mathcal{P}$ is generic, i.e., letting Δ' be the set of constants occurring in $\mathcal{P}$, for each Δ'-isomorphism h, state DB S, input DB I, and message m, $h(state(S, I, m)) = state(h(S), h(I), h(m))$ and $h(out(S, I, m)) = out(h(S), h(I), h(m))$.*

Proof. Given a triple (S, I, m), let S' and O' be the result of the computation of $\mathcal{P}$ over (S, I, m). Let S'' and O'' be the result of the computation of the Datalog encoding of $\mathcal{P}$ over (S, I, m). Thus, the rephrasing of S'' and O'' over $\mathcal{S}$ and $\mathcal{T}$ coincide with S' and O', respectively. Moreover, since Datalog is a generic query language and the constants occurring in Dat are exactly those occurring in $\mathcal{P}$, for each Δ'-isomorphism h, the computation of the Datalog encoding of $\mathcal{P}$ over $h(S) \cup h(I) \cup h(\{m\})$ returns $h(S'')$ and $h(O'')$. The computation of the DDS program over $(h(S), h(I), h(m))$ returns the rephrasing of $h(S'')$ and $h(O'')$ over $\mathcal{S}$ and $\mathcal{T}$, i.e., since isomorphisms do not affect the predicate symbols, but only their tuples, $h(S')$ and $h(O')$, respectively.   □

3.5   DDS Configuration Graphs

By combining all the previous components, we can formally define DDSs.

Definition 23. *Given a DDS network $\mathcal{N}$ and a DDS signature Λ, a DDS D is a tuple $(\mathcal{N}, \Lambda, S_0, \mathcal{P})$ where S_0 is a state DB, called* initial state DB, *and $\mathcal{P}$ is a DDS program. The* initial active domain Δ_0 *is the set of constants occurring in S_0, the set of nodes, or $\mathcal{P}$.*

We now formalize the computation cycle in Sect. 3.3 via two configuration graphs, one for the interactive and one for the autonomous input policy. In both cases, the initial configurations have the initial state DB, a non-deterministic input DB, and only the special message start, on the self-loop channel. The latter allows the execution, at start up, of step 1 of the computation cycle.

Definition 24. *Given a DDS $D = (\mathcal{N}, \Lambda, S_0, \mathcal{P})$, we denote by $\mathfrak{C}$ the set of its configurations. We say that there is an* interactive transition *from a configuration $\mathcal{C}_1 = (S_1, I_1, C_1)$ to a configuration $\mathcal{C}_2 = (S_2, I_2, C_2)$ witnessed by a message m, denoted by $\mathcal{C}_1 \rightarrow_{int}^m \mathcal{C}_2$ if:*

- *If $\mathcal{N}$ is unordered, then $m \in C$, $S_2 = state(S_1, I_1, m)$ and $C_2 = (C_1 - m) + out(S_1, I_1, m)$.*
- *If N is perfect, then $m = C[1]$, $S_2 = state(S_1, I_1, m)$ and $C_2 = (C_1 - m) + Q$ for some Q in $Queues(out(S_1, I_1, m))$.*

We write $\mathcal{C}_1 \rightarrow_{int} \mathcal{C}_2$ if there is some message m such that $\mathcal{C}_1 \rightarrow_{int}^m \mathcal{C}_2$. The interactive CG Υ_{int} *of D is $(\mathfrak{C}, E, \mathcal{M}_0)$ such that $(\mathcal{C}_1, \mathcal{C}_2) \in E$ iff $\mathcal{C}_1 \rightarrow_{int} \mathcal{C}_2$ and $\mathcal{C} = (S, I, C) \in \mathcal{M}_0$ iff $S = S_0$ and $C = [\text{start}]$, if $\mathcal{N}$ is perfect, or $C = \{\text{start}\}$, if $\mathcal{N}$ is unordered.*

For the autonomous policy, the initial configuration has, still, a non-deterministic input DB, but, afterwards, it does not change. This dynamic is captured by a single additional property on top of the definition of interactive transition.

Definition 25. *Given a DDS $D = (\mathcal{N}, \Lambda, S_0, \mathcal{P})$, we say that there is an autonomous transition from a configuration $\mathcal{C}_1 = (S_1, I_1, C_1)$ to a configuration $\mathcal{C}_2 = (S_2, I_2, C_2)$ witnessed by a message m, denoted by $\mathcal{C}_1 \to_{aut}^m \mathcal{C}_2$ if $\mathcal{C}_1 \to_{int}^m \mathcal{C}_2$ and $I_2 = I_1$. We write $\mathcal{C}_1 \to_{aut} \mathcal{C}_2$ if there is some message m such that $\mathcal{C}_1 \to_{aut}^m \mathcal{C}_2$. The autonomous CG Υ_{aut} of D is $(\mathfrak{C}, E, \mathcal{M}_0)$ such that $(\mathcal{C}_1, \mathcal{C}_2) \in E$ iff $\mathcal{C}_1 \to_{aut} \mathcal{C}_2$ and $C = (S, I, C) \in \mathcal{M}_0$ iff $S = S_0$ and $C = [\texttt{start}]$, if $\mathcal{N}$ is perfect, or $C = \{\texttt{start}\}$, if $\mathcal{N}$ is unordered.*

When the input signature is empty, the DDS CGs collapse. This special case is called closed DDS.

Definition 26. *An interactive (autonomous) DDS is a DDS interpreted over Υ_{int} (Υ_{aut}). A closed DDS is a DDS over an empty input signature. In that case, Υ_{clo} denotes the CG $\Upsilon_{int} = \Upsilon_{aut}$.*

Note that, over single-node networks, perfect closed pDDSs are deterministic, i.e., they exhibit a single run. The interactive (autonomous, closed) A- and E-termination problems are the A- and E-termination problems restricted to the CGs of interactive (autonomous, closed) DDSs. Notice that, since computation cycles start with the delivery of a message, termination occurs when a configuration with empty channels is reached. This is the reason why we do not consider lossy channels: from each initial state, there is a run that looses all messages and, thus, trivially terminates. Instead, the termination problems over unordered DDSs are undecidable, in general [10].

Theorem 6. *A- and E- termination of interactive (autonomous, closed) unordered DDSs is undecidable.*

4   Propositional DDSs

It is possible to gain decidability of termination by enforcing boundedness constraints on the DDS data-sources.

Definition 27. *A DDS is s-state bounded (c-channel bounded) if, in each reachable configuration, the state DB (the channel) contains at most b constants (c messages).*

To apply a similar constraint on the input DBs, we have to modify the input-policy, and, thus, the CGs, so that they always provide bounded input DBs.

Definition 28. *The interactive (autonomous) b-input bounded CG of a DDS D is defined as Υ_{int} (Υ_{aut}), with the provision that the set of configurations is restricted to those of the of the form (S, I, C) such that I contains at most b-constants. A DDS is bounded if it is s-state bounded, b-input bounded, and c-channel bounded, for some s, b, and c.*

Note that closed pDDSs are 0-bounded. Calvanese et al. [10] charted the impact of boundedness conditions on the decidability of formal verification of sophisticated temporal languages that can express termination. Specifically, verification turns out decidable in only three cases: bounded closed DDSs, bounded autonomous DDSs, s-state bounded and c-channel bounded interactive DDSs. All more general combinations of boundedness constraints and input policies leads to undecidability. Unfortunately, the problem of establishing if a datasource is bounded is undecidable and, thus, techniques based on boundedness cannot be easily exploited in practice.

In this paper, we study an alternative, decidable constraint that allows us to lift channel-boundedness. This is achieved by weakening the message expressiveness. In the data-centric settings of DDSs, this can be easily captured by bounding the message arities. It is known that unbounded channels on binary messages suffer of undecidable termination. Thus, the only interesting restrictions are to propositional or unary messages. In what follows, we study the first case, i.e., propositional transport signatures.

Definition 29. *Given $s, b \in \mathbb{N}$, an (s,b)-propositional-DDS is an s-state and b-input bounded DDS on a propositional channel signature. A propositional DDS (pDDS) is an (s,b)-propositional-DDS for some $s, b \in \mathbb{N}$.*

The A- and E-termination problem for pDDSs are the A- and E-termination problems restricted to the CGs of (s,b)-propositional-DDS when s and b are part of the input.

Problem (A-termination and E-termination of pDDSs)

Input. An (s,b)-propositional-DDS D, along with s and b.
Output. Whether the CG of D A-terminates (E-terminates).

In what follows, we chart the decidability boundary of the termination problems for pDDSs. We show undecidability already for perfect closed pDDSs and decidability for all unordered pDDSs.

5   Undecidability over Queues

We reduce termination of closed pDDSs over queues to termination of 2CMs. In what follows, we refer to a fixed arbitrary 2CM $K = (Q, q_0, q_f, Inst)$. We encode the 2CM state in the state DB, as a constant in a relation $s/1$, and encode the counters in the channels, as the multiplicities of message c_1 and c_2. Thus, we specify the closed pDDS $D = (\mathcal{N}, \Lambda, S_0, \mathcal{P})$ over the signatures $\mathcal{S} = \{s/1, \texttt{shuf}/0, \texttt{exec}/0, \texttt{inst}/4, \texttt{inst}'/5\}$ and $\mathcal{T} = \{c_1/0, c_2/0, \bowtie /0\}$. The initial state DB S_0 contains the initial 2CM state, an encoding of $Inst$, and the flag $\texttt{shuf}$, i.e., $S_0 = \{\texttt{s}(q_0), \texttt{shuf}\} \cup \{\texttt{inst}(+, q, q', c) \mid (+, q, q', c) \in Inst\} \cup \{\texttt{inst}'(-, q, q', q'', c) \mid (-, q, q', q'', c) \in Inst\}$. The program $\mathcal{P}$ is in Fig. 3.

Intuitively, as long as the final 2CM state is not reached (i.e., $\texttt{s}(q_f)$ is not in the state DB), the $\texttt{shuf}$ flag instructs the node to *shuffle* the content of the

```
 1 % Rules about shuf phases.
 2 s(Q); exec; ⋈ if start prev shuf, s(Q), Q≠q_f.
 3 s(Q); exec; ⋈ if ⋈ prev shuf, s(Q), Q≠q_f.
 4 s(Q); shuf; c_1 if c_1 prev shuf, s(Q), Q≠q_f.
 5 s(Q); shuf; c_1 if c_2 prev shuf, s(Q), Q≠q_f.
 6
 7 % Rules about exec phases with increment instructions.
 8 c_1; excecute; s(Q) if inst(+,Q,Q',C), c_1 prev exec, s(Q), Q≠q_f.
 9 c_2; excecute; s(Q) if inst(+,Q,Q',C), c_2 prev exec, s(Q), Q≠q_f.
10 ⋈; c_1; s(Q'); shuf if inst(+,Q,Q',1), ⋈ prev exec, s(Q), Q≠q_f.
11 ⋈; c_2; s(Q'); shuf if inst(+,Q,Q',2), ⋈ prev exec, s(Q), Q≠q_f.
12
13 % Rules about exec phase with decrement instructions over counter 1.
14 shuf; s(Q') if inst'(-,Q,Q',Q'',1), c_1 prev exec, s(Q), Q≠q_f.
15 exec; c_2;s(Q) if inst'(-,Q,Q',Q'',1), c_2 prev exec, s(Q), Q≠q_f.
16 shuf; ⋈;s(Q'') if inst'(-,Q,Q',Q'',1), ⋈ prev exec, s(Q), Q≠q_f.
17
18 % Rules about exec phase with decrement instruction's over counter 2.
19 exec; c_1; s(Q) if inst'(-,Q,Q',Q'',2), c_1 prev exec, s(Q), Q≠q_f.
20 shuf; s(Q') if inst'(-,Q,Q',Q'',2), c_2 prev exec, s(Q), Q≠q_f.
21 shuf; ⋈; s(Q'') if inst'(-,Q,Q',Q'',2), ⋈ prev exec, s(Q), Q≠q_f.
22
23 % Rules about the final phase.
24 shuf; s(q_f) if prev s(q_f).
25
26 % Rules to make inst and inst' persistent.
27 inst(X,Y,Z,W) if prev inst(X,Y,Z,W).
28 inst'(X,Y,Z,W,V) if prev inst'(X,Y,Z,W,V).
```

Fig. 3. Program of the closed pDDS D, over queues, that encodes the 2CM K.

channel-queue until a special message $⋈$ occurs only at the end of the queue (lines 2–5), i.e., it is the last message sent on the channel. When this happens, the node is in position to check (if needed) whether some message c_i is on the channel, by receiving and sending back messages until $⋈$ is received again. This is crucial, since it allows the node to perform increments, decrements, and zero-checks. Thus, by lines 2–5, when $⋈$ is received, shuf is dropped in favor of exec, which instructs the node to *execute*, possibly over several pDDS steps, a 2CM instruction (lines 8–11 for increments, 14–16 for conditional decrements on counter 1 and 19–21 for conditional decrements on counter 2). When the final 2CM configuration is reached, the node stops (line 24) and the messages are just consumed upon reception, forcing termination. Rules 27–28 make the encoding of the 2CM transitions persistent.

Since D is closed and over queue-channels, D exhibits a single run. Thus, we now prove crucial properties of this run. The first is that reachable state DBs encode only one 2CM state and have either the shuf or exec flag.

Definition 30. *A* good *configuration* $C = (S, \emptyset, C)$ *is a configuration such that* $|\{q \in \Delta \mid s(q) \in S\}| = 1$ *and either* **shuf** $\in S$ *or* **exec** $\in S$. *The 2CM state of* C *is the unique constant* q *such that* $s(q) \in S$.

Notice that the program is written in such a way that, given a good configuration $C_1 = (S_1, \emptyset, C_1)$ for which there is a transition $C_1 \to^m C_2$, then, there is a unique line $l < 25$ and a unique instantiation of its variables that make the body of l true in S_1 when receiving m. E.g., if $q_f \in S$, then $l = 24$; otherwise, if **shuf** $\in S_1$ and $m = c_1$, then $l = 4$ and, if **exec** $\in S_1$, $q \in S$, $\text{inst}(+, q, q', 1)$, and $m = \bowtie$, then $l = 10$.

Definition 31. *Given a good configuration* $C = (S, \emptyset, C)$ *and the first message* m *in* C, *the* line *of* C *is the unique line* l *of* $\mathcal{P}$ *such that* $l < 25$ *and there is an instantiation of the variables in* l *such that the instantiation of the scope of* **prev** *is true in* S *and each labeled transport literal* L *in the body of* l, *outisde the scope of* **prev**, *is true in* $\{m\}$.

Lemma 1. *Given a good configuration* $C = (S, \emptyset, C)$ *such that* $C \neq \varepsilon$, *the line of* C *exists and is unique.*

Proof. If $s(q_f) \in S$, then line 24 is clearly the only line whose instantiations of the scope of **prev** are true in S. Moreover, its body contains, outside the scope of **prev**, no labeled transport literal and no variable. Thus, only the trivial instantiation is available. Hence, the line of C is 24. We consider now the case $s(q_f) \notin S$.

If **shuf** $\in S$, being C good, only lines 2–6 have a scope of **prev** whose instantiations may be true in S. Since these lines contain only one variable Q, appearing in $s(Q)$, the instantiation is unique, i.e., it is the mapping σ such that $\sigma(Q) = q$, where q is the unique constant such that $s(q) \in S$. Moreover, m occurs in exactly one rule l among 2–6. Since the body of l contains only m, l is the line of C.

Similarly, if **exec** $\in S$, only lines 8–11, 14–16, and 19–21 have a scope of **prev** whose instantiation can be true in S. Since the scope of **prev** contains only one variable Q appearing in $s(Q)$, this instantiation is the same σ as above. Moreover, since the 2CM is deterministic, there is only one instruction δ fireable from q.

If δ is an increasing transition, after instantiating Q with $\sigma(q)$, only the instantiations of the state predicates in the bodies in lines 8–11 can be true in S. Since these rules contain only one atom over **inst**, again by determinism of the 2CM, there is only one such instantiation σ' (extending σ). If $m = c_1$, or $m = c_2$, i.e., m is the labeled transport fact in the body in line 8 or 9, respectively, then the line of C is 8 or 9. Otherwise, if $m = \bowtie$ and δ is an increment over counter 1 or 2, then, analogously, the line of C is 10 or 11, respectively.

An analogous argument proves the case for decrement transitions.   □

Reasoning with the lines of good configurations, we conclude that all reachable configurations are good.

$$\overbrace{\mathcal{C}_0 \to \mathcal{C}_1}^{\text{shuf} \quad \text{exec}} \to \cdots \to \overbrace{\mathcal{C}_i \to \ldots \mathcal{C}_{i+n} \to \mathcal{C}_{i+n+1} \to \ldots \mathcal{C}_{i+n+m}}^{\text{shuf} \quad \text{exec}} \to \cdots \to \overbrace{\mathcal{C}_j \to \cdots \to \mathcal{C}_{j+l}}^{\text{shuf and final}}$$

$$\underbrace{\phantom{\mathcal{C}_0 \to \mathcal{C}_1}}_{block} \qquad \underbrace{\phantom{\mathcal{C}_i \to \ldots \mathcal{C}_{i+n+m}}}_{block} \qquad \underbrace{\phantom{\mathcal{C}_j \to \cdots \to \mathcal{C}_{j+l}}}_{final\ block}$$

Fig. 4. The run of D organized in phases and blocks. For each block $\mathcal{B}$, all configurations in $\mathcal{B}$ have the same 2CM state and same multiplicity of messages c_1 and c_2 in the channel (Lemma 6 statement 2). Each block encodes a 2CM configuration and the execution of 2CM instructions occur in between blocks (Theoream 7), i.e., in the transition from an **exec** to a **shuf** phase. The final block exists iff the run of D is finite. The sequence of encoded 2CM configurations is the run of the 2CM (see the proof of Theoream 8).

Lemma 2. *If $\mathcal{C}_1$ is a good configuration, and $\mathcal{C}_1 \to \mathcal{C}_2$, then $\mathcal{C}_2$ is a good configuration.*

Proof. The heads of the rules in lines 1–24 deduce either **shuf** or **exec** and only one fact $s(q)$ for some constant q. By definition of line of $\mathcal{C}$, only the line of $\mathcal{C}_1$, with its unique instantiation, is relevant in the computation of $\mathcal{C}_2$. Thus, $\mathcal{C}_2$ is good. $\square$

Lemma 3. *If $\mathcal{C}$ is reachable, then $\mathcal{C}$ is good.*

Proof. Clearly, the initial configuration is a good configuration. Thus, by induction on the position of $\mathcal{C}$ in the run of D, by applying Lemma 2, each reachable configuration is good. $\square$

The line of $\mathcal{C}$ allows us to obtain a useful invariant on channels.

Lemma 4. *For each reachable configuration $\mathcal{C} = (S, \emptyset, C)$, $\mathcal{C}$ is the initial configuration, $C(\bowtie) = 1$, or $s(q_f) \in \mathcal{C}$.*

Proof. If $s(q_f) \notin S$ and $\mathcal{C}$ is not the initial configuration, then $\mathcal{C}$ is reached at least after $n0$ steps, for some $n \in \mathbb{N} \setminus \{0\}$. We proceed by induction on n. If $n = 1$, then $\mathcal{C}_0 \to \mathcal{C}$, and, since the line of $\mathcal{C}_0$, $C = [\bowtie]$ is 2. If the induction hypothesis is true for n, then, there is a configuration $\mathcal{C}_n \neq \mathcal{C}_0$ satisfying the hypothesis and $\mathcal{C}_n \to^m \mathcal{C}$, for some message m. If $m \neq \bowtie$, then the line of $(\mathcal{C}_n, m)$ does not have $\bowtie$ in the head. If $m = \bowtie$, the line of $\mathcal{C}$ has $\bowtie$ both in the body and in the head. Either case, by DDS semantics, the number of $\bowtie$ messages in $\mathcal{C}$ is the same as in $\mathcal{C}_n$, i.e., 1, by inductive hypothesis. $\square$

We organize the DDS run in phases, i.e., sub-runs in which **shuf**, **exec** and q_f are invariant, and blocks of phases, aiming at proving the picture in Fig. 4.

Definition 32. *Let $\mathcal{C}_0 \to \mathcal{C}_1 \to \ldots$ be the run of D. A **shuf** (**exec**, final) phase is a maximal, finite, and non-empty sub-run $\mathcal{C}_i \ldots \mathcal{C}_{i+n}$ for some $i, n \in \mathbb{N}$ such that, for each $j \leq n$, the state DB of $\mathcal{C}_{i+j}$ contains **shuf** (**exec**, q_f).*

For example, since the initial state DB contains shuf and, upon reception of start, shuf is not deduced (see line 2), the initial configuration forms the first phase in the run. Since reachable configurations are good, each phase is either a shuf or an exec phase. We now prove relevant properties of phases

Lemma 5. *Given two reachable configurations* $C_1 = (S_1, \emptyset, C_1)$ *and* $C_2 = (S_2, \emptyset, C_2)$ *such that* $C_1 \rightarrow C_2$, $s(q_1) \in S_1$, $s(q_2) \in S_2$, *for some constants* q_1 *and* q_2, *if* $q_1 \neq q_2$, *then* exec $\in S_1$ *and* shuf $\in S_2$.

Proof. Since C_1 is reachable, it is a good configuration and has a line l. Since $q_1 \neq q_2$, l is among lines 10, 11, 14, 16, 20, and 21, i.e., those with variable Q in the scope of prev and a different variable Q' in the head (to be instantiated with q_1 and q_2, respectively). All these rules have exec in the scope of prev and shuf in the head. Thus, exec $\in S_1$ and shuf $\in S_2$.   □

Notice that the vice-versa does not hold, since 2CM transitions do not necessarily change the state q. The statements in the next lemma is proved analogously to Lemma 5.

Lemma 6. *Given two reachable configurations* $C_1 = (S_1, \emptyset, C_1)$ *and* $C_2 = (S_2, \emptyset, C_2)$, *such that* $C_1 \rightarrow^m C_2$,

1. *If* shuf $\in S_1$, *and* exec $\in S_2$, *then* $\bowtie$ *is the last message of* C_2.
2. *If* shuf $\in S_1$ *or* exec $\in S_2$, *then* $C_1(c_1) = C_2(c_1)$, $C_1(c_2) = C_2(c_2)$, *and there is a constant* q *such that* $s(q) \in S_1 \cap S_2$.
3. *If* exec, $s(q) \in S_1$ *and* $(+, q, q', i) \in Inst$, *for some* $i \in \{1, 2\}$ *and* $q' \in Q$, *then* shuf $\in S_2$ *holds iff* $m = \bowtie$.
4. *If* exec, $s(q) \in S_1$ *and* $(-, q, q', q'', i) \in Inst$, *for some* $i \in \{1, 2\}$ *and* $q', q'' \in Q$, *then* shuf $\in S_2$ *holds iff* $m = c_i$ *or* $m = \bowtie$.

Lemma 7. *D terminates iff there is a final phase.*

Proof. If there is a final phase, then there is a reachable configuration $C_1 = (S_1, \emptyset, C_1)$ such that $s(q_f) \in S_1$. Thus, the line of $C_1 = (S_1, \emptyset, C_1)$ is 24 and, if $C_1 \rightarrow C_2 = (S_2, \emptyset, C_2)$, then $s(q_f) \in S_2$ and $|C_2| = |C_1| - 1$. Thus, by iterating this argument over the next $|C_2|$ successors, we obtain a reachable configuration with empty channels. Thus, D terminates.

Vice-versa, if D terminates, there is a non-initial reachable configuration $C = (S, \emptyset, C)$, where $C = \varepsilon$. Thus, $\bowtie \notin C$ and, by Lemma 4, $s(q_f) \in S$.   □

Lemma 8. *If there is a final phase, it occurs at the end of the run and it is a* shuf *phase.*

Proof. If there is a final phase, then the run of D is finite and ends with a non-initial reachable configuration $C = (S, \emptyset, \varepsilon)$ such that $s(q_f) \in S$. Let $C_1 = (S_1, \emptyset, C_1)$ be the first (non-initial) configuration such that $s(q_f) \in S$. Thus, the line of C is 24 and, if $C_1 \rightarrow C_2 = (S_2, \emptyset, C_2)$, $s(q_f) \in S_2$. Hence, by induction, all configurations reached after C_1 have $s(q_f)$ in their state DB, i.e., the sub-run from C_1 to the end of the run is the final phase.

Moreover, since C_1 is non-initial, there is a $C_3 = (S_3, \emptyset, C_3) \to C_1$ and $\mathsf{s}(\mathsf{q}_\mathsf{f}) \notin S_3$. Thus, by the Lemma 5, $\mathsf{exec} \in S_3$ and $\mathsf{shuf} \in S_1$. Hence, since the line of C_1 is 24 (because $\mathsf{s}(\mathsf{q}_\mathsf{f}) \in S$), all successors of C_1 have shuf in their state DB, i.e., the final phase is a shuf phase.   □

As a consequence, if D terminates, the final phase is unique.

Lemma 9. *Each phase is finite.*

Proof. If there is a final phase, then the run of D is finite and all its sub-runs are finite. Otherwise, suppose that there is no final phase, and, by contradiction, there is an infinite phase. Thus, this phase is not the first one, (which, by line 2, consists only of the initial configuration). Hence, by Lemma 4, all configurations in the phase have a message $\bowtie$ on the channel. Let $C = (S, \emptyset, C)$ be the first configuration in the phase. Say that $\bowtie$ is the n-th message in C, for some $n > 1$. Thus, the n-th configuration in the phase has $\bowtie$ as the first message on the channel, i.e., its line is among 3, 10, 11, 16, and 21 (24 cannot be its line, since there is no final phase). All these rules force a change in phase. Thus, the phase is finite, which is a contradiction.   □

Corollary 1. *Each* shuf *(*exec*) and non-final phase is followed by an* exec *(*shuf*) phase.*

Summarising, we can organize the run of D in blocks consisting either of a pair of successive shuf and exec phases or, if D terminates, of the shuf final phase. We map each block to a reachable 2CM configuration.

Definition 33. *A block $\mathcal{B}$ in the run of D is either 1) the concatenation $F_1 F_2$ of a* shuf *phase F_1 with a consecutive* exec *phase F_2 (i.e., $F_1 F_2$ is a sub-run of the run of D) or 2) the final phase. In the latter case, the block is called* final.

The picture in Fig. 4 is now proved. In fact, by Lemma 5, in each block all configurations have the same 2CM state. Moreover, if $C_1 \to C_2$ and any of the multiplicities of the c_1 or of the c_2 messages in the configurations is different, then the line of C_1 is among 10, 11, 14, 20, and 24. Except line 24, all of them force a change of block. Moreover, line 24 is the line of C_1 only if it is in a final phase. Thus, in each non-final block, the number of c_1 and of c_2 (and also of $\bowtie$) messages is invariant.

Definition 34. *A configuration $C = (S, \emptyset, C)$ encodes a 2CM configuration $\mathcal{K} = (q, k_1, k_2)$, denoted $\Gamma(C) = \mathcal{K}$ if $\mathsf{s}(q) \in S$, $C(c_1) = k_1$, and $C(c_2) = k_2$. A block $\mathcal{B}$ encodes $\mathcal{K}$, denoted $\Gamma(\mathcal{B}) = \mathcal{K}$ if each configuration C in $\mathcal{B}$ satisfies $\Gamma(C) = \mathcal{K}$.*

By studying the encodings of 2CM configurations in blocks, we obtain that D terminates iff $\mathcal{K}$ terminates. We begin by noticing that, by Lemma 6 statement 2, $\Gamma(\mathcal{B}) = \mathcal{K}$ iff there is at least one configuration C in $\mathcal{B}$ such that $\Gamma(C) = \mathcal{K}$. Moreover, since reachable configurations are good, each reachable configuration in D encodes a 2CM configuration. A simple consequence of Corollary 1 is that each block, except the final one, is followed by another block. With the next lemma, we characterize the last configuration of a block.

Lemma 10. *Given a non-final block* $\mathcal{B}$ *such that* $\Gamma(\mathcal{B}) = (q, k_1, k_2)$ *for some* $k_1, k_2 \in \mathbb{N}$ *and* $q \in Q$, *the last configuration in* $\mathcal{B}$ *is the first configuration* $C_1 = (S_1, \emptyset, C_1)$ *in the* **exec** *phase of* $\mathcal{B}$ *such that the first message in* C_1 *is, for some* $q', q'' \in Q$ *and* $i \in \{1, 2\}$:

- $\bowtie$, *if there is an instruction* $(+, q, q', i) \in Inst$, *or*
- c_i *or* $\bowtie$, *if there is an instruction* $(-, q, q', q'', i) \in Inst$.

Proof. Since $\mathcal{B}$ is non final, there is a configuration C_2 such that $C_1 \to^m C_2$. Moreover, $q \neq q_f$ and, thus, there is a transition $\delta \in Inst$ of the form $(+, q, q', i)$ or $(-, q, q', q'', i)$.

If $\delta = (+, q, q', i)$, let $\overline{C}$ be the set of configurations in the **exec** phase of $\mathcal{B}$ whose first message on the channels is $\bowtie$. By Lemma 6 statement 3, $C_1 \in \overline{C}$ and for each $C_3 \in \overline{C}$, C_3 is the last configuration of $\mathcal{B}$, i.e., $C_3 = C_1$. Thus, $\overline{C} = \{C_1\}$ and, trivially, C_1 is the first configuration C in the rn of D such that $C \in \overline{C}$.

If $\delta = (-, q, q', q'', i)$, let $\overline{C}$ be the set of configurations in the **exec** phase of $\mathcal{B}$ whose first message on the channels is $\bowtie$ or c_1. Again, by Lemma 6 statement 4, $\overline{C} = \{C_1\}$ and, trivially, C_1 is the first configuration C in the run of D such that $C \in \overline{C}$.   □

Theorem 7. *Given a block* $\mathcal{B}_1$ *whose last configuration is* $C_1 = (S_1, \emptyset, C_1)$ *and a block* $\mathcal{B}_2$ *whose first configuration is* C_2, $C_1 \to C_2 = (S_2, \emptyset, C_2)$ *iff* $\Gamma(C_1) \to \Gamma(C_2)$.

Proof. Let $s(q_1) \in S_1$, $s(q_2) \in S_2$, $\mathcal{K}_1 = \Gamma(C_1) = (q_1, k_1^1, k_2^1)$, and $\mathcal{K}_2 = \Gamma(C_2) = (q_2, k_1^2, k_2^2)$. If $q_1 = q_f$, then $\mathcal{B}_1$ is the final block and $\Gamma(C_1)$ is the final configuration in the run of K. Thus, both $C_1 \to C_2$ and $\Gamma(C_1) \to \Gamma(C_2)$ are false.

If $q_1 \neq q_f$, then there is a $\delta \in Inst$ of the form $(+, q_1, q', i)$ or $(-, q_1, q', q'', i)$. W.l.o.g., we assume $i = 1$. If $\delta = (+, q_1, q', 1)$, by Lemma 10, the first message in C_1 is $\bowtie$ and, thus, the line of C_1 is 10. Thus, $C_1 \to C_2$ iff $q_2 = q'$, $k_1^2 = C_2(c_1) = C_1(c_1) + 1 = k_1^1 + 1$, and $k_2^2 = C_2(c_2) = C_1(c_2) = k_2^1$ iff $\mathcal{K}_1 \to^\delta \mathcal{K}_2$.

If $\delta = (-, q_1, q', q'', 1)$, by Lemma 10, the first message m in C_1 is either c_1 or $\bowtie$. If $m = c_1$, then $k_1^1 > 0$ and the line of C_1 is 14. Thus, $C_1 \to C_2$ iff $q_2 = q'$, $k_1^2 = C_2(c_1) = C_1(c_1) - 1 = k_1^1 - 1$, and $k_2^2 = C_2(c_2) = C_1(c_2) = k_2^1$ iff $\mathcal{K}_1 \to^\delta \mathcal{K}_2$.

Instead, if $m = \bowtie$, assume by contradiction that $k_1^1 > 0$. Thus, there is a message c_1 in all configurations of $\mathcal{B}$. Since, in the first configuration of the **exec** phase of $\mathcal{B}$, $\bowtie$ is the last message (Lemma 6 statement 1), then there is a configuration C_3 in the **exec** phase of $\mathcal{B}$ whose first message is c_1. By Lemma 10, $C_3 = C_1$ and $\bowtie = m = c_1$, which is a contradiction. Thus, $k_1^1 = 0$. Since $m = \bowtie$, the line of C_1 is 16. Thus, $C_1 \to C_2$ iff $q_2 = q'$, $k_1^2 = C_2(c_1) = C_1(c_1) = k_1^1$, and $k_2^2 = C_2(c_2) = C_1(c_2) = k_2^1$ iff $\mathcal{K}_1 \to^\delta \mathcal{K}_2$.   □

We can finally prove that termination of D is equivalent to termination of K. Thus, we have reduced the undecidable 2CM termination to pDDS termination, which, thus, is undecidable.

Theorem 8. D *terminates iff* K *terminates.*

Proof. Clearly, the first block in the run of D encodes the initial configuration of K. By induction on n, the n-th block B_n in the run of D encodes the n-th configuration $\mathcal{K}_n$ in the run of K. In fact, Since the first block $\mathcal{B}_1$ contains the initial configuration of D, $\mathcal{B}_1$ encodes the initial configuration of K. Moreover, if B_n encodes the $n-th$ configuration $\mathcal{K}_n$ of K and there is a block B_{n+1}, then, by Theorem 7, $\mathcal{B}_n$ encodes a configuration $\mathcal{K}_{n+1}$ of K such that $\mathcal{K}_n \rightarrow \mathcal{K}_{n+1}$, i.e., $\mathcal{K}_{n+1}$ is the $n+1$ configuration in the run of K. Thus, if the run of D is infinite, then the run of K is infinite, i.e., K does not terminates. Instead, if the run of D is finite, then the final block $\mathcal{B}_f$ exists. For each configuration $\mathcal{C} = (S, \emptyset, C)$ in $\mathcal{B}_f$, $\mathbf{s}(\mathbf{q_f}) \in \mathbf{C}$ and, thus, $\mathcal{B}_f$ encodes a configuration $\mathcal{K}_f = (q_f, k_1, k_2)$ of K. Since $\mathcal{B}_f$ is the m-th block in the run of D, then $\mathcal{K}_f$ is the m-th configuration in the run of K, i.e., K reaches q_f and, thus, terminates.   □

Corollary 2. *The problem of (A- and E-) termination of pDDSs is undecidable.*

6 Decidability over Unordered Channels

We now prove decidability of termination for all input policies over multiset-channels. We start with the simplest case, i.e., closed pDDSs. In fact, since multiplicities in multiset-channels are the only source of infinity, pDDSs can be directly encoded in PNs. Then, we study the interactive input policy, which requires a preliminary abstraction to tame the infinite flow of data from the input. Finally, we solve the autonomous case with slight adaptations.

6.1 Closed pDDSs

In closed pDDSs there is no interaction with external systems or users. Thus, there is no injection of fresh values from the input DBs and, hence, the active domains of all data-sources in all reachable configurations is a subset of the initial active domain. However, this is not enough to make pDDSs finite-state systems. In fact, channels can still host an unbounded number of messages. This means that the supports of channel configurations are bounded, but the multiplicities are not. In turn, these can be naturally encoded in PNs: the support amounts to a set of places and the multiplicities to number of tokens marking them. Thus, we effectively encode pDDSs into PNs, reducing pDDS termination to PN termination. In what follows, unless explicitly stated, we work with an arbitrarily fixed pDDS $D = (\mathcal{N}, \Lambda, S_0, \mathcal{P})$.

Encoding. We can use places to encode the state DBs over the initial active domain and the messages. The current state DB S (a specific message m) can be indicated by marking the place S (the place m). We encode the dynamic enforced by the DDS program by means of several PN transitions. Each of them simulates a DDS step in front of a given state DB and incoming message. The encoding PN is defined in Definition 35, exemplified in Example 6, and depicted in Fig. 5.

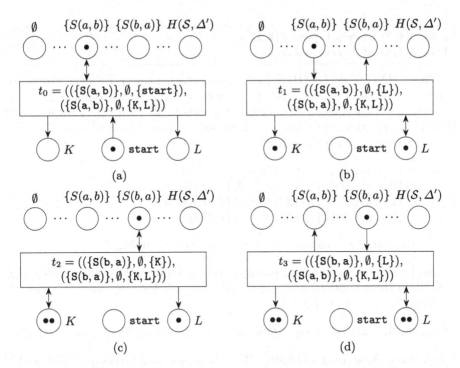

Fig. 5. Transitions of $PN(D)$ from Example 6. (a) depicts the initial marking M_0^D and the only enabled transition $t_0 = ((\{S(a,b)\}, \emptyset, \{start\}), (\{S(a,b)\}, \emptyset, \{K,L\}))$ on M_0. (b) (c) and (d) depict, respectively, the markings M_1, M_2, and M_3 and the transitions t_1, t_2, and t_3 such that, for $i \in \{0, 1, 2\}$, $M_i \to^{t_i} M_{i+1}$. The transition sequence $M_0 \to^{t_0} \cdots \to^{t_3} M_3$ of $PN(D)$ simulates the first steps of the run of D triggered by the reception of messages as in the sequence $(start, L, K, L)$.

Definition 35. $\,- P^D = \mathscr{P}(H(\mathcal{S}, \Delta_0)) \cup T$.
- $T^D \subseteq \mathfrak{C} \times \mathfrak{C}$ *is such that* $((S_1, \emptyset, C_1), (S_2, \emptyset, C_2)) \in T^D$ *if* $C_1 = \{m\}$, *for some message* m, *and* $(S_1, \emptyset, C_1) \to_{clo}^m (S_2, \emptyset, C_2)$.
- *For each* $t = ((S_1, \emptyset, \{m\}), (S_2, \emptyset, C_2)) \in T^D$ *and* $p \in P^D$: *1)* $F^D(p,t), F^D(t,p) \in \{0,1\}$, *2)* $F^D(p,t) = 1$ *iff* $p \in \{S_1, m\}$, *and 3)* $F(t,p) = 1$ *iff* $p \in \{S_2\} \cup C_2$.
- *For each* $p \in P$: *1)* $M_0^D(p) \in \{0,1\}$ *and 2)* $M_0^D(p) = 1$ *iff* $p \in \{S_0, start\}$. *We denote the CG of* $PN(D)$ *by* Υ.

We call each $S \in \mathscr{P}(H(\mathcal{S}, \Delta_0))$ a *state-place* and each $m \in T$ a *message-place*. We denote by $\mathfrak{M}$ the set of markings of $PN(D)$.

Example 6. We provide the PN (see Fig. 5) of a single-node closed pDDS D whose channel signature is $T = \{K/0, L/0\}$, state signature is $\mathcal{S} = \{S/2\}$, set of nodes is $V = \{v\}$, and initial state DB is $\{S(a,b)\}$. Each time v receives a message, both K and L are sent on the channel. When v receives the start or K message, the S tuple is maintained as it is. When v receives L, the order of the S tuple is inverted. This behavior is captured by the following program.

```
1 K;L; S(X,Y) if not L prev S(X,Y).
2 K;L; S(Y,X) if L prev S(X,Y).
```

Thus, $PN(D) = (\mathscr{P}(H(\mathcal{S}, \{a, b, v\})) \cup \{K, L, \mathtt{start}\}, T^D, F^D, \{M_0\})$ for some appropriate T^D, F^D, and M_0^D. Since $H(\mathcal{S}, \{a, b, v\})$ contains 27 facts, there are 2^{27} state-places, e.g., among the others, $\emptyset$, $\{S(a, b)\}$, $\{S(b, a)\}$, and $H(\mathcal{S}, \{a, b, v\})$. Moreover, there are 3 message-places. Thus, T^D contains $2^{27}3$ transitions, e.g., among the others,

- $t_0 = ((\{\mathtt{S(a,b)}\}, \emptyset, \{\mathtt{start}\}), (\{\mathtt{S(a,b)}\}, \emptyset, \{\mathtt{K, L}\})),$
- $t_1 = ((\{\mathtt{S(a,b)}\}, \emptyset, \{\mathtt{L}\}), (\{\mathtt{S(b,a)}\}, \emptyset, \{\mathtt{K, L}\})),$
- $t_2 = ((\{\mathtt{S(b,a)}\}, \emptyset, \{\mathtt{K}\}), (\{\mathtt{S(b,a)}\}, \emptyset, \{K, L\})),$ and
- $t_3 = ((\{\mathtt{S(b,a)}\}, \emptyset, \{\mathtt{L}\}), (\{\mathtt{S(a,b)}\}, \emptyset, \{\mathtt{K, L}\})).$

The restriction of F^D to those transitions is depicted in Fig. 5.

As can be seen in the previous example, the encoding suffers of an exponential blow up in the size of the initial state DB. Nevertheless, this issue is irrelevant for decidability. In fact, $PN(D)$ can be computed.

Theorem 9. *There is an algorithm such that, given a pDDS D, returns $PN(D)$.*

Proof. Since Δ_0 is fixed and finite, P^D is finite and can be computed. Also T^D is finite. Moreover, for each $(S_1, \emptyset, \{m\})$, the set of configurations $\mathcal{C}_2 \in \mathfrak{C}$ such that $\mathcal{C}_1 \rightarrow_{clo}^m \mathcal{C}_2$ can be computed via the DDS program. Thus, also T^D can be computed. Similarly, for each transition $t \in T^D$, the functions $F^D(\_, t), F^D(t, \_)$: $P^D \longrightarrow \{0, 1\}$ can be computed, again, by applying the DDS program. Finally, M_0^D can be computed as in Definition 35. $\square$

We now interpret configurations of D as markings in $PN(D)$.

Definition 36. *Given a configuration $\mathcal{C} = (S, \emptyset, C)$ of D, its encoding marking $M^{\mathcal{C}}$ is the marking of $PN(D)$ such that: 1) $M^{\mathcal{C}}(S) = 1$, 2) for each $q \in T$, $M^{\mathcal{C}}(q) = C(q)$, and 3) for each other place $p \notin T \cup \{S\}$, $M^{\mathcal{C}}(p) = 0$.*

By construction, the encoding marking of the initial configuration of D is the initial marking of $PN(D)$. Notice that, if a transition t is enabled on an encoding marking M and $M \rightarrow^t M'$, then, also M' is an encoding marking. Since P^D explicitly encodes the state DBs and messages without any abstraction, for each configuration there is only one encoding marking and vice-versa.

Bisimulation. The notion of encoding marking induces a bisimulation between D and $PN(D)$. This is proved by simple algebraic checks.

Theorem 10. *Υ_{clo} and Υ are bisimilar.*

Proof. Let $B = \{(\mathcal{C}, M) \in \mathfrak{C} \times \mathfrak{M} \mid M = M^{\mathcal{C}}\}$. We show that B is a bisimulation. Suppose that $\mathcal{C}_1 = (S_1, \emptyset, C_1) \to^m \mathcal{C}_2 = (S_2, \emptyset, C_2)$ and $B(\mathcal{C}_1, M_1)$. Thus, by DDS semantics, $S_2 = state(S_1, \emptyset, m)$ and $C_2 = C_1 - \{m\} + out(S_1, \emptyset, m)$. Moreover, $M_1 = M^{\mathcal{C}_1}$, $M_1(m) \geq 1$, and the transition $t = ((S_1, \emptyset, \{m\}), (S_2, \emptyset, C_2))$ is enabled. Let $M_1 \to^t M_2$. Thus, for each place p, $M_2(p) = M_1(p) - F(p, t) + F(t, p)$. By definition of F^D, $F(t, S_2) = 1$, $F(m, t) = 1$ and:

- For each state-place $p \notin \{S_1, S_2\}$, $M_1(p) = 0$ and $F(p, t) = F(t, p) = 0$; thus, $M_2(p) = 0$.
- If $S_1 = S_2$, then $M_1(S_2) = 1$ and $F(S_2, t) = 1$; thus, $M_2(S_2) = 1$.
- If $S_1 \neq S_2$, then:
  - $M_1(S_1) = 1$, $F(S_1, t) = 1$, and $F(t, S_1) = 0$; thus $M_2(S_1) = 0$.
  - $M_1(S_2) = 0$, $F(S_1, t) = 0$, and $F(t, S_1) = 1$; thus $M_2(S_2) = 1$.
- If $m \in out(S_1, \emptyset, m)$, then $C_2(m) = C_1(m) = M_1(m)$ and $F(t, m) = 1$; thus, $M_2(m) = M_1(m) = C_2(m)$.
- If $m \notin out(S_1, \emptyset, m)$, $C_2(m) = C_1(m) - 1 = M_1(m) - 1$ and $F(t, m) = 0$; thus, $M_2(m) = M_1(m) - 1 = C_2(m)$.
- For each message-place $q \neq m$, $F(q, t) = 0$:
  - If $q \in out(S_1, \emptyset, m)$, $C_2(q) = C_1(q) + 1 = M_1(q) + 1$ and $F(t, q) = 1$; thus, $M_2(q) = M_1(q) + 1 = C_2(q)$.
  - If $q \notin out(S_1, \emptyset, m)$, $C_2(q) = C_1(q) = M_1(q)$ and $F(t, q) = 0$; thus, $M_2(q) = M_1(q) = C_2(q)$.

Thus, $M_2 = M^{\mathcal{C}_2}$, i.e., $B(\mathcal{C}_2, M_2)$. The proof of condition 2 in Definition 42 is analogous. Thus, B is a bisimulation. Moreover, since the initial configuration of D is bisimilar to the initial marking of $PN(D)$, Υ_{clo} and Υ are bisimilar. $\square$

Since in closed pDDSs there is a single initial configuration, E- and A-termination of D are equivalent and we can analyze them by building $PN(D)$ and analyzing termination of $PN(D)$, which is a decidable problem.

Theorem 11. *Termination of closed pDDSs is decidable.*

6.2   Interactive pDDSs

We adapt the technique of Sect. 6.1 to the interactive input policy. In this case, even if an infinite amount of constants can flow in the system throughout an infinite run, their value is almost irrelevant: the only useful information is whether two constants are different and whether they are mentioned in the program, the network DBs, or in the initial state DB. Thus, we show how to abstract away the constants and encode the abstract system in a PN. In what follows, unless otherwise explicitly stated, we refer to a fixed, arbitrary, interactive, s-state, and b-input bounded pDDS $D = (\mathcal{N}, \Lambda, S_0, \mathcal{P})$.

Abstraction. First, we fix finite domains on which the abstraction ranges.

Definition 37. *Let Δ_s and Δ_e be set of constants such that $|\Delta_s| = s$, $|\Delta_e| = b$, and Δ_s, Δ_e, and Δ_0 are pairwise disjoint. They are called, respectively,* state *and* input abstract domain. *The* general abstract domain *is the set $\Delta_g = \Delta_s \cup \Delta_e \cup \Delta_0$. The set $Eq(D)$ is the set of equivalence relations $\sim$ on Δ_g such that, for each equivalence class K of $\sim$, $|K \cap \Delta_s| \leq 1$, $|K \cap \Delta_e| \leq 1$, and $|K \cap \Delta_0| \leq 1$.*

We use the abstract domains to rename constants in the related data-sources. The information about inequalities among the constants is captured by an equivalence relation $\sim$. Intuitively, $g_1 \sim g_2$ means that g_1 and g_2 represent the same constant in different abstract -domains.

Definition 38. *An* abstract configuration *is a tuple $\mathcal{A} = (S, I, C, \sim)$, where*

- S *is a state DB over Δ_s.*
- I *is an input DB over Δ_e.*
- C *is a multiset of messages.*
- $\sim \in Eq(D)$ *such that, for each $c \in \Delta_s \cup \Delta_e$, if $c \notin \Delta(S) \cup \Delta(I)$, $[c]_\sim = \{c\}$.*

The *set of abstract configurations* is denoted by $\mathfrak{A}$. We denote configurations by the letter $\mathcal{C}$ and abstract configurations by the letter $\mathcal{A}$, possibly with underscripts and superscripts.

Example 7. Consider an interactive, 2-state, 2-input bounded, single-node (over $V = \{p_0\}$) pDDS with one constant $p_1 \in \Delta(\mathcal{P})$. Thus, $\Delta_0 = \{p_0, p_1\}$. Suppose that the signatures are $\mathcal{S} = \{A/2\}$, $\mathcal{I} = \{B/1\}$, and $\mathcal{T} = \{Q/0\}$. Let $\Delta_s = \{s_1, s_2\}$ and $\Delta_e = \{e_1, e_2\}$. An example of abstract configuration is $\mathcal{A} = (S, I, C, \sim)$ where $S = \{A(s_1, s_2)\}$, $I = \{B(e_1), B(e_2)\}$, $C(Q) = 3$, and the classes of $\sim$ are $\{p_0, s_2, e_1, \}$, $\{s_1\}$, and $\{p_1, e_2\}$.

We now relate abstract configurations to configurations.

Definition 39. *The* concretization operator *Ω is the function $\Omega : \mathfrak{A} \longrightarrow \mathfrak{C}$ such that, for each $\mathcal{A} = (S, I, C, \sim)$, $\Omega(\mathcal{A})$ is the configuration $(\omega_\sim(S), \omega_\sim(I), C)$, where, $\omega_\sim : \Delta_g \longrightarrow \Delta_g$ is the function such that, for each $g \in \Delta_g$,*

$$\omega_\sim(g) = \begin{cases} p & \text{if } p \in [g]_\sim \cap \Delta_0 \\ s & \text{if } [g]_\sim \cap \Delta_0 = \emptyset \text{ and } s \in [g]_\sim \cap \Delta_s \\ e & \text{if } [g]_\sim \cap (\Delta_0 \cup \Delta_s) = \emptyset \text{ and } e \in [g]_\sim \cap \Delta_e \end{cases}$$

The configuration $\Omega(\mathcal{A})$ is called the concretization *of $\mathcal{A}$.*

Example 8. The concretization of the abstract configuration $\mathcal{A}$ in Example 7 is $\mathcal{C} = (S, I, C)$ where $S = \{A(s_1, p_0)\}$, $I = \{B(p_0), B(p_1)\}$, and $C(Q) = 3$.

We exploit Ω to define interactive transitions among abstract configurations.

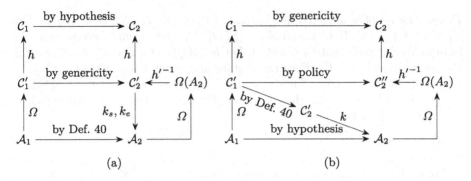

Fig. 6. Diagrams of the proof of (a) Theorem 12 and (b) Theorem 13.

Definition 40. *Given two abstract configurations* $\mathcal{A}_1 = (S_1, I_1, C_1, \sim_1)$ *and* $\mathcal{A}_2 = (S_2, I_2, C_2, \sim_2)$, *there is an* interactive abstract transition *witnessed by the message* m, *denoted by* $\mathcal{A}_1 \rightarrow^m_{int} \mathcal{A}_2$, *if, letting* $\Omega(S_1, I_1, C_1, \sim_1) = (S, I, C_1)$:

- $m \in C_1$,
- $C_2 = C_1 - \{m\} + out(S, I, m)$,
- *there is an injective function* $k : \Delta(state(S, I, m)) \hookrightarrow \Delta_s$ *such that*
  - $S_2 = k(state(S, I, m))$, *and*
  - *for each* $s \in \Delta(S_2)$ *and* $p \in \Delta_0$, $s \sim_2 p$ *iff* $p \in \Delta(state(S, I, m))$ *and* $k(p) = s$.

Remark 1. Definition 40 implies that there is some input DB J such that, letting $\mathcal{C} = (state(S, I, m), J, C_2)$, $\Omega(\mathcal{A}_1) \rightarrow^m \mathcal{C}$, i.e., $\mathcal{A}_1 \rightarrow^m \mathcal{A}_2$ if the state DB of $\mathcal{A}_2$ and corresponding part of $\sim_2$ can be viewed as an *abstraction* of the state DB of $\mathcal{C}$.

With abstract configurations and interactive abstract transitions, we define the interactive abstract configuration graph.

Definition 41. *The* interactive abstract configuration graph *is the CG* $\Upsilon^{abst}_{int} = (\mathfrak{A}, E, M)$ *such that, for each* $\mathcal{A}_1, \mathcal{A}_2 \in \mathfrak{A}$, $(\mathcal{A}_1, \mathcal{A}_2) \in E$ *iff* $\mathcal{A}_1 \rightarrow^m_{int} \mathcal{A}_2$ *for some message* m *and, for each* $\mathcal{A} = (S, I, C, \sim) \in \mathfrak{A}$, $\mathcal{A} \in M$ *if* $\omega_\sim(S'_0) = S_0$ *and* $C = \{\texttt{start}\}$.

We now define a bisimulation between Υ_{int} and Υ^{abst}_{int}.

Definition 42. *The relation* $B \subset \mathfrak{C} \times \mathfrak{A}$ *is the relation such that* $B(\mathcal{C}, \mathcal{A})$ *iff there is a* Δ_0-*isomorphism* h *such that* $\mathcal{C} = h(\Omega(\mathcal{A}))$.

Theorem 12. *Given two configurations* $\mathcal{C}_1$ *and* $\mathcal{C}_2$, *an abstract configuration* $\mathcal{A}_1$, *and a message* m, *if* $\mathcal{C}_1 \rightarrow^m \mathcal{C}_2$ *and* $B(\mathcal{C}_1, \mathcal{A}_1)$, *then there is an abstract configuration* $\mathcal{A}_2$ *such that* $\mathcal{A}_1 \rightarrow^m_{int} \mathcal{A}_2$ *and* $B(\mathcal{C}_2, \mathcal{A}_2)$.

Proof. The proof is depicted in Fig. 6a. Let $\mathcal{C}_1 = (S_1, I_1, C_1)$, $\mathcal{C}_2 = (S_2, I_2, C_2)$, $C'_1 = \Omega(\mathcal{A}_1) = (S'_1, I'_1, C_1)$, and $\mathcal{A}_1 = (S''_1, I''_1, C_1, \sim_1)$. Then, there is some Δ_0-isomorphism h such that $\mathcal{C}_1 = h(C'_1)$. Let $h^{-1}(\mathcal{C}_2) = C'_2$ and $C'_2 = (S'_2, I'_2, C_2)$. By genericity, $\mathcal{C}'_1 \to^m \mathcal{C}'_2$. Because of state and input boundedness, $|\Delta(S'_2)| \leq |\Delta_s|$ and $|\Delta(I'_2)| \leq |\Delta_e|$. Thus, there are injective functions $k_s : \Delta(S'_2) \hookrightarrow \Delta_s$ and $k_e : \Delta(I'_2) \hookrightarrow \Delta_e$. Hence, we can fix the abstract configuration $\mathcal{A}_2 = (S'_2, I'_2, C_2, \sim_2)$ such that:

- $S''_2 = k_s(S'_2)$.
- $I''_2 = k_e(I'_2)$.
- For each $s \in \Delta_s$ and $e \in \Delta_e$, $s \sim_2 e$ iff there is a $c \in \Delta(S'_2) \cap \Delta(I'_2)$ such that $s = k_s(c)$ and $e = k_e(c)$.
- For each $s \in \Delta_s$ and $p \in \Delta_0$, $s \sim_2 p$ iff $p \in \Delta(S'2)$ and $k_s(p) = s$.
- For each $e \in \Delta_e$ and $p \in \Delta_0$, $e \sim_2 p$ iff $p \in \Delta(S'2)$ and $k_e(p) = e$.

Thus, by Definition 40, $\mathcal{A}_1 \to^m_{int} \mathcal{A}_2$. However, $\mathcal{C}'_2$ and $\Omega(\mathcal{A}_2)$ may be different. Nevertheless, we now prove that they are isomorphic. In fact, let $k : \Delta(S'_2) \cup \Delta(I'_2) \to \Delta_g$ such that, for each $c \in \Delta(S'_2) \cup \Delta(I'_2)$:

$$k(c) = \begin{cases} id(c) & \text{if } c \in \Delta_0 \\ k_s(c) & \text{if } c \in \Delta(S'_2) \setminus \Delta_0 \\ k_e(c) & \text{if } c \in \Delta(I'_2) \setminus (\Delta(S'_2) \cup \Delta_0) \end{cases}$$

Notice that k is injective, since it is a piece-wise function whose pieces are injective with pairwise disjoint image sets. Moreover, k extends $id|_{\Delta_0}$. Thus, k can be extended to a Δ_0-isomorphism h'. For each $c \in \Delta(S'_2)$:

- If $c \in \Delta_0$, $k(c) = c = k_s(c) \in [k_s(c)]_{\sim_2} \cap \Delta_0$ and, hence, $\omega_{\sim_2}(k_s(c)) = k(c)$.
- If $c \notin \Delta_0$, $k(c) = k_s(c) \in \Delta_s$ and $[k_s(c)]_{\sim_2} \cap \Delta_0 = \emptyset$; hence, $\omega_{\sim_2}(k_s(c)) = k(c)$.

In either case, $\omega_{\sim_2}(k_s(c)) = k(c)$. Moreover, for each $c \in \Delta(I'_2)$:

- If $c \in \Delta_0$, $k(c) = c = k_e(c) \in [k_e(c)]_{\sim_2} \cap \Delta_0$ and, hence, $\omega_{\sim_2}(k_e(c)) = k(c)$.
- If $c \in \Delta(S'_2) \setminus \Delta_0$, $k(c) = k_s(c) \in \Delta_s$, $k_s(c) \sim_2 k_e(c)$, and $[k_s(c)]_{\sim_2} \cap \Delta_0 = [k_e(c)]_{\sim_2} \cap \Delta_0 = \emptyset$; hence, $\omega_{\sim_2}(k_e(c)) = k_s(c) = k(c)$.
- If $c \notin \Delta(S'_2) \setminus \Delta_0$, $k(c) = k_e(c)$ and $[k_e(c)]_{\sim_2} \cap (\Delta_s \cup \Delta_0) = \emptyset$; hence $\omega_{\sim_2}(k_e(c)) = k_e(c) = k(c)$.

In any case, $k_e(c) = k(c)$. Thus, $h'(C'_2) = (\omega_{\sim_2} \circ k_s(S'_2), \omega_{\sim_2} \circ k_e(I'_2), C_2) = \Omega(k_s(S'_2), k_e(I'_2), C_2, \sim_2) = \Omega(\mathcal{A}_2)$ and $C_2 = h(C'_2) = h \circ h'^{-1}(\Omega(\mathcal{A}_2))$. Since isomorphisms are closed under composition and we already proved $\mathcal{A}_1 \to^m_{int} \mathcal{A}_2$, we conclude that $B(\mathcal{C}_2, \mathcal{A}_2)$. □

Theorem 13. *Given a configuration $\mathcal{C}_1$, two abstract configurations $\mathcal{A}_1$ and $\mathcal{A}_2$, and a message m if $\mathcal{A}_1 \to^m_{int} \mathcal{A}_2$ and $B(\mathcal{C}_1, \mathcal{A}_1)$, then there is a configuration $\mathcal{C}_2$ such that $\mathcal{C}_1 \to^m \mathcal{C}_2$ and $B(\mathcal{C}_2, \mathcal{A}_2)$.*

Proof. The proof is depicted in Fig. 6b. Let $\mathcal{C}_1 = (S_1, I_1, C_1)$, $\mathcal{A}_1 = (S_1'', I_1'', C_1)$, $\mathcal{C}_1' = \Omega(\mathcal{A}_1) = (S_1', I_1', C_1)$, and $\mathcal{A}_2 = (S_2'', I_2'', C_2, \sim_2)$. Then, by Definition 40, there is a configuration $\mathcal{C}_2' = (S_2', I_2', C_2)$ such that $\mathcal{C}_1' \to^m \mathcal{C}_2'$ and an injective function $k : \Delta(S_2') \to \Delta_s$ such that $S_2'' = k(S_2')$.

The function $\omega_{\sim_2} \circ k$, with domain $\Delta(S_2')$, is injective and, for each $p \in \Delta_0 \cap \Delta(S_2'')$, $\omega_{\sim_2}(k(p)) = p$, since $p \in [k(p)]_{\sim_2}$. Thus, $\omega_{\sim_2} \circ k$ can be extended to a Δ_0-isomorphism h'. Let $\mathcal{C}_2'' = (S_2', {h'}^{-1}(\omega_{\sim_2}(I_2'')), C_2)$. Hence, $h'(\mathcal{C}_2'') = \Omega(\mathcal{A}_2)$. Moreover, since $\mathcal{C}_2'$ and $\mathcal{C}_2''$ differ only for their input DB, by the interactive input policy, $\mathcal{C}_1' \to^m \mathcal{C}_2''$ and, by genericity, $\mathcal{C}_1 \to^m h(\mathcal{C}_2'') = h({h'}^{-1}(\Omega(\mathcal{A}_2)))$. Let $\mathcal{C}_2 = h(\mathcal{C}_2'')$. Hence, $\mathcal{C}_1 \to \mathcal{C}_2$ and $B(\mathcal{C}_2, \mathcal{A}_2)$. □

Corollary 3. *The relation B is a bisimulation between Υ_{int} and Υ_{int}^{abst}.*

Proof. Thanks to Thms. 12 and Theorem 13, we only have to prove that B relates the initial configurations. As in the proof of Theorem 12, for each initial configuration $\mathcal{C}_0 = (S_0, I, \{\texttt{start}\})$ of Υ_{int}, by state and input boundedness there are k_s and k_e such that $\mathcal{A}_0 = (\omega(k_s(S_0), k_e(I), \{\texttt{start}\}))$, which, by Definition 41, is initial in Υ_{int}^{abst}, is Δ_0-isomorphic via an isomorphism h to $\mathcal{C}_0$, i.e., $B(\mathcal{C}_0, \mathcal{A}_0)$, since $\Delta(S_0) \subseteq \Delta_0$ and, $\omega_\sim(k(S_0)) = h(\omega_\sim(k(S_0))) = S_0$.

Moreover, for each an initial $\mathcal{A}_0$ of Υ_{int}^{abst}, by Definition 41, $\Omega(\mathcal{A}_0)$ is Δ_0-isomorphic to an initial configuration $\mathcal{C}_0$, i.e., $B(\mathcal{C}_0, \mathcal{A}_0)$. □

Encoding. We now encode the abstract interactive configuration graph into a PN. Since all components of abstract configurations range over finite abstract domains, the procedure is similar to that of closed pDDSs: the places represent all possible components of abstract configurations, markings are used to encode a single abstract configuration, and transitions implement the successor relation of Υ_{int}^{abst}, as formalized next. In order to encode, as distinct places, both the state and the innput empty DM, we need to add places from a form of disjoint union of state and input DBs over abstract domains.

Definition 43. *The PN $PN(D) = (P^D, T^D, F^D, \mathcal{M}_0^D)$ of D is such that:*

- $P^D = (\mathscr{P}(H(\mathcal{S}, \Delta_s)) \times \{state\}) \cup (\mathscr{P}(H(\mathcal{I}, \Delta_e)) \times \{input\}) \cup \mathcal{T} \cup (\Delta_g \times \Delta_g \times \{\top, \bot\})$, *where state and input are strings.*
- $T^D \subseteq \mathfrak{A} \times \mathfrak{A}$ *is such that* $((S_1, I_1, C_1, \sim_1), (S_2, I_2, C_2, \sim_2)) \in T^D$ *if* $C_1 = \{m\}$, *for some message m, and* $(S_1, I_1, C_1, \sim_1) \to_{int}^{abst} (S_2, I_2, C_2, \sim_2)$.
- *For each transition* $t = (S_1, I_1, \{m\}, \sim_1), (S_2, I_2, C_2, \sim_2)$:
  - *t consumes one token from S_1, I_1, m, $(g_1, g_2, \top)$ if $g_1 \sim g_2$, and $(g_1, g_2, \bot)$ if $g_1 \not\sim g_2$, i.e.,*
    - *for each $p \in (\mathscr{P}(H(\mathcal{S}, \Delta_s)) \times \{state\}) \cup (\mathscr{P}(H(\mathcal{I}, \Delta_e)) \times \{input\}) \cup \mathcal{T}$:*

$$F(p,t) = \begin{cases} 1 & \text{if } p \in \{(S_1, state), (I_1, input), m\} \\ 0 & \text{otherwise} \end{cases}$$

* *for each $g_1, g_2 \in \Delta_g$ and $\square \in \{\top, \bot\}$*

$$F((g_1, g_2, \square), t) = \begin{cases} 1 & \text{if } \square = \top \text{ and } g_1 \sim_1 g_2 \\ 1 & \text{if } \square = \bot \text{ and } g_1 \not\sim_1 g_2 \\ 0 & \text{otherwise} \end{cases}$$

- *t produces one token in S_2, I_2, each $m_2 \in C_2$, $(g_1, g_2, \top)$ if $g_1 \sim_2 g_2$, and $(g_1, g_2, \bot)$ if $g_1 \not\sim_2 g_2$, i.e.,*
  * *for each $p \in (\mathscr{P}(H(\mathcal{S}, \Delta_s)) \times \{state\}) \cup (\mathscr{P}(H(\mathcal{I}, \Delta_e)) \times \{input\}) \cup \mathcal{T}$:*

$$F(t, p) = \begin{cases} 1 & \text{if } p \in \{(S_2, state)(I_2, input)\} \cup C_2 \\ 0 & \text{otherwise} \end{cases}$$

  * *for each $g_1, g_2 \in \Delta_g$ and $\square \in \{\top, \bot\}$*

$$F((g_1, g_2, \square), t) = \begin{cases} 1 & \text{if } \square = \top \text{ and } g_1 \sim_2 g_2 \\ 1 & \text{if } \square = \bot \text{ and } g_1 \not\sim_2 g_2 \\ 0 & \text{otherwise} \end{cases}$$

- *$\mathcal{M}_0$ is the set of markings encoding the initial abstract configurations of Υ_{int}^{abst}, where, for each abstract configuration $\mathcal{A} = (S, I, C, \sim)$, $\mathcal{A}$ is encoded by a marking M if:*
  - *For each $p \in (\mathscr{P}(H(\mathcal{S}, \Delta_s)) \times \{state\}) \cup (\mathscr{P}(H(\mathcal{I}, \Delta_e)) \times \{input\})$,*

$$M(p) = \begin{cases} 1 & \text{if } p \in \{(S, state), (I, input)\} \\ 0 & \text{otherwise} \end{cases}$$

  - *For each message $T \in \mathcal{T}$, $M(T) = C(T)$.*
  - *For each $g_1, g_2 \in \Delta_g$ and $\square \in \{\top, \bot\}$*

$$F((g_1, g_2, \square), t) = \begin{cases} 1 & \text{if } \square = \top \text{ and } g_1 \sim g_2 \\ 1 & \text{if } \square = \bot \text{ and } g_1 \not\sim g_2 \\ 0 & \text{otherwise} \end{cases}$$

We denote the CG of $PN(D)$ by Υ.

The CGs Υ and Υ_{int}^{abst} are bisimilar. The proof is analogous to that of Theorem 10, which states the bisimilarity between a closed pDDS and its PN. Thus, we omit the proof of the next theorem.

Theorem 14. *Υ is bisimilar to Υ_{int}^{abst}.*

As for the closed case, $PN(D)$ can be computed. This holds because the successors of an abstract configuration $\mathcal{A}$ can be computed directly, without computing the successors of $\Omega(\mathcal{A})$, which, in turn, are in infinite number because of the interactive input policy.

Theorem 15. *There is an algorithm such that, given an interactive pDDS D with abstract domains, returns PN(D).*

Proof. As in Theorem 9, P^D is finite and computable, since the abstract domains are given as input. Moreover, the set of abstract configurations with only one message in the channel is finite and, for each such configuration $\mathcal{A}$, the set of successors can be computed: according to Definition 43, it suffices to 1) compute $\Omega(\mathcal{A}) = (S, I, C)$, 2) for each message $m \in C$, compute $C' = out(S, I, m)$ and $S' = state(S, I, m)$, and 3) for each function k and equivalence relation $\sim_2$ as in Definition 43, and for each input DB I over Δ_e, build the successor $\mathcal{A}_2 = (k(S'), I, C', \sim_2)$. Clearly, this procedure computes all and only the abstract configurations $\mathcal{A}_2$ as in Definition 43, i.e., it computes the set of successors of $\mathcal{A}$. Moreover, the procedure terminates because the sets of functions k, relations $\sim_2$, and input DBs I over Δ_e are finite and enumerable (since they range over the finite and fixed abstract domains). Finally, the functions $F^D(\_, t), F^D(t, \_) : P^D \longrightarrow \{0, 1\}$ can be computed according to the algebraic conditions in Definition 43 and $\mathcal{M}_0$ can be computed by checking, for each abstract configuration $\mathcal{A}$ of the form $(S, I, \{\texttt{start}\}, \sim)$, whether $\Omega(\mathcal{A})$ is an initial configuration of D. $\square$

Thus, again, we can analyze A- or E-termination of D by building $PN(D)$ and then checking whether $PN(D)$ A- or E-terminates.

Theorem 16. *Both E- and A-termination are decidable for interactive pDDSs.*

6.3   Autonomous pDDSs

Autonomous pDDSs can be analyzed with the same technique. In what follows, we refer to a fixed autonomous pDDS $D = (\mathcal{N}, \Lambda, S_0, \mathcal{P})$. First, we define autonomous abstract transitions in place of interactive ones.

Definition 44. *Given two abstract configurations $\mathcal{A}_1 = (S_1, I_1, C_1, \sim_1)$ and $\mathcal{A}_2 = (S_2, I_2, C_2, \sim_2)$, there is an autonomous abstract transition witnessed by the message m, denoted by $\mathcal{A}_1 \to^m_{aut} \mathcal{A}_2$ if, letting $\Sigma(S_1, I_1, C_1, \sim_1) = (S, I, C_1)$, on top of the conditions in Definition 40 for $\mathcal{A}_1 \to^m_{int} \mathcal{A}_2$, there is an injective function $k' : \Delta(I) \hookrightarrow \Delta_e$ such that:*

- $I_2 = k'(I)$.
- *For each $e \in \Delta(I_2)$ and $p \in \Delta_0$, $e \sim_2 p$ iff $p \in \Delta(I)$ and $k'(p) = e$.*
- *For each $e \in \Delta(I_2)$ and $s \in \Delta(S_2)$, $e \sim_2 s$ iff there is a $c \in \Delta(S) \cap \Delta(I)$ such that $k(c) = s$ and $k'(c) = e$.*

This allows us to define the abstract autonomous CG.

Definition 45. *The autonomous abstract configuration graph is the CG $\Upsilon^{abst}_{aut} = (\mathfrak{A}, E, M)$ such that, for each $\mathcal{A}_1, \mathcal{A}_2 \in \mathfrak{A}$, $(\mathcal{A}_1, \mathcal{A}_2) \in E$ iff $\mathcal{A}_1 \to^m_{aut} \mathcal{A}_2$ for some message m and, for each $A \in \mathcal{A}$, $A \in M$ if there is a Δ_0-isomorphism h such that $h(\Omega(\mathcal{A}))$ is an initial configuration of Υ_{aut}.*

The relation B in Definition 42 is a bisimulation also between $\varUpsilon_{aut}$ and $\varUpsilon_{aut}^{abst}$.

Theorem 17. *Given two configurations $\mathcal{C}_1, \mathcal{C}_2$ and an abstract configuration $\mathcal{A}_1$ such that $\mathcal{C}_1 \rightarrow_{aut}^m \mathcal{C}_2$ and $B(\mathcal{C}_1, \mathcal{A}_1)$, there is an abstract configuration $\mathcal{A}_2$ such that $\mathcal{A}_1 \rightarrow_{aut}^m \mathcal{A}_2$ and $B(\mathcal{C}_2, \mathcal{A}_2)$.*

Proof. The proof is analogous to the one of Theorem 12. In fact, the new conditions in Definition 44 are the same used in the proof of Theorem 12 to define the abstract configuration $\mathcal{A}_2$.   □

Theorem 18. *Given a configuration $\mathcal{C}_1$ and two abstract configurations $\mathcal{A}_1, \mathcal{A}_2$ such that $\mathcal{A}_1 \rightarrow_{aut}^m \mathcal{A}_2$ and $B(\mathcal{C}_1, \mathcal{A}_1)$, there is a configuration $\mathcal{C}_2$ such that $\mathcal{C}_1 \rightarrow_{aut}^m \mathcal{C}_2$ and $B(\mathcal{C}_2, \mathcal{A}_2)$.*

Proof. The proof is analogous to the one of Theorem 13 with the provision that, since the transitions comply to the autonomous input policy both in $\varUpsilon_{aut}$ and $\varUpsilon_{aut}^{abst}$, $\Omega(\mathcal{A}_2)$ is isomorphic directly to $\mathcal{C}_2'$ via the same isomorphism k defined in the proof of Theorem 12.   □

Corollary 4. *$\varUpsilon_{aut}$ is bisimilar to $\varUpsilon_{aut}^{abst}$.*

Finally, the encoding of $\varUpsilon_{aut}^{abst}$ is exactly the one used for interactive pDDSs, with the provision that the set of PN transitions is defined according to autonomous abstract transitions, instead of interactive abstract transitions. Specifically, $T^D \subseteq \mathfrak{A} \times \mathfrak{A}$ is such that $((S_1, I_1, C_1 \sim_1), (S_2, I_2, C_2 \sim_2))$. If $C_1 = \{m\}$, for some message m, and $(S_1, I_1, C_1 \sim_1) \rightarrow_{aut}^m (S_2, I_2, C_2 \sim_2)$. Again, for the same reasons as for interactive pDDSs, the PN can be effectively built and termination of autonomous pDDSs can be analyzed via the PN.

Theorem 19. *E- and A-termination of autonomous pDDSs is decidable.*

7   Conclusions

Our investigation on the impact of weak message expressiveness led us to consider a family of DDSs with bounded input and state, unbounded channels, and propositional or unary messages. We provided complete proofs of the fact that the termination problems on DDSs, with single-node networks and deterministic and non-recursive programs, share the same decidability boundary of reachability of CFSMs, i.e., perfect closed pDDSs suffer of undecidability, while unordered pDDSs (irrespective of the input policy) enjoy decidability.

These results can be easily generalized to full DDSs and beyond. In fact, concerning undecidability over perfect channels, since full pDDSs are more general than those we studied above, we immediately obtain undecidability also for full DDSs over perfect networks. Instead, for decidability, we have to lift both the single-node network topology and the deterministic, non-recursive programs. The former issue can be seamlessly solved by, e.g.:

- adapting the abstract configuration graphs to arbitrary networks; the configurations should now be represented via functions that map nodes and channels to their content, the abstract configuration graph should now exploit replicated abstract domains (one for each node in the topology), and, consequently,
- by introducing, in the PN, state-DB places dedicated to each node, message-places for each channel, and related transitions.

The latter issue can be solved without even modifying the technique. In fact, taking advantage of genericity, the abstract transitions and the PN transitions we introduced completely hide the DDS program. Thus, as long as we deal with programming languages that enjoy genericity, of reformulations of Definition 40 and Definition 44 (of abstract transitions), and of computable functions *state* and *out* (which make the corresponding PN computable), we can analyze the extended program with the same technique. This is clearly the case of full DDS programs and, actually, even beyond (e.g., with sophisticated non-deterministic mechanisms based on negation under stable-model semantics, in the style of Answer Set Programming [19]).

Having reduced unordered pDDSs to PNs, we can analyze properties beyond termination. For example, we can consider convergence properties (whether it is possible to reach a configuration where the state DBs does not change anymore, despite, possibly, continuing to send messages) by checking whether it is possible to reach a marking that *freezes* the token marking the state-DB place.

A natural next step is the study of DDSs with unary messages, which seems non-reducible to standard PNs: the relations between the unbounded values on the channels cannot be encoded via an equivalence relation encoded over a finite, fixed set of places. A possible solution would be the tune of reductions to Data-Aware PNs, e.g., ν-PNs [27]. In case this strategy proves itself effective, we would obtain an indication that the decidability and complexity boundary for DDSs with unary messages is significantly different than the boundary for pDDSs, since, in ν-PNs, reachability is undecidable and coverability is non-elementary [18].

Another direction for future works is the study of the implementability of our technique. In fact, since, on PNs, the form of termination we studied (i.e., whether there is a terminating run) is as complex as reachability (which, in turn, is non-elementary), it seems unlikely that practical cases can be analyzed this way. However, because of the restricted shape of the PNs we built, good performances may still be observed, at least on the average-case. Moreover, the picture could be simpler for other problems amounting to PN properties with lower complexity (e.g., checking whether there is a non-terminating run, which is EXPSPACE-complete [20,25]). Finally, this implementation could be achieved by exploiting available tools dedicated to PN analysis (see, e.g., [17]).

References

1. Abiteboul, S., Abrams, Z., Haar, S., Milo, T.: Diagnosis of asynchronous discrete event systems: datalog to the rescue! In: Proceedings of PODS, pp. 358–367. ACM Press (2005)
2. Abiteboul, S., Bienvenu, M., Galland, A., Antoine, É.: A rule-based language for web data management. In: Proceedings of PODS, pp. 293–304. ACM Press (2011)
3. Abiteboul, S., Hull, R., Vianu, V.: Foundations of Databases. Addison-Wesley, Boston (1995)
4. Aiswarya, C.: On network topologies and the decidability of reachability problem. In: Georgiou, C., Majumdar, R. (eds.) NETYS 2020. LNCS, vol. 12129, pp. 3–10. Springer, Cham (2021). https://doi.org/10.1007/978-3-030-67087-0_1
5. Ameloot, T.J., Geck, G., Ketsman, B., Neven, F., Schwentick, T.: Parallel-correctness and transferability for conjunctive queries. In: Proceedings of PODS, pp. 47–58 (2015)
6. Ameloot, T.J., Ketsman, B., Neven, F., Zinn, D.: Weaker forms of monotonicity for declarative networking: a more fine-grained answer to the CALM-conjecture. In: Proceedings of PODS, pp. 64–75 (2014)
7. Ameloot, T.J., Neven, F., Van den Bussche, J.: Relational transducers for declarative networking. JACM **60**(2), 15:1–15:38 (2013)
8. Bagheri Hariri, B., Calvanese, D., De Giacomo, G., Deutsch, A., Montali, M.: Verification of relational data-centric dynamic systems with external services. In: Proceedings of PODS, pp. 163–174 (2013)
9. Bagheri Hariri, B., Calvanese, D., De Giacomo, G., Deutsch, A., Montali, M.: Verification of relational data-centric dynamic systems with external services. In: Hull, R., Fan, W. (eds.) Proceedings of the 32nd ACM SIGMOD-SIGACT-SIGART Symposium on Principles of Database Systems, PODS 2013, New York, NY, USA, 22–27 June 2013, pp. 163–174. ACM (2013)
10. Calvanese, D., Di Cosmo, F., Lobo, J., Montali, M.: Convergence verification of declarative distributed systems. In: Monica, S., Bergenti, F. (eds.) Proceedings of the 36th Italian Conference on Computational Logic, Parma, Italy, 7–9 September 2021, CEUR Workshop Proceedings, vol. 3002, pp. 62–76. CEUR-WS.org (2021)
11. Calvanese, D., Montali, M., Lobo, J.: Verification of fixed-topology declarative distributed systems with external data. In: Proceedings of AMW-2018.,CEUR, ceur-ws.org, vol. 2100 (2018)
12. Chambart, P., Schnoebelen, P.: Mixing lossy and perfect fifo channels. In: van Breugel, F., Chechik, M. (eds.) CONCUR 2008. LNCS, vol. 5201, pp. 340–355. Springer, Heidelberg (2008). https://doi.org/10.1007/978-3-540-85361-9_28
13. Chen, C., Jia, L., Xu, H., Luo, C., Zhou, W., Loo, B.T.: A program logic for verifying secure routing protocols. In: Ábrahám, E., Palamidessi, C. (eds.) FORTE 2014. LNCS, vol. 8461, pp. 117–132. Springer, Heidelberg (2014). https://doi.org/10.1007/978-3-662-43613-4_8
14. Chen, C., Loh, L.K., Jia, L., Zhou, W., Loo, B.T.: Automated verification of safety properties of declarative networking programs. In: Proceedings of PPDP, pp. 79–90 (2015)
15. Czerwinski, W., Lasota, S., Lazic, R., Leroux, J., Mazowiecki, F.: The reachability problem for petri nets is not elementary. J. ACM **68**(1), 7:1–7:28 (2021). https://doi.org/10.1145/3422822
16. Di Cosmo, F.: Verification of sometimes termination of lazy-bounded declarative distributed systems. CoRR arxiv:2308.10007 (2023). https://doi.org/10.48550/arXiv.2308.10007

17. Jensen, K., Kristensen, L.M.: Colored petri nets: a graphical language for formal modeling and validation of concurrent systems. Commun. ACM **58**(6), 61–70 (2015). https://doi.org/10.1145/2663340
18. Lazic, R., Schmitz, S.: The complexity of coverability in ν-petri nets. In: Grohe, M., Koskinen, E., Shankar, N. (eds.) Proceedings of the 31st Annual ACM/IEEE Symposium on Logic in Computer Science, LICS '16, New York, NY, USA, 5–8 July 2016, pp. 467–476. ACM (2016). https://doi.org/10.1145/2933575.2933593
19. Lifschitz, V.: Thirteen definitions of a stable model. In: Blass, A., Dershowitz, N., Reisig, W. (eds.) Fields of Logic and Computation. LNCS, vol. 6300, pp. 488–503. Springer, Heidelberg (2010). https://doi.org/10.1007/978-3-642-15025-8_24
20. Lipton, R.: The reachability problem requires exponential space. Research Report 62. Department of Computer Science, Yale University (1976)
21. Loo, B.T., et al.: Declarative networking. CACM **52**(11), 87–95 (2009)
22. Ma, J., Le, F., Wood, D., Russo, A., Lobo, J.: A declarative approach to distributed computing: specification, execution and analysis. Theory Pract. Logic Program. **13**, 815–830 (2013)
23. Murata, T.: Petri nets: properties, analysis and applications. Proc. IEEE **77**(4), 541–580 (1989). https://doi.org/10.1109/5.24143
24. Nigam, V., Jia, L., Loo, B.T., Scedrov, A.: Maintaining distributed logic programs incrementally. Comput. Lang. Syst. Struct. **38**(2), 158–180 (2012)
25. Rackoff, C.: The covering and boundedness problems for vector addition systems. Theor. Comput. Sci. **6**, 223–231 (1978). https://doi.org/10.1016/0304-3975(78)90036-1
26. Ren, Y., et al.: FSR: formal analysis and implementation toolkit for safe interdomain routing. Comput. Commun. Rev. **41**(4), 440–441 (2011)
27. Rosa-Velardo, F., de Frutos-Escrig, D.: Decidability and complexity of petri nets with unordered data. Theor. Comput. Sci. **412**(34), 4439–4451 (2011). https://doi.org/10.1016/j.tcs.2011.05.007
28. Zaychik Moffitt, V., Stoyanovich, J., Abiteboul, S., Miklau, G.: Collaborative access control in WebdamLog. In: Proceedings of ACM SIGMOD, pp. 197–211. ACM (2015)
29. Zhou, W., et al.: Distributed time-aware provenance. PVLDB **6**(2), 49–60 (2012)

Formalizing Henkin-Style Completeness of an Axiomatic System for Propositional Logic

Asta Halkjær From$^{(\boxtimes)}$

Technical University of Denmark, Kongens Lyngby, Denmark
ahfrom@dtu.dk

Abstract. I formalize a Henkin-style completeness proof for an axiomatic system for propositional logic in the proof assistant Isabelle/HOL. The formalization precisely details the structure of this proof method.

Keywords: Propositional logic · Henkin-style completeness · Isabelle/HOL

1 Introduction

Hilbert proved the completeness of an axiomatic system for propositional logic in 1917–18 [32], Gödel proved the completeness of first-order logic in 1929 [13] and Henkin [14] simplified this proof in 1947, thus devising what we now know as the Henkin-style method. In this paper I study the structure of a Henkin-style completeness proof for an axiomatic Hilbert system for propositional logic by formalizing it in the proof assistant Isabelle/HOL [21].

Isabelle is a generic proof assistant and Isabelle/HOL is the instance based on higher-order logic. With it, we can state every definition, proposition and proof in the precise language of higher-order logic rather than in natural language. Our proof language is then completely formal, which makes it possible for the machine to assist us in our endeavor. By writing our proofs in the Isar language, an acronym of *intelligible semi-automated reasoning* [31], we can have Isabelle check everything that we type. In particular, Isar contains commands such as **assume** to introduce assumptions, **have** to state a partial result and **moreover** to chain several of these together. After these commands, we typically write so-called ⟨cartouches⟩, delimited by angle brackets, that contain our higher-order logic terms: definitions, statements and so on [21]. Our proofs are checked by the trusted Isabelle/HOL kernel but we do not typically use the kernel's axioms and inference rules directly. Instead we give the name of e.g. a tableaux or resolution prover that will generate the proof for us. By formalizing our proofs like this we know that our conclusions always follow from our assumptions.

Of course, Isabelle cannot verify that our definitions match our intentions, that part is up to us, but formalization still reduces the possibility of mistakes.

A. Pavlova et al. (Eds.): ESSLLI 2019/2020/2021, LNCS 14354, pp. 80–92, 2024.
https://doi.org/10.1007/978-3-031-50628-4_5

In particular, it reduces the surface area where mistakes can happen, since the proofs themselves are checked by the machine. Not only does a formalization like this one increase the trust in the result, it can also serve as a reference to understand the proof since every detail is given: no case can be omitted as "trivial" or left as an "exercise for the reader." The work can also act as a starting point for formalizing other results based on the same techniques.

The full formalization, just below 400 lines, is available online:

$$\text{https://github.com/logic-tools/axiom}$$

I reproduce the essential pieces of it here and introduce parts of the syntax as needed, but forgo any thorough explanation of the Isabelle commands [21].

1.1   Structure of the Paper

After a brief history of formalized completeness proofs, the paper continues with a formalization of the syntax and semantics of propositional logic (Sect. 2) and a sound proof system (Sect. 3). The idea of the completeness proof is as follows: given a formula ϕ valid under assumptions $\psi_1, \ldots, \psi_k$, assume for the sake of contradiction that there is no corresponding derivation of ϕ under $\psi_1, \ldots, \psi_k$:

$$\nvdash \psi_1 \longrightarrow \ldots \longrightarrow \psi_k \longrightarrow \phi$$

This means we cannot derive falsity, $\bot$, when also assuming $\neg\phi$, so:

$$\nvdash \neg\phi \longrightarrow \psi_1 \longrightarrow \ldots \longrightarrow \psi_k \longrightarrow \bot$$

The set $\{\neg\phi, \psi_1, \ldots, \psi_k\}$ is therefore *consistent* and can be turned into a *maximal consistent set* (Sect. 4) through an *extension* (Sect. 5). Such sets are *Hintikka* sets (Sect. 6) and their elements have a model. This contradicts the validity assumption, proving that a derivation must exist. The proof system is therefore complete (Sect. 7) and the paper concludes with possible extensions (Sect. 8).

1.2   A History of Formalized Completeness Proofs

The formalization is part of a long line of formalized completeness proofs.

Completeness proofs can generally be split into two categories based on their approach: semantic proofs in the style of Gödel [13] and Henkin [14] on the one hand and syntactic proofs in the style of Beth and Hintikka [17] and Gallier [12] on the other. Fitting and Mendelsohn call the semantic proofs "synthetic" because they start from a formula and *synthesize* new ones, building up larger and larger sets of formulas that are consistent with the starting point [9]. Formulas in such sets are then shown to have a model and this is the approach presented here. Fitting and Mendelsohn contrast this with the syntactic proofs that they dub "analytic" because they work by *analyzing* the given formula, breaking it into smaller and smaller subformulas and reasoning from those. In these proofs we typically construct a counterexample from the open leaves or an infinite path of a failed derivation attempt. The synthetic approach is remarked to have a *mathematical*, abstract feeling whereas the analytic approach is more *computational* and often resembles an actual prover for the logic [5].

The Henkin-style completeness method has been applied to modal logic from the beginning, notably to system S5 as early as 1959 by Bayart [1] (in French). Bentley [2] recently formalized such a proof in the proof assistant Lean. Jørgensen et al. [16] adapted the synthetic approach to a tableau system for hybrid logic and I formalized this proof [10] in Isabelle/HOL.

In 1985, Shankar [27] formalized Shoenfield's first-order logic and axiomatic proof system in the Boyer-Moore theorem prover. He showed propositional completeness of the system analytically by defining a tautology checker for a fragment of the syntax based on negation and disjunction.

In 1996, Persson [24] showed completeness for intuitionistic first-order logic in Martin-Löf type theory using the proof assistant ALF. His proof had a synthetic flavor and the result was constructive: he obtained a program that transforms a proof of validity into a natural deduction or sequent calculus derivation. Persson also formalized an axiomatic system without proving completeness.

By early 2000, Margetson formalized the completeness of first-order logic and the cut elimination theorem for sequent calculus in Isabelle/HOL and Ridge later updated the formalization to the Isar language [18]. Their completeness proof, in the Beth-Hintikka style, was based on analyzing failing branches in proof trees.

In 2005, Braselmann and Koepke [6] followed in the Mizar system but using a Henkin-style argument for their sequent calculus.

In 2007, Berghofer [3] formalized Fitting's synthetic work on natural deduction [8] in Isabelle/HOL. The formalized model existence theorem was based on Smullyan's abstract consistency properties [29] and Berghofer followed Fitting in reusing the result to show the Löwenheim-Skolem theorem. I extended the formalized completeness result to also cover open formulas [3]. Inspired by Berghofer, Schlichtkrull [26] proved the completeness of first-order resolution in 2016.

In 2010, Ilik [15] investigated Henkin-style arguments for both classical and intuitionistic first-order logic in the proof assistant Coq.

In 2017, Michaelis and Nipkow [19,20] formalized a number of proof systems for propositional logic in Isabelle/HOL: natural deduction, sequent calculus, an axiomatic Hilbert system and resolution. They gave a syntactic completeness proof for the sequent calculus and showed that sequent calculus derivations can be translated into natural deduction and further into their Hilbert system, obtaining completeness for the three proof systems. Independently of this approach, they formalized the propositional model existence theorem by Fitting [8] and used this result to reprove completeness of the sequent calculus and Hilbert system, respectively. Their formalization is more ambitious than this one and therefore more involved. I start from a smaller syntax and focus on one proof system and one approach. This leads to a simpler formalization that helps us understand the essential pieces of the method.

Blanchette, Popescu and Traytel [5] recently advanced the state of completeness proofs for sequent calculus and tableau systems in Isabelle/HOL. They deliberately chose the Beth-Hintikka style and used codatatypes to model possibly infinite derivation trees. Their result can be instantiated for different variations of sequent calculus or tableau systems and various flavors of first-order logic.

Blanchette [4] gave an overview of the formalized metatheory of various other logical calculi and automatic provers in Isabelle.

If we move to Gödel's incompleteness theorems, the first one was formalized in the Boyer-Moore theorem prover by Shankar in 1986 [28] and in Coq by O'Connor in 2003 [22]. Both incompleteness theorems have been formalized in Isabelle/HOL by Paulson in 2013 [23] and by Popescu and Traytel in 2019 [25].

In summary, the Henkin style is ubiquitous and we have seen it applied to examples such as sequent calculus and natural deduction for first-order logic, system S5 for modal logic and a tableau system for hybrid logic. Most work either extends the technique to cover more advanced logics or abstracts it so that it applies to several at once. My contribution is to boil this proof style down to its essence, motivate each step as it is presented and to use a proof assistant to ensure precision, correctness and comprehensiveness. The paper may also serve as a fast-paced introduction to Isabelle/HOL on a concrete example.

2   Syntax and Semantics

The syntax is minimal and consists of a logical constant representing falsity, natural numbers as propositional symbols and implication. The datatype *form* models it in Isabelle/HOL with a constructor for each case (falsity, propositional symbols and implication) separated by "|":

datatype *form* = *Falsity* ($\langle \bot \rangle$) | *Pro nat* | *Imp form form* (**infixr** $\langle \longrightarrow \rangle$ 25)

The annotations in parentheses allow us to construct formulas using standard notation (in bold, to avoid conflict with built-in Isabelle syntax). The definition of negation as an abbreviation makes use of this:

abbreviation *Neg* ($\langle \neg \; \text{-}\rangle$ [40] 40) **where** $\langle \neg \; p \equiv p \longrightarrow \bot \rangle$

The meaning of formulas is given by their interpretation in the meta-logic, where the higher-order logic type *bool* gives the truth of the formula. The semantics are thus a primitive recursive predicate on formulas given an interpretation of propositional symbols:

primrec *semantics* :: $\langle (nat \Rightarrow bool) \Rightarrow form \Rightarrow bool \rangle$ ($\langle \text{-} \models \text{-} \rangle$ [50, 50] 50) **where**
  $\langle (I \models \bot) = False \rangle$
  | $\langle (I \models Pro \; n) = I \; n \rangle$
  | $\langle (I \models (p \longrightarrow q)) = ((I \models p) \longrightarrow (I \models q)) \rangle$

The first line gives the type and infix notation while the remaining lines define the predicate by each case of the syntax. The first case states that no interpretation models $\bot$, the second case that the semantics of a propositional symbol is given by the interpretation and finally the meta-logical implication $\longrightarrow$ interprets the object logic implication $\longrightarrow$.

3   Proof System

Church's axiom system P_1 [7] is delightfully simple. It consists of modus ponens and three axiom schemas and can be defined in Isabelle/HOL as follows:

inductive *Axiomatics* :: ⟨*form* $\Rightarrow$ *bool*⟩ (⟨$\vdash$ -⟩ [50] 50) **where**
  MP: ⟨$\vdash$ p $\Longrightarrow$ $\vdash$ ($p \longrightarrow q$) $\Longrightarrow$ $\vdash$ q⟩
| *Imp1*: ⟨$\vdash$ ($p \longrightarrow q \longrightarrow p$)⟩
| *Imp2*: ⟨$\vdash$ (($p \longrightarrow q \longrightarrow r$) $\longrightarrow$ ($p \longrightarrow q$) $\longrightarrow$ $p \longrightarrow r$)⟩
| *Neg*: ⟨$\vdash$ ((($p \longrightarrow \bot$) $\longrightarrow \bot$) $\longrightarrow$ p)⟩

The specification defines the inductive predicate *Axiomatics* with the symbolic name $\vdash$. The judgment holds for a given formula if the formula can be derived from the specified rule and axioms in a finite number of steps.

This proof system is sound with respect to the semantics, which means that every derivable formula is true under any interpretation:

theorem *soundness*: ⟨$\vdash$ p $\Longrightarrow$ $I \models p$⟩
  by (*induct rule*: *Axiomatics.induct*) *simp-all*

The **by** command completes the proof in two proof method invocations. The *induct* part states that the proof should be performed by induction over the rules of the proof system, transforming the one goal into a subgoal for each case of the predicate. Next, the simplifier, *simp-all*, easily discharges these subgoals.

4   Consistency and Maximality

A list of formulas is *consistent* when we cannot derive $\bot$ from it. The judgment $\vdash$ has no notion of such entailment but implication, $\longrightarrow$, can serve the same purpose. The below technique is widely applicable, whereas extending the judgment $\vdash$ would make the result harder to translate to e.g. modal logic. The following function, *imply*, builds a chain of implications from a list of assumptions to a conclusion. Here, a list is a finite sequence that is either empty, [], or built from an element, the separator #, and a smaller list. We then say that q can be *derived from ps* when we can derive $\vdash$ *imply ps q*.

primrec *imply* :: ⟨*form list* $\Rightarrow$ *form* $\Rightarrow$ *form*⟩ **where**
  ⟨*imply* [] q = q⟩
| ⟨*imply* (p # ps) q = ($p \longrightarrow$ *imply ps q*)⟩

A potentially infinite set S is consistent exactly when all its finite subsets are consistent. That is, when there is no list S' that, when treated as a *set*, is a subset of S and that entails $\bot$ in the sense of *imply*:

definition *consistent* :: ⟨*form set* $\Rightarrow$ *bool*⟩ **where**
⟨*consistent* $S \equiv \nexists S'.\ set\ S' \subseteq S \land\ \vdash imply\ S'\ \bot$⟩

A set is *maximal* when any proper extension makes it inconsistent:

definition *maximal* :: ⟨*form set* $\Rightarrow$ *bool*⟩ **where**
⟨*maximal* $S \equiv \forall p.\ p \notin S \longrightarrow \neg\ consistent\ (\{p\} \cup S)$⟩

Note that, to separate concerns, this allows for inconsistent maximal sets.

5   Extension

We want to grow a consistent set into a *maximal* one while preserving consistency. According to Lindenbaum's lemma, attributed to him by Tarski [30], we can always do this. First, given an enumeration of formulas, (ϕ_n), construct a corresponding sequence of consistent sets (S_n) in the following way.

Assuming S_n has been constructed, its immediate extension is given by

$$S_{n+1} = \begin{cases} \{\phi_n\} \cup S_n & \text{if } \{\phi_n\} \cup S_n \text{ is consistent,} \\ S_n & \text{otherwise.} \end{cases}$$

That is, we only add the corresponding formula to the previous set if consistency is preserved. In the Isabelle code, the function *extend S f n* constructs S_n from $S = S_0$ given an enumeration of formulas represented by f:

primrec *extend* :: ⟨*form set* $\Rightarrow$ (*nat* $\Rightarrow$ *form*) $\Rightarrow$ *nat* $\Rightarrow$ *form set*⟩ **where**
⟨*extend S f 0 = S*⟩
| ⟨*extend S f (Suc n)* =
  (*if consistent* ($\{f\ n\} \cup extend\ S\ f\ n$)
  then $\{f\ n\} \cup extend\ S\ f\ n$
  else extend S f n)⟩

To construct the *maximal consistent set*, take the infinite union $\bigcup S_n$:

definition *Extend* :: ⟨*form set* $\Rightarrow$ (*nat* $\Rightarrow$ *form*) $\Rightarrow$ *form set*⟩ **where**
⟨*Extend S f* $\equiv \bigcup n.\ extend\ S\ f\ n$⟩

It is easy to see that the starting set is a subset of the union:

lemma *Extend-subset*: ⟨$S \subseteq Extend\ S\ f$⟩
unfolding *Extend-def* **by** (*metis Union-upper extend.simps(1) range-eqI*)

And, by induction, that any element S_m is a superset of previous elements:

lemma *extend-bound*: ⟨$(\bigcup n \leq m.\ extend\ S\ f\ n) = extend\ S\ f\ m$⟩
by (*induct m*) (*simp-all add: atMost-Suc*)

5.1   Consistency

When the initial set S is consistent, so is any S_n by construction:

lemma *consistent-extend*: ⟨*consistent S* $\implies$ *consistent* (*extend S f n*)⟩
  by (*induct n*) *simp-all*

Finally, the limit, $\bigcup S_n$, is also consistent:

lemma *consistent-Extend*:
  assumes ⟨*consistent S*⟩
  shows ⟨*consistent* (*Extend S f*)⟩

The proof starts by classical contradiction using the *ccontr* rule:

unfolding *Extend-def*
proof (*rule ccontr*)

Assume, towards a contradiction, that the union is inconsistent. Then we can derive $\bot$ from some subset S':

assume ⟨¬ *consistent* ($\bigcup n.$ *extend S f n*)⟩
  then obtain S' **where** ⟨⊢ *imply S'* $\bot$⟩ ⟨*set S'* $\subseteq$ ($\bigcup n.$ *extend S f n*)⟩
    unfolding *consistent-def* **by** *blast*

This subset is finite so it must be a subset of a finite segment of the union, say, $S_0 \cup \ldots \cup S_m$ for some m:

then obtain m **where** ⟨*set S'* $\subseteq$ ($\bigcup n \leq m.$ *extend S f n*)⟩
    using *UN-finite-bound* **by** (*metis List.finite-set*)

But every element in (S_n) is a subset of the next, so S' is a subset of S_m:

then have ⟨*set S'* $\subseteq$ *extend S f m*⟩
    using *extend-bound* **by** *blast*

And we already established that any such element is consistent:

moreover have ⟨*consistent* (*extend S f m*)⟩
    using *assms consistent-extend* **by** *blast*

So there cannot be an inconsistent subset S' and we have our contradiction:

ultimately show *False*
    unfolding *consistent-def* **using** ⟨⊢ *imply S'* $\bot$⟩ **by** *blast*
qed

In conclusion, $\bigcup S_n$ is consistent when S_0 is.

5.2 Maximality

Importantly, the union $\bigcup S_n$ is also maximal (regardless of the choice of S_0) when the enumeration f is surjective. That is, when it enumerates every formula:

lemma *maximal-Extend*:
  assumes ⟨*surj f*⟩
  shows ⟨*maximal (Extend S f)*⟩
  (proof omitted)

The proof is similar to the one for consistency. If the union is not maximal then there is some $\phi_k \notin \bigcup S_n$ such that $\{\phi_k\} \cup \bigcup S_n$ is consistent. Since $\phi_k \notin \bigcup S_n$, it was not added to the sequence, i.e. $\phi_k \notin S_{k+1}$, and by construction this must be because $\{\phi_k\} \cup S_k$ is inconsistent. But $\{\phi_k\} \cup \bigcup S_n$ is a superset of $\{\phi_k\} \cup S_k$, so $\{\phi_k\} \cup \bigcup S_n$ must be inconsistent too, contradicting the assumption.

6 Hintikka Sets

The completeness proof works by showing that every maximal consistent set is a Hintikka set, where Hintikka sets are defined by the following four conditions:

locale *Hintikka* =
  fixes H :: ⟨*form set*⟩
  assumes
    NoFalsity: ⟨$\bot \notin H$⟩ **and**
    Pro: ⟨*Pro* $n \in H \Longrightarrow (\neg\ Pro\ n) \notin H$⟩ **and**
    ImpP: ⟨$(p \longrightarrow q) \in H \Longrightarrow (\neg\ p) \in H \lor q \in H$⟩ **and**
    ImpN: ⟨$(\neg\ (p \longrightarrow q)) \in H \Longrightarrow p \in H \land (\neg\ q) \in H$⟩

The idea is to ensure that every formula in a set is satisfiable through syntactic criteria. This is done by making the set *downwards saturated* [29] such that the satisfiability of any complex formula is guaranteed by conditions on its subformulas. Since $\bot$ is unsatisfiable it should never occur (*NoFalsity*), and if a propositional symbol occurs then its negation should not (*Pro*). An implication is satisfied if either the antecedent is false or the consequent is true, so if an implication occurs in a Hintikka set, then either the negated antecedent or the consequent should too (*ImpP*). If a negated implication occurs in a Hintikka set then so should both the antecedent and negated consequent (*ImpN*).

6.1 Model Existence

The downwards saturation ensures that if we interpret every proposition in a Hintikka set as true, then every larger formula in the set will be modelled inductively by this interpretation. Therefore, the model is based on set membership:

abbreviation (*input*) ⟨*model H n* ≡ *Pro* $n \in H$⟩

This satisfies any formula in a Hintikka set (and falsifies its negation):

lemma *Hintikka-model*:
⟨*Hintikka H* ⟹ (*p* ∈ *H* ⟶ *model H* ⊨ *p*) ∧ ((¬ *p*) ∈ *H* ⟶ ¬ *model H* ⊨ *p*)⟩
by (*induct p*) (*simp*; *unfold Hintikka-def*, *blast*)+

The proof goes by induction on the structure of the formula and standard proof methods to handle each resulting case. We need to prove both satisfaction and falsification at the same time to obtain a strong enough induction hypothesis.

6.2   Maximal Consistency

The penultimate task is to show that a maximal consistent set is a Hintikka set:

lemma *Hintikka-Extend*:
  assumes ⟨*maximal S*⟩ ⟨*consistent S*⟩
  shows ⟨*Hintikka S*⟩

The proof has four similar cases based on the cases of the Hintikka definition. The following gives the essence. Consider first propositional symbols:

  fix *n*
  assume ⟨*Pro n* ∈ *S*⟩
  moreover have ⟨⊢ *imply* [*Pro n*, ¬ *Pro n*] ⊥⟩
    by (*simp add*: *FalsityE*)
  ultimately show ⟨(¬ *Pro n*) ∉ *S*⟩
    using *assms*(*2*) **unfolding** *consistent-def*
    by (*metis bot.extremum empty-set insert-subset list.set*(*2*))

Assume a fixed but arbitrary propositional symbol *n* that occurs positively in *S*. We can derive ⊥ from this in combination with a negative occurrence. Thus, the latter cannot appear in the consistent *S* and this case of the Hintikka definition is proved.

Next, assume that a negated implication occurs in *S*. By contradiction, so does the antecedent:

  assume *∗*: ⟨(¬ (*p* ⟶ *q*)) ∈ *S*⟩
  show ⟨*p* ∈ *S* ∧ (¬ *q*) ∈ *S*⟩
  proof (*rule conjI*; *rule ccontr*)

The set *S* is maximal, so if it does not contain *p* there must be some finite subset *S'* of *S* that we can derive falsity from when adding *p*:

  assume ⟨*p* ∉ *S*⟩
  then obtain *S'* **where** *S'*: ⟨⊢ *imply* (*p* # *S'*) ⊥⟩ ⟨*set S'* ⊆ *S*⟩
    using *assms inconsistent-head* **by** *blast*

But *p* follows from the negated implication so we can *cut* out *p* in favor of it:

  moreover have ⟨⊢ *imply* ((¬ (*p* ⟶ *q*)) # *S'*) *p*⟩
    using *add-imply ImpE1 deduct* **by** *blast*
  ultimately have ⟨⊢ *imply* ((¬ (*p* ⟶ *q*)) # *S'*) ⊥⟩
    using *cut'* **by** *blast*

These assumptions, however, are a subset of S, contradicting its consistency:

moreover have ⟨*set* $((\neg\ (p \longrightarrow q))\ \#\ S') \subseteq S$⟩
  using $*(1)\ S'(2)$ **by** *fastforce*
ultimately show *False*
  using *assms* **unfolding** *consistent-def* **by** *blast*

7 Completeness

Isabelle can automatically prove the countability of formulas, providing a surjective function *from-nat* for obtaining specific elements of the enumeration (ϕ_n):

instance *form* :: *countable* **by** *countable-datatype*

With this we finally reach the completeness lemma itself. If we assume that p is valid under the assumptions ps, then p can be derived from ps:

lemma *imply-completeness*:
  assumes *valid*: ⟨$\forall I\ s.\ list\text{-}all\ (\lambda q.\ I \models q)\ ps \longrightarrow I \models p$⟩
  shows ⟨$\vdash imply\ ps\ p$⟩

The proof proceeds by contradiction and a similar derivation rule:

proof (*rule ccontr*)
  assume ⟨$\neg \vdash imply\ ps\ p$⟩
  then have $*$: ⟨$\neg \vdash imply\ ((\neg\ p)\ \#\ ps)\ \bot$⟩
    using *Boole* **by** *blast*

Abbreviate the starting consistent set $?S$ and its maximal extension $?H$:

let $?S = $ ⟨*set* $((\neg\ p)\ \#\ ps)$⟩
let $?H = $ ⟨*Extend* $?S$ *from-nat*⟩

Then use the previous results to show that $?H$ is a Hintikka set:

have ⟨*consistent* $?S$⟩
  unfolding *consistent-def* **using** $*$ *imply-weaken* **by** *blast*
then have ⟨*consistent* $?H$⟩ ⟨*maximal* $?H$⟩
  using *consistent-Extend maximal-Extend surj-from-nat* **by** *blast+*
then have ⟨*Hintikka* $?H$⟩
  using *Hintikka-Extend* **by** *blast*

We have seen that we have a model for any formula in such an $?H$:

have ⟨*model* $?H \models p$⟩ **if** ⟨$p \in ?S$⟩ **for** p
  using *that Extend-subset Hintikka-model* ⟨*Hintikka* $?H$⟩ **by** *blast*

So in particular for $\neg p$ and all of ps:

then have ⟨*model* $?H \models (\neg\ p)$⟩ ⟨*list-all* $(\lambda p.\ model\ ?H \models p)\ ps$⟩
  unfolding *list-all-def* **by** *fastforce+*

The validity assumption then gives us that *model ?H* also models *p*:

then have ⟨*model ?H* ⊨ *p*⟩
  using *valid* **by** *blast*

But this is a contradiction:

then show *False*
  using ⟨*model ?H* ⊨ (¬ *p*)⟩ **by** *simp*
qed

As such, any valid formula must be derivable:

theorem *completeness*: ⟨∀ *I*. *I* ⊨ *p* ⟹ ⊢ *p*⟩
  using *imply-completeness*[**where** *ps*=⟨[]⟩] **by** *simp*

8 Conclusion

We have seen how to formalize the soundness and completeness of a simple axiomatic proof system for propositional logic in Isabelle/HOL. The proof assistant is sophisticated enough to do the soundness proof almost automatically and enables constructions like infinite sets in the proof of completeness.

The choice of propositional logic means that we missed out on an aspect of Henkin's original proof: the use of special constants to witness existential statements. I have included this in a larger formalization of first-order logic [11].

The formalization is simple to extend. The supplementary material contains a file with binary disjunction and conjunction operators added to the syntax, proof system and completeness proof. The result is around 130 lines longer and only adds new lines. The biggest changes are in the Hintikka definition and maximal consistency lemma while model existence remains completely automatic.

Acknowledgements. I thank Jørgen Villadsen, Alexander Birch Jensen, Frederik Krogsdal Jacobsen, Anders Schlichtkrull, Agnes Moesgård Eschen and the anonymous reviewers for valuable comments.

References

1. Bayart, A.: Quasi-adéquation de la logique modale du second ordre S5 et adéquation de la logique modale du premier ordre S5. Logique et Anal. (N.S.) **2**(6/7), 99–121 (1959)
2. Bentzen, B.: A Henkin-style completeness proof for the modal Logic S5. In: Baroni, P., Benzmüller, C., Wáng, Y.N. (eds.) CLAR 2021. LNCS (LNAI), vol. 13040, pp. 459–467. Springer, Cham (2021). https://doi.org/10.1007/978-3-030-89391-0_25
3. Berghofer, S.: First-Order Logic According to Fitting. Archive of Formal Proofs (2007). https://isa-afp.org/entries/FOL-Fitting.html
4. Blanchette, J.C.: Formalizing the metatheory of logical calculi and automatic provers in Isabelle/HOL (invited talk). In: Mahboubi, A., Myreen, M.O. (eds.) Proceedings of the 8th ACM SIGPLAN International Conference on Certified Programs and Proofs, CPP 2019, pp. 1–13. ACM (2019)

5. Blanchette, J.C., Popescu, A., Traytel, D.: Soundness and completeness proofs by coinductive methods. J. Autom. Reason. **58**(1), 149–179 (2017)
6. Braselmann, P., Koepke, P.: Gödel's completeness theorem. Formal. Math. **13**(1), 49–53 (2005)
7. Church, A.: Introduction to Mathematical Logic. Princeton Mathematical Series, Princeton University Press, Princeton (1956)
8. Fitting, M.: First-Order Logic and Automated Theorem Proving. Graduate Texts in Computer Science, 2nd edn. Springer, Heidelberg (1996). https://doi.org/10.1007/978-1-4612-2360-3
9. Fitting, M., Mendelsohn, R.L.: First-Order Modal Logic. Springer, Heidelberg (2012). https://doi.org/10.1007/978-94-011-5292-1
10. From, A.H.: Formalizing a Seligman-style tableau system for hybrid logic. Archive of Formal Proofs (2019). https://isa-afp.org/entries/Hybrid_Logic.html
11. From, A.H.: Soundness and completeness of an axiomatic system for first-order logic. Archive of Formal Proofs (2021). https://isa-afp.org/entries/FOL_Axiomatic.html
12. Gallier, J.H.: Logic for Computer Science: Foundations of Automatic Theorem Proving. Courier Dover Publications, Mineola (2015)
13. Gödel, K.: Über die Vollständigkeit des Logikkalküls. Ph.D. thesis, University of Vienna (1929)
14. Henkin, L.: The discovery of my completeness proofs. Bull. Symb. Logic **2**(2), 127–158 (1996)
15. Ilik, D.: Constructive completeness proofs and delimited control. Ph.D. thesis, École polytechnique (2010)
16. Jørgensen, K.F., Blackburn, P., Bolander, T., Braüner, T.: Synthetic completeness proofs for Seligman-style tableau systems. In: Proceedings of the 11th Conference on Advances in Modal Logic, pp. 302–321 (2016)
17. Kleene, S.C.: Mathematical Logic. Wiley, London (1967)
18. Margetson, J., Ridge, T.: Completeness theorem. Archive of Formal Proofs (2004). https://isa-afp.org/entries/Completeness.html
19. Michaelis, J., Nipkow, T.: Propositional proof systems. Archive of Formal Proofs (2017). https://isa-afp.org/entries/Propositional_Proof_Systems.html
20. Michaelis, J., Nipkow, T.: Formalized proof systems for propositional logic. In: Abel, A., Forsberg, F.N., Kaposi, A. (eds.) 23rd International Conference on Types for Proofs and Programs (TYPES 2017). LIPIcs, vol. 104, pp. 6:1–6:16. Schloss Dagstuhl - Leibniz-Zentrum fuer Informatik (2018)
21. Nipkow, T., Wenzel, M., Paulson, L.C. (eds.): Isabelle/HOL. LNCS, vol. 2283. Springer, Heidelberg (2002). https://doi.org/10.1007/3-540-45949-9
22. O'Connor, R.: Essential incompleteness of arithmetic verified by coq. In: Hurd, J., Melham, T. (eds.) TPHOLs 2005. LNCS, vol. 3603, pp. 245–260. Springer, Heidelberg (2005). https://doi.org/10.1007/11541868_16
23. Paulson, L.C.: A machine-assisted proof of Gödel's incompleteness theorems for the theory of hereditarily finite sets. Rev. Symb. Logic **7**(3), 484–498 (2014)
24. Persson, H.: Constructive completeness of intuitionistic predicate logic. Licenciate thesis, Chalmers University of Technology (1996)
25. Popescu, A., Traytel, D.: A formally verified abstract account of Gödel's incompleteness theorems. In: Fontaine, P. (ed.) CADE 2019. LNCS (LNAI), vol. 11716, pp. 442–461. Springer, Cham (2019). https://doi.org/10.1007/978-3-030-29436-6_26
26. Schlichtkrull, A.: Formalization of the resolution calculus for first-order logic. J. Autom. Reason. **61**(1–4), 455–484 (2018)

27. Shankar, N.: Towards mechanical metamathematics. J. Autom. Reason. **1**(4), 407–434 (1985)
28. Shankar, N.: Metamathematics, machines, and Gödels's proof, Cambridge tracts in theoretical computer science, vol. 38. Cambridge University Press, Cambridge (1994)
29. Smullyan, R.M.: First-Order Logic. Springer, Heidelberg (1968). https://doi.org/10.1007/978-3-642-86718-7
30. Tarski, A.: Logic, Semantics, Metamathematics: Papers from 1923 to 1938. Hackett Publishing, Indianapolis (1983)
31. Wenzel, M.: Isabelle/Isar-a generic framework for human-readable proof documents. From Insight Proof-Festschrift Honour Andrzej Trybulec **10**(23), 277–298 (2007)
32. Zach, R.: Completeness before post: Bernays, Hilbert, and the development of propositional logic. Bull. Symb. Logic **5**(3), 331–366 (1999)

Hope for Epistemic Reasoning
with Faulty Agents!

Krisztina Fruzsa$^{(\boxtimes)}$

TU Wien, Vienna, Austria
`krisztina.fruzsa@tuwien.ac.at`

Abstract. In this paper, we study a new epistemic modal operator, termed hope, which has been introduced recently in the context of a novel epistemic reasoning framework for distributed multi-agent systems with arbitrarily ("byzantine") faulty agents. It has been proved that both preconditions of actions used in agent protocols, as well as assertions about the epistemic states of agents obtained for analysis purposes, need to be restricted in a particular way for such systems. Hope has been proposed as the most promising candidate for analysis purposes, and defined in terms of the standard knowledge operator. To support the challenging next step of defining the semantics of common hope and eventual common hope, which are crucial for the analysis of fault-tolerant distributed agreement algorithms, we provide a suitable axiomatization of individual hope that avoids knowledge altogether, and prove its (strong) soundness and (strong) completeness.

Keywords: epistemic logic · fault-tolerant distributed systems · byzantine agents · axiomatization · soundness and completeness

1 Introduction

In [9–11], a comprehensive framework for epistemic reasoning in distributed multi-agent systems has been introduced, where agents (processing units) may misbehave. It extends Fagin et al.'s [4] classic runs-and-systems framework by also incorporating so-called *byzantine* agents [13]. Byzantine agents may arbitrarily deviate from their protocols (and may or may not be aware of doing so): they may "lie", send deceiving messages, and collude to fool the nonfaulty agents in the most malicious ways in order to achieve some (presumably sinister) goal. In addition to acting outside their protocols, byzantine agents may also have false memories as a consequence of incorrectly recording their own performed actions and/or witnessed events.

The utility of the framework was illustrated in [10], by exposing the limitations on what can be known by asynchronous agents in byzantine fault-tolerant distributed systems. In particular, as even the *brain-in-a-vat* scenario can be

PhD student in the Austrian Science Fund (FWF) doctoral program LogiCS (W1255).

A. Pavlova et al. (Eds.): ESSLLI 2019/2020/2021, LNCS 14354, pp. 93–108, 2024.
https://doi.org/10.1007/978-3-031-50628-4_6

modeled in such systems, the Knowledge of Preconditions Principle [15] reveals that preconditions of actions used in agent protocols must be restricted accordingly. Indeed, if an agent tried to act based on a simple precondition, such as, e.g., an occurrence of some event of interest in the system, this would lead to no actions being taken at all: Even when an asynchronous agent is correct, it can never discount the scenario of being a "brain-in-a-vat", i.e., that the observed event is only a fictitious result of its malfunction. Interestingly, the possibility to model the *brain-in-a-vat* scenario later turned out to be a widespread phenomenon. Not only that it can be modeled in systems with synchronous agents as well, but even the perfectly synchronized clocks available in lockstep synchronous systems cannot be used to avoid it [18].

A natural attempt to alleviate this problem is to have agents act as if *everything is fine* (see [14] for discussion). This led to the so-called *defeasible* knowledge of the precondition, formally $B_i\varphi := K_i(correct_i \rightarrow \varphi)$, a generalized version of which has been considered in detail in [16]. Herein, K_i denotes the standard knowledge operator [4], and $correct_i$ is an atomic proposition which is used to state that, by the time of evaluation, agent i did not violate its protocol (through improper action or improper inaction) and has correctly recorded its actions and witnessed events.

A typical specification for a distributed computing problem does not impose any restrictions on byzantine agents. For instance, in distributed agreement (consensus) [13], all correct agents must agree on a value, whatever byzantine agents do. Consequently, in a correctness proof for a particular protocol, it is common to verify $B_i\varphi$ only for correct agents. In effect, the precondition actually required for correctness analysis is $H_i\varphi := correct_i \rightarrow K_i(correct_i \rightarrow \varphi)$, which has been introduced as *hope* that φ holds in [10]. Note that hope is not a local property, because, as also shown in [10], no agent can ever ascertain its own correctness. Moreover, for fault-free systems, hope collapses to knowledge, as one would expect.

In [9], the framework of [11] has been applied to provide a thorough epistemic analysis of causality in asynchronous systems with byzantine agents. For that purpose, a byzantine analog of Lamport's causal cone [12] has been introduced, as well as a communication structure, called *multipede*, which is necessary for verifying hope regarding the occurrence of some event of interest in the system.[1]

Part of our ongoing work is devoted to the epistemic analysis of byzantine fault-tolerant agreement algorithms [13], where hope plays a crucial role. Actually, it is well-known that in case of benign faults (like agents that just stop operating or lose messages [3,8,17]) agreement is connected with certain forms of common knowledge. Consequently, it was to be expected that some forms

---

[1] In case of synchronous systems, a causal structure called *centipede* is both necessary and sufficient for verifying knowledge (when considering *full-information* protocols) as shown in [1].

of common hope would appear in case of byzantine faults; defining a suitable semantics turned out to be a challenge, however.[2]

Contributions: The aim of this paper is to support the above work, by improving our knowledge of the hope modality. More specifically, we give a suitable axiomatization of H_i that is independent of K_i and provide a self-contained proof of (strong) soundness and (strong) completeness.

Paper Organization: In Sect. 2, we introduce the formal language and its semantics in order to express hope of an agent. In Sect. 3, we propose an axiomatic system which fully captures the hope modality. In Sects. 4, we give the respective soundness and completeness results along with their proofs. Some conclusions and directions for further research in Sect. 5 complete our paper.

2 Basic Concepts

Throughout the whole paper, we will assume that we have a group of n agents (processing units), named $1, \ldots, n$.

Syntax. We start with a nonempty countable set of atomic propositions *Prop* and continue by forming formulas by closing under the Boolean connectives $\neg$ and $\wedge$ and also under the unary modal operators (one for each agent) $H_1, \ldots, H_n$ to obtain the language $\mathcal{L}_H^n$, i.e., the language $\mathcal{L}_H^n$ is generated by the following BNF:

$$\varphi ::= p \mid \neg\varphi \mid (\varphi \wedge \varphi) \mid H_i\varphi,$$

where $p \in Prop$ and $i \in \{1, \ldots, n\}$. We take $\top$ to be an abbreviation for some fixed propositional tautology, and take $\bot$ to be an abbreviation for $\neg\top$. Also, we use the following standard abbreviations from propositional logic: $\varphi \vee \psi$ for $\neg(\neg\varphi \wedge \neg\psi)$, $\varphi \to \psi$ for $\neg\varphi \vee \psi$, and $\varphi \leftrightarrow \psi$ for $(\varphi \to \psi) \wedge (\psi \to \varphi)$. For each $i \in \{1, \ldots, n\}$, we designate the following atomic proposition from *Prop* as special: $correct_i$, and we introduce an abbreviation for its negation as well: $faulty_i := \neg correct_i$.

Remark 1. We use $K_1, \ldots, K_n$ modalities instead of $H_1, \ldots, H_n$ modalities to obtain the language $\mathcal{L}_K^n$.

---

[2] We note that this paper has been accepted to ESSLLI2019 Student Session. Since then (building on top of the results presented here), new results have been obtained. See [5] for an example of a distributed computing problem analyzed using epistemic logic where the notion of eventual common hope shows up. See [2] where it is shown how one can make the logic of hope (introduced here) not depend on the *correct_i* atomic propositions. It turns out that, essentially, the logic of KB4_n can be taken as an alternative logic for hope. Interestinly, in [6] Goubault et al. show that the logic of KB4_n also plays a crucial role in studying systems with *crash failures*. See [2] for further discussion.

Semantics. We define the semantics for the $\mathcal{L}_H^n$ language in terms of *possible worlds*, which we formalize in terms of *Kripke models*

$$M = (W, \pi, \mathcal{H}_1, \ldots, \mathcal{H}_n),$$

where W is a nonempty set of *states* or *possible worlds* representing the domain of M (we will also sometimes write $\mathcal{D}(M)$ to refer to W), $\pi : W \to (Prop \to \{true, false\})$ is an interpretation that associates with each state $w \in W$ a truth assignment to the atomic propositions from *Prop*, and $\mathcal{H}_i$ are binary relations on W for all $i \in \{1, \ldots, n\}$.

Definition 1. *A binary relation $\mathcal{R}$ on a set S is*

- *reflexive if, for all $s \in S$, $(s, s) \in \mathcal{R}$ holds,*
- *transitive if, for all $s, t, u \in S$, if $(s, t) \in \mathcal{R}$ and $(t, u) \in \mathcal{R}$, then $(s, u) \in \mathcal{R}$,*
- *Euclidean if, for all $s, t, u \in S$, if $(s, t) \in \mathcal{R}$ and $(s, u) \in \mathcal{R}$, then $(t, u) \in \mathcal{R}$.*

A Kripke model $M = (W, \pi, \mathcal{H}_1, \ldots, \mathcal{H}_n)$ is called *epistemic* if all $\mathcal{H}_i$ relations are equivalence relations, i.e., reflexive, transitive, and Euclidean. We will denote the class of all epistemic models with n relations by $\mathsf{S5_n}$.

Definition 2. *By $M, w \models \varphi$ we denote the fact that formula φ is satisfied at state w of the model M and define the $\models$ relation inductively as follows for all $i \in \{1, \ldots, n\}$:*

1. *For atomic propositions $p \in Prop$, $M, w \models p$ iff $\pi(w)(p) = true$,*
2. *$M, w \models \varphi \wedge \psi$ iff $M, w \models \varphi$ and $M, w \models \psi$,*
3. *$M, w \models \neg\varphi$ iff $M, w \models \varphi$ does not hold,*
4. *$M, w \models H_i\varphi$ iff $M, w' \models \varphi$ for all w' such that $(w, w') \in \mathcal{H}_i$.*

We will write $M, w \not\models \varphi$ to denote that $M, w \models \varphi$ does not hold. By $M \models \varphi$ we will denote the fact that φ is satisfied at all states w of the model M, i.e., that φ is *valid* in M. We will also use $\mathcal{C} \models \varphi$ to denote that φ is valid in all model M from the class of models $\mathcal{C}$.

Remark 2. We will sometimes want to interpret the language $\mathcal{L}_K^n$ on the class of epistemic models $\mathsf{S5_n}$, in which case, for all $i \in \{1, \ldots, n\}$, the modality K_i is treated the same way as the modality H_i (as described above in Definition 2).

3 Axiomatizing Hope

In this section, we provide an axiomatic system for hope (in Definition 3), which we will prove in Sect. 4 to be equivalent (in the sense made precise by Corollary 1) to the translation

$$H_i\varphi := correct_i \to K_i(correct_i \to \varphi) \tag{1}$$

proposed in [10], where K_i is the standard knowledge operator [4].

Definition 3. *The axiomatic system $\mathcal{H}$ consists of the following axioms:*

$$
\begin{aligned}
P : \quad & \text{All propositional tautologies} \\
K : \quad & H_i(\varphi \to \psi) \wedge H_i\varphi \to H_i\psi \\
4 : \quad & H_i\varphi \to H_iH_i\varphi \\
5 : \quad & \neg H_i\varphi \to H_i\neg H_i\varphi \\
T' : \quad & correct_i \to (H_i\varphi \to \varphi) \\
F : \quad & faulty_i \to H_i\varphi \\
H : \quad & H_i\, correct_i
\end{aligned}
$$

and the following inference rules :

$$
\begin{aligned}
\text{Modus Ponens}: \quad & \text{From } \vdash_{\mathcal{H}} \varphi \text{ and } \vdash_{\mathcal{H}} \varphi \to \psi, \text{ infer } \vdash_{\mathcal{H}} \psi. \\
\text{Necessitation}: \quad & \text{From } \vdash_{\mathcal{H}} \varphi, \text{ infer } \vdash_{\mathcal{H}} H_i\varphi.
\end{aligned}
$$

The first four axioms are standard in the literature on epistemic logic. The additional axioms for hope are T', which states that for a correct agent, factivity of hope holds; F, which states that a faulty agent hopes for everything; and H, which states that an agent always hopes to be correct. Albeit these axioms appear reasonable in view of the intended meaning of hope, and have actually been inspired by the axiomatization of defeasible knowledge B_i given in [16], they are certainly not the only possible choice. And even more importantly, it is not clear *a priori* whether our axioms really capture the intended meaning. In the remainder of the paper, we will show that this is indeed the case.

We start with a translation according to (1) and some of its properties when employed in $S5_n$ models:

Definition 4. *For any $p \in Prop$, any $\varphi, \psi \in \mathcal{L}_H^n$, and any $i \in \{1, \ldots, n\}$, the translation function $t : \mathcal{L}_H^n \to \mathcal{L}_K^n$ is defined recursively in the following way:*

1. $t(p):=p$,
2. $t(\neg\varphi):=\neg t(\varphi)$,
3. $t(\varphi \wedge \psi):=t(\varphi) \wedge t(\psi)$,
4. $t(H_i\varphi):=correct_i \to K_i(correct_i \to t(\varphi))$.

Lemma 1. *For all $\varphi, \psi \in \mathcal{L}_H^n$, all $M^K \in S5_n$ and all $i \in \{1, \ldots, n\}$:*

1. *If φ is an instance of a propositional tautology, then $M^K \models t(\varphi)$,*
2. $S5_n \models t(H_i(\varphi \to \psi) \wedge H_i\varphi \to H_i\psi)$,
3. $S5_n \models t(H_i\varphi \to H_iH_i\varphi)$,
4. $S5_n \models t(\neg H_i\varphi \to H_i\neg H_i\varphi)$,
5. $S5_n \models t(correct_i \to (H_i\varphi \to \varphi))$,
6. $S5_n \models t(faulty_i \to H_i\varphi)$,
7. $S5_n \models t(H_i\, correct_i)$,
8. *If $M^K \models t(\varphi)$ and $M^K \models t(\varphi \to \psi)$, then $M^K \models t(\psi)$,*
9. *if $M^K \models t(\varphi)$, then $M^K \models t(H_i\varphi)$.*

Proof. We will prove only 5., 6. and 7. here; the remaining cases follow from the corresponding properties of defeasible knowledge established in [16].

For 5., let us apply the translation function:

$$t(correct_i \rightarrow (H_i\varphi \rightarrow \varphi)) = correct_i \rightarrow ((correct_i \rightarrow K_i(correct_i \rightarrow t(\varphi))) \rightarrow t(\varphi)).$$

Take an arbitrary model $M^K = (W, \pi, \mathcal{K}_1, \ldots, \mathcal{K}_n) \in \mathsf{S5}_n$ and an arbitrary state $w \in W$. We need to show that $M^K, w \not\models correct_i$ or $M^K, w \models (correct_i \rightarrow K_i(correct_i \rightarrow t(\varphi))) \rightarrow t(\varphi)$ holds. Let us assume $M^K, w \models correct_i$. We now need to show $M^K, w \models (correct_i \rightarrow K_i(correct_i \rightarrow t(\varphi))) \rightarrow t(\varphi)$, that is, $M^K, w \not\models correct_i \rightarrow K_i(correct_i \rightarrow t(\varphi))$ or $M^K, w \models t(\varphi)$. Let us further assume $M^K, w \models correct_i \rightarrow K_i(correct_i \rightarrow t(\varphi))$. By combining this with $M^K, w \models correct_i$, we get $M^K, w \models K_i(correct_i \rightarrow t(\varphi))$. Using the factivity property of knowledge, we now obtain $M^K, w \models correct_i \rightarrow t(\varphi)$. Finally, using the assumption $M^K, w \models correct_i$ one more time, we obtain $M^K, w \models t(\varphi)$. Since $M^K = (W, \pi, \mathcal{K}_1, \ldots, \mathcal{K}_n) \in \mathsf{S5}_n$ and $w \in W$ were chosen arbitrarily, 5. follows.

For 6., let us apply the translation function as well:

$$t(faulty_i \rightarrow H_i\varphi) = faulty_i \rightarrow (correct_i \rightarrow K_i(correct_i \rightarrow t(\varphi))).$$

Take an arbitrary model $M^K = (W, \pi, \mathcal{K}_1, \ldots, \mathcal{K}_n) \in \mathsf{S5}_n$ and an arbitrary state $w \in W$. Since $faulty_i = \neg correct_i$, we immediately obtain $M^K, w \models faulty_i \rightarrow (correct_i \rightarrow K_i(correct_i \rightarrow t(\varphi)))$ because the translated formula is an instance of a propositional tautology. Since $M^K = (W, \pi, \mathcal{K}_1, \ldots, \mathcal{K}_n) \in \mathsf{S5}_n$ and $w \in W$ were chosen arbitrarily, 6. indeed holds.

For 7., by applying the translation function we obtain:

$$t(H_i correct_i) = correct_i \rightarrow K_i(correct_i \rightarrow t(correct_i)) = correct_i \rightarrow K_i(correct_i \rightarrow correct_i).$$

Take an arbitrary model $M^K = (W, \pi, \mathcal{K}_1, \ldots, \mathcal{K}_n) \in \mathsf{S5}_n$ and an arbitrary state $w \in W$. Since $correct_i \rightarrow correct_i$ is an instance of a propositional tautology, $M^K, w \models K_i(correct_i \rightarrow correct_i)$ holds (agents know all propositional tautologies). Therefore, $M^K, w \models correct_i \rightarrow K_i(correct_i \rightarrow correct_i)$ also holds. Both the model $M^K = (W, \pi, \mathcal{K}_1, \ldots, \mathcal{K}_n) \in \mathsf{S5}_n$ and the state $w \in W$ were chosen arbitrarily, hence 7. follows.   □

Using Lemma 1, it is not difficult to prove that every formula derivable in $\mathscr{H}$ is valid in $\mathsf{S5}_n$ when translated according to Definition 4:

Theorem 1. *For any formula $\varphi \in \mathcal{L}_H^n$ holds the following:*

$$\vdash_{\mathscr{H}} \varphi \implies \mathsf{S5}_n \models t(\varphi).$$

Proof. It is straightforward to prove by induction on the length of the derivation of φ in $\mathscr{H}$.   □

4 Soundness and Completeness

The proof of completeness uses standard techniques of completeness proofs in modal logics for knowledge and belief, which can be found, for example, in [7].

Definition 5. *The class $\mathcal{C}^H$ consists of all Kripke models of the form*

$$M^H = (W, \pi, \mathcal{H}_1, \ldots, \mathcal{H}_n),$$

where for every $i \in \{1, \ldots, n\}$, and every $w \in W$:

1. $\mathcal{H}_i$ is transitive and Euclidean,
2. if $M^H, w \models correct_i$, then $w \in \mathcal{H}_i(w)$,
3. if $M^H, w \models faulty_i$, then $\mathcal{H}_i(w) = \emptyset$, and
4. for all pairs $(w, w') \in \mathcal{H}_i$, it is the case that $M^H, w' \models correct_i$,

where $\mathcal{H}_i(w) := \{w' : (w, w') \in \mathcal{H}_i\}$.

The following Theorem 2 provides a collection of formulas that are valid in models from $\mathcal{C}^H$. Note the one-to-one correspondence of these formulas with the axioms and inference rules of Definition 3.

Theorem 2. *For all $\varphi, \psi \in \mathcal{L}_H^n$, all $M^H \in \mathcal{C}^H$, and all $i \in \{1, \ldots, n\}$:*

1. *if φ is an instance of a propositional tautology, then $M^H \models \varphi$,*
2. $\mathcal{C}^H \models H_i\varphi \wedge H_i(\varphi \to \psi) \to H_i\psi$,
3. $\mathcal{C}^H \models H_i\varphi \to H_i H_i\varphi$,
4. $\mathcal{C}^H \models \neg H_i\varphi \to H_i \neg H_i\varphi$,
5. $\mathcal{C}^H \models correct_i \to (H_i\varphi \to \varphi)$,
6. $\mathcal{C}^H \models faulty_i \to H_i\varphi$,
7. $\mathcal{C}^H \models H_i correct_i$,
8. *If $M^H \models \varphi$ and $M^H \models \varphi \to \psi$, then $M^H \models \psi$,*
9. *if $M^H \models \varphi$, then $M^H \models H_i\varphi$.*

Proof. We will prove only 5., 6. and 7., because the proofs of the remaining cases are standard.

For 5., take an arbitrary model $M^H = (W, \pi, \mathcal{H}_1, \ldots, \mathcal{H}_n) \in \mathcal{C}^H$ and an arbitrary state $w \in W$. Assume $M^H, w \models correct_i$. According to Definition 5 (2), it follows that $w \in \mathcal{H}_i(w)$, i.e., $(w, w) \in \mathcal{H}_i$. Now suppose that $M^H, w \models H_i\varphi$ holds as well. This means that, for any state $v \in W$ such that $(w, v) \in \mathcal{H}_i$, $M^H, v \models \varphi$ holds. Since we do have that $(w, w) \in \mathcal{H}_i$, it follows that $M^H, w \models \varphi$ holds, as desired. The state w was chosen arbitrarily from W, therefore we can conclude $M^H \models correct_i \to (H_i\varphi \to \varphi)$, and since $M^H = (W, \pi, \mathcal{H}_1, \ldots, \mathcal{H}_n)$ was chosen arbitrarily from $\mathcal{C}^H$, 5. follows.

For 6., as before, take any model $M^H = (W, \pi, \mathcal{H}_1, \ldots, \mathcal{H}_n) \in \mathcal{C}^H$ and any state $w \in W$. Assume that $M^H, w \models faulty_i$ holds. According to Definition 5 (3), it follows that $\mathcal{H}_i(w) = \emptyset$, i.e., there exists no $v \in W$ such that $(w, v) \in \mathcal{H}_i$. To prove $M^H, w \models H_i\varphi$, we have to show that $M^H, v \models \varphi$ holds for all $v \in W$ such that $(w, v) \in \mathcal{H}_i$. Since there are no such $v \in W$, we have that $M^H, w \models H_i\varphi$

vacuously holds. Since $M^H = (W, \pi, \mathcal{H}_1, \ldots, \mathcal{H}_n) \in \mathcal{C}^H$ and $w \in W$ were chosen arbitrarily, 6. follows.

For 7., take again an arbitrary model $M^H = (W, \pi, \mathcal{H}_1, \ldots, \mathcal{H}_n) \in \mathcal{C}^H$ and an arbitrary state $w \in W$. To prove $M^H, w \models H_i correct_i$, we need to show that $M^H, v \models correct_i$ holds for all $v \in W$ such that $(w, v) \in \mathcal{H}_i$. But, this follows immediately from Definition 5 (4). Since $M^H = (W, \pi, \mathcal{H}_1, \ldots, \mathcal{H}_n) \in \mathcal{C}^H$ and $w \in W$ were chosen arbitrarily, 7. follows.   □

Our main technical tool will be Lemma 2 which relies on the notion and the properties of *maximal AX-consistent sets* of formulas in a given language $\mathcal{L}$, where AX is some axiomatic system. First of all, we say that a formula $\varphi \in \mathcal{L}$ is *AX-consistent* if $\neg\varphi$ is not AX-provable, i.e., there does not exist a proof of $\neg\varphi$ in AX. A finite set $\{\varphi_1, \ldots, \varphi_k\} \subseteq \mathcal{L}$ of formulas is AX-consistent exactly if $\varphi_1 \wedge \cdots \wedge \varphi_k$ is AX-consistent, and an infinite set of formulas is AX-consistent exactly if all of its finite subsets are AX-consistent. A set $F \subseteq \mathcal{L}$ of formulas is a *maximal AX-consistent* set with respect to $\mathcal{L}$ if

1. it is AX-consistent, and
2. for all φ in $\mathcal{L}$ but not in F, the set $F \cup \{\varphi\}$ is not AX-consistent.

The proof of the following lemma can be found in [4].

Lemma 2. *Suppose the language $\mathcal{L}$ consists of a countable set of formulas and is closed with respect to propositional connectives. In any axiomatic system AX that includes every instance of propositional tautologies and the Modus Ponens inference rule for the language $\mathcal{L}$, every AX-consistent set $F \subseteq \mathcal{L}$ can be extended to a maximal AX-consistent set with respect to $\mathcal{L}$.[3] In addition, if F is a maximal AX-consistent set with respect to $\mathcal{L}$, then it satisfies the following properties:*

1. *for every formula $\varphi \in \mathcal{L}$, exactly one of φ and $\neg\varphi$ is in F,*
2. *$\varphi \wedge \psi \in F$ iff $\varphi \in F$ and $\psi \in F$,*
3. *if φ and $\varphi \to \psi$ are both in F, then ψ is in F,*
4. *if φ is AX-provable, then $\varphi \in F$.*

Definition 6. *We define the so called canonical Kripke model*

$$M^c = (W^c, \pi, \mathcal{H}_1^c, \ldots, \mathcal{H}_n^c)$$

for the axiomatic system $\mathscr{H}$ in the following way:

$$W^c = \{w_S : S \text{ is some maximal } \mathscr{H}\text{-consistent set}\},$$
$$\pi(w_S)(p) = \begin{cases} true, & \text{if } p \in S, \\ false, & \text{if } p \notin S, \end{cases}$$
$$\mathcal{H}_i^c = \{(w_S, w_T) : S/H_i \subseteq T\},$$

where $S/H_i = \{\varphi : H_i\varphi \in S\}$.

---

[3] In literature on modal logics, a statement of this type is called *Lindenbaum's Lemma*.

Lemma 3. *For any formula $\varphi \in \mathcal{L}_H^n$ holds the following:*[4]

$$M^c, w_S \models \varphi \quad \textit{iff} \quad \varphi \in S. \tag{2}$$

Proof. We proceed by induction on the structure of φ.

Base case: If φ is an atomic proposition p, then the statement of the lemma follows immediately from the definition of $\pi(w_S)$.

Induction step: Proofs of the cases where φ is a negation or a conjuction are easy to obtain using propositional reasoning and Lemma 2.

Assume that φ is of the form $H_i \psi$.

($\Longleftarrow$): Let $H_i \psi \in S$. This means that $\psi \in S/H_i$ holds according to the definition of the S/H_i set. Take an arbitrary $w_T \in W^c$ such that $(w_S, w_T) \in \mathcal{H}_i^c$. We now have that $\psi \in T$ must also hold according to the definition of the $\mathcal{H}_i^c$ relation. By applying the induction hypothesis, we obtain $M^c, T \models \psi$. Therefore, $M^c, w_S \models H_i \psi$ indeed holds.

($\Longrightarrow$): Let $M^c, w_S \models H_i \psi$. It is easy to prove that the set $(S/H_i) \cup \{\neg\psi\}$ must be $\mathcal{H}$-inconsistent: Assume the opposite, i.e., $(S/H_i) \cup \{\neg\psi\}$ is $\mathcal{H}$-consistent. According to Lemma 2, there exists a maximal $\mathcal{H}$-consistent set T extending it. Thus, by construction, we have $(w_S, w_T) \in \mathcal{H}_i^c$. Using the induction hypothesis, however, we obtain $M^c, w_T \not\models \psi$, and so $M^c, w_S \not\models H_i \psi$, contradicting our original assumption. Since $(S/H_i) \cup \{\neg\psi\}$ is hence indeed $\mathcal{H}$-inconsistent, some finite subset, say $\{\varphi_1, \dots \varphi_k, \neg\psi\}$, must be $\mathcal{H}$-inconsistent. This means that $\neg(\varphi_1 \wedge \cdots \wedge \varphi_k \wedge \neg\psi)$ is $\mathcal{H}$-provable. Thus, by propositional reasoning, we have

$$\vdash_{\mathcal{H}} \varphi_1 \rightarrow (\varphi_2 \rightarrow (\cdots \rightarrow (\varphi_k \rightarrow \psi) \dots)). \tag{3}$$

From (3), by Necessitation, we further obtain

$$\vdash_{\mathcal{H}} H_i(\varphi_1 \rightarrow (\varphi_2 \rightarrow (\cdots \rightarrow (\varphi_k \rightarrow \psi) \dots))). \tag{4}$$

By induction on k, using axiom K and propositional reasoning, it is straightforward to prove

$$\vdash_{\mathcal{H}} H_i(\varphi_1 \rightarrow (\varphi_2 \rightarrow (\cdots \rightarrow (\varphi_k \rightarrow \psi) \dots))) \rightarrow$$
$$(H_i\varphi_1 \rightarrow (H_i\varphi_2 \rightarrow (\cdots \rightarrow (H_i\varphi_k \rightarrow H_i\psi) \dots))). \tag{5}$$

Now, by Modus Ponens, from (4) and (5), we finally get

$$\vdash_{\mathcal{H}} H_i\varphi_1 \rightarrow (H_i\varphi_2 \rightarrow (\cdots \rightarrow (H_i\varphi_k \rightarrow H_i\psi) \dots)).$$

Therefore, it follows that the set $\{H_i\varphi_1, \dots, H_i\varphi_k, \neg H_i\psi\}$ is $\mathcal{H}$-inconsistent as well. By the definition of the S/H_i set, since $\varphi_1, \dots, \varphi_k \in S/H_i$, it must be $H_i\varphi_1, \dots, H_i\varphi_k \in S$. As either $H_i\psi$ or $\neg H_i\psi$ is in S according to Lemma 2, we must in fact have $H_i\psi \in S$ or else S would not be (maximal) $\mathcal{H}$-consistent. $\square$

---

[4] In literature on modal logics, a statement of this type is called *Truth Lemma*.

Lemma 4. $M^c \in \mathcal{C}^H$.[5]

Proof. We need to show that the four conditions from Definition 5 are satisfied for $M^c = (W^c, \pi, \mathcal{H}_1^c, \ldots, \mathcal{H}_n^c)$:[6]

1. Assume $(w_S, w_T) \in \mathcal{H}_i^c$. Let us first show that, in this case, $S/H_i = T/H_i$: Assume $\varphi \in S/H_i$. Then $H_i\varphi \in S$, according to the definition of the S/H_i set. Axiom 4 and Lemma 2 imply $H_i H_i\varphi \in S$, which further implies $H_i\varphi \in S/H_i$. Using the definition of the $\mathcal{H}_i^c$ relation, we also obtain $H_i\varphi \in T$. Thus, $\varphi \in T/H_i$ follows, which implies that $S/H_i \subseteq T/H_i$ holds. Assume now $\varphi \notin S/H_i$. Then $H_i\varphi \notin S$, according to the definition of the S/H_i set. Axiom 5 and Lemma 2 imply $H_i\neg H_i\varphi \in S$, which further implies $\neg H_i\varphi \in S/H_i$. Using the definition of $\mathcal{H}_i^c$, we also obtain $\neg H_i\varphi \in T$. Since T is a maximal $\mathcal{H}$-consistent set, we now have $H_i\varphi \notin T$ according to Lemma 2. Thus, $\varphi \notin T/H_i$ follows, which implies that $T/H_i \subseteq S/H_i$ holds as well. Transitivity and Euclideanity now easily follow using the fact that $(w_S, w_T) \in \mathcal{H}_i^c$ implies $S/H_i = T/H_i$. For transitivity, assume $(w_S, w_T) \in \mathcal{H}_i^c$ and $(w_T, w_U) \in \mathcal{H}_i^c$. By definition, $T/H_i \subseteq U$ follows ($S/H_i \subseteq T$ follows as well). From $T/H_i \subseteq U$ and $S/H_i = T/H_i$ we obtain $S/H_i \subseteq U$, which implies $(w_S, w_U) \in \mathcal{H}_i^c$, as desired. The proof of Euclideanity is similiar.

2. Let $w_S \in W^c$ be a state satisfying $M^c, w_S \models correct_i$ and let $\varphi \in S/H_i$, that is, $H_i\varphi \in S$. Using (2), we obtain $correct_i \in S$. From axiom T' and Lemma 2 it follows that $\varphi \in S$. Since φ was chosen arbitrarily, this means that $S/H_i \subseteq S$ holds. By the definition of the $\mathcal{H}_i^c$ relation, this implies $w_S \in \mathcal{H}_i^c(w_S)$.

3. Let $w_S \in W^c$ be a state satisfying $M^c, w_S \models faulty_i$. Using (2), we obtain $faulty_i \in S$. From axiom F and Lemma 2 it follows that $H_i\varphi \in S$ holds for every formula $\varphi \in \mathcal{L}_H^n$. This means that the set S/H_i contains all formulas. Since there does not exist a maximal $\mathcal{H}$-consistent set T such that $S/H_i \subseteq T$ holds, we obtain $\mathcal{H}_i^c(w_S) = \emptyset$.

4. Let $(w_S, w_T) \in \mathcal{H}_i^c$. Since $H_i correct_i$ is axiom H, from Lemma 2 we get $H_i correct_i \in S$ and, consequently, $correct_i \in S/H_i$. Using the definition of the $\mathcal{H}_i^c$ relation, we conclude that $correct_i \in T$ holds as well. Using (2), we thus obtain $M^H, w_T \models correct_i$. □

Theorem 3 (Soundness and Completeness). *The axiomatic system $\mathcal{H}$ is sound and complete with respect to the language $\mathcal{L}_H^n$ and the class of models $\mathcal{C}^H$.*

Proof. Soundness: For an arbitrary $\varphi \in \mathcal{L}_H^n$, using the close correspondence of Theorem 2 and Definition 3, it is straightforward to prove by induction on the length of the derivation of φ in $\mathcal{H}$.

Completeness: We prove the contrapositive. Assume $\nvdash_{\mathcal{H}} \varphi$. Therefore, $\nvdash_{\mathcal{H}} \neg\neg\varphi$ holds as well, which by definition means that $\neg\varphi$ is $\mathcal{H}$-consistent. Using Lemma 2, we now obtain that $\neg\varphi$ is contained in some maximal $\mathcal{H}$-consistent

---

[5] In literature on modal logics, a statement of this type is called *Correctness Lemma*.
[6] Note that $W^c \neq \emptyset$ since any $\mathcal{H}$-consistent set can be extended to a maximal $\mathcal{H}$-consistent set according to Lemma 2.

set S. According to (2), it thus follows $M^c, w_S \models \neg\varphi$, i.e., $M^c, w_S \not\models \varphi$, where M^c is the canonical Kripke model for $\mathcal{H}$ defined in Definition 6. Therefore, $\mathcal{C}^H \not\models \varphi$ since $M^c \in \mathcal{C}^H$ as shown in Lemma 4. $\qquad\square$

We can now turn to proving the completeness part of $\mathcal{H}$ with respect to $S5_n$ models using the translation from Definition 4, as started in Sect. 3.

Theorem 4. *For any model* $M^H = (W, \pi, \mathcal{H}_1, \ldots, \mathcal{H}_n) \in \mathcal{C}^H$ *there exists a corresponding model* $M^K = (W, \pi, \mathcal{K}_1, \ldots, \mathcal{K}_n) \in S5_n$, *such that the following holds for any formula* $\varphi \in \mathcal{L}_H^n$ *and any state* $w \in W$:

$$M^H, w \models \varphi \quad \text{iff} \quad M^K, w \models t(\varphi). \tag{6}$$

Proof. Let $M^H = (W, \pi, \mathcal{H}_1, \ldots, \mathcal{H}_n) \in \mathcal{C}^H$. We define $M^K = (W, \pi, \mathcal{K}_1, \ldots, \mathcal{K}_n)$ by taking

$$\mathcal{K}_i := \mathcal{H}_i \cup \{(w, w) \mid M^K, w \models \text{faulty}_i\}$$

for all $i \in \{1, \ldots, n\}$. We show (6) by induction on the structure of φ.

Base case: If φ is an atomic proposition p, then $t(p) = p$ according to Definition 4. Now (6) follows immediately based on the fact that π is same in M^H and M^K.

Induction step: Proofs of the cases where φ is a negation or a conjunction are easy to obtain using Definition 4 and the induction hypothesis.

Assume that φ is of the form $H_i\psi$. We need to show

$$M^H, w \models H_i\psi \quad \text{iff} \quad M^K, w \models \text{correct}_i \to K_i(\text{correct}_i \to t(\psi)).$$

($\Longrightarrow$): Let $M^H, w \models H_i\psi$. This means that for all $v \in W$ such that $(w, v) \in \mathcal{H}_i$, $M^H, v \models \psi$ holds. Assume now $M^K, w \models \text{correct}_i$. Take an arbitrary $v \in W$ such that $(w, v) \in \mathcal{K}_i$. By the definition of the $\mathcal{K}_i$ relation, this means that either $(w, v) \in \mathcal{H}_i$ or ($v \equiv w$ and $M^K, w \models \text{faulty}_i$). Since, by assumption, $M^K, w \models \text{correct}_i$ (i.e., $M^K, w \not\models \text{faulty}_i$), it follows that $(w, v) \in \mathcal{H}_i$ must hold. Therefore, $M^H, v \models \psi$ follows by assumption. From this, by applying the induction hypothesis, we obtain $M^K, v \models t(\psi)$. Consequently, $M^K, v \models \text{correct}_i \to t(\psi)$ also holds. Since $v \in W$ was chosen arbitrarily, we get $M^K, w \models K_i(\text{correct}_i \to t(\psi))$. Thus, $M^K, w \models \text{correct}_i \to K_i(\text{correct}_i \to t(\psi))$ follows.

($\Longleftarrow$): Let $M^K, w \models \text{correct}_i \to K_i(\text{correct}_i \to t(\psi))$. This means that either $M^K, w \not\models \text{correct}_i$ or $M^K, w \models K_i(\text{correct}_i \to t(\psi))$. If $M^K, w \not\models \text{correct}_i$, that is, $M^K, w \models \text{faulty}_i$, then $M^H, w \models \text{faulty}_i$ as well, as shown in the base case. Thus, $M^H, w \models H_i\psi$ follows according to Theorem 2. Assume now $M^K, w \models K_i(\text{correct}_i \to t(\psi))$. This means that for all $v \in W$ such that $(w, v) \in \mathcal{K}_i$, $M^K, v \models \text{correct}_i \to t(\psi)$ holds, that is, either $M^K, v \not\models \text{correct}_i$ or $M^K, v \models t(\psi)$. In particular, for all $v \in W$ such that $(w, v) \in \mathcal{H}_i$, either $M^K, v \not\models \text{correct}_i$ or $M^K, v \models t(\psi)$. If $M^K, w \not\models \text{correct}_i$, that is, $M^K, w \models \text{faulty}_i$, then $M^H, w \models \text{faulty}_i$ holds too, as shown in the base case. Since there exists no $v \in W$ such that $(w, v) \in \mathcal{H}_i$ and $M^H, w \models \text{faulty}_i$ according to Definition 5 (4), it follows that for all $v \in W$ such that $(w,v) \in \mathcal{H}_i$, $M^K, v \models t(\psi)$ holds. By applying the induction hypothesis now, we obtain that $M^H, v \models \psi$ holds for all $v \in W$ such that $(w,v) \in \mathcal{H}_i$. Thus, $M^H, w \models H_i\psi$ follows.

It remains to show that $M^K \in \mathsf{S5_n}$, that is, it remains to show that the relations $\mathcal{K}_i$ are reflexive, transitive and Euclidean. Transitivity and Euclideanity follow based on the fact that $\mathcal{H}_i$ satisfy these properties. To show reflexivity, let $w \in W$. If $M^K, w \models correct_i$, then $M^H, w \models correct_i$ holds too, thus $(w,w) \in \mathcal{H}_i$ follows by Definition 5 (2). Therefore, $(w,w) \in \mathcal{K}_i$ holds too according to the definition of $\mathcal{K}_i$. If $M^K, w \models faulty_i$, then $(w,w) \in \mathcal{K}_i$ immediately follows from the definition of the $\mathcal{K}_i$ relation. □

Theorem 5. *For any formula $\varphi \in \mathcal{L}_H^n$ holds the following:*

$$\mathsf{S5_n} \models t(\varphi) \quad \implies \quad \vdash_{\mathscr{H}} \varphi.$$

Proof. We prove the contrapositive. Let $\nvdash_{\mathscr{H}} \varphi$. Theorem 3 implies now that $\mathcal{C}^H \nvDash \varphi$ must also hold. This means that there exists a model $M^H \in \mathcal{C}^H$ such that $M^H \nvDash \varphi$. By definition, we now have that there exists a state $w \in \mathcal{D}(M^H)$ such that $M^H, w \nvDash \varphi$. According to Theorem 4, there exists a corresponding model $M^K \in \mathsf{S5_n}$ such that $M^K, w \nvDash t(\varphi)$. Therefore, $M^K \nvDash t(\varphi)$ holds as well. Finally, we obtain $\mathsf{S5_n} \nvDash t(\varphi)$, as desired. □

We gather the results stated in Theorem 1 and Theorem 5 in the following corollary:

Corollary 1. *For any formula $\varphi \in \mathcal{L}_H^n$,*

$$\vdash_{\mathscr{H}} \varphi \quad \Longleftrightarrow \quad \mathsf{S5_n} \models t(\varphi).$$

Corollary 1 finally allows us to conclude:

$$\mathcal{C}^H \models \varphi \quad \Longleftrightarrow \quad \vdash_{\mathscr{H}} \varphi \quad \Longleftrightarrow \quad \mathsf{S5_n} \models t(\varphi) \quad \Longleftrightarrow \quad \vdash_{\mathsf{S5_n}} t(\varphi).$$

Strong Soundness and Strong Completeness

We will now show that the axiomatic system $\mathscr{H}$ is also strongly sound and strongly complete with respect to the $\mathcal{C}^H$ class of models.

First, we need to know how to derive a formula from a set of premises.

Definition 7. *An $\mathscr{H}$-derivation from premises $\Gamma \subseteq \mathcal{L}_H^n$ is a sequence of formulas $\varphi_1, \ldots, \varphi_k \in \mathcal{L}_H^n$ such that for each $i = 1, \ldots, k$:*

1. *$\varphi_i = H_{a_m} \ldots H_{a_1} \xi$ for some $m \geq 0$ and some axiom ξ of $\mathscr{H}$, or*
2. *φ_i follows from $\varphi_{j_1} = \varphi_{j_2} \to \varphi_i$ and φ_{j_2} by Modus Ponens for some $j_1, j_2 < i$, or*
3. *$\varphi_i \in \Gamma$.*

We will write $\Gamma \vdash_{\mathscr{H}} \varphi_k$ to denote the fact that φ_k can be derived from Γ in $\mathscr{H}$.

The following lemma states that $\vdash_{\mathscr{H}}$ is closed with respect to Modus Ponens.

Lemma 5. *Let* $\Gamma \subseteq \mathcal{L}_H^n$ *and* $\varphi, \psi \in \mathcal{L}_H^n$. *If* $\Gamma \vdash_{\mathscr{H}} \varphi$ *and* $\Gamma \vdash_{\mathscr{H}} \varphi \to \psi$, *then* $\Gamma \vdash_{\mathscr{H}} \psi$.

Proof. Follows immediately from Definition 7. □

Theorem 6 (Deduction theorem). *Let* $\Gamma \subseteq \mathcal{L}_H^n$ *and* $\varphi, \psi \in \mathcal{L}_H^n$. *Then*

$$\Gamma \cup \{\varphi\} \vdash_{\mathscr{H}} \psi \quad \Longrightarrow \quad \Gamma \vdash_{\mathscr{H}} \varphi \to \psi.$$

Proof. We proceed by induction on the length of the derivation of ψ from $\Gamma \cup \{\varphi\}$ in $\mathscr{H}$. Let $\psi_1, \ldots, \psi_k$ be a proof of the formula ψ from $\Gamma \cup \{\varphi\}$ in $\mathscr{H}$. If $k = 1$, then we have the following three possibilities:

- $\psi = H_{a_m} \ldots H_{a_1}\xi$ for some $m \geq 0$ and some axiom ξ of $\mathscr{H}$. Using the fact that $\psi \to (\varphi \to \psi)$ is an instance of a propositional tautology, we obtain $\Gamma \vdash_{\mathscr{H}} \psi \to (\varphi \to \psi)$. By applying Lemma 5, we obtain $\Gamma \vdash_{\mathscr{H}} \varphi \to \psi$.
- $\psi \in \Gamma$. Analogously to the previous case, we obtain $\Gamma \vdash_{\mathscr{H}} \varphi \to \psi$.
- $\psi = \varphi$. Using the fact that $\varphi \to \varphi$ is an instance of a propositional tautology, we obtain $\Gamma \vdash_{\mathscr{H}} \varphi \to \varphi$.

Assume now that the desired statement holds for every formula which has a proof of length shorter than k and consider a formula ψ which has a proof of length k. This means that the last formula in the proof is ψ. There are four possibilities: $\psi = H_{a_m} \ldots H_{a_1}\xi$ for some $m \geq 0$ and some axiom ξ of $\mathscr{H}$, or $\psi \in \Gamma$, or $\psi = \varphi$, or ψ follows by an application of Modus Ponens. We already dealt with the first three possibilities in the base case, so let us consider the remaining possibility: ψ follows by an application of Modus Ponens to some formulas, for example ψ_i and $\psi_i \to \psi$. Since these two formulas are earlier in the proof, they have proofs whose lengths are shorter than k. By applying the induction hypothesis on them, we get $\Gamma \vdash_{\mathscr{H}} \varphi \to \psi_i$ and $\Gamma \vdash_{\mathscr{H}} \varphi \to (\psi_i \to \psi)$. Using Lemma 5 and propositional reasoning, we obtain $\Gamma \vdash_{\mathscr{H}} \varphi \to \psi$. □

Next, we need to know when a formula is a logical consequence of a set of formulas.

Definition 8. *Let* $\mathcal{C}$ *be a collection of Kripke models. Let* $\Gamma \subseteq \mathcal{L}_H^n$ *and* $\varphi \in \mathcal{L}_H^n$. *We say that* φ *is a local logical consequence of* Γ *and write* $\Gamma \models_{\mathcal{C}} \varphi$ *if, for any* $M \in \mathcal{C}$ *and any* $w \in \mathcal{D}(M)$, *we have*

$$M, w \models \psi \quad \text{for all} \quad \psi \in \Gamma \quad \Longrightarrow \quad M, w \models \varphi.$$

Lemma 6. *Let* $\mathcal{C}$ *be a collection of Kripke models. Let* $\Gamma \subseteq \mathcal{L}_H^n$ *and* $\varphi \in \mathcal{L}_H^n$. *If* $\varphi \in \Gamma$, *then* $\Gamma \models_{\mathcal{C}} \varphi$.

Proof. Follows immediately from Definition 8. □

The following lemma states that $\models_{\mathcal{C}_H}$ is closed with respect to Modus Ponens too.

Lemma 7. *Let $\Gamma \subseteq \mathcal{L}_H^n$ and $\varphi, \psi \in \mathcal{L}_H^n$. If $\Gamma \models_{\mathcal{C}^H} \varphi$ and $\Gamma \models_{\mathcal{C}^H} \varphi \to \psi$, then $\Gamma \models_{\mathcal{C}^H} \psi$.*

Proof. Assume $\Gamma \models_{\mathcal{C}^H} \varphi$ and $\Gamma \models_{\mathcal{C}^H} \varphi \to \psi$. Take an arbitrary $M^H = (W, \pi, \mathcal{H}_1, \ldots, \mathcal{H}_n) \in \mathcal{C}^H$ and an arbitrary $w \in W$. Assume $M^H, w \models \xi$, for all $\xi \in \Gamma$. Since $\Gamma \models_{\mathcal{C}^H} \varphi$, $M^H, w \models \varphi$ follows. Since $\Gamma \models_{\mathcal{C}^H} \varphi \to \psi$, $M^H, w \models \varphi \to \psi$ follows too. By applying Modus Ponens now, we obtain $M^H, w \models \psi$, as desired. Since $M^H = (W, \pi, \mathcal{H}_1, \ldots, \mathcal{H}_n) \in \mathcal{C}^H$ and $w \in W$ were chosen arbitrarily, $\Gamma \models_{\mathcal{C}^H} \psi$ follows. □

Theorem 7 (Strong soundness and strong completeness). *Let $\Gamma \subseteq \mathcal{L}_H^n$ and $\varphi \in \mathcal{L}_H^n$. Then*

$$\Gamma \vdash_{\mathcal{H}} \varphi \quad \Longleftrightarrow \quad \Gamma \models_{\mathcal{C}^H} \varphi.$$

Proof. Strong soundness: We proceed by induction on the length of the derivation of φ from Γ in $\mathcal{H}$. Let $\varphi_1, \ldots, \varphi_k$ be a proof of the formula φ from Γ in $\mathcal{H}$. If $k = 1$, then we have the following two possibilities:

- $\varphi = H_{a_m} \ldots H_{a_1} \xi$ for some $m \geq 0$ and some axiom ξ of $\mathcal{H}$. Since ξ is an axiom of $\mathcal{H}$, according to Theorem 2 it follows that $\mathcal{C}^H \models \xi$. This means that $M^H \models \xi$ for all $M^H = (W, \pi, \mathcal{H}_1, \ldots, \mathcal{H}_n) \in \mathcal{C}^H$. By repeatedly applying Theorem 2, we now obtain $M^H \models H_{a_m} \ldots H_{a_1} \xi$, i.e., $M^H \models \varphi$, for all $M^H = (W, \pi, \mathcal{H}_1, \ldots, \mathcal{H}_n) \in \mathcal{C}^H$. In other words, $M^H, w \models \varphi$ for all $M^H = (W, \pi, \mathcal{H}_1, \ldots, \mathcal{H}_n) \in \mathcal{C}^H$ and all $w \in W$. Therefore, $\Gamma \models_{\mathcal{C}^H} \varphi$ trivially holds.
- $\varphi \in \Gamma$. By Lemma 6, we obtain the desired.

Assume now that the desired statement holds for every formula which has a proof of length shorter than k and consider a formula φ which has a proof of length k. This means that the last formula in the proof is φ. There are three possibilities: $\varphi = H_{a_m} \ldots H_{a_1} \xi$ for some $m \geq 0$ and some axiom ξ of $\mathcal{H}$, or $\varphi \in \Gamma$, or φ follows by an application of Modus Ponens. We already dealt with the first two possibilities in the base case, so let us consider the remaining possibility: φ follows by an application of Modus Ponens to some formulas, for example φ_i and $\varphi_i \to \varphi$. Since these two formulas are earlier in the proof, they have proofs whose lengths are shorter than k. By applying the induction hypothesis on them, we get $\Gamma \models_{\mathcal{C}^H} \varphi_i$ and $\Gamma \models_{\mathcal{C}^H} \varphi_i \to \varphi$. Thus, $\Gamma \models_{\mathcal{C}^H} \varphi$ follows from Lemma 7.

Strong completeness: We prove the contrapositive. Assume $\Gamma \nvdash_{\mathcal{H}} \varphi$. Then it is easy to prove that $\Gamma \cup \{\neg\varphi\}$ must be $\mathcal{H}$-consistent: Assume the opposite, i.e., $\Gamma \cup \{\neg\varphi\}$ is $\mathcal{H}$-inconsistent. Thus, from Definition 7, $\Gamma \cup \{\neg\varphi\} \vdash_{\mathcal{H}} \bot$ follows. Theorem 6 now implies $\Gamma \vdash_{\mathcal{H}} \neg\varphi \to \bot$. Using propositional reasoning, from this we further obtain $\Gamma \vdash_{\mathcal{H}} \varphi$ contradicting our original assumption. Since $\Gamma \cup \{\neg\varphi\}$ is indeed $\mathcal{H}$-consistent, it is contained in some maximal $\mathcal{H}$-consistent set S according to Lemma 2. From (2) we thus obtain

$$M^c, w_S \models \neg\varphi \quad \text{and} \quad M^c, w_S \models \psi \quad \text{for all} \quad \psi \in \Gamma,$$

where M^c is the canonical Kripke model for $\mathscr{H}$ defined in Definition 6. According to Definition 2, $M^c, w_S \models \neg\varphi$ means that $M^c, w_S \models \varphi$ does not hold. Therefore, $\Gamma \not\models_{CH} \varphi$. □

5 Conclusions

We studied a new epistemic modality called hope, which has been introduced for the analysis of distributed multi-agent systems which allow byzantine faults. In contrast to its original definition, we treated the hope modality separately, i.e., without the use of the knowledge modality. We provided a suitable axiomatization for this purpose, which we proved to be (strongly) sound and (strongly) complete in an independent way.

Regarding future work, our next step is to fully describe the relationships between modal logics containing only the knowledge operator, modal logics containing only the hope operator, and bi-modal logics containing both of the operators. Moreover, we will study group extensions of hope, in particular, common hope.[7]

Acknowledgments. I am immensely grateful to Ulrich Schmid and Roman Kuznets for inspiring discussions, suggestions and constructive comments on earlier versions of this paper. I would also like to thank the anonymous reviewers for their very much appreciated suggestions, in particular, regarding the need to justify the axiomatization, which allowed me to considerably strengthen the paper.

References

1. Ben-Zvi, I., Moses, Y.: On interactive knowledge with bounded communication. J. Appl. Non Class. Logics **21**(3–4), 323–354 (2011). https://doi.org/10.3166/jancl. 21.323-354
2. van Ditmarsch, H., Fruzsa, K., Kuznets, R.: A new hope. In: Fernández-Duque, D., Palmigiano, A., Pinchinat, S. (eds.) Advances in Modal Logic, AiML 2022, Rennes, France, 22–25 August 2022, pp. 349–370. College Publications (2022)
3. Dwork, C., Moses, Y.: Knowledge and common knowledge in a Byzantine environment: crash failures. Inf. Comput. **88**, 156–186 (1990). https://doi.org/10.1016/ 0890-5401(90)90014-9
4. Fagin, R., Halpern, J.Y., Moses, Y., Vardi, M.Y.: Reasoning About Knowledge. MIT Press (1995)
5. Fruzsa, K., Kuznets, R., Schmid, U.: Fire! In: Halpern, J., Perea, A. (eds.) Proceedings Eighteenth Conference on Theoretical Aspects of Rationality and Knowledge. EPTCS, vol. 335, pp. 139–153. Open Publishing Association (2021). https://doi. org/10.4204/EPTCS.335.13

---

[7] We again note that this paper has been accepted to ESSLLI2019 Student Session. Since then (building on top of the results presented here), new results have been obtained. See [2] where a logic containing both individual knowledge and individual hope has been introduced as well as a logic containing both common knowledge and common hope.

6. Goubault, É., Ledent, J., Rajsbaum, S.: A simplicial model for **KB4$_n$**: Epistemic logic with agents that may die. In: Berenbrink, P., Monmege, B. (eds.) 39th International Symposium on Theoretical Aspects of Computer Science (STACS 2022). Leibniz International Proceedings in Informatics (LIPIcs), vol. 219, pp. 33:1–33:20. Schloss Dagstuhl - Leibniz-Zentrum für Informatik (2022). https://doi.org/10.4230/LIPIcs.STACS.2022.33

7. Halpern, J.Y., Moses, Y.: A guide to completeness and complexity for modal logics of knowledge and belief. Artif. Intell. **54**, 319–379 (1992). https://doi.org/10.1016/0004-3702(92)90049-4

8. Halpern, J.Y., Moses, Y., Waarts, O.: A characterization of eventual Byzantine agreement. SIAM J. Comput. **31**, 838–865 (2001). https://doi.org/10.1137/S0097539798340217

9. Kuznets, R., Prosperi, L., Schmid, U., Fruzsa, K.: Causality and epistemic reasoning in byzantine multi-agent systems. In: Moss, L.S. (ed.) TARK 2019. EPTCS, vol. 297, pp. 293–312. Open Publishing Association (2019). https://doi.org/10.4204/EPTCS.297.19

10. Kuznets, R., Prosperi, L., Schmid, U., Fruzsa, K.: Epistemic reasoning with byzantine-faulty agents. In: Herzig, A., Popescu, A. (eds.) FroCoS 2019. LNCS (LNAI), vol. 11715, pp. 259–276. Springer, Cham (2019). https://doi.org/10.1007/978-3-030-29007-8_15

11. Kuznets, R., Prosperi, L., Schmid, U., Fruzsa, K., Gréaux, L.: Knowledge in Byzantine message-passing systems I: Framework and the causal cone. Tech. Rep. TUW-260549, TU Wien (2019). https://publik.tuwien.ac.at/files/publik_260549.pdf

12. Lamport, L.: Time, clocks, and the ordering of events in a distributed system. Commun. ACM **21**, 558–565 (1978). https://doi.org/10.1145/359545.359563

13. Lamport, L., Shostak, R., Pease, M.: The Byzantine generals problem. ACM Trans. Program. Lang. Syst. **4**, 382–401 (1982). https://doi.org/10.1145/357172.357176

14. McKinsey, M.: Skepticism and content externalism. In: Stanford Encyclopedia of Philosophy (2018). https://plato.stanford.edu/entries/skepticism-content-externalism/

15. Moses, Y.: Relating knowledge and coordinated action: the knowledge of preconditions principle. In: Ramanujam, R. (ed.) TARK 2015, pp. 231–245 (2015). https://doi.org/10.4204/EPTCS.215.17

16. Moses, Y., Shoham, Y.: Belief as defeasible knowledge. Artif. Intell. **64**, 299–321 (1993). https://doi.org/10.1016/0004-3702(93)90107-M

17. Moses, Y., Tuttle, M.R.: Programming simultaneous actions using common knowledge. Algorithmica **3**, 121–169 (1988). https://doi.org/10.1007/BF01762112

18. Schlögl, T., Schmid, U., Kuznets, R.: The persistence of false memory: brain in a vat despite perfect clocks. In: Uchiya, T., Bai, Q., Marsá-Maestre, I. (eds.) PRIMA 2020. LNCS, vol. 12568, pp. 403–411. Springer, Cham (2020). https://doi.org/10.1007/978-3-030-69322-0_30

Sentential Negativity and Anaphoric Polarity-Tags: A Hyperintensional Account

Lisa Hofmann$^{(\boxtimes)}$ (iD)

Institute of Linguistics, University of Stuttgart, Stuttgart, Germany
lisa.hofmann@ling.uni-stuttgart.de

Abstract. Certain propositional anaphora, like the Polarity Particles and Polar Additives discussed in this paper, are sensitive to the polarity of their antecedent clause. The paper establishes that discourse polarity—the polarity of the antecedent clause for the purposes of licensing subsequent anaphora—is influenced by complex factors, some of them syntactic, semantic, and pragmatic in nature.

The hyperintensional dynamic framework presented here gives a formal foundation to a distinction of polarity for propositional discourse referents and captures some of the central generalizations. It uses discourse referents for hyperintensional propositions, providing a level of representation that connects information from the discourse context, the proposition's semantic content, and the information about the polarity of the antecedent clause. Therefore, it constitutes a step towards an analysis capturing the heterogeneous factors influencing discourse polarity.

Keywords: Propositional Anaphora · Discourse negation · Polarity Particles

1 Introduction

This paper gives a hyperintensional dynamic analysis of polarity-sensitive anaphoric particles, in particular polar additives (e.g. English *neither/so*, Klima 1964) and polarity particles (e.g. English *yes/no*, Pope 1972; Ginzburg and Sag 2000; Farkas and Bruce 2010). The licensing of these (discourse) polarity-tags is contingent on the polarity of their antecedent clause (1)+(2).

(1) **Polar additives**
    a. *Mary slept.*
        (i)   *So did Dalia.*
        (ii) # *Neither did Dalia.*

    b. *Mary didn't sleep.*
        (i) # *So did Dalia.*
        (ii)   *Neither did Dalia.*

(2) **Agreeing uses of polarity particles**
    a. *Mary slept.*
        (i)   *Yes, she did.*
        (ii) # *No, she did.*

    b. *Mary didn't sleep.*
        (i)   *Yes, she didn't.*
        (ii)   *No, she didn't.*

© The Author(s), under exclusive license to Springer Nature Switzerland AG 2024
A. Pavlova et al. (Eds.): ESSLLI 2019/2020/2021, LNCS 14354, pp. 109–135, 2024.
https://doi.org/10.1007/978-3-031-50628-4_7

Polar additives are polarity-sensitive in their licensing: Positive polar additives with *so* are available with a positive antecedent (1a), but not with a negative one (1b), whereas *neither* shows the opposite pattern. Polarity particles (PolPs) are polarity-sensitive in their interpretation. In a positive context (2a), only *yes*, but not *no* can be used to agree with the antecedent. In the negative context (2b), this contrast is neutralized and either polarity particle can be used to agree (see e.g. Ginzburg and Sag 2000; Roelofsen and Farkas 2015). These asymmetries lead me to two questions: **1.** *How can the polarity-sensitivity of anaphoric polarity-tags be accounted for?* **2.** *What renders a sentence positive/negative for the purposes of discourse and how can it be captured theoretically?*

1. Polarity-tags: This work treats polarity-tags as anaphoric to propositional content (following Ginzburg and Sag 2000; Farkas and Bruce 2010; Krifka 2013; van Elswyk 2018 for PolPs; and Ahn 2015 for additives[1]). A minimal semantic theory would be based on a standard conception of propositions as sets of worlds. However, sets of worlds constitute an unstructured representation that could not make the relevant polarity distinctions. This paper introduces a hyperintensional representation for propositions, treating them as ontologically basic (Thomason 1980), while using a function relating them to their truth-conditional content formalized intensionally as sets of worlds (as in Pollard 2015). By incorporating this into a dynamic framework, we obtain discourse referents (in the sense of Karttunen 1976; Kamp 1981; Heim 1982) for hyperintensional propositions, which store both the propositional content and the polarity of the clause introducing them.

2. Discourse Polarity: The phenomenon of discourse negativity is influenced by syntactic, semantic, and pragmatic factors. Klima (1964) argued that licensing contexts for negativity-tags should be characterized in syntactic terms, based on the fact that they could not be licensed by lexical entailments (see Roelofsen and Farkas 2015, where this observation is given for PolPs).

(3)   **Non-licensing by entailment**

    a.   A: *Susan failed the exam.*
              ↔ Susan didn't pass the exam.
    b.   B: # *Neither did I.*
              (I didn't pass the exam either)
    c.   B: # *No, she did not pass.* (agreeing)

A's utterance in (3a) introduces the proposition that *Susan failed the exam.* Given satisfaction of the presuppositions, this is truth-conditionally equivalent to the negative paraphrase *Susan didn't fail the exam.* If polarity-tags involved propositional anaphora that could be formalized purely in terms of the set of

---

[1] Ahn (2015) suggests that additive *either/too* is anaphoric to a proposition in the discourse which serves as grounds for satisfying the additive presupposition, which we adopt here for *neither/so*. Additive *so* is semantically distinct from propositional *so*-anaphora, which can occupy CP-positions (e.g. *I believe so*). The latter do not come with an additive inference (see e.g. Hankamer and Sag 1976).

worlds in which the proposition is true, we might expect this context to license negativity-tags. However, negative additives (3b) and agreement with 'no' (3c) are not acceptable in this context.

This observation led Klima (1964) to assume a more structural generalization, proposing that utterances which license negativity-tags include sentential negation. Roelofsen and Farkas (2015), providing an analysis where propositional discourse referents (drefs) bear $[+/-]$ features indicating the polarity of the clause that introduced them, tie the occurrence of negative features to Jackendoff's (1969) semantic notion of sentential negation: Contradictory negation as the highest-scoping operator in the clause.

However, cases like the following (4) indicate that negativity-tags may be licensed by sentences in which negation is in the scope of another operator.

(4)   **Narrow-scope negation**

    a.   High-scoping modals:
        A: *I shouldn't go alone.* $(\Box > \neg), (\neg \not> \Box)$
        B: *Me neither.* (I shouldn't go alone either.)
           No, you really shouldn't.
    b.   Quantified pronominal subjects:
        A: *We all didn't sleep.* $(\forall > \neg), (\neg \not> \forall)$
        B: *Me neither.* (I didn't sleep either.)
           No, you truly didn't.

Horn (1989) suggests that cases like (4a) pose problems for any semantic account of sentential negation that does not make reference to syntax. Note that negation is outscoped not only in the antecedent but also in the interpretation of the anaphoric expression. The content that is picked up anaphorically includes the meaning components introduced by negation *and* the outscoping operator. Therefore, this data provides a challenge to semantic accounts, which assume that negativity-tags are anaphoric to a proposition in the scope of negation.

Cases of non-licensing by entailment, and licensing by narrow-scope negation both indicate that discourse-negativity is associated with a more structural representation than possible worlds can offer. Making reference to a syntactic notion of sentential negation, as Klima (1964) originally suggested (see e.g. the ellipsis-based accounts of polarity-tags Kramer and Rawlins 2009; Holmberg 2013; Hofmann 2018; Zaitsu 2021), could address both cases: It can distinguish the positive sentence in (3) from its negative paraphrase, and subsume the cases in (4) under the umbrella of sentential negation in a syntactic sense (in the sense of e.g. Klima 1964; Haegeman and Zanuttini 1991; Ladusaw 1992; Zanuttini 1997; Zeijlstra 2004).

However, there are licensing contexts which pressure against a purely syntactic account, i.e. ones where negativity-tags are licensed by antecedents that do not contain overt negation. These include contexts that Kroll (2019) identifies as licensing polarity-reversals in sluicing, like the neg-raising context in (5).

(5)   **Neg-raising**
       I don't think Mary slept, ...
       a.   *... and neither did Dalia.*   (Dalia didn't sleep either.)
       b.   *... No, she really didn't.*   (Mary really didn't sleep.)

The negativity-tags in (5) are anaphoric to the affirmative embedded clause. Assuming that neg-raising can be derived pragmatically (Gajewski 2007; Collins and Postal 2018), this shows that the discourse-polarity of a potential antecedent clause can be influenced its semantic and pragmatic context. Further evidence for this claim comes from cases of neg-raising in island contexts, which are uncontroversially derived pragmatically (Collins and Postal 2018), and anti-veridical attitudes, where the lexical semantics affects the anaphoric potential of the embedded content (Hofmann 2022).

(6)   a.   Island Neg-raising:
             I didn't get the impression that Mary exercises.
       b.   Anti-veridical attitudes:
             I don't remember being scared. And neither was my dog.

While acceptability of some examples of this kind is mixed, results from an experimental study in Hofmann (2022) suggest that neg-raising in island contexts and anti-veridical attitude predicates can license negativity-tags, although less robustly than sentential negation.

The cases discussed here suggest that polarity-tags cannot be licensed by entailment alone, but they can be semantically and pragmatically licensed by anti-veridically interpreted embedded content. The cases of licensing where clausal negation in the antecedent is outscoped by another semantic operator, on the other hand, suggest that surface-based generalizations need to be taken into account.

The heterogeneity of factors influencing discourse polarity suggests a semantic level of representation that may capture both contextual influences and relevant morphosyntactic factors. To achieve this, I introduce a representation of the polarity of propositional anaphora in the framework of Compositional Discourse Representation Theory (CDRT, cf. Muskens 1996) enriched with hyperintensional propositional drefs (based on Thomason 1980). This allows me to give a formal foundation for the interpretation of polarity-features for propositional drefs assumed in Farkas and Bruce (2010); Roelofsen and Farkas (2015).

Section 2 presents the account informally, as a way of representing polarity on the level of propositional drefs. Section 3 gives an outline of the formal account and shows how it captures discourse negativity and negativity-tags. I illustrate that the analysis captures non-licensing by entailment and licensing in outscoping cases. However, as presented here, the account relies on a morphosyntactic representation of negation to introduce a negative propositional dref. It, therefore, cannot account directly for neg-raising cases. Despite this shortcoming, the presented analysis presents a step forward from existing accounts of discourse negativity, accounting for central generalizations about the heterogeneous properties of licensing contexts. These issues are discussed in Sect. 4, which also provides a comparison with previous accounts of PolPs. Section 5 concludes.

2   Reference to Negative Propositions

CDRT with hyperintensional propositional drefs offers a way to distinguish reference to positive and negative propositions in discourse. This framework uses hyperintensional propositional drefs as a representation connecting information from the linguistic context, the semantic content of the proposition, and the information whether the proposition was introduced by a negative sentence. Roelofsen and Farkas (2015) (R&F) suggest representing polarity on the level of propositional drefs, analogously to Farkas and Zec's (1995) treatment of gender features on pronouns, where drefs function as a level of representation that incorporates both semantic and morphosyntactic sources of gender specification. The account presented here gives a formal foundation to the $[+/-]$ distinction for polarity for propositional anaphora suggested in R&F.

Farkas and Zec (1995) propose that (morphosyntactic) phi-features are interpreted as properties of drefs. Now, if we want to understand polarity as a property of propositional drefs (in a model-theoretic and truth-conditional formalization), we cannot have them refer to intensional propositions. That is due to cases like (3a), repeated here: utterances of sentences which have equivalent paraphrases of opposite polarity.

(3-a)   *Susan failed the exam.*
            ↔ Susan didn't pass the exam.

If propositional drefs were understood intensionally, how would we characterize the set of worlds in which Susan failed the exam (or equivalently: didn't pass it)? It appears it should be both positive and negative, in which case the distinction is not very useful, or not really a distinction at all. To get at the licensing contrasts for anaphoric polarity-tags, the sets of positive and negative propositions should be mutually exclusive. Since the intensional content of positive and negative sentences can be equivalent, finer grained distinctions are needed. Hyperintensionality can offer that (Thomason 1980, see also Pollard,2015).

Here, the distinction between positive and negative propositions is conceptualized on a semantic level in terms of drefs for hyperintensional propositions in the sense of Thomason (1980), i.e., atomic propositional objects. In Thomason's spirit, I add not one, but two basic types for positive and negative propositions. Propositions are related to their truth-conditional content (a set of worlds) by a content-function (as in Pollard 2015). This mechanism allows for referencing propositional content in discourse while also indicating whether the propositional dref was introduced by a positive or negative sentence.

The lexical entries of natural language expressions ensure that sentences containing negation introduce negative propositional drefs and sentences without negation introduce positive propositional drefs (illustrated in some detail in Sect. 3, below). This is achieved on the level of type-theory, as the interpretation of the discourse would otherwise result in a type-mismatch. An alternative formal implementation of this distinction in terms of relations over hyperintensional propositions, rather than positive and negative propositional types, is briefly discussed in Sect. 3.5.

3   Outline of the Formal Account

3.1   Hyperintensional CDRT

Thomason (1980) introduced hyperintensionality to account for non-closure under entailment for complements of belief-statements. Entailment is defined over sets of worlds, and introducing a basic type of propositions p as primitive objects achieves that propositions do not participate in entailment relations anymore.

Similarly, we can distinguish propositional polarity on the level of type theory by assuming a two-sorted domain of basic propositional objects: D_{p^+}, D_{p^-}. We yield hyperintensional propositional drefs, enabling reference to propositions of a specific polarity in discourse. Negative drefs cannot be derived from positive ones and vice versa, capturing the selective nature of polarity-tags and ruling out cases where they are not licensed as type mismatches.

Hyperintensional propositions are related to their truth-conditional content (a set of worlds) through a content-function, as in Pollard (2015), which assigns a set wt for each proposition $p \in D_{p^+} \cup D_{p^-}$.

(7)   **Content function**
Cont$_{p(wt)}$, for $p \in \{p^+, p^-\}$, s.t. for any proposition p, **Cont**(p) is the set of worlds that is the 'content' of p, i.e. the set of worlds in which p is true.

(7) only defines the shape of the function, that is, its type. The particular set of worlds associated with a basic propositional object is constrained by the interpretation of linguistic expressions in discourse.

The proposed hyperintensional dynamic system adapts the dynamic Ty2 Logic introduced as the Logic of Change in Muskens (1996), including reference to propositions. I am closely following Brasoveanu's (2006) implementation of this system (Brasoveanu's Dyamic Ty2, see also Brasoveanu's 2006; 2010a Intensional Plural CDRT, and Hofmann's 2019; 2022 Intensional CDRT for intensional versions).

The system uses six basic types: t (truth-values), e (entities), w (possible worlds), p^+ (positive propositions), p^- (negative propositions), and s (variable assignments). A dref for individuals v is a function of type se from assignments i_s to individuals x_e (subscripts on terms indicate their type). Accordingly, the individual $v_{se}(i_s)$ is the individual that the assignment i assigns to the dref v. A dref for positive propositions π^+ is a function of type sp^+ from assignments i_s to positive propositions p^+, and a dref for negative propositions π^- is a function of type sp^- from assignments i_s to negative propositions p^-.

Natural language sentences are interpreted as DRSs, which are defined as binary relations of type $s(st)$ between input state i_s and output state j_s, where discourse states are variable assignments. A DRS contains a list of new drefs $(v_1, \ldots, v_n)$, and a series of conditions of type st, i.e., properties of discourse states $(C_1, \ldots, C_n)$, and is defined as (8):

(8)   **Sentence Meanings**
$$[v_1, \ldots, v_n \mid C_1, \ldots, C_n] :=$$
$$\lambda i_s . \lambda j_s . i[v_1, \ldots, v_n]j \wedge C_1(j) \wedge \cdots \wedge C_n(j)$$

The dynamic variable update $(i[v]j)$ specifies a relation between variable assignments and is defined as random assignment of values to a variable v. This relation holds between discourse states i_s and j_s, iff they differ at most wrt the values assigned to v (Groenendijk and Stokhof 1991; Muskens 1996). (8) makes use of the introduction of multiple drefs, which relies on dynamic conjunction, which in turn is defined as relation composition.

(9)   a.   Introducing multiple drefs:
$$[v_1, \ldots, v_n] := [v_1]; \ldots; [v_n]$$
       b.   Dynamic conjunction:
$$\mathcal{D}; \mathcal{D}' := \lambda i_s . \lambda j_s . \exists h_s . \mathcal{D}(i)(h) \wedge \mathcal{D}'(h)(j)$$

DRS-conditions are properties of the output state (type st). They include dynamic predicates with their arguments, which abbreviate a condition an assignment i_s. This abbreviation is illustrated in (10), relating a dynamic predicate to the corresponding static predicate, and its argument drefs to their referents in the context of i.

(10)   **DRS-conditions**
$Sleep_\pi \{v\} :=$
$\lambda i_s . \forall w \in \mathbf{Cont}(\pi(i)).sleep_{e(wt)}(v(i))(w)$ [2]

The dynamic predicate *Sleep* takes two arguments: an individual dref v, and a propositional dref π (indicated as a subscript on the predicate). The condition is true of an assignment i iff the referent of $v(i)$ sleeps in all the worlds in the content of $\pi(i)$. While the above definition of the content-function in (7) specifies its type, predication over hyperintensional drefs imposes constraints on the possible mappings between propositions and their content, according to the interpretation of linguistic expressions. This is so, because the content of the propositional argument will provide the intensional context of evaluation for the static predicate.

Although this system uses Thomason's (1980) basic idea of introducing a basic type of propositions, hyperintensional CDRT is different from the logical system Thomason introduces (intentional logic). Unlike the meaning postulates of intentional logic, the content-function in hyperintensional CDRT does not

---

[2] for $v \in \mathbf{Term}_{s(we)}$, $\pi \in \mathbf{Term}_{sp}$, where $p \in \{p^+, p^-\}$

relate hyperintensional propositions to truth-values directly, but instead to the set of worlds in which they are true.[3]

3.2   Deriving Discourse Polarity in Hyperintensional CDRT

With this system in place, the assertion of a positive sentence receives the interpretation in (11):

(11)   *Mary slept.*   ⤳

π^+, υ
$\upsilon = Mary_\mathbf{e}$
$sleep_{\pi^+}\{\upsilon\}$

(11) introduces two new drefs: A positive propositional dref π^+ referring to the proposition expressed by the sentence, and an individual dref υ referring to 'Mary'. The condition $\upsilon = Mary_\mathbf{e}$ ensures that υ refers to the individual $mary_e$. The condition $sleep_{\pi^+}\{\upsilon\}$ states that the referent of υ sleeps in all worlds in the content of π^+.

An affirmative sentence, i.e., one that doesn't have negation, will always introduce a positive propositional dref. To see how this is guaranteed, we take a look at the compositional semantics:

Following Brasoveanu's (2006) implementation of Muskens's (1996) CDRT, sub-clausal semantic composition in a Montegovian/Fregean sense follows from the underlying type logic. A standard Montegovian compositional system makes use of semantic types for individuals and sentences, which we might abbreviate using the 'meta-types' **e** and **t**. An intensional system in addition makes reference to possible worlds, abbreviated as **w**. In an intensional static logic, **e** corresponds to type e, **w** corresponds to type w, and **t** to type t. The English predicate *sleep* would be translated as an intensional property of individuals of type **e(wt)**, accordingly: sleep ⤳ $\lambda x_e.\lambda w_w.sleep_{e(wt)}(x)(w)$.

In our dynamic hyperintensional system, replace these compositional types with their dynamic and hyperintensional counterparts. **e** will correspond to individual drefs of type se, and **t** to dynamic sentence meanings of type $s(st)$. The intensional argument that provides the worlds of evaluation for a predicate is a propositional dref in this system. Since we now have a two-sorted domain of propositions, we are dropping the type **w** and instead abbreviating the two types of drefs for positive and negative propositions as $\mathbf{p}^+$ (short for sp^+) and $\mathbf{p}^-$ (short for sp^-), respectively. Occasionally, the compositional system will need to make

---

[3] An anonymous reviewer points out that Fox and Lappin (2008) show that Thomason's intentional logic cannot do what it is intended to do, viz. distinguishing between distinct, but logically equivalent, propositions. This is shown based on the algebraic properties of the used meaning postulates, which relate hyperintensional propositions to truth-values ($D_p \mapsto 2$). Unlike intentional logic, hyperintensional CDRT has an intensional layer, and a content-function $((D_{p^+} \cup D_{p^-}) \mapsto D_{wt})$. This allows distinct propositional objects to be related to the same content and avoids the problems Fox and Lappins identify for Thomason's intentional logic.

reference to cases where arguments of certain relations can have either type. In these cases, the optionality is abbreviated as **p**, where $\mathbf{p} \in \{\mathbf{p^+}, \mathbf{p^-}\}$.[4] Lexical items corresponding to predicates can now receive translations as in (12).

(12) $sleep \rightsquigarrow \lambda v_{\mathbf{e}}.\lambda \pi_{\mathbf{p}}^{++}.[Sleep_{\pi^+}\{v\}]$

The verb *sleep* is formalized as dynamic hyperintensional property of individuals (type $\mathbf{e(p^+t)}$). It takes an individual dref v and a positive propositional dref π^+ as arguments and predicates that the static relation $sleep_{e(wt)}$ holds of the individual referred to by v in all worlds in the content of π^+ (at a given assignment). The DP *Mary* contributes the following:

(13) $Mary \rightsquigarrow \lambda P_{\mathbf{e(p^+t)}}.\lambda \pi_{\mathbf{p^+}}^+.\ [v \mid v = Mary_{\mathbf{e}}]; P(v)(\pi^+)$
$$(\text{s.t. } \forall i_s.Mary(i) = mary_e)$$

(13) is a dynamic quantifier over individuals (type $\mathbf{(e(p^+t))(p^+t)}$). It combines with a property P and a positive proposition π^+, introduces an individual dref that is equal to the discourse constant $Mary_e$, and requires that P holds of v in the content of π^+. In (11), the two items (12) and (13) combine as (14):

(14) $[Mary \; sleep] \rightsquigarrow \lambda \pi_{\mathbf{p^+}}^+.[v \mid v = Mary_{\mathbf{e}}]; [Sleep_{\pi^+}\{v\}]$

I assume that a sentential operator introduces the propositional dref corresponding to the clause, as given in (15). For concreteness, I follow Bittner (2009); Snider (2017) in associating this contribution with declarative sentential mood. The introduction of a propositional dref is the only part of this operator's semantics relevant to the points made here, so I am glossing over other semantic contributions of sentential mood here.

(15)   Declarative sentential mood:
         $\text{DEC} \rightsquigarrow \lambda \mathcal{P}_{\mathbf{pt}}.[\pi_{\mathbf{p}}]; \mathcal{P}(\pi)$

Crucially, the declarative operator is assumed to flexibly introduce a positive or negative propositional dref, depending on the requirements of its prejacent. In combination with (14), which requires a positive propositional argument, this guarantees that affirmative sentences will introduce a positive propositional dref.

3.3   The Discourse-Effect of Negative Sentences

The introduction of a negative propositional dref in a simple negative sentence (16) is ensured by the semantics of sentential negation.

(16)   *Mary didn't sleep.*

---

[4] This could be given a cleaner formal foundation in terms of Carpenter's (1997) union types, or potentially a richer type theory like Type Theory with Records, see e.g. Cooper (Jul 2005; 2012).

The semantics of negation introduces a propositional dref π^+, the content of which is the set of worlds in which its prejacent is true. The result of combining negation with its prejacent requires another propositional argument, which is negative due to an argument restriction of the negative operator, with the semantics in (17).

(17)   NOT $\rightsquigarrow \lambda \mathcal{P}_{\mathbf{pt}}.\lambda \pi_{1\mathbf{p}}^{-}.[\pi_{2\mathbf{p}}^{+} \mid \mathbf{Cont}\{\pi_1^-\} = \overline{\mathbf{Cont}\{\pi_2^+\}}]; \mathcal{P}(\pi_2^+)$

The truth-functional meaning of negation is introduced by the condition that the content of the positive propositional dref corresponding to the prejacent and the content of the negative propositional dref corresponding to the matrix sentence are complements of each other.

Because the negative operator requires its hyperintensional argument to be negative, and the declarative operator will introduce a propositional dref of the required type, the matrix propositional dref corresponding to a negated sentence will be negative. The representation of (16), modulo tense, is given in (18):

(18)   *Mary didn't sleep.* $\rightsquigarrow$

$\pi_1^-, \pi_2^+, \upsilon$
$\mathbf{Cont}\{\pi_1^-\} = \overline{\mathbf{Cont}\{\pi_2^+\}}$
$\upsilon = Mary_\mathbf{e}$
$sleep_{\pi_2^+}\{\upsilon\}$

(18) introduces three new drefs: A negative propositional dref π_1^- referring to the proposition expressed by the sentence, a positive propositional dref π_2^+ corresponding to the prejacent of negation, and an individual dref υ. The condition $\upsilon = Mary_\mathbf{e}$ ensures that υ refers to the individual $mary_e$. The condition $sleep_{\pi_2^+}\{\upsilon\}$ states that the referent of υ sleeps in all worlds in the content of π_2^+. The condition $\mathbf{Cont}\{\pi_1^-\} = \overline{\mathbf{Cont}\{\pi_2^+\}}$ requires that the contents of π_1^- and π_2^+ are complementary opposites.

This system also allows for an account of cases where negation is outscoped by making use of the type restrictions on the propositional argument because they are passed up to the declarative operator across an outscoping operator. This is illustrated for the negative sentence with a quantified pronominal subject in (19a), assuming the semantics for *we all* in (19b).

(19)   a.   *We all didn't sleep.*
        b.   we all $\rightsquigarrow \lambda \mathcal{P}_{\mathbf{e(pt)}}.\lambda \pi_\mathbf{p}.[\mathbf{all}(WE_\pi, \mathcal{P}(\pi))]$
               where WE_π is (the property that characterizes) the set
               of (drefs that map i to) entities denoted by 'we' in $\pi(i)$

For concreteness (and simplicity), we can assume that the $\mathbf{all}_{\mathbf{e(pt)},(\mathbf{e(pt)},\mathbf{pt})}$ specifies a condition on the output state as a generalized quantifier over drefs, i.e. over mappings from the output state to entities (see van den Berg 1993; Brasoveanu 2006 for fully dynamic generalized quantification).

(20) $\mathbf{all}_\pi \ (A_{\mathbf{e(pt)}}, B_{\mathbf{e(pt)}}) := \lambda s.(\lambda \upsilon.B_\pi(\upsilon(s)) \subseteq \lambda \upsilon.A_\pi(\upsilon(s)))$

The particular semantics for the quantifier does not bear on the analysis here, as long as it compositionally behaves as in (19b).

The quantifier (19b) takes two arguments: A dynamic property of individuals $\mathcal{P}$ as its nuclear scope, and a propositional argument π. Note that π is flexible in type: it could be positive or negative. Further, the same π that the quantifier receives as an argument is passed on as propositional argument for the nuclear scope $\mathcal{P}$. The requirements that $\mathcal{P}$ imposes on the type of π will therefore also be requirements on the argument of *we all*.

Because the subject plausibly has moved across negation and rigidly scopes from its surface position, I am assuming the structure in (21) along with the semantics for the moved quantifier and its lower copy in (22), based on a standard semantics for movement.

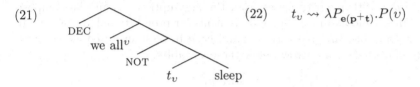

(21) / (22) $\quad t_v \rightsquigarrow \lambda P_{\mathbf{e(p+t)}}.P(v)$

Accordingly, the interpretation of (19a) can be given as (23).

(23) a.   *We all didn't sleep.* ($\forall > \neg$)

b.

$$\text{all}\left(\begin{array}{c|c} & \pi_1^- \\ \hline WE_{\pi_1^-}, \lambda v_{\mathbf{e}}. & \begin{array}{c} \pi_2^+ \\ \hline \mathbf{Cont}\{\pi_1^-\} = \overline{\mathbf{Cont}\{\pi_2^+\}} \\ \hline Sleep_{\pi_2^+}\{v\} \end{array} \end{array}\right)$$

In (23), the quantifier takes scope over negation. The propositional argument of the quantifier is fed forward to its nuclear scope, and thus has to be of the right type to satisfy the type requirement of the nuclear scope. As a result, the propositional dref introduced by DEC has to be negative in order to avoid a type mismatch.

Because **all** is a universal generalized quantifier over drefs, the condition $\mathbf{all}(WE_{\pi_1^-}, \lambda v_{\mathbf{e}}.[\pi_2^+ \mid \mathbf{Cont}\{\pi_1^-\} = \overline{\mathbf{Cont}\{\pi_2^+\}}]; [Sleep_{\pi_2^+}\{v\}])$ states that the set of drefs that point to a member of the set denoted by *we* in the content of π_1^- is a subset of the set of possible drefs for which the update of the restrictor argument could be made.[5]

---

[5] Since this is a hypothetical local update in the scope of the quantifier, the embedded π_2^+ is predicted to never be accessible outside of the scope of the quantifier. The current system does not provide a way of capturing the constraints (and possibilities) for anaphora to quantified content. See Brasoveanu (2006; 2010b) for an account that can handle anaphora to quantified content by making use of selectively distributive dynamic quantification and structural dependencies between plural drefs.

3.4   Polar Additives

With our two types of propositional drefs, we can capture the anaphoric requirements of discourse polarity tags.

Following Ahn (2015), I assume that additives are propositional relations, where one argument is provided by the prejacent, and another interpreted anaphorically. Further, I assume that *so*, a positive additive like *too*, requires two positive propositional arguments, while *neither* provides the semantic contribution of NOT + *either*, and requires two negative propositional arguments.

Differently from treatments of *either* as an NPI (Rullmann 2003; Ahn 2015), I treat both *either* and *so* as additives taking scope over negation, defined in terms of a relation $\mathbf{add}(\pi_1)(\pi_2)$, which is assumed to be satisfied if the additive presupposition in the sense of Heim (1992) is satisfied.[6] Here, the interaction of *so* and *neither* with polarity arises from the assumptions about the compositional semantics and assumed type requirements for propositional arguments. In (24), the π_2-variables are free variables and need to be interpreted as discourse anaphora, indicated by an arrow below these variables.

(24)   a.   so $\rightsquigarrow \lambda \mathcal{P}_{\mathbf{p}+\mathbf{t}}.\lambda \pi_1^+.\mathcal{P}(\pi_1^+); [\mathbf{add}\{\pi_1^+, \underset{\leftarrow}{\pi_2^+}\}]$

b.   neither $\rightsquigarrow \lambda \mathcal{P}_{\mathbf{p}+\mathbf{t}}.\lambda \pi_1^-.\text{NOT}(\mathcal{P})(\pi_1^-); [\mathbf{add}\{\pi_1^-, \underset{\leftarrow}{\pi_2^-}\}]$

Consider (25) and (26), a discourse where a *neither*-tag is licensed.

(25)   *Mary didn't sleep.*

$\pi_1^-, \pi_2^+, \upsilon_1$
$\mathbf{Cont}\{\pi_1^-\} = \overline{\mathbf{Cont}\{\pi_2^+\}}$
$\upsilon_1 = Mary_{\mathbf{e}}$
$sleep_{\pi_2^+}\{\upsilon_1\}$

(26)   *Neither did Dalia* ~~sleep~~.

$\pi_3^-, \pi_4^+, \upsilon_2$
$\mathbf{Cont}\{\pi_3^-\} = \overline{\mathbf{Cont}\{\pi_4^+\}}$
$\upsilon_2 = Dalia_{\mathbf{e}}$
$sleep_{\pi_4}\{\upsilon_2\}$
$\mathbf{either}\{\pi_3^-, \underset{\leftarrow}{\pi_5^-}\}$

Crucially, (25) introduces a negative propositional dref π_1^-, s.t. Mary didn't sleep in the content of π_1^-. (26) involves a negative propositional anaphor π_5^-, requiring a negative antecedent in discourse, which it finds in π_1^-. Its resolution is illustrated in (27).

---

[6] A formal treatment of the additive presupposition requires additional machinery to deal with presuppositions, and focus alternatives, and is glossed over here. I am also not accounting for (interaction with) VP-ellipsis at this point.

(27)   Merging DRSs and resolving anaphor:

$$\boxed{\begin{array}{l} \pi_1^-, \pi_2^+, \upsilon_1, \pi_3^-, \pi_4^+, \upsilon_2 \\ \hline \mathbf{Cont}\{\pi_1^-\} = \overline{\mathbf{Cont}\{\pi_2^+\}} \\ \upsilon_1 = Mary_{\mathbf{e}} \\ sleep_{\pi_2^+}\{\upsilon_1\} \\ \mathbf{Cont}\{\pi_3^-\} = \overline{\mathbf{Cont}\{\pi_4^+\}} \\ \upsilon_2 = Dalia_{\mathbf{e}} \\ sleep_{\pi_4}\{\upsilon_2\} \\ \mathbf{either}\{\pi_3^-, \pi_1^-\} \end{array}}$$

In a positive context (28), *neither* is not licensed (29).

(28)   *Mary slept.*

$$\boxed{\begin{array}{l} \pi_1^+, \upsilon_1 \\ \hline \upsilon_1 = Mary_{\mathbf{e}} \\ sleep_{\pi_1^+}\{\upsilon_1\} \end{array}}$$

(29)   *Neither did Dalia ~~sleep~~.*

$$\boxed{\begin{array}{l} \pi_2^-, \pi_3^+, \upsilon_2 \\ \hline \mathbf{Cont}\{\pi_2^-\} = \overline{\mathbf{Cont}\{\pi_3^+\}} \\ \upsilon_2 = Dalia_{\mathbf{e}} \\ sleep_{\pi_3}\{\upsilon_2\} \\ \mathbf{either}\{\pi_2^-, \overleftarrow{\pi_4^-}\} \end{array}}$$

(28) is the representation of a positive sentence, crucially only introducing one positive propositional dref π_1^+, s.t. Mary slept in the content of π_1^+. As above, the anaphor introduced by *neither* (π_4^-), requires a negative antecedent, which is not available here.

To account for the unavailability of *so* in negative contexts, there needs to be a restriction that the propositional anaphora of interest can only make reference to drefs introduced on matrix level, but not to embedded drefs.

(30)   Mary didn't sleep.

$$\boxed{\begin{array}{l} \pi_1^-, \pi_2^+, \upsilon_1 \\ \hline \upsilon_1 = Mary_{\mathbf{e}} \\ sleep_{\pi_2^+}\{\upsilon_1\} \\ \mathbf{Cont}\{\pi_1^-\} = \overline{\mathbf{Cont}\{\pi_2^+\}} \end{array}}$$

(31)   So did Dalia ~~sleep~~.

$$\boxed{\begin{array}{l} \pi_3^+, \upsilon_2 \\ \hline \upsilon_2 = Dalia_{\mathbf{e}} \\ sleep_{\pi_3^+}\{\upsilon_2\} \\ \mathbf{parallel}\{\pi_3^+, \overleftarrow{\pi_4^+}\} \end{array}}$$

(30) makes two propositional drefs available: π_1^-, corresponding to the full sentence, and π_2^+, corresponding to the prejacent of negation.

A restriction is needed to explain the non-licensing of the anaphor introduced by *so*: It could not be anaphoric to the embedded positive proposition. This kind of restriction is not accounted for here, but could potentially be understood in terms of accessibility over structural discourse coherence relations (Asher 1993; Asher and Lascarides 2003), or by invoking a notion of propositional salience in QUD-based frameworks, where it might be operationalized in terms of at-issueness (as Snider 2017 considers based on e.g. Murray 2010; Tonhauser 2012, but argues against), or discourse-expectedness (based on Tönnis 2021; 2022). While such a constraint is necessary to account for the unavailability of (31) following (30), the factors which constrain propositional anaphora to embedded content fall outside of the scope of the current paper.

3.5   Interim Discussion

This section has illustrated how the system captures the polarity-sensitivity of discourse polarity tags in a basic way. The account put forward in this paper is a fully formal analysis of polarity for propositional drefs in discourse. This is achieved by introducing an intermediate representation of hyperintensional propositions, following Thomason (1980). This is implemented here using a two-sorted domain of positive and negative hyperintensional propositions as a way of making reference to propositional content in discourse while preserving the information whether the propositional dref was introduced by a positive or a negative sentence.

As pointed out by a reviewer, understanding properties of drefs in terms of type-distinctions comes with non-trivial ontological assumptions about model domains. The worry is that this approach opens the gates for other properties associated with drefs (such as e.g. those marked by phi-features discussed in Farkas and Zec 1995) to be understood in the same way, allowing for further subdivision of the domain. Alternatively, we might give an isomorphic treatment, which formalizes the relevant properties in terms of two relations **positive**(π) and **negative**(π). These relations would have to be mutually exclusive and jointly exhaustive over the domain of hyperintensional propositions in every possible model. It is this feature that lends some conceptual justification to a type-theoretic treatment.

It is important to note that propositional polarity (independent of whether it is implemented in terms of semantic relations or type-theoretically) could not be a property of intensional propositions (as shown in Sect. 1), but requires the additional distinctions made possible by hyperintensional propositions. Setting aside the ontological considerations for now, the approach taken here has a practical advantage: The type-restrictions provide a basic way of addressing the relevant restrictions in the compositional system.

Since hyperintensionality essentially provides a way of making reference to morphosyntactic structure in the semantic representation, the basic analysis relies on overt negation to introduce discourse-negativity. This account is well-suited for cases where negation is outscoped by another operator and for non-licensing by entailment. However, capturing the contextual introduction of negativity in neg-raising contexts is a challenge for this account, which will be discussed further in Sect. 4.4.

4   Comparison with Analyses of PolPs

This section compares the suggested account with previous analyses of the interaction of negation and propositional anaphor in polarity-tags, particularly with accounts of PolPs. While these previous studies have focused on analyzing the relevant anaphoric expressions to explain variation in patterns of polarity-sensitivity, I will focus the discussion here on the empirical coverage concerning different kinds of licensing contexts.

4.1   Roelofsen and Farkas (2015)

Roelofsen and Farkas (2015) (R&F) propose that PolPs take two propositional arguments: one from a prejacent clause and one retrieved anaphorically. PolPs may bear two kinds of features that constrain the polarity of their propositional arguments. Absolute polarity features $[+/-]$ which introduce a presupposition that the prejacent be positive or negative, respectively. Relative polarity features [AGREE/REVERSE] introduce a presupposition that the prejacent have the same polarity (and propositional content) as the prejacent or opposite polarity (and contradictory content), respectively.

I take the system presented here to be a faithful implementation of the $[+/-]$ polarity distinction of R&F, embedding polarity distinctions for propositional drefs in a fully formalized system. It allows capturing more fine-grained generalizations about what makes a propositional dref positive or negative, precisely specifying the conditions for evaluating presuppositions imposed by polarity features, and extends the empirical coverage of licensing contexts to those in which negation is outscoped.

R&F account for the typology of particle-based answering systems by assuming that PolPs in any given language may lexicalize absolute or relative polarity features, or a combination of both. The presented formalization, paired with R&F's assumptions about the morphological typology of answering systems, can capture cross-linguistic variation in an isomorphic way. The basic mechanism of this implementation is illustrated here for cases of agreeing uses of *no* in English.

English PolPs in Hyperintensional CDRT. To implement R&F in Hyperintensional CDRT, we give a semantics for absolute features that impose conditions on the polarity of their prejacent:

(32)   a. $[+] \rightsquigarrow \lambda \mathcal{P}_{\mathbf{p}^+ \mathbf{t}}.\lambda \pi^+_{\mathbf{p}^+}.\mathcal{P}(\pi^+)$

      b. $[-] \rightsquigarrow \lambda \mathcal{P}_{\mathbf{p}^- \mathbf{t}}.\lambda \pi^-_{\mathbf{p}^-}.\mathcal{P}(\pi^-)$

The lexical entries in (32) restrict the hyperintensional argument of their prejacent (and therefore of the response) to have either positive or negative polarity, resulting in a type mismatch otherwise. While this is not enforced via a pragmatic presupposition, it is required for interpretability, achieving the same effect.

Relative features impose conditions on the relationship between the prejacent and antecedent. R&F's [AGREE]-feature requires them to be truth-conditionally equivalent and to have the same polarity. This is captured in (33).

(33)   [AGREE] $\rightsquigarrow \lambda \mathcal{P}_{\mathbf{pt}}.\lambda \pi_{1\mathbf{p}}.[\pi_1 = \underleftarrow{\pi_2}]; \mathcal{P}(\pi_1)$

(33) anaphorically retrieves a propositional dref and states that it is equal to the hyperintensional argument of its prejacent. The propositional anaphor, being flexible in type, can be either positive or negative. Importantly, the prejacent will have the same polarity and truth-conditional content as the antecedent.

The [REVERSE]-feature requires the antecedent and prejacent to be truth-conditional complements and of opposite polarity. We can achieve this with the semantics in (34):

(34)   a. $[\text{REVERSE}] \rightsquigarrow \lambda \mathcal{P}_{\mathbf{p}+\mathbf{t}}.\lambda \pi_1^+.[\mathbf{Cont}\{\pi_1^+\} = \overline{\mathbf{Cont}\{\underset{\leftarrow}{\pi_2^-}\}}]; \mathcal{P}(\pi_1^+)$

      b. $[\text{REVERSE}] \rightsquigarrow \lambda \mathcal{P}_{\mathbf{p}\text{-}\mathbf{t}}.\lambda \pi_1^-.[\mathbf{Cont}\{\pi_1^-\} = \overline{\mathbf{Cont}\{\underset{\leftarrow}{\pi_2^+}\}}]; \mathcal{P}(\pi_1^-)$

The relative features constrain the relationship between the prejacent and antecedent, so the type-restrictions on the anaphor depend on the polarity of the prejacent. Thus, implementing the [REVERSE]-feature requires two versions: A positive prejacent is compatible with (34a), which requires its content to be the complement of the content of a negative antecedent. A negative prejacent is compatible with (34b), which demands a positive antecedent.

R&F suggest that the meaning contribution of English Polarity Particles can be accounted for by assuming that they lexicalize the feature combinations shown in Table 1, which also gives their semantics in Hyperintensional CDRT.

Table 1. Feature Combinations and Lexical Entries associated with English PolPs

Antecedent	Response	Feature combination	PolP	Lexical Entry
+	+	[AGREE, +]	yes	$\lambda \mathcal{P}_{\mathbf{pt}}.\lambda \pi_{1\mathbf{p}+}^+.[\underset{\leftarrow}{\pi_1^-} = \pi_2]; \mathcal{P}(\pi_1^-)$
−	−	[AGREE, −]	yes/no	$\lambda \mathcal{P}_{\mathbf{pt}}.\lambda \pi_{1\mathbf{p}\text{-}}^-.[\underset{\leftarrow}{\pi_1} = \pi_2]; \mathcal{P}(\pi_1)$
−	+	[REVERSE, +]	yes/no	$\lambda \mathcal{P}_{\mathbf{p}+\mathbf{t}}.\lambda \pi_1^+.[\mathbf{Cont}\{\pi_1^+\} = \overline{\mathbf{Cont}\{\underset{\leftarrow}{\pi_2^-}\}}]; \mathcal{P}(\pi_1^+)$
+	−	[REVERSE, −]	no	$\lambda \mathcal{P}_{\mathbf{p}\text{-}\mathbf{t}}.\lambda \pi_1^-.[\mathbf{Cont}\{\pi_1^-\} = \overline{\mathbf{Cont}\{\underset{\leftarrow}{\pi_2^+}\}}]; \mathcal{P}(\pi_1^-)$

The English PolP 'no' can be used to agree with a negative antecedent as it can realize the feature combination [AGR, -]. This results in the following representation for agreeing uses of 'no'.

(35)   *Mary didn't sleep.*

$\pi_1^-, \pi_2^+, \upsilon_1$
$\upsilon_1 = Mary_{\mathbf{e}}$
$sleep_{\pi_2^+}\{\upsilon_1\}$
$\mathbf{Cont}\{\pi_1^-\} = \overline{\mathbf{Cont}\{\pi_2^+\}}$

(36)   *No$_{[\text{AGR}, -]}$, she didn't sleep.*

π_3^-, π_4^+
$sleep_{\pi_4^+}\{\underset{\leftarrow}{\upsilon_2}\}$
$\mathbf{Cont}\{\pi_3^-\} = \overline{\mathbf{Cont}\{\pi_4^+\}}$
$\mathbf{Cont}\{\pi_3^-\} = \overline{\mathbf{Cont}\{\underset{\leftarrow}{\pi_5^+}\}}$

(36) involves two anaphoric expressions: The pronoun *she* introduces the discourse variable $\underset{\leftarrow}{v_2}$, for which v_1 is a suitable antecedent. The PolP *no* introduces the discourse variable π_5^-, for which $\underset{\leftarrow}{\pi_1^-}$ is a suitable antecedent. The resolution of these anaphora in the context of (35) is illustrated in (37).

(37)   Merging DRSs and resolving anaphora:

$$
\begin{array}{|c|}
\hline
\pi_1^-, \pi_2^+, v_1, \pi_3^-, \pi_4^+ \\
\hline
v_1 = Mary_e \\
sleep_{\pi_2^+}\{v_1\} \\
\mathbf{Cont}\{\pi_1^-\} = \mathbf{Cont}\{\pi_2^+\} \\
sleep_{\pi_4^+}\{v_1\} \\
\mathbf{Cont}\{\pi_3^-\} = \mathbf{Cont}\{\pi_4^+\} \\
\mathbf{Cont}\{\pi_3^-\} = \mathbf{Cont}\{\pi_1^-\} \\
\hline
\end{array}
$$

In contrast, *'no'* could not be used to agree with a positive assertion. It could not do so with a [AGR, +] feature-combination, since the assumption is that *no* cannot realize these features. It also cannot do so with the combinations [REV, +] or [AGR, -], as these combinations require a negative antecedent, but only a positive one is available in the context of a positive assertion.

Discussion. The feature-based account of R&F and the presented implementation in hyperintensional CDRT rely on propositional drefs introduced by linguistic expressions, and can, therefore, account for non-licensing by entailment. R&F suggest that a propositional dref is negative if negation is the highest-scoping operator in the clause that introduces it. The present account extends the empirical coverage of licensing contexts to those in which negation is outscoped. However, since the analysis require overt negation, it is not able to account for contextually introduced negativity in cases of neg-raising.

R&F give a unified account for responses to declarative assertions and polar questions by suggesting that both introduce a single highlighted proposition within a table model of these discourse moves. I assume that the introduction of a highlighted proposition is analogous to the introduction of a propositional dref, and that polar questions can be subsumed under the analysis given here, by assuming that they also introduce a propositional dref for the content of the interrogative clause.[7]

---

[7] An anonymous reviewer suggests that instead of sentential mood, one might attribute the introduction of a propositional dref to a TP-level sentential operator, as in e.g. Roeper (2011; Krifka (2013); van Elswyk (2018). This may have some empirical weaknesses as noted in Snider (2017), but it would include polar interrogatives in the analysis more straightforwardly.

4.2 Intensional Propositions and Discourse Coherence

The propositional anaphor approach in Krifka (2013) is a purely semantic account of the anaphoric component of PolPs. Krifka characterizes negative antecedents based on an independent characteristic of negative sentences in discourse: While simple sentences without negation only introduce one propositional dref corresponding to the proposition expressed by the sentence, a negative sentence licenses propositional anaphora to the full proposition, as well as to the proposition in the scope of negation (38):[8]

(38) $[^{\phi_1}$ *Ede didn't* $[^{\phi_2}$ ~~*Ede*~~ *steal the cookie*]],   [Krifka (2013): 24]

    a.   *and he can actually prove it*$_{\phi_1}$.
       (he can prove that he didn't steal the cookie.)

    b.   *even though people believed it*$_{\phi_2}$.
       (people believed that he stole the cookie.)

PolPs like *'yes'* and *'no'* are simply taken to assert the affirmation or negation of their propositional antecedent. In R&F's terms, PolPs only encode the relative polarity between the antecedent and the response under Krifka's view. Accordingly, the necessity of two separate lexical entries for reversing features in (34), above, would be avoided in favor of more simplistic lexical assumptions.

The neutralization of the contrast between positive and negative polarity particles in the context of negative antecedents is accounted for by assuming that polarity particles may pick up either the matrix propositional dref or the counterfactual one corresponding to the prejacent of negation.

(39)   A: $^{\phi_1}$ Ede didn't$^{\phi_2}$ steal the cookie.

    a.   B: Yes$_{\phi_1}$, he didn't. (agreement)

    b.   B: Yes$_{\phi_2}$, he did. (disagreement)

    c.   B: No$_{\phi_2}$, he didn't. (agreement)

    d.   B: No$_{\phi_1}$, he did. (disagreement)

Accordingly, a positive PolP can affirm the matrix propositional dref or the negated one introduced in the scope of negation. A negative one could similarly assert the negation of either antecedent. The resulting ambiguity is resolved based on contextual information and the relative salience between the two propositional drefs introduced by a negative sentence.

One issue with the salience-based approach to disambiguating PolPs is that the notion of salience is not operationalized in Krifka's account, and it is not obvious how to do so. Further, experimental studies in Claus et al. (2017), have not found an effect of manipulating the salience of potential antecedents for PolPs. However, some facts about the resolution of the ambiguities giving rise to the pattern in (39) could be understood in terms of a contextual licensing requirement and basic assumptions about discourse consistency (Hofmann 2022).

---

[8] The superscript ϕ-variables indicate the introduction of (here not necessarily hyperintensional) propositional drefs, and the lowercase instances of these variables indicate that they are being picked up anaphorically.

Specifically, an intensional account of polarity-tags may assume that the interpretation of a propositional anaphor leads to contextual entailment of its referent in its local context (in the sense of Heim 1982, see Kroll 2019 for a similar requirement for clausal ellipsis, and discussion in Hofmann 2022 applying this to pronominal propositional anaphora).[9] In combination with the assumption that a discourse contains only non-contradictory information, this could provide an understanding of the fact that (39a), for instance, is an agreeing use of *yes*: If the anaphorically retrieved proposition ϕ_1 is contextually entailed in the context of B's utterance, while A is also committed to their assertion of ϕ_1, A and B are in agreement. In contrast, if ϕ_2 is entailed in the context of B's utterance (39b), the opposite is the case. By relativizing contextual entailment to local contexts, we get the reverse situation for anaphora under negation (39c+d).

Whether an utterance involving a PolP is interpreted as agreeing or disagreeing with its antecedent is determined in interdependence with the question how the anaphor is resolved, and whether the anaphorically retrieved proposition is asserted or negated. This interdependence can be understood in the context of Hobbs's (1985) view that reference resolution and establishing discourse coherence are inter-dependent and mutually constraining processes (see also Kehler 2002; Asher and Lascarides 2003). In the spirit of R&F, we can say that possible meanings of PolPs arise as combinations of the polarity of the response, and the relationship between response and antecedent utterance, although both of these factors are understood differently from R&F under the intensional account. The polarity of the response is understood here in terms of whether the particle involves the negation or affirmation of the anaphoric proposition. The relationship between response and antecedent utterance may also be understood as a by-product of reference resolution.

Farkas and Roelofsen (2019) present some arguments against this type of account: Cross-linguistic data from languages where PolPs do not exhibit ambiguity or neutralization of contrast in the context of negative antecedents require additional assumptions to rule out that the dref introduced in the scope of negation could be a possible antecedent. They note that these assumptions would have to be made specifically in these languages and specifically for PolPs to the exclusion of other propositional anaphora. Further, certain polarity particles like German '*doch*', French '*si*', as well as the Romanian rejecting responses '*ba da*' and '*ba nu*' require their antecedent to be of a certain polarity. Therefore, Farkas and Roelofsen (2019) argue that absolute polarity needs to be encoded in addition to relative polarity to gain a general account of the phenomenon.

Considering the kinds of licensing contexts discussed here, Krika's semantic characterization of negative utterances faces problems with cases where a negativity-tag picks up propositional content that includes an the meaning con-

---

[9] The idea that anaphoric accessibility is constrained in terms of local contextual entailment of a referent is also found for individual anaphora in Stone (1999); Brasoveanu (2010a); Hofmann (2019). See also work in Elliott (2020; 2022); Mandelkern (2022), which develops the intuition of contextual entailment for individual anaphora on a global discourse level.

tribution of operators taking scope over negation. That is because this kind of account relies on the distinction between propositional content in the scope of negation vs. matrix propositions.

On the other hand, the account is based on semantic properties of the antecedent rather than the morphosyntactic expression of negation, and therefore it could more straightforwardly include neg-raising cases. Discourse negativity is characterized by the presence of a propositional dref that the speaker takes to be false, rather than the presence of morphosyntactic negation. Since in neg-raising, the proposition introduced by the neg-raising verb's complement will be interpreted as false, this can quite readily be extended to neg-raising cases.

4.3   Ellipsis Accounts

Ellipsis-based accounts of PolPs (e.g. Kramer and Rawlins 2009; Holmberg 2013) assume that they are anaphoric to propositional content because they are accompanied by clausal ellipsis, and that the anaphoric polarity-sensitivity comes about due to a syntactic dependency of polarity-features (e.g. in the sense of Zeijlstra 2004) between the PolP and negation within the ellipsis site. For instance in Kramer and Rawlins (2009), agreeing *no*-responses are analyzed by assuming the particle is accompanied by an uninterpretable negative feature which enters into an agree-relation with an interpretable negative feature in the ellipsis site (based on Zeijlstra 2004), illustrated in (40).

(40)   a.   *Mary didn't sleep.*
        b. $\text{No}_{[uNeg]}$ [~~Mary did not~~$_{[iNeg]}$ ~~sleep~~]

Under this type of account, agreeing *no*-responses require a negative antecedent, because the $[uNeg]$ feature on the PolP is licensed by an interpretable instance of negation in the ellipsis site, and because ellipsis parallelism requires the same of the antecedent. Therefore, this kind of analysis relies on a morphosyntactic realization of sentential negation in the antecedent (in the sense of Klima 1964; Haegeman and Zanuttini 1991; Ladusaw 1992; Zanuttini 1997; Zeijlstra 2004; Penka 2013, among others). As such, it could account for non-licensing by entailment, as well as the narrow-scope negation cases discussed here, while it seems like these kinds of analyses could not be extended to pragmatic cases of neg-raising.

4.4   Neg-Raising and Discourse Inferences

To summarize the above discussion, the presented analysis is on a par with ellipsis approaches on account of deriving non-licensing by entailment, and licensing in outscoped negation cases. When it comes to licensing in neg-raising cases, it is at a disadvantage compared to approaches that treat polarity-tags as intensional propositional anaphora. To motivate the kind of approach taken here, I have suggested that the chosen discourse-level representation is one that keeps track of some morphosyntactic information, while also allowing for discourse inferences to interact with the represented information. To illustrate how this is the case, this section gives a brief sketch of a possible way that licensing by neg-raising might be addressed in this system, by allowing neg-raising inferences on a discourse-level to license negativity-tags by bridging.

The fact that the introduction of a negative propositional dref is tied to an overt instance of negation in Hyperintensional CDRT poses a challenge in analyzing neg-raising cases like (5), repeated here.

(5)   *I don't think Mary slept, ...*

   a.   *... and neither did Dalia.*   (Dalia didn't sleep either.)
   b.   *... No, she really didn't.*   (Mary really didn't sleep.)

The negativity-tags in (5) anaphorically pick up the embedded content, but the semantic contribution of a neg-raising utterance does not provide a negative propositional antecedent corresponding to the embedded content. This is illustrated in (41), analyzing *think* as a doxastic attitude in a Hintikkan semantics for propositional attitudes, following Heim (1992). (41) gives the semantic contribution of the update, without the pragmatic contribution of the neg-raising inference, under which the attitude holder is unopinionated about the truth of the embedded content.

(41)   **Neg-raising**

   a.   *I don't think that Mary slept.* $\rightsquigarrow$

$$\begin{array}{|c|}
\hline
\pi_1^-, \pi_2^+, \pi_3^+, \upsilon \\
\hline
\mathbf{Cont}\{\pi_1^-\} = \overline{\mathbf{Cont}\{\pi_2^+\}} \\
Think_{\pi_2^+}\{\mathbf{sp}, \pi_3^+] \\
\upsilon = Mary_{\mathbf{e}} \\
sleep_{\pi_3^+}\{\upsilon\} \\
\hline
\end{array}$$

   b.   *think* as a doxastic attitude:

$Think_{\pi_1^+}\{\upsilon, \pi_2^+\} := \lambda i_s. \forall w \in \mathbf{Cont}\{\pi_1^+\} : \mathrm{Dox}_{\upsilon(i)}(w) \subseteq \mathbf{Cont}\{\pi_2^+\}$
(where Dox is the set of worlds that conform with what $\upsilon(i)$ believes in each $w \in \mathbf{Cont}\{\pi_1^+\}$)

An update with (41) introduces a negative propositional dref π_1^-, corresponding to the matrix sentence, s.t. the speaker does not think that Mary slept in the content of π_1^-. Importantly, the embedded clause introduces a positive propositional dref π_3^+, s.t. Mary slept in the content of π_3^+. As a result, the representation in (41) cannot explain why neg-raising contexts may license negativity-tags that are anaphoric to the embedded content.

There are some possibilities for addressing that in this system. One would involve a syntactic analysis of neg-raising, under which negation is underlyingly introduced in the lower clause (see Collins and Postal 2014). Another possibility would be a bridging-analysis, under which a negative propositional dref corresponding to the neg-raising complement is introduced via a bridging-inference. Given that neg-raising seems to be derived pragmatically, at least in some cases (e.g. cases of island neg-raising discussed in Collins and Postal 2018), we would want to include the possibility that a negative propositional antecedent may be introduced by an update that is licensed by the kind of discourse-inference contributed by neg-raising.

Following Gajewski (2007), we may assume that a neg-raising interpretation can be derived on the basis of an excluded-middle presupposition associated with neg-raising verbs like *think*. Informally, this presupposition in the context of (41) will be that the speaker either believes the embedded content to be true (that Mary slept), or its negation. Since the former is not the case by virtue of the assertion, the contextual inference supported by this presupposition is that the speaker believes that it's not the case that Mary slept.

While a treatment of presupposition is not included here, we can represent the kind of bridging update that the neg-raising inference would need to support, in order to license subsequent negativity-rags with reference to the embedded clause. This is given in (42):

(42)   Bridging update:
$$[\pi_4^- \mid \mathbf{Cont}\{\pi_4^-\} = \overline{\mathbf{Cont}\{\pi_3^+\}}]$$

To understand how an update like (42) may be introduced by a bridging mechanism that is constrained enough to rule out the previously discussed cases of non-licensing by entailment, we may consider a bridging-analysis for negativity-tag anaphora to neg-raising antecedents, along the lines of Nouwen's (2003) bridging analysis for complement anaphora.

Nouwen (2003) suggests that *'pronominal complement anaphors [. . .] link to their antecedents by inference'* (p. 102), proposing that anaphoric pronouns may introduce a new dref, provided the conditions in (43) are satisfied.

(43)   Nouwen's constraints on bridging:
    a.   **Inferability:** The referent of the pronoun is inferable.
    b.   **Uniqueness:** *'[T]here should be no other similarly inferable entities with the same semantic features.'* (p. 105)
    c.   **Use of semantically available information:**
        World-knowledge cannot be used to support bridging inferences
    d.   **Support of discourse coherence by the anaphoric link:**
        The bridging inference is only available, if the interpretation of the pronoun would otherwise lead to an inconsistent discourse.

In our case, inferability (43a) is satisfied: The context (by neg-raising) supports the inference that there exists a proposition π, s.t. Mary didn't sleep in the content of π, and the speaker believes π. The uniqueness-condition (43b) can be understood in the context of our anaphoric expressions in (5): For both the additive tag and the PolP, the so inferred proposition would be the only possible antecedent here (provided it is interpreted as a negative proposition).

The condition (43c) is given by Nouwen to rule out bridging based on inferences supported by world knowledge. In light of neg-raising, this may need to be
extended slightly: While the supporting inference may be considered pragmatic,
the involved excluded-middle presupposition is assumed to be part of the content conventionally associated with neg-raising verbs. The coherence condition
(43d) addresses the fact that bridging anaphora (and complement anaphora)
have antecedents that are less salient than is usually the case for pronominal
anaphora. Therefore, these are only available if no other consistent interpretation is possible.

Now, these constraints are well motivated in Nouwen's discussion of bridging
cases, but still not yet restrictive enough for our purposes. In particular, the
conditions in (43) alone cannot yet distinguish a neg-raising context (41) from
cases of non-licensing by entailment (3), repeated here.

(3)   Non-licensing by entailment:

    a.   A: *Susan failed the exam.*
                    ↔ Susan didn't pass the exam.
    b.   B: # *Neither did I.*
                    (I didn't pass the exam either)
    c.   B: # *No, she did not pass.* (agreeing)

Similarly to the neg-raising case, an utterance of (3a) entails the existence of a
uniquely inferable proposition π (s.t. Susan didn't pass the exam), based on the
semantic information available, while the anaphora in (3b)+(3c) have no other
coherent resolution. Provided that π can be interpreted as a negative proposition,
we might expect negativity-tags to be licensed here as well.

To distinguish between (41) and (3), we need to explicitly develop some
assumptions about the relationship between a bridging anaphor and its
antecedent. The bridging-update in (42) connects the bridged dref and its
antecedent via the semantic relation contributed by negation: A relation between
a positive and negative proposition s.t. their contents are complements of each
other. In contrast, a bridging-update that could license negativity-tags in (3)
would need to include a hypothetical relation between a positive and negative
proposition that have the same content.

While bridging for nominal anaphora often requires semantic or lexical relations between antecedent and bridging-anaphora (see Zhao 2014 for an overview
of studies on bridging), our bridging-analysis would rely on the assumption that
a propositional relation that can be lexically expressed (e.g. by negation) can
provide a bridge between antecedent and anaphor, while our hypothetical relation needed for (3) could not.

A full investigation of this suggested restriction falls outside of the scope
of this paper, but the assumed representation of propositional polarity on the
level of drefs may interact with certain kinds of contextual information along the
lines suggested here, in order to allow for discourse-negativity to be introduced
contextually, in some cases.

Another way of dealing with the licensing of negativity-tags through neg-raising would be abandoning an account that represents morphosyntactic infor-mation for a more semantic account. Given that the purely semantic account of discourse-polarity in terms of propositional anaphora also faces problems (partic-ularly for narrow-scope negation), I suggest that further research should address the question of which routes may lead to an explanatory analysis.

5   Conclusion

This paper establishes that the phenomenon of discourse polarity, particularly discourse negativity, is influenced by complex factors, some of them syntac-tic, semantic, and pragmatic in nature. The empirical data impose conflicting demands: The possibility of contextual introduction of discourse negativity poses a challenge for accounts that reference the morphosyntactic realization of nega-tion. In contrast, negativity-tags licensed by sentences with negation in the scope of another operator pose challenges for accounts that do not.

This tension is also reflected in the literature on PolPs: While R&F assume that a polarity-tag needs to be able to reference the information about the contri-bution of sentential negation in its antecedent, Krifka's approach suggests a way to account for polarity-tags that does not reference a sentential representation of the antecedent. This divide in the literature invites further research to com-bine the opposing accounts' advantages and insights and address the challenges imposed by different licensing contexts.

The proposed hyperintensional framework was developed to advance under-standing of polarity-sensitivity in discourse. It offers a formal foundation for distinguishing positive and negative propositional discourse referents, and cap-tures some of the central generalizations. Hyperintensional drefs link proposi-tional polarity to the discourse context, the semantic content of the proposition, and surface-based information about whether the proposition was introduced by a negative sentence. While more work needs to be done to analyze discourse-level semantic licensing in cases like neg-raising, the analysis offers a level of representation that is equipped to incorporate discourse information.

Acknowledgments. This paper is a revised version of Hofmann (2019), presented at ESSLLI student session 2019. It grew out of work during my graduate studies at UCSC. I am grateful for Adrian Brasoveanu's and Donka Farkas' invaluable guidance and feedback. Thank you also to Jorge Hankamer, Amanda Rysling, Chris Barker, Morwenna Hoeks for helpful comments and discussion, the participants of the UCSC 2019 Research Seminar, and anonymous reviewers from ESSLLI for insightful feedback. Special thanks to Jim McCloskey for inspiring my interest in this phenomenon.

References

Ahn, D.: The semantics of additive either. In: Proceedings of Sinn und Bedeutung, vol. 19, pp. 20–35 (2015)

Asher, N.: Reference to Abstract Objects in Discourse, Studies in Linguistics and Philosophy, vol. 50. Springer, Netherlands, Dordrecht (1993). https://doi.org/10.1007/978-94-011-1715-9

Asher, N., Lascarides, A.: Logics of Conversation. Cambridge University Press, Cambridge (2003)

van den Berg, M.: Full dynamic plural logic. Citeseer (1993)

Bittner, M.: Tense, mood, and centering (2009). manuscript, Rutgers University

Brasoveanu, A.: Structured Nominal and Modal Reference. Doctoral dissertation, Rutgers University (2006)

Brasoveanu, A.: Decomposing modal quantification. J. Semant. **27**(4), 437–527 (2010). https://doi.org/10.1093/jos/ffq008

Brasoveanu, A.: Structured anaphora to quantifier domains. Inf. Comput. **208**(5), 450–473 (2010). https://doi.org/10.1016/j.ic.2008.10.007

Carpenter, B.: Type-logical Semantics. MIT Press (1997). https://doi.org/10.7551/mitpress/6945.001.0001

Claus, B., Meijer, A.M., Repp, S., Krifka, M.: Puzzling response particles: an experimental study on the German answering system. Semant. Pragmat. **10**(19) (2017)

Collins, C., Postal, P.: Classical NEG Raising: An Essay on the Syntax of Negation. MIT Press (2014)

Collins, C., Postal, P.M.: Disentangling two distinct notions of NEG raising. Semant. Pragmat. **11**, 5 (2018)

Cooper, R.: Austinian truth, attitudes and type theory. Res. Lang. Comput. **3**(2–3), 333–362 (2005). https://doi.org/10.1007/s11168-006-0002-z

Cooper, R.: Type theory and semantics in flux. In: Philosophy of Linguistics, pp. 271–323. Elsevier (2012)

Elliott, P.D.: Towards a principled logic of anaphora (2020), manuscript, LingBuzz

Elliott, P.D.: Partee conjunctions: projection and possibility: manuscript. LingBuzz, Submitted (2022)

Elswyk, P.: Propositional anaphors. Philos. Stud. **176**(4), 1055–1075 (2018). https://doi.org/10.1007/s11098-018-1042-6

Farkas, D., Bruce, K.: On reacting to assertions and polar questions. J. Semant. **27**(1), 81–118 (2010). https://doi.org/10.1093/jos/ffp010

Farkas, D., Zec, D.: Agreement and pronominal reference. In: Cinque, G., Giusti, G. (eds.) Advances in Roumanian Linguistics, pp. 83–101. John Benjamins, Philadelphia (1995)

Farkas, D.F., Roelofsen, F.: Polarity particles revisited. Semant. Pragmat. **12**, 15 (2019). number: 0

Fox, C., Lappin, S.: Foundations of Intensional Semantics. Wiley, Malden (2008)

Gajewski, J.: Neg-raising and polarity. Linguist. Philos. **30**, 289–328 (2007). https://doi.org/10.1007/s10988-007-9020-z

Ginzburg, J., Sag, I.: Interrogative Investigations. CSLI Publications, Stanford (2000)

Groenendijk, J., Stokhof, M.: Dynamic predicate logic. Linguist. Philos. **14**(1), 39–100 (1991). https://doi.org/10.1007/BF00628304

Haegeman, L., Zanuttini, R.: Negative heads and the neg criterion. Linguist. Rev. **8**, 233–251 (1991). https://doi.org/10.1515/tlir.1991.8.2-4.233, publisher: Walter de Gruyter, Berlin/New York Berlin, New York

Hankamer, J., Sag, I.: Deep and surface anaphora. Linguistic Inquiry **7**, 391–428 (1976)

Heim, I.: The Semantics of Definite and Indefinite Noun Phrases. Doctoral dissertation, University of Massachusetts Amherst (1982)

Heim, I.: Presupposition projection and the semantics of attitude verbs. J. Semant. **9**(3), 183–221 (1992). https://doi.org/10.1093/jos/9.3.183

Hobbs, J.R.: On the coherence and structure of discourse (1985)

Hofmann, L.: Why not? - Polarity ellipsis in why-questions (2018). uCSC Manuscript

Hofmann, L.: The anaphoric potential of indefinites under negation and disjunction. In: Proceedings of the 22nd Amsterdam Colloquium, pp. 181–190 (2019)

Hofmann, L.: Sentential negativity and polarity-sensitive anaphora. In: ESSLLI 2019 Student Session (2019)

Hofmann, L.: Anaphora and Negation. Doctoral dissertation, UC Santa Cruz (2022)

Holmberg, A.: The syntax of answers to polar questions in English and Swedish. Lingua **128**, 31–50 (2013). https://doi.org/10.1016/j.lingua.2012.10.018

Horn, L.: A Natural History of Negation. University of Chicago Press, Chicago (1989)

Jackendoff, R.: An interpretive theory of negation. Found. Lang. **5**(2), 218–241 (1969)

Kamp, H.: A theory of truth and semantic representation. In: Groenendijk, J., Janssen, T., Stokhof, M. (eds.) Formal Methods in the Study of Language, pp. 277–322. Mathematical Centre Tracts, Amsterdam (1981)

Karttunen, L.: Discourse Referents. In: Notes from the linguistic underground, pp. 363–385. Brill (1976). https://doi.org/10.1163/9789004368859_021

Kehler, A.: Coherence, Reference, and the Theory of Grammar. CSLI Publications, Stanford (2002)

Klima, E.: Negation in English. In: Fodor, J., Katz, J. (eds.) The Structure of Language, pp. 232–246. Prentice Hall, New Jersey (1964)

Kramer, R., Rawlins, K.: Polarity particles: an Ellipsis Account. In: Schardl, A., Walkow, M., Abdurrahman, M. (eds.) Proceedings of NELS (2009)

Krifka, M.: Response particles as propositional anaphors. Semant. Linguist. Theory (SALT) **23**, 1–18 (2013). https://doi.org/10.3765/salt.v23i0.2676

Kroll, M.: Polarity reversals under sluicing. Semant. Pragmat. **12**, 18 (2019). https://doi.org/10.3765/sp.12.18

Ladusaw, W.A.: Expressing negation. In: Semantics and Linguistic Theory, vol. 2, pp. 237–260 (1992). https://doi.org/10.3765/salt.v2i0.3030

Mandelkern, M.: Witnesses. Linguistics and Philosophy pp. 1–27. Springer (2022)

Murray, S.E.: Evidentiality and the structure of speech acts. Doctoral dissertation, Rutgers The State University of New Jersey-New Brunswick (2010). https://doi.org/10.1007/BF00635836

Muskens, R.: Combining Montague semantics and discourse representation. Linguist. Philos. **19**(2), 143–186 (1996)

Nouwen, R.: Complement anaphora and interpretation. J. Semant. **20**(1), 73–113 (2003). https://doi.org/10.1023/A:1022941407162

Pollard, C.: Agnostic hyperintensional semantics. Synthese **192**(3), 535–562 (2013). https://doi.org/10.1007/s11229-013-0373-2

Pollard, C.: Agnostic hyperintensional semantics. Synthese **192**(3), 535–562 (2015)

Pope, E.: Questions and answers in English. Ph.D. thesis, Diss. Massachusetts Institute of Technology (1972)

Roelofsen, F., Farkas, D.: Polarity particle responses as a window onto the interpretation of questions and assertions. Language **91**(2), 359–414 (2015). https://doi.org/10.1353/lan.2015.0017

Roeper, T.: How the emergence of propositions separates strict interfaces from general interface. In: Proceedings of Sinn und Bedeutung. vol. 15, pp. 55–78 (2011)

Rullmann, H.: Additive particles and polarity. J. Semant. **20**(4), 329–401 (2003). https://doi.org/10.1093/jos/20.4.329

Snider, T.N.: Anaphoric Reference to Propositions. Doctoral dissertation, Cornell University (2017)

Stone, M.: Reference to possible worlds. RuCCS Report 46 (1999)

Thomason, R.H.: A model theory for propositional attitudes. Linguist. Philos. **4**(1), 47–70 (1980). https://doi.org/10.1007/BF00351813

Tonhauser, J.: Diagnosing (not-) at-issue content. In: Proceedings of Semantics of Under-represented Languages of the Americas (SULA) **6**, 239–254 (2012). publisher: UMass; GLSA Amherst

Tönnis, S.: German es-clefts in discourse. A question-based analysis involving expectedness. Doctoral dissertation, Graz University (2021)

Tönnis, S.: It is not the obvious question that a cleft addresses. In: Özgün, A., Zinova, Y. (eds.) TbiLLC 2019. LNCS, vol. 13206, pp. 128–147. Springer, Cham (2022). https://doi.org/10.1007/978-3-030-98479-3_7

Zaitsu, A.: High negation and ellipsis in English No-answers. In: Bakay, Ö., Pratley, B., Neu, E., Deal, P. (eds.) Proceedings of NELS, vol. 3, 265–278 (2022)

Zanuttini, R.: Negation and Clausal Structure. Oxford University Press, New York and Oxford (1997)

Zeijlstra, H.: Sentential Negation and Negative Concord. Doctoral dissertation, University of Amsterdam, Utrecht: LOT Publications (2004)

Zhao, W.: A survey of studies of bridging anaphora. Can. Soc. Sci. **10**(3), 130–139 (2014)

Temporal Modification of Event Kinds

Zi Huang[(✉)] [iD]

Universitat Pompeu Fabra, Roc Boronat 138, 08018 Barcelona, Spain
zi.huang@upf.edu

Abstract. As the counterpart to kinds of entities or objects [5], event kinds are used to account for a variety of linguistic facts in the event domain. The modification of event kinds is usually considered to be restricted, and temporal modifiers are claimed to be hardly acceptable [18]. In this paper I focus on verbal gerunds in English, which have been analyzed as event kind descriptions [15], and demonstrate that they accept temporal modification but remain kind-referring. I extend the analysis of frequency adjectives [13] to interpret both temporal and frequency modifiers in verbal gerunds, showing that the modification of event kinds is less restricted than commonly assumed.

Keywords: Event kind · Temporal modification · Verbal gerunds · Frequency adverbs

1 Introduction

The notion of kinds has been crucial in semantic theory since Carlson's [5] analysis of bare plurals in English as kinds. It is also known that kind formation is not unrestricted: a kind has to identify a class of objects with a regular function or behavior. In the Neo-Carlsonian analysis developed by Chierchia [7], kinds are represented as individual concepts that correspond to functions from worlds to the maximum sum of instances of that kind in each world. A property-denoting expression can be shifted to its corresponding kind-denoting expression through $\cap$ only if the largest member of its extension is found in the set of kinds K:

(1) For any property P and world/situation s,

$$\cap P = \begin{cases} \lambda s \; \iota P_s, \text{if } \lambda s \; \iota P_s \text{ is in K} \\ \text{undefined, otherwise} \end{cases}$$

where P_s is the extension of P in s. [7, p. 351]

It follows that not all bare plurals that correspond to some property denote kinds. For example, *lions in my backyard* is not a good kind expression because the property of being a lion at a certain location does not intuitively indicate any regular behavior. Such an expression has to denote individual lions, thus being incompatible with kind-level predicates such as *be widespread*.

A. Pavlova et al. (Eds.): ESSLLI 2019/2020/2021, LNCS 14354, pp. 136–151, 2024.
https://doi.org/10.1007/978-3-031-50628-4_8

(2)   ??Lions in my backyard are widespread.

What makes a bare plural unable to denote kinds? Chierchia makes it clear that a property that is necessarily instantiated by only one individual, such as being the denotation of a proper name, does not qualify as a kind. Another restriction, as discussed by Mueller-Reichau [21], is spatiotemporal localization. The subject in (2) is not a kind because its referent is restricted to what is *in my backyard*.

A similar effect is seen with the definite singular,[1] another typical kind expression in English:[2]

(3)   The (African/*injured) lion is widespread.

It has been proposed that definite singular kind expressions are restricted to what Krifka et al. [17] call well-established kinds, but it is also observed [4,8] that such a constraint is not a linguistic one, but depends on pragmatic or encyclopaedic information.

This paper is concerned with how temporal modifiers, as a means of temporal localization, affect event kind expressions. In natural language ontology, events are concrete entities that are perceptible, can be located in time and space, and can vary in the way they are realized [19]. In analogy to kinds in the nominal domain (hereafter, nominal kinds), event kinds enable us to talk about types of events as sortal concepts,[3] without making reference to individual, or token, events. Event kinds are a crucial concept in the analyses of various phenomena, such as anaphora to manner adverbials [18] and adjectival passives in German [9–11,14,20], where spatiotemporal modification is unavailable. In Sect. 2, I present the evidence for setting such a restriction on event kinds and the arguments supporting the view that temporal modifiers are not formally limited to modifying tokens.

This paper focuses on English verbal gerunds, which have been analyzed as event kind descriptions [15] but freely take temporal modifiers. I will summarize the kind-based analysis of verbal gerunds in Sect. 3 and report an experiment in Sect. 4 on the effect of temporal modification. In Sect. 5, I present an interpretation of temporal modifiers inspired by the treatment of frequency adjectives

---

[1] According to Borik & Espinal [4], the generic reading of expressions like *the lion* is a direct combination of the definite article with a property of kinds. It does not have a Number projection, and is therefore numberless. I refer to such expressions as definite singular solely because of their surface non-plural form.

[2] The definite singular is commonly used to encode genericity, but it is not analyzed as a kind-denoting expression in all the accounts. For example, Chierchia [7] analyzes *the lion* as a group-denoting expression that comprises both singular and plural denotations of the noun *lion*.

[3] In the literature on nominal kinds, there are at least two different views: one is based on the instances of a kind, such as the view of kinds as individual concepts corresponding to functions from worlds to the sum of all the instances of the named kind in each world [7], and the other sees kinds as an intergral sortal concept [4,21]. In this paper I am not committed to a specific view of event kinds other than that they are intensional objects.

by Gehrke & McNally [13], which also accounts for frequency modifiers in event kind expressions.

2 Do Temporal Modifiers Modify Event Kind Descriptions?

Event kinds have been used in the analyses of different phenomena that do not share a recognizable surface form [12]. Landman & Morzycki [18] analyze anaphora to manner modifiers across languages, illustrated below by *so* 'thus' in German (4). They propose that words like *so* denote a property of event tokens, such that they realize (by Carlson's [5] realization relation **R**) a contextually salient event kind denoted by *so*'s antecedent, represented by e_{ki} in (5).

(4) Er hat so   getanzt.
     He has thus danced

     'He danced like that.' [18, p. 1]

(5) $[\![so]\!] = \lambda e[\mathbf{R}(e, e_{ki})]$

Therefore, (4) describes a token event of him dancing, which realizes a salient event kind. The antecedent of *so* can be provided by a manner adverbial, like *clumsily*, when it appears in the context preceding (4). The authors demonstrate that anaphora to temporal adverbials using *so*, however, is unacceptable:

(6) * Maria hat am Dienstag getanzt und Jan   hat auch so   getanzt.
     Mary has on Tuesday danced and John has also thus danced

     'Mary danced on Tuesday, and John danced like that too.' [18, p. 9]

Unlike manner adverbials like *clumsily*, which specify a way some action is carried out, temporal adverbials locate an event token at a certain time. The authors argue that temporal modifiers restrict a set of events to having happened at a specific time, and therefore do not make for a good event kind.

Landman & Morzycki's paper does not suggest a particular formalization for adverbials in general. On a common view, event kinds are contributed by verbal phrases [6] and adverbials restrict them, facilitating reference to subkinds. This requires modifiers to denote properties of event kinds, and therefore apply to event kind descriptions:

(7) *clumsily*: $\lambda P \lambda e_k[\mathbf{clumsily}(P)(e_k)]$

I use the following Neo-Davidsonian notation to illustrate how, according to the idea of [18], *clumsily* contributes to forming a subkind, and *yesterday* does not. In (8b), there is an event kind satisfying the predicate **clumsily(dance)**. In (9b), τ is the temporal trace relation and **y** stands for the time interval corresponding to the day before the time of utterance. What is asserted is that there is an event token of Clay dancing, which is located within yesterday; there is no event kind corresponding to *dance yesterday*.

(8)   a. Clay danced clumsily.

      b. $\exists e, e_k[\mathbf{Agent}(\mathbf{c}, e) \wedge \mathbf{R}(e, e_k) \wedge \mathbf{clumsily}(\mathbf{dance})(e_k)]$

      c. $\forall e, e_k[\mathbf{R}(e, e_k) \wedge \mathbf{clumsily}(\mathbf{dance})(e_k) \leftrightarrow \mathbf{dance}(e) \wedge \mathbf{clumsy}(e)]$

(9)   a. Clay danced yesterday.

      b. $\exists e, e_k[\mathbf{Agent}(\mathbf{c}, e) \wedge \mathbf{R}(e, e_k) \wedge \mathbf{dance}(e_k) \wedge \tau(e) \subseteq \mathbf{y}]$

      c. Not possible: $\exists e, e_k[\mathbf{Agent}(\mathbf{c}, e) \wedge \mathbf{R}(e, e_k) \wedge \mathbf{yesterday}(\mathbf{dance})(e_k)]$ in which $\forall e, e_k[\mathbf{R}(e, e_k) \wedge \mathbf{yesterday}(\mathbf{dance})(e_k) \leftrightarrow \mathbf{dance}(e)$ $\wedge \tau(e) \subseteq \mathbf{y}]$

Intuitively, any event token that realizes the kind *dance clumsily* is a dancing event that is clumsy, as shown in (8c). (9c) is a disallowed representation which interprets *dance yesterday* as naming a subkind, only to reinterpret it using the relation τ. It is different from *dance clumsily* in that it cannot be targeted by manner anaphora, but is there a formal obstacle to constructing such a kind?

It would be convenient to claim that temporal adverbials apply exclusively to event tokens, making them formally distinguished from manner modifiers. However, examples from the German adjectival passive show that this distinction is not clear-cut. Event kinds are a crucial concept in the study of adjectival passives in German [9–11,14,20], in which some adverbials are licensed, but not others:

(10)   Das Haar war schlampig gekämmt.
      The hair was sloppily   combed   [9, p. 242]

(11)   * Das Kind war im   Badezimmer gekämmt.
      The child was in.the bathroom   combed   [9, p. 247]

Most researchers agree that adjectival passives represent the result state type of an event kind. Those adverbials licensed in adjectival passives are event kind modifiers, and event token modifiers are unacceptable. Maienborn, Gese & Stolterfoht [20] notice that the distinction is not made between manner and spatiotemporal adverbials, because the same type of adverbials could be acceptable in some cases and unacceptable in others:

(12)   Das Manuskript ist in einer Nacht geschrieben.
      The manuscript is in one   night written   [20, p. 324]

(13)   * Sie ist im   Nachbarwald   umgebracht.
      She is in.the neighboring forest killed   [20, p. 302]

The authors claim that the structure is constrained by pragmatics: the adverbial should informatively affect the result state type, for example, the manuscript being written in one night implies that it is either ingenious or very messy. In this sense, *in einer Nacht* 'in one night' has a non-specific reading and essentially becomes a manner modifier. If the temporal modifier were specific, such as *on Tuesday night*, it would still be seen as a token modifier because it is unclear how it affects the result state. Syntactically, they claim that acceptable event kind modifiers attach low to the verbal cluster. More specific restrictions on adjectival passives have also been discussed in the literature, such as the event kind employed should be a well-established one [11].

This paper supports the idea that temporal modifiers are not formally restricted to modifying tokens by focusing on the temporal modification of a different kind of expression: verbal gerunds in English. It has been argued [15] that verbal gerunds are event kind descriptions, but such expressions can take temporal modification freely.

3   Verbal Gerunds as Kind Descriptions

There are two types of so-called verbal gerunds in English in which the -ing form takes a direct complement: POSS-ing (*Clay's/his winning the game*) and ACC-ing (*Clay/him winning the game*). Unlike nominal gerunds (also referred to as -ing$_{of}$, e.g. *Clay's/his/the winning of the game*), verbal gerunds are incompatible with certain contexts which Vendler [26] calls narrow containers. For Vendler, containers are sentence roots with a gap suited for a nominal. Loose containers accept both nominal and verbal gerunds, while narrow containers are only compatible with nominal ones. Predicates in the class of narrow containers include eventive predicates (*occur, begin*) and extensional adjectives (*be fast, be slow*), among others. Vendler's judgments make a contrast between the following sentences:

(14)   *Clay('s) killing the enemies* was fast/happened at midnight.

(15)   *Clay's killing of the enemies* was fast/happened at midnight.

The distributional data have motivated many researchers to make an ontological distinction between the denotations of nominal and verbal gerunds. The compatibility between nominal gerunds and narrow containers suggest that the denotation of nominal gerunds has properties of (token) events: they can *happen*, can be located in space and time, and can be realized in a certain manner. The denotation of verbal gerunds lacks such properties. As a result, most theories agree that nominal gerunds denote events and narrow containers only select for events, but propose different ontological objects for verbal gerunds, such as facts [3,26], states of affairs [28] and sets of minimal situations [24].

The theory relevant to the current discussion about event kinds is by Grimm & McNally [15], who apply a parsimonious ontology with only event kinds and tokens in their analysis. Inspired in Zamparelli [27], Grimm & McNally take common nouns and -ing forms to be kind-denoting. They assume that in nominal gerunds, like in definite NPs, kinds can be converted to either descriptions of subkinds or token-level descriptions via Number Phrase. Verbal gerunds, as event kinds descriptions, may merely *entail* a token via interaction with the matrix tense or, in the case of POSS-ing, through Possessive Existential Import [22].

Instead of setting a selectional restriction on containers, Grimm & McNally [15] explain the narrow container phenomenon, such as the unacceptability of (16), with the pragmatic assumption that it is unlikely that all the instances of a kind have the same property (e.g. *started at nine*). While some kind-referring expressions, such as English bare plurals, produce an existential reading in episodic contexts, this explanation is in line with Carlson's [5] analysis of the kind reading of English definite singular, where he notices that when paired with an episodic context, the definite singular should help to report something significant about the entire kind (17a), not just any trivial event involving instances of the kind (17b).

(16)   *Clay's singing the song* started at nine.

(17)   a. *The horse* came to America with Columbus. [5, p. 278]

        b. ?*The horse* arrived on my doorstep yesterday. [5, p. 279]

A kind-based analysis brings into question the acceptability of sentences that are predicted to be unacceptable by most other analyses. For example, (18) involves a narrow container in a generic context:

(18)   ?*Alex's practicing the violin* usually starts at eight.

I used (18) as a filler in the acceptability judgment task reported in the next section. It received an average score of 4.37 on a 7-point Likert scale with a large deviation among participants, indicating that such sentences remain in an uncertain status. It is not the goal of the present study to fully explain the distribution of verbal gerunds on the kind-based analysis, so I will simply assume that verbal gerunds do not offer direct access to the event tokens bearing the same description. Therefore, although one easily understands from (19), thanks to the matrix clause in past tense and the presupposition of *surprise*, that there was (at least) one token event of Clay killing the enemies, the fact that the same expression does not appear in narrow containers, as shown in (14), requires that it stay an event kind expression in (19).

(19)   *Clay('s) killing the enemies* greatly surprised George.

4   Data

If verbal gerunds describe event kinds and temporal modification of kinds are restricted, we should expect temporal modifiers to either not appear with verbal gerunds or turn them into token-referring expressions. In this Sect. 1 present corpus and experimental data to show that such expectation is not met.

    Data from the British National Corpus (BNC) [25][4] show that POSS-*ing* occurs with temporal modifiers:

(20)   A chance encounter, that's all. Not one he'd remember. Not one I'd have remembered, but for *his losing his temper with me this afternoon*. (BNC)

---

[4] My data were collected from a copy of BNC previously parsed with part-of-speech tags and dependency relations using MALTParser (http://www.maltparser.org/).

(21) [...] in the hope that Edward would eventually get launched again on crusade, a hope stimulated by *his taking the cross in 1287* when he vowed to depart in June 1293 and by the fall of Acre in 1291. (BNC)

Extracting ACC-*ing* data from the corpus is challenging for various reasons (see for example [16]). ACC-*ing* is attested to appear with temporal modifiers, but in this particular case, *before now* is ambiguous between modifying *it crashing* and the clause:

(22) He said that, besides reducing the tower's elasticity – which may have prevented *it crashing before now* – the weight of the steel and lead could lead to disaster by causing the soggy ground to give way. (BNC)

I attempted to test the preference between temporally modified POSS-*ing* and ACC-*ing* in a pilot study, where I took original sentences with POSS-*ing* from the BNC along with their context and replaced the target expression by a blank space. I offered three options for native English speakers to choose from: POSS-*ing*, the corresponding ACC-*ing* and "both are possible". The following two sentences were shown to two different groups, of 20 and 22 participants respectively:

(23) Does _____ now mean that I am a little bit reconciled to myself?
      me writing this down 4/20
      my writing this down 2/20
      both are possible 14/20

(24) Very roughly, _____ a moment ago is to be understood not only in terms of the stuffiness of the room [...]
      me wanting the window open 9/22
      my wanting the window open 3/22
      both are possible 10/22

The results did not show an absolute preference for either POSS-*ing* or ACC-*ing*, and both seem to be able to take temporal modifiers and remain felicitous with loose containers.[5] However, the assumption that temporal modifiers locate an event token raises the question of whether they turn verbal gerunds into token-referring expressions. For example, in comparison to *his losing his temper with me*, *his losing his temper with me this afternoon* is much more likely to have a unique event corresponding to the description. If temporal modifiers make verbal

---

[5] An anonymous reviewer pointed out that in the case of both verbal gerunds being acceptable with temporal modifiers, almost all the participants should have chosen "both are possible". I believe that the current results are due to a general preference towards ACC-*ing*. In a different pilot experiment, I observed that participants assigned high scores to ACC-*ing* preceded by *as a result of* and *because of*, which are both predicted and attested in the corpus to take both verbal gerunds, while assigning low scores to the POSS-*ing* counterpart in the same sentence. The explanation for this preference will be left for future research.

gerunds token-referring, temporally modified gerunds should become compatible with narrow containers.

In order to examine the potential effect of temporal modification on verbal gerunds, I designed an acceptability judgment task[6] with two independent variables: type of gerund (POSS-*ing*, ACC-*ing*, -*ing*$_{of}$) and modifier (no modifier or with temporal modifier) which produced 6 conditions, as illustrated by (25):

(25) {George's performing/George performing/George's performing of} the song {∅/three days ago} took place in public.

To create the test items, I used 12 lexical combinations consisting of a narrow container in the past tense as matrix predicate and a gerund based on an accomplishment predicate, where the subject of the gerund was a personal proper name and the object was a definite singular NP. Every lexical combination was presented in all 6 conditions and distributed in 6 lists according to a Latin square design, so that each lexicalization appeared in each list in exactly one condition, and each list contained 2 items for each condition. 5 practice items and 12 fillers that were similar to the test items were used in all the lists. Each of them had an NP or a gerund starting with a personal proper name as subject, and the matrix predicates showed more variety than those in test items. Participants were asked to rate each sentence on a 7-point Likert scale, with 1 representing "unacceptable" and 7 "acceptable".

60 self-reported native speakers of English, located in the USA and the UK, were recruited from Prolific. Each list was completed by exactly 10 participants and none of them was excluded after examining their performance on fillers.

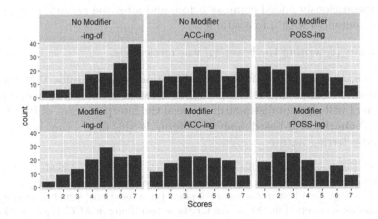

Fig. 1. Distribution of data points in each condition.

Figure 1 shows the distribution of all the data points across 6 conditions. Every condition contains 120 data points. As an event-denoting expression,

---

[6] The material and the original data of this experiment can be found at https://osf.io/pbhyt/.

$-ing_{of}$ is compatible with narrow containers as predicted, both without (M=5.23, SD=1.75) and with temporal modifiers (M=4.83, SD=1.65). POSS-ing (without modifier: M=3.51, SD=1.86; with modifier: M=3.48, SD=1.82) and ACC-ing (without modifier:M=4.27, SD=1.92; with modifier: M=3.95, SD=1.73) score lower and show higher variation.

A Cumulative Link Mixed Model was fit to the data with type of gerund and modifier as independent variables, with random intercepts for participant and item, as well as random slopes for type of gerund and modifier. The results indicate a significant overall effect of temporal modification ($z = -2.25, p = 0.025$) which is negative, with an estimate of -0.376. Negative estimates are associated with lower judgments of acceptability and positive estimates with higher judgments of acceptability. The type of gerund also shows a significant effect: taking $-ing_{of}$ as reference, the effect of ACC-ing has an estimate of -1.337 ($z = -4.812, p < 0.001$), and POSS-ing has an estimate of -2.240 ($z = -8.314, p < 0.001$). Pairwise comparisons between the three types of gerund indicate that they are all different from one another. A likelihood ratio test was performed to compare the current model with one that takes into account the interaction between type of gerund and modifier. Results indicate that said interaction does not significantly improve the model ($\chi^2(2) = 3.348, p = 0.19$).

One will note that, although both verbal gerunds are described as being incompatible with narrow containers, ACC-ing seems to get a higher score than POSS-ing. This is unexpected and even contradicts Asher's [3, p. 192] observation that POSS-ing is not completely infelicitous with prototypical event predicates like *take place* and *happen* but ACC-ing is particularly bad with such predicates. One possibility is that when judging ACC-ing items, some participants subconsciously added commas before and after the gerund, making them felicitous sentences with a free adjunct:[7]

(26)   Dave*(,) writing the letter*(,) was meticulous.

With a negative effect of temporal modification, I will assume that temporal modifiers do not improve the compatibility between verbal gerunds and narrow containers. I will also not distinguish between the interpretations of POSS-ing or ACC-ing.[8] On the kind-based analysis of gerunds, this means that both preserve their kind-referring nature.

---

[7] Most of the test items in this experiment have a matrix predicate that accepts human subjects: *take* (time), *begin/finish at* (time), *be fast/slow/sloppy/meticulous*, *go fast/slowly*. Two test items use *take place* (at a location), which is incompatible with human subjects, but the scores for these two items in ACC-ing conditions are not lower than POSS-ing conditions.

[8] This does not mean that there is no difference between POSS-ing and ACC-ing. For example, Portner [24] proposes that POSS-ing is definite and ACC-ing indefinite, making them different from a discourse pragmatic aspect. Grimm & McNally [15] argue that POSS-ing is a possessive structure, and that therefore it tends to imply the existence of an event token, but note that POSS-ing can be selected by predicates like *prevent*, which denies the existence of any event tokens: *George prevented Clay's winning the game.*

Temporal modification poses a challenge for the event kind analysis because as presented in Sect. 2, the modification of kinds in order to create subkinds typically involves only manner adverbs, or is constrained in other ways [11, 20]. Here the temporally modified event kinds are rather ad hoc: they are not well-established kinds and have no specific implications as in those in adjectival passives do.

Since event tokens are spatiotemporally localized instances of corresponding event kinds, token-referring expressions can be modified by temporal adverbials. An event kind, in contrast, cannot be an argument of the temporal trace function, so it needs to be instantiated by a token for the temporal modification to be interpreted; however, the experiment shows that the resulting expression is still kind-referring (insofar as it is incompatible with narrow containers). This type of data can even be used to argue in favor of other ontological proposals for verbal gerunds. For example, in the theories where the denotation of verbal gerunds is based on their corresponding propositions, *that Clay won the game yesterday* is not very different from *that Clay won the game*.

In sum, verbal gerunds present a conflict between kind-referring expressions and temporal modifiers which depend on event tokens to be interpreted.[9] In the next section, I demonstrate how this conflict is solved in the interpretation of frequency adjectives.

5   Frequency Adjectives and Adverbs

Corpus data show that verbal gerunds can also be modified by frequency adverbs (see also [23] for verbal gerunds without a preceding NP), which present a similar problem:

(27)   So when he rehearsed the scene he based it on his experience at the chemist's, an example of his *always* having to make contact with a real, lived emotion. (BNC)

Frequency adverbs are not discussed in the literature on *so* anaphora or adjective passives [18,20], but they are obviously no better event kind modifiers than are other temporal adverbials. German-speaking informants confirm that they cannot be targeted by German *so* 'thus' either:[10]

---

[9] With the limited amount of corpus data, one could pursue an alternative hypothesis that avoids the problem of event kind modification: that temporal modifiers occur with verbal gerunds only because the corresponding nominal gerund is not available. Many cases in the BNC, like (23) and (24), cannot be expressed with $-ing_{of}$: *my *wanting of the window open*. It is possible that the attested cases are a measure of last resort, and when an $-ing_{of}$ form is available, like in (25) and other test items in my experiment, the verbal gerund would be blocked resulting in low acceptability. More data and experiments will be needed to support this hypothesis.

[10] An anonymous reviewer pointed out that frequency adverbs are acceptable in German adjectival passives if they target the consequent state instead of the underlying event kind: *Das Fenster ist oft geöffnet.* 'The window is often open(ed).' See [10] for a discussion about two types of modifiers in adjectival passives.

(28)   * Maria hat oft   getanzt und Jan   hat auch so   getanzt.
        Mary has often danced and John has also thus danced
        'Mary often danced, and John danced like that too.'

Using a simpler example to illustrate, the conflict presented by such adverbs is that intuitively, *Clay('s) winning the game frequently* is not a subkind of *Clay('s) winning the game* because it does not narrow down the kind, but involves quantification over, e.g. events of Clay participating in the game and him winning it. Moreover, *Clay('s) winning the game* can be instantiated by a single event of Clay winning, but *Clay('s) winning the game frequently* cannot, because a single token of Clay winning does not justify *frequently*, unless one knows that such event tokens occur in high frequency. Again, the interpretation of *frequently* requires the access to event tokens, while the modified expression must remain type-referring in order to explain the narrow container facts:

(29)   ?Clay('s) frequently winning the parkour race started from the first season of the tournament.

In order to interpret such modifiers in verbal gerunds, we can turn to a similar situation involving frequency adjectives modifying NPs. A typical example in the literature is as follows:

(30)   An occasional sailor strolled by.

(30) is understood not as an episodic sentence, but the assertion that the event of a sailor strolling by happened occasionally. Although the interpretation of *occasional* is based on token events of "a sailor strolled by" and it asserts that such events are loosely distributed, the modified NP does not refer to a single instantiation of the kind "sailor".

Gehrke & McNally [13] propose that frequency modifiers in NPs are event kind modifiers. They describe the distribution of token realizations of the kind at an index i. The following shows the interpretation of *frequent* as in *a frequent downdraft* [13, p. 27]:

(31) $[\![\text{frequent}]\!] = \lambda P \lambda e_k\, [P(e_k) \wedge \textbf{frequent}(e_k)]$ where
        $\forall e_k, i[\textbf{frequent}(e_k)$ at $i \leftrightarrow \textbf{distribution}(\{e : \mathbf{R}(e, e_k)$ at $i\}) = high]$

This analysis, adapted to the adverbial counterpart of such adjectives, can be easily applied to verbal gerunds. *Clay('s) winning the game frequently* is interpreted as follows, where (32) shows the denotation of POSS-*ing* according to [15], ignoring the potential differences between POSS-*ing* and ACC-*ing*, and the adverb has the same interpretation and meaning postulate as the adjective above:

(32) $[\![\text{Clay('s) winning the game}]\!] = \lambda e_k[^{\cup}\textbf{winning}(e_k) \wedge \textbf{Agent}(\mathbf{c}, e_k) \wedge \textbf{Theme}(\mathbf{g}, e_k)]$

(33) $[\![\text{Clay('s) winning the game frequently}]\!] = \lambda e_k[^{\cup}\textbf{winning}(e_k) \wedge \textbf{Agent}(\mathbf{c}, e_k) \wedge \textbf{Theme}(\mathbf{g}, e_k) \wedge \textbf{frequent}(e_k)]$

This analysis has a welcome consequence: tokens of the modified kind are still tokens of the original unmodified kind, but with the additional information that such tokens are distributed in a certain way. Therefore, *his always having to make contact with a real, lived emotion* in (27) denotes a kind whose realization is any token from a set of tokens in the "always" distribution. The matrix clause of (27), which describes the event of basing one's performance on his own experience, stands in an *example* relation to such a kind, which is roughly the relation between a token and the kind it realizes.

I propose that, similar to frequency adverbs, temporal adverbs restrict the possible instantiations of the event kind by setting their temporal trace in a specific period. In (34), *yesterday* combines with an event kind description P and specifies that all its realizations must be located within "yesterday", which is a temporal interval $\mathbf{y}$ valued indexically with respect to the index i.

(34) $[\![\text{yesterday}]\!] = \lambda P \lambda e_k [P(e_k) \wedge \forall e, i[\mathbf{R}(e, e_k) \text{ at } i \rightarrow \tau(e) \subseteq \mathbf{y} \text{ at } i]]$

(35) $[\![\text{Clay('s) winning the game yesterday}]\!] = \lambda e_k[^{\cup}\mathbf{winning}(e_k) \wedge \mathbf{Agent}(\mathbf{c}, e_k) \wedge \mathbf{Theme}(\mathbf{g}, e_k) \wedge \forall e, i[\mathbf{R}(e, e_k) \text{ at } i \rightarrow \tau(e) \subseteq \mathbf{y} \text{ at } i]]$

(36) $[\![\text{Clay('s) winning the game yesterday surprised George}]\!]$
$= \lambda t, j \exists e_k, e', e'_k[^{\cup}\mathbf{winning}(e_k) \wedge \mathbf{Agent}(\mathbf{c}, e_k) \wedge \mathbf{Theme}(\mathbf{g}, e_k) \wedge$
$\forall e, i[\mathbf{R}(e, e_k) \text{ at } i \rightarrow \tau(e) \subseteq \mathbf{y} \text{ at } i] \wedge \mathbf{surprise}(e'_k) \wedge \mathbf{Theme}(e_k, e'_k) \wedge$
$\mathbf{Experiencer}(\mathbf{ge}, e'_k) \wedge \mathbf{R}(e', e'_k) \wedge \tau(e') = t \wedge t < \mathbf{now} \text{ at } j]$ which entails
$\exists e, e_k[^{\cup}\mathbf{winning}(e_k) \wedge \mathbf{Agent}(\mathbf{c}, e_k) \wedge \mathbf{Theme}(\mathbf{g}, e_k) \wedge \mathbf{R}(e, e_k) \wedge \tau(e) \subseteq \mathbf{y}]$

The application of the modifier to the event kind description results in (35). Note that while we have temporally located the possible event tokens, (35) is still a kind-referring expression and does not entail the existence of such tokens. In the following examples, the existence can be cancelled:

(37) George is unconvinced about Clay's winning the game yesterday. In fact, Clay did not win.

(38) Clay winning the game yesterday would have been great. It was a pity that Clay did not win.

When used in a past tense assertion, e.g. (36), the existence of an event token in the interval "yesterday" is entailed. When (35) serves as an argument, a corresponding event kind e_k is provided by Existential Closure. The treatment of the matrix predicate *surprise* follows [15] in that it also starts as the description of a kind e'_k. By taking on the past tense, e'_k is realized by e', which is located at time t and world j. The event token corresponding to (35) is entailed by (36) because, as the kind described by the matrix predicate e'_k gets instantiated, its theme e_k is also realized.

Let us now turn to a more complicated case. Portner [23] raises the issue of adverbial quantification within gerunds, where he advocates for replacing David-sonian event semantics with a situation-based one. He argues that in sentences like (39), on a Davidsonian approach, the event variable of *eating beans* cannot be bound both within the gerund and in the matrix clause, thus producing a problem.

(39)   Clay hates always eating beans.

With the focus on *beans, always eating beans* quantifies over instances of Clay eating and all such instances involve him eating beans. For Portner, the gerund denotes the set of situations such that whenever Clay eats something in that situation, he eats beans. On our approach, quantification is also possible internally. More generally, *always* quantifies over contextually relevant events, stating that all such events are events of Clay eating beans.

(40)   ⟦Clay always eating beans⟧ $= \lambda e_k[C(e_k) \wedge \forall e[\mathbf{R}(e, e_k)$ at $i \rightarrow$
$\exists e'_k[^\cup\mathbf{eating\text{-}beans}(e'_k) \wedge \mathbf{Agent}(\mathbf{c}, e'_k) \wedge \mathbf{R}(e, e'_k)]]]$

What Clay hates, then, is contexually determined event kind of which all the instances involve himself eating beans. Since the resulting gerund is still a kind description, it can be used in a quantified matrix clause, such as *Always eating beans never makes Clay happy.*

6   Discussion

This proposal has several implications for the characteristics of event kind descriptions. First, it suggests that event kind descriptions can be more specific than usually assumed: not only can they be modified by manner adverbials, but they can be restricted by the time or frequency of their instances at a certain index. Unlike in adjectival passives [11,20], the formation of event kind descriptions using verbal gerunds is free and not constrained by pragmatics.

Note that on the kind-based view of verbal gerunds, event kinds are already more specific than the same concept involved in manner anaphora or adjectival passive in that they specify at least one participant of the event kind through the possessor or accusative subject, so they do not involve much regularity to begin with. I have shown how temporal modifiers can be fit in such an analysis and not be seen as an important counterargument to it.

Second, it shows that there are at least two types of modification of event kind descriptions. Manner modifiers create subkinds of the original kind. As already shown in (7), they can be applied directly to kind predicates. Temporal and frequency adverbs, united under this proposal, need access to the tokens at a certain index. Just as *an occasional sailor* in (30) is not a subkind of *sailor*, temporal and frequency modifiers do not create event subkinds: instead, they provide additional information for the instantiations of the original kind. They may still seem to be modifying tokens, but the fact that they appear in verbal gerunds show that they provide a means of locating or describing tokens without forcing kind-referring expressions to denote tokens.

This may lead to a deeper look at the realization relation $\mathbf{R}$. One can potentially propose a predicate for temporal adverbs as properties of kinds, that works the same as manner adverbs: *yesterday* interpreted as $\lambda P \lambda e_k [\textbf{yesterday}(P)(e_k)]$. However, this cannot be done with event kind descriptions modified by frequency adverbs, because they are not instantiated by a single token but a set of tokens in order to meet the distribution requirement. The same thing happens with internally quantified gerunds. The realization relation $\textbf{R}$ does not make such a distinction.[11]

Third, this analysis of temporal adverbs is also applicable to contexts other than verbal gerunds. It can be extended to the modification of matrix verbs if, as illustrated in (36), all verbal predicates begin as kind-referring expressions. It is not necessary for a temporal modifier to be always interpreted as an event kind modifier, but this could be convenient at times. For example, in an appropriate context, *dance on Tuesday* can be seen as a event kind description with a temporal modifier, which provides the antecedent for *so* and *it*:

(41)   Clay danced on Tuesday and George did so too. It was a dangerous action because the enemies had claimed earlier that they would attack anyone that danced on Tuesday (but not on Monday or Wednesday).

This interpretation can also be useful in some cases of German *so* 'thus' anaphora. In the following case, "by full moon" can be seen as a special way to plant things:

(42)   Maria hat die Erdbeeren   bei Vollmond gepflanzt, und Paul hat die
        Maria has the strawberries at   full-moon planted   and Paul has the
        Tomaten auch so gepflanzt.
        tomatoes also so planted

        'Maria planted the strawberries by full moon and Paul also planted the tomatoes that way.' [20, p. 330]

Therefore, the formation of event kind descriptions is essentially free, and it is the possibility of anaphora to temporal adverbials that is restricted. The question is what determines the possiblity of using an episodic temporal modifier. Anderson & Morzycki [2] propose that manner is the "distinguished property" of events, so words like *so* 'thus' only target manner when modifying event descriptions. This would mean that (6) can be explained by a stricter selectional requirement of *so*, which is not incompatible with analyzing temporal adverbials as modifying event kinds.

Syntactically, Gehrke [11] argues that the crucial difference is the attaching site of the modifier. Since event kinds are generally assumed to be introduced on the VP level [6] and episodic temporal modifiers attach higher, they are not available as event kind modifiers unless they are lowered as a manner modifier. What is different about verbal gerunds is that they are usually analyzed as a richer verbal structure up to AspectP [1] or IP [3].[12] From this perspective, it is

---

[11] An account of gerunds based on propositions still has an advantage in this regard, because this distinction is as simple as deciding whether the original proposition is an episodic or a generic one.

[12] Grimm & McNally [15] treat them as VP.

not surprising that they allow for higher modifiers; but again, the restriction on event kind modification is imposed in the syntax, and not by the semantics of kind descriptions.

7 Conclusion

This study proposes an interpretation for temporal modifiers of event kinds, which allows for temporally modifying an event kind-describing expression without having the result refer to a token. It suggests that the formation of event kind descriptions is freer than usually assumed [18,20], and that the distinction between manner and temporal modification shown by some linguistic data is not due to constraints on event kind modification.

Temporal modification may be used as an argument in favor of other theories of gerunds, e.g. analyzing verbal gerunds as facts [3,26] or propositional entities [24], because temporal adverbials are more easily interpreted in a proposition. My analysis shows that temporal modification should not be a problem for the event kind analysis.

Acknowledgements. I would like to thank two anonymous reviewers. This study is supported by an FI-AGAUR grant (2019FI-B00397), the grant FFI2016-76045-P (AEI/FEDER, EU) and an ICREA Academia award to Louise McNally.

References

1. Alexiadou, A., Iordăchioaia, G., Schäfer, F.: Scaling the variation in Romance and Germanic nominalizations. In: Sleeman, P., Perridon, H. (eds.) The noun phrase in Romance and Germanic, pp. 25–40. John Benjamins, Amsterdam/Philadelphia (2011)
2. Anderson, C., Morzycki, M.: Degrees as kinds. Nat. Lang. Linguist. Theory **33**(3), 791–828 (2015)
3. Asher, N.: Reference to abstract objects in discourse. Kluwer Academic Publishers, Dordrecht (1993)
4. Borik, O., Espinal, M.T.: Reference to kinds and to other generic expressions in Spanish: definiteness and number. Linguist. Rev. **32**(2), 167–225 (2015)
5. Carlson, G.: Reference to kinds in English. PhD thesis, University of Massachusetts, Amherst (1977)
6. Carlson, G.: Weak indefinites. In: Coene, M., D'hulst, Y. (eds.) From NP to DP, pp. 195–210. John Benjamins, Amsterdam/Philadelphia (2003)
7. Chierchia, G.: Reference to kinds across languages. Nat. Lang. Seman. **6**(4), 339–405 (1998)
8. Dayal, V.: Number marking and (in)definiteness in kind terms. Linguist. Philos. **27**(4), 393–450 (2004)
9. Gehrke, B.: Stative passives and event kinds. In: Reich, I., Horch, E., Pauly, D. (eds.) Proceedings of Sinn und Bedeutung, vol. 15, pp. 241–257. Universaar - Saarland University Press, Saarbrücken (2011)
10. Gehrke, B.: Still puzzled by adjectival passives. In: Folli, R., Sevdali, C., Truswell, R. (eds.) Syntax and its limits, pp. 175–191. Oxford University Press, Oxford (2013)

11. Gehrke, B.: Adjectival participles, event kind modification and pseudo-incorporation. Nat. Lang. Linguist. Theory **33**(3), 897–938 (2015)
12. Gehrke, B.: Event kinds. In: Truswell, R. (ed.) The Oxford handbook on event structure, pp. 205–233. Oxford University Press, Oxford (2019)
13. Gehrke, B., McNally, L.: Distributional modification: the case of frequency adjectives. Language **91**(4), 837–870 (2015)
14. Gese, H.: Events in adjectival passives. In: Reich, I., Horch, E., Pauly, D. (eds.) Proceedings of Sinn und Bedeutung, vol. 15, pp. 259–274. Universaar - Saarland University Press, Saarbrücken (2011)
15. Grimm, S., McNally, L.: The - ing dynasty: rebuilding the semantics of nominalizations. In: D'Antonio, S., Moroney, M., Little, C.R. (eds.) Proceedings of the 25th Semantics and Linguistic Theory Conference (SALT), vol. 25, pp. 82–102. LSA and CLC Publications, Ithaca, NY (2015)
16. Grimm, S., McNally, L.: Nominalization and natural language ontology. Annual Rev. Linguist. **8**, 257–277 (2022)
17. Krifka, M., Pelletier, F.J., Carlson, G., ter Meulen, A., Link, G., Chierchia, G.: Introduction. In: Carlson, G., Pelletier, F.J. (eds.) The Generic Book, pp. 1–124. The University of Chicago Press, Chicago (2015)
18. Landman, M., Morzycki, M.: Event-kinds and the representation of manner. In: Agbayani, B., Samiian, V., Tucker, B.V. (eds.) Proceedings of the Western Conference in Linguistics (WECOL), vol. 11, pp. 1–12. Department of Linguistics, California State University, Fresno, Fresno (2003)
19. Maienborn, C.: Event semantics. In: Maienborn, C., von Heusinger, K., Portner, P. (eds.) Semantics: an international handbook of natural langauge meaning, pp. 802–829. De Gruyter Mouton, Berlin/Boston (2011)
20. Maienborn, C., Gese, H., Stolterfoht, B.: Adverbial modifiers in adjectival passives. J. Semant. **33**(2), 299–358 (2016)
21. Mueller-Reichau, O.: Sorting the world: On the relevance of the kind/object-distinction to Referential Semantics. Walter de Gruyter, Berlin (2011)
22. Peters, S., Westerståhl, D.: The semantics of possessives. Language **89**, 713–759 (2013)
23. Portner, P.: Gerunds and types of events. In: Moore, S.K., Wyner, A.Z. (eds.) Proceedings from Semantics and Linguistic Theory I, pp. 189–208. Cornell University, Ithaca, NY (1991)
24. Portner, P.: Situation Theory and the semantics of propositional expressions. Ph.D. thesis, University of Massachusetts at Amherst, Amherst, MA (1992)
25. The British National Corpus, version 3 (BNC XML Edition): Distributed by Bodleian Libraries, University of Oxford, on behalf of the BNC Consortium (2007). http://www.natcorp.ox.ac.uk/
26. Vendler, Z.: Linguistics in philosophy. Cornell University Press, Ithaca, NY (1967)
27. Zamparelli, R.: Layers in the determiner phrase. Phd thesis, University of Rochester, Rochester, NY (1995). published in 2000 by Garland Publishing, New York
28. Zucchi, A.: The language of propositions and events: issues in the syntax and the semantics of nominalization. Kluwer Academic Publishers, Dordrecht (1993)

Assessing the Effect of Text Type on the Choice of Linguistic Mechanisms in Scientific Publications

Iverina Ivanova[(✉)] [iD]

Goethe University Frankfurt, Norbert-Wollheim-Platz 1, 60323 Frankfurt am Main,
Germany
I.Ivanova@em.uni-frankfurt.de

Abstract. In this paper, we report a qualitative and quantitative evaluation of a hand-crafted set of discourse features and their interaction with different text types. To be more specific, we compared two distinct text types—scientific abstracts and their accompanying full texts—in terms of linguistic properties, which include, among others, sentence length, coreference information, noun density, self-mentions, noun phrase count, and noun phrase complexity. Our findings suggest that abstracts and full texts differ in three mechanisms which are size and purpose bound. In abstracts, nouns tend to be more densely distributed, which indicates that there is a smaller distance between noun occurrences to be observed because of the compact size of abstracts. Furthermore, in abstracts we find a higher frequency of personal and possessive pronouns which authors use to make references to themselves. In contrast, in full texts we observe a higher frequency of noun phrases. These findings are our first attempt to identify text type motivated linguistic features that can help us draw clearer text type boundaries. These features could be used as parameters during the construction of systems for writing evaluation that could assist both tutors and students in text analysis, or as guides in linguistically-controllable neural text generation systems.

Keywords: Linguistic Mechanisms · Discourse Coherence · Text Types · Linguistic Features for Text Generation · Noun Density · Self-mentions

1 Introduction

Writing is a creative process which involves not only the generation of a sequence of sentences, but also a mechanism of how these sentences relate to each other. In fact, how to produce a coherent text has always been a challenge for all those who are actively involved in the creative writing process, for example, instructors,

Supplementary Information The online version contains supplementary material available at https://doi.org/10.1007/978-3-031-50628-4_9.

researchers working on scientific papers, as well as students who make their first endeavours in academic writing (Flower & Hayes, 1981) [4].

The recent development in neural transformer-based language modeling (Vaswani et al. 2017 [16]; Devlin et al. 2018) [3] has made tremendous progress in automatic generation of coherent texts. Radford et al. (2019) [14], for instance, have successfully demonstrated that neural text generation can produce syntactically valid and meaningful texts. Justified concerns about the large-scale generation of disinformation have been raised already[1] and it is quite certain that sequence prediction models will soon find their way also into the fields of computer-assisted writing. First interactive editors, for example, the one by Wolf et al. (2019) [19] propose automatic completion of text fragments and incorporate next sentence prediction objectives in their underlying models (Devlin et al., 2018) [3].[2]

Although these text predictions incorporate some notion of "discourse understanding", they still suffer from being controllable as text productions are greedily chosen and typically represent only random predictions. Keskar et al. (2019) [10] make one of the first attempts to encode a control mechanism in their language model objectives, however, to date it is still an unresolved problem how these powerful models can be used to conform to text-level coherence and what exactly the linguistic factors are that determine text coherence for neural language models. In this paper, we try to fill the gap between the formal theoretical approaches to modeling discourse coherence on the one hand, for example, the one by Grosz et al. (1995) [5], and the latest neural advancements on the other, which do not incorporate any linguistic signals other than plain n-grams. We set the scope of our work into the context of Benz & Jasinskaja (2017) [2], who argue that a text is produced as an answer to a question and that the text structure, as well as the choice of language expression in terms of information packaging and the use of cohesive devices, is constrained by the communicative goal of the **type of text**, which has also been pointed out by von Stutterheim & Klein (1989) [17].

The goal and contribution of our present study is to verify this claim and to **identify distinctive linguistic features** for two different text types. These features can be applied to other text genres, for example, academic essays, or even to discourse segments in scientific publications such as introductions, methods, discussions, conclusions, and used as parameters during the development of tools for automated writing evaluation (McNamara & Graesser, 2011) [12] or automated essay scoring (Jin et al. 2018) [8]. To be more specific, such distinctive features could provide a better understanding of the typical underlying linguistic characteristics that set one text type or discourse segment apart from another one. This could facilitate the development of more informative tools that can provide hints about the features that are expected to be found in a concrete text type or segment. The presence or the absence of the target features could assist tutors in the analysis and evaluation of the text quality. Furthermore, such

---

[1] https://openai.com/blog/better-language-models/.
[2] https://transformer.huggingface.co/ (July 4 2020).

linguistic features can be employed as an interpretable guiding signal that controls the output of neural text generation systems across the sentence boundary. In this paper, we focus on their identification; their integration into downstream applications is left for future work.

1.1 Related Work

Various attempts have been made to extract distinctive features from different text types, both in purely linguistic contexts and in text classification settings. Previous studies have focused, for example, on the linguistic characteristics that distinguish scientific English from literary English. Ahmad (2012) [1], for instance, found that scientific language differs from non-scientific language in the use of impersonal constructions marked by the passive voice, which makes the authors' expression objective; the use of nominalizations, which adds to the technicality in scientific discourse, and the use of hedging as a means of achieving a consensus among scientists on the subject matter under discussion. Other researchers, by contrast, have found out that academic expression is not entirely devoid of authors' presence. In fact, Hyland (2001) [7] and Yazilarda et al. (2017) [20] analyze the frequency of self-mentions in research articles and emphasize that authors make use of self-referring words to achieve various rhetorical purposes such as to present the aim of the study, to explain the research procedure, to elaborate on an argument, or to make claims. Others investigate the internal organization of information in academic abstracts by analyzing the grammatical and lexical patterns that indicate the problem–solution–evaluation–conclusion moves. Such patterns can be implemented in models that measure the overall text coherence in abstracts by means of automated detection of the moves (Orasan, 2001) [13]. von Stutterheim & Klein (1989) [17] analyze how the nature of the question constrains the text structure and the choice of referential movements, i.e. what type of information is transferred from one utterance to another and what linguistic devices are adopted to signal these movements by comparing narrative with descriptive texts.

Unlike previous studies which contrast the linguistic characteristics of texts representing different genres and disciplines, our study examines two different text types - pairs of an abstract and its accompanying full text - which both appear in the same corpus of a scientific article, but because of the differences in their size and purpose are considered distinct text types. Therefore, the current research seeks, on the one hand, to elaborate on the linguistic mechanisms present in scientific discourse and, on the other hand, to verify if the choice of these mechanisms can be constrained by the text type. To achieve this, we compare the text types in terms of a set of features which are automatically extracted. Thus, we will find out which of the analyzed features are text-specific and will try to explain what justifies their dominance.

2   Experimental Setup

We analyze the two text types on the basis of a predefined, linguistically-motivated set of features reflecting the size and purpose constraints imposed by the text type. In order to extract these features from the target texts, we use automated annotations as a proof-of-concept for the feasibility of experiments involving more data and more features, which is currently beyond the scope of this present study. The purpose of this experiment is to obtain distinctive features that can help us draw clearer text type boundaries that can facilitate both text generation and text evaluation/analysis.

For the purposes of our research we analyze the abstracts and the accompanying full texts of 1,761 scientific papers in the field of computational linguistics available from the ACL Anthology Reference Corpus[3]. The analysis involves an automatic extraction of a set of linguistic features using the `StanfordCoreNLP` module.[4] CoreNLP is a tool for Natural Language Processing (NLP) in Java which processes the input texts and generates linguistic annotations such as parts of speech, dependency and constituency parses of sentences, coreference resolution.

Table 1. Our linguistic features involved in this study and how they are measured.

	Feature	Description
1	Sentence length	The total number of tokens normalized by the total number of sentences.
2	Coreference	The total number of coreference chains normalized by the total number of sentences.
3	Noun density	The sum of the difference in number of tokens between noun occurrences normalized by the number of noun occurrences.
4	Self-mentions	The total number of self-mention occurrences normalized by the total number of noun phrases.
5	Noun phrase count	The total number of noun phrases per document normalized by the total number of tokens.
6	Noun phrase complexity — The total number of embedded past participle clauses normalized by the total number of noun phrases (excluding pronouns). — The total number of embedded to-infinitive clauses normalized by the total number of noun phrases (excluding pronouns).	— The total number of embedded that-clauses in the noun phrases normalized by the total number of noun phrases (excluding pronouns).

---

[3] https://aclanthology.org/.
[4] https://stanfordnlp.github.io/CoreNLP/index.html.

Table 2. Overview of analyzed text types, mean size in tokens, and mean number of sentences.

Text type	Avg length	Avg # of sentences
Abstract	104 tokens	4.97
Main Part	3,262 tokens	151.8

A paper's abstract and its main part are considered two distinctive text types as they clearly differ in size (see Table 2) and purpose. The hypothesized intentions of abstracts are to inform the target reader about the aim, the methods, the results, and the contributions of the study in a concise fashion, as well as to convince them to read the paper's main part (Orasan, 2001) [13]. Thus, the question that abstracts answer can be *What are the purpose, the methods, the results, and the contributions of the study in short?* The main part, by contrast, is intended to inform the reader about the findings of the study in an extended form by providing a comprehensive description of the background, the adopted methods, the results, and the possible conclusions that can be drawn from them. The hypothesized questions that the main part answers can be *What is the scope of this study and in what ways it differs from previous works?, How was the study conducted?, What are the results of the current study?, What claims can be made on the basis of the research results?*

2.1 Linguistic Features Under Consideration

Our features include sentence length, coreference, noun density, self-mentions, noun phrase (NP) count, and noun phrase complexity; see Table 1 for a full overview of the features. Such lexical, syntactic, and discourse signals can inform us about the lexical and syntactic sophistication of the texts and could therefore be employed as predictors of text quality and writing proficiency in automated writing tools (McNamara et al., 2009) [11]. In this study, sentence length is measured by the mean number of tokens per sentence and the feature is used for normalization purposes. Coreference is a type of grammatical cohesive device (Halliday & Hassan, 1976) [6] which provides insights into the topic persistence in the texts indicated by the presence of coreferential relations that hold between threads of meaning. The `StanfordCoreNLP` module displays these relations between entities in the form of coreference chains. A coreference chain stands for the relation between an anaphora and its antecedent and a chain can contain two or more mentions of the same entity. Our expectations are that full texts will contain a higher frequency of coreference chains, which could be size motivated, i.e. the longer the text, the higher the frequency of coreference chains. Noun density refers to the mean distance between noun occurrences in the text. Following Witte & Faigley (1981) [18], we measure density by calculating the mean number of tokens that occur between nouns–thus, the smaller the distance, the greater the density of nouns. We expect that in abstracts nouns will be more densely distributed, which could be both size and purpose bound.

Self-mentions are occurrences of personal pronouns such as *I, me, we, us* and possessive pronouns such as *my, mine, our, ours* that authors use to make self references. Taking Hyland's (2001) [7] and Yazilarda et al.'s (2017) [20] findings into account, we expect that in abstracts there will be a higher occurrence of self-mentions since authors use them to mark rhetorical moves, for example, to introduce their research topic, to explain the research procedure, to emphasize the significance of their research, and to make conclusions based on the research results. NP count refers to the number of NP occurrences in texts. By an NP occurrence we understand the noun head along with its dependents. Since nominalization is a distinctive feature of scientific language (Ahmad, 2012) [1], we believe that there are NP occurrences in both text types, but their frequency will be higher in full texts due to their length. The NP complexity measures the types of modification that are present in the internal structure of NPs. We extract the frequency of embedded finite and non-finite clauses from the NP structures. Considering the nominalization feature, we expect that noun heads in NPs are heavily modified by that-clauses or non-finite clauses introduced by to-infinitive or a past participle in both abstracts and full texts. We would like to check which type of NP modification is predominant in the two target texts.

3   Evaluation

3.1   Quantitative Assessment

The distinctive features are shown in Fig. 1. The current results indicate that the two text types differ significantly in three of the analyzed features: noun density, NP count, and self-mentions. The abstract and full text samples for each feature were compared pairwise. Abstracts and full texts differ in terms of noun density. The mean number of tokens that appear between nouns in abstracts is lower than that in the accompanying full text. In abstracts, a noun occurs once every 2.91 tokens, whereas in full texts - once every 3.28 tokens. Since the data in both samples was normally distributed, a paired t-test (Kalpíc et al., 2011) [9] with 0.95 percent confidence interval was conducted. The test result confirmed that the means of the two samples differ significantly with a p-value < 0.05, t $= -48.402$ and df $= 1712$. Another distinctive feature is the frequency of NP occurrences. This frequency in full texts is higher (0.46) than that in abstracts (0.41). The data in both samples was normally distributed and the paired t-test confirmed that the difference is again statistically significant with a p-value < 0.05, t $= -30.722$ and df $= 2912.8$. Finally, a third distinctive feature is the frequency of self-mentions, which is higher in abstracts (0.07) than in full texts (0.03). The Wilcoxon test (Rey & Neuhäuser, 2011) [15] was used since the data in the abstract sample was non-normally distributed and its result showed that the difference in means is statistically significant ($p < 0.05$, V $= 1170812$). For all the rest of the features, the tests did not reveal any statistically significant differences (cf. Table 3).

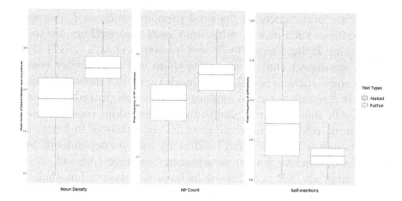

Fig. 1. Distinctive linguistic features between two text types: Abstracts exhibit a lower number of tokens between noun occurrences and a higher frequency of self-mentions, whereas full texts have a higher frequency of noun phrases.

Table 3. All linguistic features and their computed mean values per text type.

Feature	Abstract	Main Part
Sentence length	21.14	21.56
Coreference	0.33	0.35
Noun density	2.91	3.28
Self-mentions	0.07	0.03
NP count	0.41	0.46
Embedded finite clauses	0.05	0.06
Embedded past part clauses	0.08	0.07
Embedded to-inf clauses	0.03	0.03

3.2   Discussion

Our findings support the observations of previous work by von Stutterheim & Klein (1989) [17] that the communicative goal of the text places constraints on the text structure and the selection of linguistic devices that add to the overall text coherence. It also confirms our preliminary expectations that there are genre-bound differences in terms of linguistic mechanisms. The results from our quantitative study suggest that nouns in abstracts are more densely distributed than those in full texts. This could be explained, on the one hand, by the compact size of abstracts in which authors tend to present the essential points of their research by using nominal forms that are information burdened like in the following examples: *an **approach** for **opinion role induction** for verbal **predicates**, a new manually-compiled **opinion role lexicon**, etc.* (see Fig. 2). On the other hand, it could also be motivated by the text purpose, i.e. abstracts have to be informative per se in order to persuade the reader into the significance and credibility of the conducted research. Moreover, abstracts and their

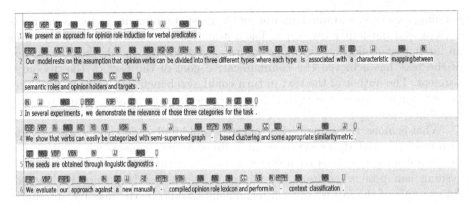

Fig. 2. An example of an abstract annotated with the parts of speech of the tokens using CoreNLP: The "NN" and "NNS" labels stand for a noun in singular and plural form respectively.

accompanying full texts also differ in the frequency of NP occurrences. The frequency of NPs could correlate with the text size. The longer the text, the higher the frequency. In abstracts there might be fewer NPs, but these NPs might contain a sequence of nouns that modify the noun head, as illustrated with the NP examples in Fig. 2. This could also be a possible explanation for the high noun density in abstracts. Finally, the third feature on the basis of which the two text types differ is the high frequency of self-mentions in abstracts, which means that authors tend to refer to themselves more often in abstracts than in the main part of the article. This could be motivated by the purpose of abstracts, namely, to convince the reader of the significance of the conducted research. By referring to themselves, authors focus readers on their own research efforts and emphasize the significance of their research aim, the approach they have adopted/the model they have used, the results they have achieved, and the claims they can make in light of the presented results. Figure 2 illustrates the focusing function of self-mentions: *we present, we show, we demonstrate, we evaluate, our model, our approach*. The use of self-mentions also makes the expression more personal and thus improves the writer-reader interaction by implicitly inviting the reader to participate in the interpretation of the presented research results.

Contrary to our initial assumptions, the two text types did not display any significant differences in terms of sentence length, the frequency of coreferential relations, or the complexity of NPs marked by embedded finite and non-finite clauses. This could be due to the data sparsity. Nevertheless, we believe that these findings provide more insights into the text-specific linguistic mechanisms and help us understand better how the aim of the text imposes constraints on the language expression. They also make us more confident in our claims that automated tools for writing evaluation or text generation can greatly benefit from such text-specific characteristics. The integration of such pre-defined distinctive features in natural language processing tools could improve their functionality by enabling a more fine-grained analysis of the most common linguistic mechanisms present in a particular text type. The automated detection of these features in an input text could give tutors an informative feedback on whether the author of the text has achieved the communicative goal of the text or the discourse segment. The author of the text in turn could also benefit from this feedback by being informed about the typical linguistic mechanisms that are expected in a particular text type.

What is more, these linguistic properties could find a good application as predictors of the underlying syntactic and discourse mechanisms when integrated in natural language generation systems. However, the potential risks that such systems can pose when used for unintended purposes should not be ignored. An example of the misuse of such technologies would be the massive automatic generation of academic essays or scientific papers. In order to avoid such practices and to support the design of innovations from which those involved in the writing process can truly benefit and which foster the development of their writing competencies, there should be transparency and control of the purposes for which these technologies are designed.

4   Conclusion and Future Work

We have investigated the effect of text type on the choice of linguistic mechanisms. By comparing scientific abstracts and their accompanying full texts, we found that the size and the communicative goal of the text type could influence the linguistic devices that are employed in the text. The results showed that the features of noun density and self-mentions are predominant mechanisms in abstracts and are both size and purpose bound. The high frequency of noun phrases is a predominant feature of the full text, which turned out to be size bound.

The current study requires further investigation in various directions. First, we would like to investigate other types of features which are related to the internal structure of the NP such as the mean NP length measured by the mean number of tokens, as well as the frequency of nominal and adjectival modification. Second, another feature that is associated with scientific language is hedging. Hedging expresses the degree of confidence with which authors present the information in their studies. Our expectation is that there will be a higher occurrence of hedges in full texts, especially in the Discussion part where authors present their interpretation of the research results. Third, since relations between utterances can be signaled not only by means of reference, but also by lexical markers such as repetitions, synonyms, and antonyms, we would like to see which are the predominant lexical cohesive devices and what is their distribution in abstracts and in the different sections of the accompanying full texts. Finally, the mechanisms and the proposed research methodology of acquiring linguistic features described in this study will be further extended and applied to larger text corpora and other academic genres.

*The paper submission is accompanied with **supplementary material which includes the source code and the dataset with the computed values of the features per text type**.*

Acknowledgements. I would like to thank Dr. Niko Schenk for his constant support, inspiration, and supervision of the extracted and analyzed data. Sincere gratitude to Prof. Gert Webelhuth, Dr. Janina Radó, and Prof. Manfred Sailer for their guidance and assistance in the interpretation of the research results.

References

1. Ahmad, J.: Stylistic features of scientific English: a study of scientific research articles. English Lang. Literat. Stud. **2**(1), 47–55 (2012). https://doi.org/10.5539/ells.v2n1p47

2. Benz, A., Jasinskaja, K.: Questions under discussion: from sentence to discourse. Discourse Proc. **54**(3), 177–186 (2017). https://doi.org/10.1080/0163853X.2017.1316038. (04.07.2020)

3. Devlin, J., Chang, M.-W., Lee, K., Toutanova, K.: Bert: pre-training of deep bidirectional transformers for language understanding (2018). https://arxiv.org/abs/1810.04805 (04.07.2020)

4. Flower, L., Hayes, J.R.: A cognitive process theory of writing. College Compos. Commun. **32**(4), 365–387 (1981)

5. Grosz, B.J., Joshi, A.K., Weinstein, S.: Centering: a framework for modeling the local coherence of discourse. Comput. Linguist. **21**(2), 203–225 (1995)

6. Halliday, M., Hasan, R.: Cohesion in English. Longman Group Ltd London (1976)

7. Hyland, K.: Humble servants of the discipline? self-mention in research articles. Engl. Specif. Purp. **20**(3), 207–226 (2001). https://doi.org/10.1016/S0889-4906(00)00012-0. (04.07.2020)

8. Jin, C., He, B., Hui, K., Sun, L.: TDNN: a two stage deep neural network for prompt-independent automated essay scoring. In Proceedings of the 56th Annual Meeting of the Association for Computational Linguistics (Volume 1, Long Papers), pp. 1088–1097 (2018). https://doi.org/10.18653/v1/P18-1100(04.07.2020)

9. Kalpić, D., Hlupić, N., Lovrić, M.: Student's tTests, pp. 1559–1563. Springer, Berlin (2011)

10. Keskar, N.S., McCann, B., Varshney, L.R., Xiong, C., Socher, R.: CTRL: a conditional transformer language model for controllable generation (2019). https://doi.org/10.48550/arXiv.1909.05858 (Oct 7 2020)

11. McNamara, D.S., Crossley, S.A., Mccarthy, P.M.: Linguistic features of writing quality. Written Commun. **27**(1), 57–86 (2009). https://doi.org/10.1177/0741088309351547

12. McNamara, D.S. Graesser, A.C.: Coh-metrix: an automated tool for theoretical and applied natural language processing. In McCarthy, P., Boonthum-Denecke, C. (eds.) Applied Natural Language Processing: Identication, Investigation and Resolution, pp. 188–205. IGI Global, Hershey, PA (2011). https://doi.org/10.4018/978-1-60960-741-8.ch011(10.07.2020)

13. Orasan, C.: Patterns in scientific abstracts. In: Proceedings Corpus Linguistics, pp. 433–445 (2001)

14. Radford, A., Wu, J., Child, R., Luan, D., Amodei, D., Sutskever, I.: . Language models are unsupervised multitask learners. https://d4mucfpksywv. cloudfront.net/better-language-models/language_models_are_unsupervised_ multitask_learners.pdf (4 July 2020)

15. Rey, D., Neuhäuser, M.: Wilcoxon-Signed-Rank Test. In: International Encyclopedia of Statistical Science, pp. 1658–1659. Springer, Heidelberg (2011). https://doi. org/10.1007/978-3-642-04898-2

16. Vaswani, A., et al.: Attention is all you need. In: Guyon, I., et al. (eds.) Advances in Neural Information Processing Systems, vol. 30, pp. 5998– 6008. Curran Associates, Inc. (2017). https://papers.nips.cc/paper/2017/file/ 3f5ee243547dee91fbd053c1c4a845aa-Paper.pdf (July 4 2020)

17. von Stutterheim, C., Klein, W.: Referential movement in descriptive and narrative discourse, **54**, 39–76 North-Holland Linguistic Series: Linguistic Variations. Elsevier (1989). https://doi.org/10.1016/B978-0-444-87144-2.50005-7

18. Witte, S.P., Faigley, L.: Coherence, cohesion, and writing quality. Coll. Compos. Commun. **32**(2), 189–204 (1981)

19. Wolf, T., et al.: HuggingFace's transformers: State-of-the-art natural language processing (2019). https://arxiv.org/abs/1910.03771v4 (4 July 2020)

20. Yazilarda, A., İşaret, Y., Kullanlml, E.S., Kafes, H.: The use of authorial self-mention words in academic writing. Inter. J. Language Academy **5**(3), 165–180 (2017). https://doi.org/10.18033/ijla.3532

Limited Symmetry

Alexandros Kalomoiros[✉][iD]

University of Pennsylvania, Philadelphia, PA 19104, USA
akalom@sas.upenn.edu

Abstract. This paper aims to tackle some of the basic (a-)symmetries of presupposition projection in a pragmatic, bivalent, and incrementally-oriented framework. The main data point that we are trying to capture is that projection from the first conjunct of a conjunction is asymmetric, while projection from the first disjunct of a disjunction can be symmetric. We argue that a solution where there are effectively two filtering mechanisms, one symmetric and one asymmetric, [11], is not tenable given recent experimental evidence, [4,7]. Instead, we propose a bivalent system, where at each point during the incremental interpretation of a sentence S, the comprehender is trying to compute the sets of worlds in the context where the truth value of S has already been determined. This computation plays out differently in the case of conjunction vs the case of disjunction, and coupled with appropriate definitions of the incremental interpretation process and of what it means for a presupposition to project in the current system, it leads to asymmetric conjunction, but symmetric disjunction.

Keywords: Presupposition Projection · (A-)symmetries · Connectives

1 Introduction

This paper is concerned with the projection problem for presuppositions. Certain lexical items impose conditions (presuppositions) on the context in which they are uttered, (see e.g. [13] among many others):

(1)   a.   ***Context:*** We do not know whether or not John used to have research interests in Tolkien.
        b. #John continues having research interests in Tolkien.

'Continue having research interests in Tolkien' presupposes 'used to have research interests in Tolkien', hence infelicity arises when (1-b) is uttered in a (global) context that does not entail this presupposition.

Thanks to Florian Schwarz for many helpful discussions and comments on this work. Thanks also to Phillipe Schlenker, Jacopo Romoli, Julie Legate, Anna Papafragou, Ryan Budnick, Andrea Beltrama, Spencer Caplan, and to the members of the Penn Semantics Lab for helpful comments and suggestions. Thanks also to the ESSLLI reviewers for useful feedback and suggestions. All errors are my own.

A. Pavlova et al. (Eds.): ESSLLI 2019/2020/2021, LNCS 14354, pp. 163–176, 2024.
https://doi.org/10.1007/978-3-031-50628-4_10

The projection problem, [15], enters the stage when presuppositions are embedded under various operators:

(2)   **Projection Problem:** How are the presuppositions of a complex sentence derived from the presuppositions of its parts?

To see the motivation for the problem consider the following sentences:

(3)   a.   *Context:* We do not know whether or not John used to have research interests in Tolkien.
       b.   #John continues having research interests in Tolkien and he used to have interests in Tolkien.
       c.   John used to have research interests in Tolkien and he continues having research interests in Tolkien.

Example (3-b) is felt to carry the presupposition that 'John used to have research interests in Tolkien'; in this case we say that the presupposition **projects**. Hence, when (3-b) is uttered in a context where we have ignorance about whether or not John used to have such research interests, infelicity arises.

On the other hand, the conjunction in (3-c) is not felt to carry the presupposition that John used to have research interests in Tolkien. In this case we say that the presupposition is **filtered** (in the terminology of Karttunen, [5]). The only difference between (3-b) and (3-c) is the order of the conjuncts: in (3-b) the presupposition-bearing conjunct comes first (see also [7] on experiments that confirm this difference for conjunction).

Thus, conjunction represents a case where the filtering of presuppositions is asymmetric. An intuitive explanation for this is that the first conjunct in (3-c) is evaluated first [13], just by virtue of the fact that one encounters it first as the sentence unfolds in time. Thus the information carried by it is integrated in the context before the second conjunct is evaluated. In this way, the second conjunct is evaluated against a context that entails its presupposition. That's why no projection arises.

Conversely, in (3-b) the first conjunct is evaluated in a context which does not entail the presupposition that John used to have research interests in Tolkien. That information only comes later, in the second conjunct, and is not in principle accessible for the evaluation of the first conjunct.

While conjunction behaves asymmetrically, this is not universally true across connectives. A famous example is disjunction. Presuppositions in the second disjunct of a disjunction are filtered if the negation of the first disjunct entails the presupposition, [5]:

(4)   Either John never had research interests in Tolkien or he continues to have such research interests.

However, reversing the disjuncts does not change the filtering pattern ([3], see also Partee's 'bathroom sentences'):[1]

(5)   Either John continues to have research interests in Tolkien or he never had such interests.

Neither (4) nor (5) are felt to presuppose that John used to have research interests in Tolkien. This raises the following conundrum: projection from conjunction would appear to imply that the mechanism determining projection/filtering is fundamentally asymmetric, with the asymmetry perhaps rooted in the left-to-right incrementality inherent in the way we parse a sentence as it unfolds in time. Disjunction though appears to provide an argument for a symmetric filtering mechanism. The question is then is whether need two different filtering mechanisms, one symmetric and one asymmetric, to account for this landscape (as proposed by [11]); or whether it is possible to unify the phenomena as instances of one general filtering algorithm.

The rest of this paper is organised as follows: Sect. 2 briefly reviews [11]'s theory of local contexts, which aims to tackle the problem in a pragmatic, incrementally-oriented framework, by having two filtering mechanisms, one symmetric and one asymmetric. We argue that recent experimental evidence points to the existence of a single filtering mechanism. Section 3 takes on the task of building such a single mechanism (dubbed 'Limited Symmetry') within the a pragmatic, incrementally-oriented, bivalent framework, and shows how it derives asymmetry for conjunction, but symmetry for disjunction. Section 4 concludes.

2   Schlenker 2009

We give a brief introduction to Schlenker's approach to the projection problem [11], as our own solution in Sect. 3 follows the spirit of this approach. Schlenker provides a reconstruction of Karttunen's notion of 'local context', [5], and uses it to state the classic constraint that **the presupposition of sentence S must be entailed by its local context**.

At the core of Schlenker's proposal is the idea that in determining what counts as a local context, there's an underlying strategy of only evaluating presuppositions relative to those possible worlds in which the truth value of the complex sentence overall is not already determined by other parts of the sentence. How precisely this plays out will, of course, depend on the truth-functional properties of the connective in question, which ultimately accounts for differences in local contexts, e.g., with conjunction involving consideration of information of

---

[1] The reason that these disjunctions are known as 'bathroom disjunctions' is that they resemble certain Partee sentences involving symmetric anaphora resolution:

(i)   Either it's in a funny place or this house has no bathroom.

another conjunct, whereas disjunction requires consideration of the negation of another disjunct.

Schlenker assumes a language with a classical bivalent semantics. Here, we focus on the propositional fragment of this language (see Sect. 3.2 for a statement of this fragment). Following Stalnaker, a context C is modelled as a set of possible worlds, [14]. The notation $C \models p$ means that the proposition expressed by p is true in every world in C. Here's the definition for the asymmetric local context of an sentence S:

Definition 1. Asymmetric Local Context:[2] The asymmetric local context of a sentence S in a syntactic environment $a \_ b$ and global context C, is the strongest proposition r such that for all sentences D and good finals b', $C \models a(r \text{ and } D)b' \leftrightarrow a(D)b'$

Now consider a conjunction like $(p \text{ and } q)$, and say we want to calculate the local context for q in a global context C. Applying the definition, we need to calculate the strongest proposition r such that for all sentences D and good finals b', $C \models (p \text{ and } (r \text{ and } D)b' \leftrightarrow (p \text{ and } (D)b'$. The only possible good final here is a closing parenthesis,). One proposition that does the job is the proposition expressed by p: $C \models (p \text{ and } (p \text{ and } D)b' \leftrightarrow (p \text{ and } (D)b'$, since conjoining the first conjunct to the second conjunct is not going to change the truth conditions of the conjunction. To show that p is the strongest proposition that we could conjoin here, suppose that there is a proposition r that excludes a C-world w' that satisfies p, i.e. r is false in w'. Suppose also that D is true in w'. In this case, $(p \text{ and } D)$ is true in w', but $(p \text{ and } (r \text{ and } D))$ is false; so it does not hold that $C \models (p \text{ and } D) \leftrightarrow (p \text{ and } (r \text{ and } D))$. Therefore, the local context for a second conjunct is the first conjunct.

Applying similar reasoning, we can calculate the local context for the second disjunct q of a disjunction $(p \text{ or } q)$: $C \models (p \text{ or } (D)b' \leftrightarrow (p \text{ or } ((not \ p) \text{ and } D)b'$.[3] $(not \ p)$ is the strongest proposition we could conjoin here: suppose we also conjoin r such that there is a C-world w, where r is false, p is false, but D is true (again the only possible good-final here is the closing parenthesis). In this world, $(p \text{ or } ((not \ p) \text{ and } D)$ is true but $(p \text{ or } ((not \ p) \text{ and } r \text{ and } D)$ is not. So, the local context of a second disjunct is the negation of the first disjunct, thus correctly predicting filtering in cases like (5).

So far, this system predicts correct filtering conditions for presuppositions in the second conjunct/disjunct. However, it predicts the same filtering conditions for presuppositions in the first conjunct/disjunct, as in both cases the asymmetric local context is the global context. The reason for this is that in both cases we are calculating the strongest r that can be conjoined to a first conjunct/disjunct D such that $C \models ((D)b' \leftrightarrow ((r \text{ and } D)b'$, for all possible good finals b'. It does not matter what the connective is, as the connective essentially 'hides' in b', which quantifies over all possible good finals. Therefore, the only

---

[2] This definition focuses on the propositional case and is borrowed from [6]. See [11] for full definitions generalized to a more expressive language.

[3] $(p \lor q) \leftrightarrow (p \lor ((\neg p) \land q))$ is a tautology.

possible restriction of the first conjunct/disjunct is $r = C$ (which is no restriction contextually). If we try to conjoin something stronger than C, then we get into trouble: consider a proposition r which is false in some C-world w, while D is true in w and $b' = and\ \top$), where $\top$ is a tautology. Then $(r\ and\ D\ and\ \top)$ is false in w, but $(D\ and\ \top)$ is true in w, so the equivalence between them fails. Thus, a presupposition in the first conjunct/disjunct creates a problem unless it is entailed by C.

The result about first disjuncts/conjuncts seems to be contradicted by cases like (5), where the second disjunct is apparently filtering the presupposition of the first disjunct. To account for this, [11] proposes a symmetric definition of local contexts:

Definition 2. Symmetric Local Context: The symmetric local context of a sentence S in a syntactic environment $a \_ b$ and global context C is the strongest proposition r such that for all sentences D, $C \models a(r\ and\ D)b \leftrightarrow a(D)b$.

Now we are no longer quantifying over all possible good finals, but rather allow access to the actual sentence completion b. This allows the actual continuation of the first disjunct (namely, $or\ q$)) to be taken into account. Applying similar reasoning as in the case of the asymmetric local context of a second disjunct, the symmetric local context of a first disjunct is $(not\ q)$, which is what we need here. This definition also predicts a symmetric local context for a first conjunct, namely the second conjunct, which predicts cases of symmetric filtering in conjunction. To account for the fact that symmetric filtering in conjunction seems much rarer, [11] posits that asymmetric local contexts are the default (it is in this sense that the system is parsing-oriented), while accessing symmetric contexts involves overriding this default and hence carries a processing cost.

Nevertheless, recent experimental evidence casts doubt on this claim. Recent work by Mandelkern et al, [7], has shown that it is not possible to prevent a presupposition projecting from the first conjunct, even in situations where the only way to prevent infelicity would be to access a symmetric mechanism. Moreover, the idea that symmetric filtering is costly makes a prediction that disjunctions like (4) where the presupposition is in the second disjunct are more felicitous than disjunction like (5), where the presupposition is in the first disjunct. [4] tested this prediction by adapting the Mandelkern et al. design to disjunctions: the results showed no asymmetry between the two types of disjunction; both were equally felicitous. Therefore, it seems preferable to derive the projection (a-)symmetries via a single mechanism.

3   Limited Symmetry

3.1   The System Informally

We develop a pragmatic, bivalent, incrementally-oriented system, which we dub 'Limited Symmetry', inspired by Schlenker's approach, but where the asymmetry of conjunction and the symmetry of disjunction follow from a single mechanism.

We start with an informal version of the system; the formal definitions and main results are in Sects. 3.2, 3.3.

Part of the reason that the asymmetric definition of local contexts could not differentiate between the first conjunct vs the first disjunct was that one does not have access to the connective when calculating those local contexts, as the connective comes after the first conjunct/disjunct. To overcome this, we need our projection algorithm to be able to have access to the $(p$ and, $(p$ or substrings of a conjunction and a disjunction (i.e., access to the connectives).[4]

To do this we will assume that when encountering a sentence, e.g. a conjunction like $S = (p$ and $q)$, comprehenders parse the symbols of S incrementally: [$($, $(p$, $(p$ and, $(p$ and q, $(p$ and q$)$]. Similarly, a disjunction of the form $(p$ or $q)$ is parsed as [$($, $(p$, $(p$ or, $(p$ or q, $(p$ or q$)$].[5] Each entry in these lists represents a parsing step for the given sentence. Let's assume that at each parsing step the comprehender is attempting to calculate all the sets of worlds where the truth value of the whole sentence is already determined (as either true or false) for all possible sentence completions (good finals). The aim is to update, i.e. to get rid of the worlds in the global context C where the sentence is false as fast as possible, while keeping the worlds where it is true. At each parsing step, the set of worlds where the sentence is already false is removed from the global context C and the update process restarts with $C' = C - \{w|$ the $sentence$ is $already$ $false$ in $w\}$ as the new global context.

Our treatment of presuppositions is very much related to Schlenker's. Recall that a (symmetric) local context is the strongest proposition one can conjoin to a sub-constituent D without changing the overall truth conditions of the sentence S in which D is embedded (for any D). One can add or remove a local context to its sub-constituent $salva$ $veritate$, no matter the identity of the sub-constituent. Presuppositions of D then must be entailed by the local context. Equivalently, a local context is the strongest proposition that D can presuppose; presuppositions then are essentially subject to a constraint that says that they can be removed without changing the truth conditions of S.[6,7]

---

[4] Throughout the rest of this paper, the **verbatim** font is used to mark partial syntactic objects.

[5] Note that I sometimes use the term 'parsing' to mean roughly 'getting access to bits of syntactic structure during incremental interpretation', which deviates from the common usage of the term somewhat. Nonetheless, within the presuppositions literature, approaches like that of [11] that work by manipulating partial strings of expressions, are often referred to as 'parsing-based' (see e.g. [6]), and it is this usage I have in mind here.

[6] Schlenker himself originally stated his constraint on presuppositions in such terms, in the context of his Transparency theory, [9,10]. The local contexts theory is an equivalent reformulation of the Transparency theory, as shown in Schlenker 2009.

[7] There are similarities here with the Strong Kleene algorithm, [2], where projection (i.e., the third truth value) results when the other sentences of a larger sentence are not enough for determining the classical truth value, given the semantics of the connective. In fact, as discussed for instance in [8], the predictions of Strong Kleene and symmetric Local Contexts are very close to one another.

We will assume that some sentences carry presuppositions, represented as $p'p$, where p' is the presuppositional component of the sentence, and p the assertive component. Following [11], we will understand such sentences as the conjunction of p' and p in a bivalent classical logic. Consider the effect of the constraint we described in the previous paragraph on $p'p$; it says that for any $p,$[8] p' can be added or removed from p without change in truth conditions:

(6) $\forall p : C \models p'p \leftrightarrow p$

We can re-write this in the following way:

(7)   For all p:
        a. $\{w \in C| \ p' = 1 \ and \ p = 1\} \subseteq \{w \in C| \ p = 1\}$ (this is simply $C \models p'p \rightarrow p$)
        b. $\{w \in C| \ p' = 0 \ or \ p = 0\} \subseteq \{w \in C| \ p = 0\}$ (this is the contrapositive of $C \models p \rightarrow p'p$)

So, this Schlenkerian constraint boils down to saying that for all p, all of the worlds in the context where the sentence with the presupposition p' is true should be worlds where the sentence without p' is true, and similarly for false. It can be shown (see Observation 1 in Sect. 3.3) that this constraint is satisfied just in case $C \models p'$, i.e. just in case the context entails the presuppositions of the sentence, which is the desired result.

Here's now our twist on this idea: the aim of the comprehender is indeed to show that for every presuppositional component $p'p$ of a sentence S, for all p the version of S with the presupposition p' (the [+presup] version), is equivalent to the version without p' (the [-presup] version). However, instead of waiting until they have access to the whole of S before attempting to check this equivalence, they try to build it incrementally as they are getting access to the worlds where S is true or false.

For example, suppose that $S = (p'p \ and \ q)$. The general requirement is that in a context C, $(p'p \ and \ q)$ should be equivalent to $(p \ and \ q)$, for all p. So, all worlds in C where $(p'p \ and \ q)$ is true should be worlds where $(p \ and \ q)$ is true (for all p); and similarly all worlds where $(p'p \ and \ q)$ is false should be worlds where $(p \ and \ q)$ is false (for all p).

The key is that a comprehender doe not need access to the whole of S to start calculating whether this equivalence holds. At the point in parse where the comprehender has access only to the (p'p and part of S they already know that the sentence is false in all C-worlds where $p'p$ is false. Therefore, for these worlds the comprehender can already at this point check whether they satisfy the condition that they should also be worlds where the [-presup] version of S is false. The [-presup] version that the comprehender has access to at this point is (p and. The question then is whether for all p: $\{w|p' = 0 \ or \ p = 0\}$ is (contextually) a subset of $\{w|p = 0\}$. It can be shown (see Sect. 3.3) that this happens just in case $C \models p'$, which is the desired result.

---

[8] This is just the 'for any D' part in the definitions of local contexts.

Conversely, given a disjunction $S = (p'p\ or\ q)$, at parsing step (p'p or, we can determine a set of worlds where the disjunction is true for all possible continuations: all the worlds where p' is true and p is true: $\{w|\ p' = 1\ and\ p = 1\}$, which for all p, is a subset of $\{w|\ p = 1\}$ (the corresponding set if we only consider the [-presup] version of S at the corresponding parsing point). This already shows that our system distinguishes between conjunction and disjunction: they have different points where the conditions imposed on presuppositions can create trouble (see Sect. 3.3 for how exactly symmetry comes about). We now turn to formalizing 'Limited Symmetry'.

3.2   Formalization

We restrict ourselves to a propositional language $\mathcal{L}$ (inspired by [11]):

(8)   a.   **Propositions** $:= p_i\ |\ p'_j p_k$ (subscripts are natural numbers)
         b.   **Formulas** $\phi := (not\ \phi)\ |\ (\phi\ and\ \ \phi)\ |\ (\phi\ or\ \phi)\ |\ (if\ \phi.\ \phi)$

In $p'_j p_k$, p'_i is meant to be understood as the an entailment that is marked as a presupposition (hence the prime), while p_k as the non-presuppositonal entailment (the asserted content). Below, we will omit subscripts and will be using lower case letters to name propositions $(p, q, r, \ldots$ etc.)

The intended models of this language are pairs $\langle W, F \rangle$, where W is a set of worlds, and F is a function assigning to each propositional constant of $\mathcal{L}$ a set of worlds. Our semantics is bivalent and follows the standard truth tables. Presupposition-bearing sentences are treated as conjunctions:

Definition 3. Satisfaction

- $w \models p$ iff $w \in F(p)$
- $w \models p'p$ iff $w \in F(p')$ and $w \in F(p)$
- $w \models (not\ \phi)$ iff $w \not\models \phi$
- $w \models (\phi\ and\ \psi)$ iff $w \models \phi$ and $w \models \psi$
- $w \models (\phi\ or\ \psi)$ iff $w \models \phi$ or $w \models \psi$
- $w \models (if\ \phi.\ \psi)$ iff $w \not\models \phi$ or $w \models \psi$

We follow [11] in taking a sentence S to be evaluated against a context C (the global context), where C is a set of worlds (intuitively, the set of worlds that are live options in the current conversation). Recall that we want access to the *parsing steps* of a sentence S, which we represent as a sequence of substrings of S. We define this list in three steps. First we define the notion of an *atomic parsing unit*:

Definition 4. Atomic Parsing Unit: The atomic parsing units are:

- The left and right parentheses: (,)
- The connectives: *and, or, not*
- The symbol: *if*
- The dot: .

We will look at a sentence S as a sequence of atomic parsing units. The length of S ($length(S)$) will be the number of atomic parsing units in S. We then define the *Parse* of a sentence S:

Definition 5. Parse: The Parse of a sentence S, written as $P(S)$, is a list $[\alpha_1, \ldots, \alpha_{length(S)}]$, such that each a_i is the ith atomic parsing unit of S.

For instance, for $S = (p'p\ or\ q)$, $P(S)$ will be [(, p'p, or, q,)]. We will use the notation $L[i]$ to refer to the ith element of a list L. We now define the parsing steps of a sentence S:

Definition 6. Parsing Steps: The Parsing Steps of a sentence S, written as $PS(S)$, are a list $[\alpha_1, \ldots, \alpha_n]$ such that:

- $PS(S)[1] = P(S)[1]$
- $PS(S)[i] = PS(S)[i-1] \frown P(S)[i]$, where $1 < i \le length(S)$, and $\frown$ indicates concatenation

Thus, the parsing steps of a sentence S is the list that results by starting from the first atomic parsing unit of S, and successively concatenating to it the next parsing unit. Thus, for $S = (p'p\ or\ q)$, $PS(S) = [(, (p, (p\ or, (p\ or\ q, (p\ or\ q)]$.

At each parsing step of S, we want to be calculating the worlds (in a given context C) where S is true/false for all possible continuations (good finals). We will call the set of worlds where S is already true, the *Includable Context*, while the set of worlds where the sentence is already false the *Excludable Context*.

Definition 7. Includable Context: The Includable Context given a context C and Parsing Step t, written as $IC(C,t)$, is the set $\{w|\ w \in C, and\ for\ all\ good\ finals\ d,\ w \models td\}$.

Definition 8. Excludable Context: The Excludable Context given a context C and Parsing Step t, written as $EC(C,t)$, is the set $\{w|\ w \in C, and\ for\ all\ good\ finals\ d,\ w \not\models td\}$.

The constraint we described earlier depends on comparing the version of the sentence with the presupposition to the version of the sentence where presuppositional sentences have been replaced by their non-presuppositional counterparts. It will be useful to stipulate that every instance of a presuppositional constant in a sentence S is unique.[9] We define a substitution operation, $S_{p'p/p}$, that substitutes an atomic sentence of the form $p'p$ in S with p. Since sentences of the $p'p$ form are unique in S, every substitution has only one instance:[10]

Definition 9. $S_{p'p/p}$**:** Given a sentence S and an atomic proposition $p'p$:

---

[9] This leads to no loss of generality. Every time a sentence contains the same $p'_i p_j$ symbol in two different positions, just rewrite S with one of the $p'_i p_j$ instance changed to $p_k p_j$, where $i \ne k$, with the stipulation that F assigns to both p_i and p_k the same set of worlds.

[10] A reviewer points out that this way of thinking about presuppositions (as *representationally distinct* from assertions) is not necessarily compatible with triggering

- If S has the form p, $S_{p'p/p} = p$.
- If S has the form $p'p$, $S_{p'p/p} = p$.
- If S has the form $(not\ \alpha)$, $S_{p'p/p} = (not\ \alpha_{p'p/p})$.
- If S has the form $(\alpha * \beta)$, where $* \in \{and,\ or\}$, $S_{p'p/p} = (\alpha_{p'p/p} * \beta_{p'p/p})$.
- If S has the form $(if\ \alpha.\ \beta)$, $S_{p'p/p} = (if\ \alpha_{p'p/p}.\ \beta_{p'p/p})$.

Finally, we can state our update algorithm more precisely:

Definition 10. Update: The update of a context C with a sentence S is defined via the following algorithm:

$Update(C, S)$:

   Set $C_0 := C$

   For $i \in [1, length(PS(S))]$:

      For every $p'p$ in $PS(S)[i]$:

      If $\forall p:\ EC(C_{i-1}, PS(S)[i]) \nsubseteq EC(C_{i-1}, PS(S_{p'p/p})[i])$
      or $IC(C_{i-1}, PS(S)[i]) \nsubseteq IC(C_{i-1}, PS(S_{p'p/p})[i])$
      then return $\#$

      Else continue with the loop

      Set $C_i := C_{i-1} - EC(C_{i-1}, PS(S)[i])$

   Return C_i

The algorithm takes a sentence S and an initial context C, and for each parsing step $PS(S)[i]$, it attempts to find the worlds where the sentence is already false, and exclude them. It doing this, it checks whether for all $p'p$ in S up to that point in the parse, for all p:

(9)   All the worlds that are excluded/included by the [+presup] version of S at parsing step $PS(S)[i]$ are also excluded/included by the [-presup] version of S, namely $S_{p'p/p}$, at parsing step $PS(S_{p'p/p})[i]$.

If yes, then the algorithm moves to parsing step $[i + 1]$, taking as the new global context the previous global context, minus all the worlds that were excluded at the previous step. If no, the update fails (it returns an undefinedness value $\#$). Thus, presupposition projection is modeled as update failure; updating here is a pragmatic process, so this failure is to be understood as infelicity.

---

algorithms (e.g., [1,12]), which view presuppositions as entailments of the overall proposition that are selected by the triggering algorithm and marked as presuppositions. Nevertheless, I think one could view the process I'm describing here as what happens *once an entailment has been triggered as a presupposition*, essentially taking triggering for granted and focusing on a representation where what is to be presupposed has been already marked; in effect this follows [11] in separating conceptually the triggering problem from the projection problem.

3.3   Results

We now turn to the derivation of some results regarding the projection behavior of the connectives.

Observation 1: Given a context C **and** $S = p'p$, **Update**$(C, S) \neq \#$ **just in case** $C \models p'$.
For the update process to return $\#$ the constraint on presuppositions built into the updating process must fail. The parsing step where we can start reasoning about Includable and Excludable contexts is $p'p$. Focus on the EC. Since a presupposition is interpreted as conjoined to the assertion, the EC for the [+presup] version is $\{w|\ p' = 0\ or\ p = 0\}$. The EC for the $S_{p'p/p} = p$ is $\{w|\ p = 0\}$. Our constraint checks whether:

(10) $\forall p : \{w|\ p' = 0\ or\ p = 0\} \subseteq \{w|\ p = 0\}$

Suppose this holds. Then it holds for all p, e.g. for $p = \top$ (where $\top$ is a tautology). The constraint then becomes:

(11) $\{w|\ p' = 0\} \subseteq \emptyset$

For (11) to hold, the context needs to contain no p' worlds, i.e. $C \models p'$. Now suppose that $C \models p'$. In this case the EC for the [+presup] version is $\{w|\ p = 0\}$. It is easy to see then that the condition in (10) holds. For the IC, it clearly holds for all p that $\{w|\ p' = 1\ and\ p = 1\} \subseteq \{w|\ p = 1\}$.

Observation 2: Given a context C **and** $S = (not\ p'p)$, **Update**$(C, S) \neq \#$ **just in case** $C \models p'$.
The reasoning is exactly parallel to **Observation 1** only now the set of worlds $\{w|\ p' = 0\ or\ p = 0\}$ is the IC instead of the EC.

**Observation 3:   Given   a   context   C   and $S = (p'p\ and\ q)$,
Update**$(C, S) \neq \#$ **just in case** $C \models p'$.
The first step where we can start reasoning about IC and EC is $(p'p\ and.$ At this point we can calculate an EC: for the [+presup] version it is $\{w|\ p' = 0\ or\ p = 0\}$. The [-presup] version, $S_{p'p/p}$ at the corresponding point is $(p\ and.$ so its EC is $\{w|\ p = 0\}$. The then constraint demands that:

(12) $\forall p : \{w|\ p' = 0\ or\ p = 0\} \subseteq \{w|\ p = 0\}$

At this point, the reasoning follows **Observation 1**.

Note that for both S and $S_{p'p/p}$, at this parsing point the ICs are the empty set (there are no worlds in the context where the sentence is true regardless of continuation yet), so the ICs here are equal.

**Observation   4:   Given   a   context   C   and $S = (q\ and\ p'p)$,
Update**$(C, S) \neq \#$ **just in case** $C \models q \to p'$.
Again, the first step where we can start reasoning about IC and EC is $(q\ and.$ Since q carries no primed bits, the EC and the IC for the [+presup] version

and the [-presup] will be equal, since the [+presup] version is the same as the [-presup] version.

Note that we can calculate an EC at this point: $\{w|\ q = 0\}$. Per our update algorithm, we remove all these worlds from C, and we go on with the update taking $C' = C - \{w|\ q = 0\}$ as the new context.

We then move on to ⟨q and p'p. The only possible good final here is). The IC for the [+presup] version is $\{w|q = 1\ and\ p' = 1\ and\ p = 1\}$. The IC for the [-presup] is $\{w|q = 1\ and\ p = 1\}$. Since clearly for all p: $\{w|q = 1\ and\ p' = 1\ and\ p = 1\} \subseteq \{w|q = 1\ and\ p = 1\}$, no issue arises.

The EC at the same parsing step for [+presup] is $\{w|\ q = 0\ or\ p' = 0\ or\ p = 0\}$. For the [-presup] version, it is $\{w|\ q = 0\ or\ p = 0\}$. But note that at this stage in the update, all the worlds where q is false have been removed, so the context only contains worlds where q is true; therefore, the constraint demands that:

(13) $\forall p: \{w|\ (q = 1\ and\ p' = 0)\ or\ (q = 1\ and\ p = 0)\} \subseteq \{w|\ q = 1\ and\ p = 0\}$

Assume that this holds. Then it holds for the case where $p = \top$. So, we have:

(14) $\forall p: \{w|\ q = 1\ and\ p' = 0\} \subseteq \emptyset$

This holds just in case there are no worlds in C where $q = 1$ and $p' = 0$, or equivalently, iff $C \models q \to p'$. It is easy to check that if $C \models q \to p'$, then the condition in (13) holds.

Observation 5: Given a context C and S = (p'p or q), Update(C, S) ≠ # **just in case C ⊨ ¬q → p'.**

At parsing step ⟨p'p or we cannot yet compute a set of worlds where the entire sentence is false for all possible continuations. But we can compute an IC. For the [+presup] version, $IC = \{w|\ p' = 1\ and\ p = 1\}$. The corresponding set for the [-presup] version is $\{w|\ p = 1\}$. Since clearly $\forall p : \{w|\ p' = 1\ and\ p = 1\} \subseteq \{w|\ p = 1\}$, no issue arises.

We move to ⟨p'p or q. The only good final here is). The IC for the [+presup] version is $\{w|\ (p' = 1\ and\ p = 1)\ or\ q = 1\}$. For the [-presup] version, it is $\{w|\ p = 1\ or\ q = 1\}$. Since clearly $\forall p : \{w|\ (p' = 1\ and\ p = 1)\ or\ q = 1\} \subseteq \{w|\ p = 1\ or\ q = 1\}$, no issue arises.

Things are more interesting when we consider the EC. For the [+presup] version it is $\{w|\ (p' = 0\ or\ p = 0)\ and\ q = 0\} = \{w|(p' = 0\ and\ q = 0)\ or\ (p = 0\ and\ q = 0)\}$. For the [-presup] version, it is $\{w|\ p = 0\ and\ q = 0\}$. The constraint demands that:

(15) $\forall p : \{w|(p' = 0\ and\ q = 0)\ or\ (p = 0\ and\ q = 0)\} \subseteq \{w|\ p = 0\ and\ q = 0\}$

Assume that this holds. Then it needs to hold for the case where $p = \top$. Then the condition becomes:

(16) $\{w|p' = 0 \text{ and } q = 0\} \subseteq \emptyset$

This holds iff there are no worlds in C where $q = 0$ and $p' = 0$, or in other words $C \models q \vee p'$ which is equivalent to $C \models \neg q \rightarrow p'$. Similarly, it is easy to establish that if $C \models \neg q \rightarrow p'$, then the condition in (15) holds.

A similar argument establishes this result for the (q or $p'p$) case.

Observation 6: Given a context C and S = (if p'p. q), Update(C, S) $\neq$ # just in case C $\models$ p'.

At parsing step (if p'p. we can calculate an IC, for [+presup], namely $\{w|p' = 0 \text{ or } p = 0\}$, since in all worlds where the antecedent fails, the entire conditional is automatically true. The corresponding set for [-presup] is $\{w|\ p = 0\}$. The constraint then demands:

(17) $\forall p : \{w|p' = 0 \text{ or } p = 0\} \subseteq \{w|\ p = 0\}$

Again, the reasoning here is the same as in Observation 1.

Observation 7: Given a context C and S = (if (not p'p). q), Update(C, S) $\neq$ # just in case C $\models$ ¬q $\rightarrow$ p'.

At parsing step (if (not p'p, we can calculate an IC: for the [+presup] version, this will be $\{w|\ p' = 1 \text{ and } p = 1\}$; for the [-presup] version, this is $\{w|p = 1\}$. Since subsethood is in the correct direction, no issue arises.

At parsing step (if (not p'p. q, we can calculate both an IC and an EC. The [+presup] IC is $\{w|\ (p' = 1 \text{ and } p = 1) \text{ or } q = 1\}$. The corresponding [-presup] set is $\{w|\ p = 1 \text{ or } q = 1\}$. The direction of subsethood in this case then is the correct one.

Consider now the EC. For [+presup], it is $\{w|\ (p' = 0 \text{ or } p = 0) \text{ and } q = 0\} = \{w|\ (p' = 0 \text{ and } q = 0) \text{ or } (p = 0 \text{ and } q = 0)\}$. For the [-presup] version, it is $\{w|\ p = 0 \text{ and } q = 0\}$. At this point, the reasoning follows the disjunction case in **Observation 5** exactly.

Note that such cases of non-projection where the negation of q entails the presupposition p' exist (essentially 'bathroom conditionals'; see also [11]):

(18)   If the bathroom is not hidden, then there is no bathroom. (no projection of the presupposition in the antecedent that 'there is a bathroom')

Thus, our system derives correct results for the projection behavior of presuppositions embedded under the connectives: presuppositions project from negation, the first conjunct, and the antecedent of conditionals, while at the same time the mechanism allows enough flexibility to avoid projection in cases of 'bathroom disjunctions/conditionals'.

4 Conclusion

We have developed a **bivalent system** for presupposition projection that is **incrementally-oriented**, and captures the basic projection behavior of the connectives in a way that makes **conjunction asymmetric, but disjunction symmetric through a single mechanism**. The system can also capture cases of symmetric conditionals. However, it is limited to the propositional case. A question to pursue in the future is how to generalize these intuitions to handle projection from the scope of quantifiers. Moreover, it's important to apply the system to more complex cases beyond conjunction and disjunction (e.g. antecedent-final conditionals (see [6])), and experimentally test the system's predictions in these cases, as this will afford a clearer view of the system's empirical 'bite'.

References

1. Abrusán, M.: Predicting the presuppositions of soft triggers. Linguist. Philos. **34**(6), 491–535 (2011)
2. George, B.: Presupposition repairs: a static, trivalent approach to predicting projection. UCLA MA thesis (2008)
3. Hausser, R.: Presuppositions in montague grammar. Theor. Linguist. (3), 245–280 (1976)
4. Kalomoiros, A., Schwarz, F.: Presupposition projection from disjunction is symmetric. Proc. Linguist. Soc. Am. **6**(1), 556–571 (2021)
5. Karttunen, L.: Presuppositions of compound sentences. Linguist. Inquiry **4**(2), 169–193 (1973)
6. Mandelkern, M., Romoli, J.: Parsing and presuppositions in the calculation of local contexts. Semant. Pragmat. **10**, 7 (2017)
7. Mandelkern, M., Zehr, J., Romoli, J., Schwarz, F.: We've discovered that projection across conjunction is asymmetric (and it is!). Linguist. Philos. **43**(5), 473–514 (2020)
8. Rothschild, D.: Presupposition projection and logical equivalence. Philos. Perspect. **22**, 473–497 (2008)
9. Schlenker, P.: Anti-dynamics: presupposition projection without dynamic semantics. J. Logic Lang. Inform. **16**, 325–356 (2007)
10. Schlenker, P.: Be articulate: a pragmatic theory of presupposition projection. Theor. Linguist. 157–212 (2008)
11. Schlenker, P.: Local contexts. Semant. Pragmat. **2**, 3–1 (2009)
12. Schlenker, P.: Triggering presuppositions. Glossa J. General Linguist. **6**(1) (2021)
13. Stalnaker, R.: Pragmatic presuppositions. In: Munitz, M.K., Unger, P.K. (eds.) Semantics and Philosophy, pp. 197–213. New York University Press, New York (1974)
14. Stalnaker, R.: Assertion. Syntax and Semantics, vol. 9, pp. 315–332. New York Academic Press, New York (1978)
15. Terence Langendoen, D., Savin, H.: The projection problem for presuppositions. In: Fillmore, C.J., Terence Langendoen, D. (eds.) Studies in Linguistic Semantics, pp. 54–60. Irvington (1971)

A Problem for Downward Closure in the Semantics of Counterfactuals

Dean McHugh[(✉)] [iD]

Department of Philosophy and Institute for Logic,
Language and Computation (ILLC), University of Amsterdam,
Amsterdam, The Netherlands
d.m.mchugh@uva.nl

Abstract. Ciardelli et al. [2018b] adopt the framework of inquisitive semantics to provide a novel semantics for counterfactuals. They argue in favour of adopting inquisitive semantics based on experimental evidence that De Morgan's law, which fails in inquisitive semantics, is invalid in counterfactual antecedents. We show that a unique feature of inquisitive semantics—the fact that its meanings are downward closed—leads to difficulties for Ciardelli et al.'s semantic account of their data. The scenarios we consider suggest either adopting a semantic framework other than inquisitive semantics, or developing a non-semantic explanation of the phenomena Ciardelli et al. [2018b] seek to explain.

1 Introduction

Inquisitive semantics is a semantic framework that provides a uniform treatment of declarative and interrogative utterances. (For a comprehensive introduction to inquisitive semantics, see Ciardelli et al. 2018a.) In this paper we consider a recent application of inquisitive semantics to conditionals, proposed by Ciardelli [2016] and Ciardelli et al. [2018b].

According to inquisitive semantics, the meaning of a term is given by a set of propositions, which is constructed around a primitive notion of *resolution conditions*. Intuitively, the resolution conditions of an utterance are the set of propositions that resolve the issue it raises.[1]

1.1 Downward Closure

As Ciardelli et al. (2018a, §2.3) point out, one formal consequence of framing meanings in terms of resolution conditions is that meanings are *downward closed*:

Thanks to Ivano Ciardelli, Alexandre Cremers, Morwenna Hoeks, Hana Möller Kalpak, Jonathan Pesetsky, Floris Roelofsen, Katrin Schulz and Zhuoye Zhao for very helpful comments. Thanks also to the participants of the ILLC inquisitive semantics seminar.
[1] Other recent discussions of inquisitive semantics of conditionals include Romoli et al. [2022] and Güngör [2022].

A. Pavlova et al. (Eds.): ESSLLI 2019/2020/2021, LNCS 14354, pp. 177–186, 2024.
https://doi.org/10.1007/978-3-031-50628-4_11

for any expression A, if a proposition p is an element of $[\![A]\!]$ (the meaning inquisitive semantics assigns to A), then any more informative proposition $p' \subseteq p$ is also an element of $[\![A]\!]$. After all, if p resolves the issue raised by A, every more informative proposition must too.

The property of downward closure distinguishes inquisitive semantics from other frameworks with a similar empirical range as inquisitive semantics, such as alternative semantics (e.g. Hamblin 1973; Kratzer and Shimoyama 2002) and truthmaker semantics (Briggs 2012; Fine 2012, 2014). Downward closure restricts the range of meanings that inquisitive semantics admits. Compare, for instance, a logical form (LF) given by an atomic sentence B with one of the form $B \vee (A \wedge B)$. In alternative semantics and truthmaker semantics, where meanings are not downward closed, these sentences receive a different interpretation. For, let $|S|$ be the the set of worlds where an LF S is true. Then alternative semantics interprets B as $\{|B|\}$, but $B \vee (A \wedge B)$ as $\{|B|, |A \wedge B|\}$. While these interpretations are distinct, their downward closures are identical. Thus, without further enrichment, these sentences receive the same denotation according to inquisitive semantics.

The comparison between LFs of the form B and $B \vee (A \wedge B)$ will serve as a central example in what follows. For now we continue our introduction with inquisitive semantics for conditionals.

Inquisitive semantics has recently been applied to conditionals through the work of Ivano Ciardelli and collaborators. Ciardelli [2016] and Ciardelli et al. [2018b] assume alongside others (Alonso-Ovalle 2006, 2009; Fine 2012; Santorio 2018) that the hypothetical scenarios raised by a counterfactual antecedent are a matter of semantics. However, unlike Alonso-Ovalle's approach which relies on alternative semantics, since inquisitive meanings are downward closed—and hence typically contain infinitely many elements—inquisitive semantics needs an additional operator to extract the alternatives raised by a counterfactual antecedent, which then serve as input in the process of making counterfactual assumptions. Ciardelli [2016] and Ciardelli et al. [2018b] achieve this by taking only the weakest elements (with respect to entailment) of the meaning inquisitive semantics assigns to the antecedent and consequent. These weakest elements are called its *alternatives*.

(1) $\mathsf{alt}(A) = \{p \subseteq W \mid p \in [\![A]\!] \text{ and for no } q \supsetneq p \text{ is } q \in [\![A]\!]\}$

Ciardelli [2016]'s semantics for conditionals also involves a conditional connective $\Rightarrow$ holding between propositions, to be defined in terms of one's favourite semantics of conditionals, such as similarity among worlds (Lewis 1973; Stalnaker 1968) or causal models (Briggs 2012; Ciardelli et al. 2018b; Santorio 2019). Writing $>$ for the conditional construction, the clause is as follows.

(2)   A counterfactual $A > C$ is supported at a state s just in case for every $p \in \mathsf{alt}(A)$ there is a $q \in \mathsf{alt}(C)$ such that $s \subseteq p \Rightarrow q$ (Ciardelli 2016)

As Ciardelli explains, "The intuition is that in order to support [a conditional], a state needs to contain information that implies, for every alternative for the antecedent, that if that alternative were to obtain, then some corresponding alternative for the consequent would obtain" (2016, 741).

In the following section we consider a recent application of inquisitive semantics to counterfactuals. This analysis will serve as the focus of our discussion to come.

2   De Morgan's Law in Counterfactual Antecedents

Ciardelli et al. [2018b] present experimental evidence against De Morgan's law in counterfactual antecedents. De Morgan's law is the equivalence of $\neg(A \wedge B)$ and $\neg A \vee \neg B$. Many semantic frameworks that have been applied to conditionals validate De Morgan's law, such as possible-worlds semantics (Lewis 1973; Stalnaker 1968) and truthmaker semantics (Briggs 2012; Fine 2012). In contrast, inquisitive semantics—alongside alternative semantics (Alonso-Ovalle 2006) and intuitionistic truthmaker semantics (Fine 2014)—does not validate De Morgan's law.

The experimental data in Ciardelli et al. [2018b] concern the scenario below featuring two switches, A and B, connected to a light. As the wiring diagram in Fig. 1 shows, the light is on just in case both switches are in the same position (i.e. both up or both down). Currently, both switches are up, so the light is on.

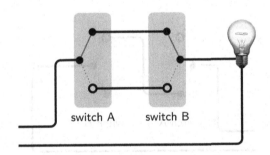

switch A   switch B

Fig. 1. Scenario used in Ciardelli et al. [2018b]'s experiment.

(3)   a.   If switch A or switch B was down, the light would be off.
       b.   If switch A and switch B were not both up, the light would be off.

Comparing 1425 responses, Ciardelli et al. [2018b] found a significant difference between the two sentences in (3). (3-a) was judged true by a wide majority (True $\approx$ 70%), whereas (3-b) was generally judged false or indeterminate (True $\approx$ 22%).

Ciardelli et al. [2018b] choose to offer a *semantic* explanation for the difference in acceptability between (3-a) and (3-b). In their framework, it is the difference in semantic value between $[\![\neg(A \wedge B)]\!]$ and $[\![\neg A \vee \neg B]\!]$, together with their method of adopting hypothetical assumptions, which leads to (3-a) and

(3-b) raising different counterfactual scenarios. Specifically, in Ciardelli et al.'s framework, evaluating (3-b) but not (3-a) requires considering the scenario where both switches are down.

In the following section we turn to an addition inquisitive semantics requires to make the correct predictions regarding counterfactuals. In Sect. 4 we will see that this addition raises a problem for the account in (Ciardelli et al. 2018b).

3   Exclusification

Earlier we saw how downward closure makes B equivalent to $B \vee (A \wedge B)$. In this section we consider a variant of the scenario in Fig. 1 which shows that the equivalence of B and $B \vee (A \wedge B)$ is not valid in counterfactual antecedents. Though we will see in Sect. 3.2 that there is a natural proposal available to inquisitive semantics to resolve the problem.

3.1   A Scenario with New Wiring

Consider the following variant of the scenario in Fig. 1. As the wiring in Fig. 2 depicts, the light is on just in case switch A is down and B is up. Suppose that currently, both switches are down, so the light is off, and consider (4).

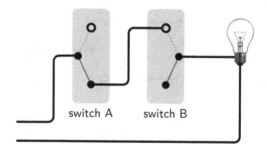

Fig. 2. The light is on just in case A is down and B is up.

(4)   a.   If switch B was up, the light would be on. $B >$ On
      b.   If switch B was up, or switches A and B were up, the light would be on. $B \vee (A \wedge B) >$ On

Intuitively, when we interpret (4-a) we keep the position of switch A fixed while imagining switch B up, in which case the light is on. But when we consider both switches being up we find that the light is off. Thus in the scenario raised by (4-a)'s antecedent, the light is on, making the conditional (4-a) as a whole true. But in one scenario raised by (4-b)'s antecedent the light is off, making (4-b) false.

Since B is equivalent to $B \vee (A \wedge B)$ according to inquisitive semantics, without further refinement inquisitive semantics predicts both (4-a) and (4-b) to be true. However, there is an attractive story available to inquisitive semantics that avoids the equivalence of (4-a) and (4-b), which we turn to now.

3.2   Embedded Exclusivity Operators

A promising proposal is that the disjunction in $B \vee (A \wedge B)$ is interpreted *exclusively*. This would make *B is up or A and B are up* no longer equivalent to *B is up*, but instead to something paraphrasable as, *Only B is up, or A and B are up*, which is arguably further paraphrasable as *B is up and A is not up, or A and B are up*.

A further argument inquisitive semantics can make in favour of an exclusive interpretation of the disjunction in (4-b) comes from Hurford's constraint (Hurford 1974), illustrated in (5).

(5)   # If John were from France or Paris, he would speak French.

Many authors explain the infelicity of (5) in terms of *redundancy* (Ciardelli et al. 2017; Katzir and Singh 2013; Meyer 2013, 2014; Simons 2001). Since every Parisian is French, the disjunct *or Paris* in (5) is redundant, being already included in the assumption of John being French. By the same reasoning, one would expect the disjunction $B \vee (A \wedge B)$ in (4-b) to be infelicitous because the disjunct $A \wedge B$, which entails B, is redundant.

However, unlike (5), clearly (4-b)'s antecedent *If switch B was up, or switches A and B were up* is acceptable. We can explain this by pointing out that, while $B \vee (A \wedge B)$ contains a redundant disjunct, its exclusive interpretation $(B \wedge \neg A) \vee (A \wedge B)$ does not. This is analogous to the explanation of good Hurford disjunctions, such as (6), in terms of a local embedded exhaustivity operator (Chierchia 2004).

(6)   Nancy ate EXH(some) or all of the chocolate.

Roelofsen and van Gool [2010] define an exhaustivity operator EXH that is suitable for inquisitive semantics, which Aloni and Ciardelli [2011] have already put to use in the interpretation of imperatives. Applying this operator to $B \vee (A \wedge B)$ produces $(B \wedge \neg A) \vee (A \wedge B)$, which is intuitively the correct result. Under any adequate semantics for counterfactuals, this interpretation also makes (4-b) false, as desired.

Thus, with sufficient enrichment inquisitive semantics for counterfactuals can provide the correct judgements in the scenario of Fig. 2. In so doing, the analysis renders $B \vee (A \wedge B)$ as $(B \wedge \neg A) \vee (A \wedge B)$. It turns out the difference between $B \vee (A \wedge B)$ and $(B \wedge \neg A) \vee (A \wedge B)$, though subtle, gives rise to a difference in the truth value of conditionals in certain environments. This is because $|B \wedge \neg A|$ is a stronger proposition than $|B|$. In terms of conditional antecedents, we might loosely describe the difference by saying that imagining switch B up does not say anything about switch A, whereas imagining $B \wedge \neg A$ involves considering switch A not up.

In what follows we design a situation making the difference between $B \vee (A \wedge B)$ and $(B \wedge \neg A) \vee (A \wedge B)$ explicit, even when switch A is already not up.

4   When Exclusification is Too Strong

Consider the scenario below (Fig. 3) where switch A can take three positions: up, in the middle or down. We might imagine that switch A is a caretaker's 'master switch', which can fix the light on by being up, fix the light off by being down, or let a user decide by being in the middle. Switch B is then the user's switch, which as before can only be up or down.[2] Currently, switch A is in the middle and switch B is down, so the light is off.

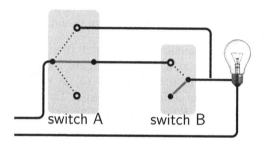

Fig. 3. The light is on just in case A is up, or A is in the middle and B is up.

With respect to the scenario of Fig. 3, consider the counterfactuals in (7).

(7) a.   If switch B was up, the light would be on. B
     b.   If switch B was up, or switches A and B were up, the light would be on. $B \vee (A \wedge B)$
     c.   If switch B was up and switch A was not up, or switches A and B were up, the light would be on. $(B \wedge \neg A) \vee (A \wedge B)$

If we are asked to imagine switch B up, and asked nothing about switch A, it seems intuitively we keep the position of switch A fixed. This is different from being asked to imagine switch A not up, as in (7-c), even though switch A is already not up. Loosely, we can say that (7-c)'s antecedent raises the possibility of switch A being down, and hence the light being off.

In the previous paragraph we phrased the interpretation of (7-b) and (7-c) purely in terms of intuition. There is nonetheless experimental evidence in its favour. In a similar scenario to those considered here, Schulz [2018] presents experimental evidence that in counterfactual antecedents, mentioning something

---

[2] Thanks to Alexandre Cremers for coming up with this description of the scenario.

that is already true does not make the same contribution as not mentioning it at all.

In the second scenario we considered (Fig. 2), where switch A can only take two positions, inquisitive semantics can avoid the problems posed by downward closure by appealing to the exclusification story above. But here this same story predicts the equivalence of (7-b) and (7-c). In contrast, a semantic framework in which meanings are not downward closed, such as alternative semantics (Alonso-Ovalle 2006) and truthmaker semantics (Fine 2014, 2017), can reproduce the correct judgements here since they do not appeal to exclusification in the first place. Thus, for example, alternative semantics can distinguish between the antecedents of (4-a) and (4-b) in the first scenario, and of (7-b) and (7-c) in the second, all under their usual interpretation.

One avenue available to inquisitive semantics is to propose that overt negation has additional effects in conditional antecedents beyond its semantic contribution. Inquisitive semantics could still interpret $\textsc{exh}B \lor \textsc{exh}(A \land B)$ as $(B \land \neg A) \lor (A \land B)$, but propose that the operator $\textsc{exh}$ does not have the same effect as an overt negation. Of course, inquisitive semantics already has a semantic entry for negation, so this additional effect would have to be non-semantic.

However, this proposal on behalf of inquisitive semantics undermines the semantic explanation of violations of De Morgan's law in counterfactual antecedents that Ciardelli et al. [2018b] provide. To preserve the explanatory value of inquisitive semantics in such cases, one would have to ensure that the proposed additional effects of overt negation do not explain what Ciardelli et al. [2018b] wish to explain in purely semantic terms. This is a challenging task given the structural similarities between the scenario Ciardelli et al. [2018b] originally tested (Fig. 1) and the scenario just considered (Fig. 3), both of which involve the effects of negation in raising additional counterfactual scenarios.

5 Counterfactual Exhaustification

In the previous section we saw that inquisitive semantics of conditionals faces a dilemma: not exhaustifying (7-b)'s antecedent, downward closure wrongly predicts the equivalence of (7-a) and (7-b). But exhaustifying (7-b)'s antecedent wrongly predicts the equivalence of (7-b) and (7-c). The problem is that, intuitively, these three sentences all seem to receive a distinct interpretation. One way to solve this problem on behalf of inquisitive semantics is to rethink the notion of exhaustification, an avenue we explore in this section.

The potential rescue is to make the $\textsc{exh}$ operator sensitive to counterfactual alternatives.[3] Loosely, the idea is to exhaustify with respect to the *changes* one makes when moving from the actual world to the hypothetical scenarios raised by a conditional antecedent, rather than with respect to the positions of the switches.

---

[3] I am grateful to Floris Roelofsen for suggesting this proposal.

It is generally agreed that the contribution of exhaustification is determined with respect to a set of alternatives. If these alternatives are given by a question under discussion, then we can embed this proposal into standard accounts of exhaustifiation by making EXH sensitive to a question under discussion that asks explicitly about counterfactual alternatives. Up to now we have exhaustified with respect to the positions of the switches, assuming a question under discussion such as *What are the positions of switches A and B?*. In contrast, one could propose that the question under discussion is in fact something like $Q = What$ *happened to the switches in the hypothetical scenarios generated by the given counterfactual antecedent?*.

We can formalise the idea of 'nothing happening' in terms of the counterfactual selection function f, defined in terms of one's favourite semantics of counterfactuals. Here is how the proposal would work on the first disjunct of (4-b), repeated as (8-a).

(8) a. If switch B was up or switches A and B were up, the light would be on.
     b. $\text{EXH}_Q(\text{switch B is up})$
     c. Paraphrase: Switch B is up, and nothing happened to switch A
     d. $\forall w' \in f(\underline{\text{switch B is up}}, w)$: switch B is up in w', and w' agrees with w on the position of switch A.

Note that, for reasons of compositionality, the interpretation of EXH—appearing at the level of the counterfactual antecedent—cannot depend directly on the mechanism of making counterfactual assumptions, which only enters the computation at the level of the entire conditional. To see this, consider the following LF for (4-b) according to the restrictor analysis of conditionals (or, the Lewis/Kratzer/Heim approach, as dubbed by Partee [1991]).

(9) [Modal [if [EXH(B is up) or EXH(A and B are up)]]]] [the light is on]

EXH appears below *if* and the modal. Thus the introduction of the selection function f in the calculation of EXH_Q cannot come from the presence of these constituents. However, we could say that EXH features λf in its semantic entry, although this seems highly costly, requiring the introduction of a special 'counterfactual exhaustification operator' tailor-made for counterfactual antecedents. Alternatively, we could say that f is indicated by the presence of counterfactual morphology, in particular the X-marking on the antecedent.

The intriguing idea of counterfactual exhaustification deserves to be considered in full detail, for which there is not space here. It would certainly require a much more sophisticated kind of exhaustification, one that does not interfere with the unique subtleties of the selection function, such as keeping some aspects of the actual world fixed while allowing others to vary. Rewriting the notion of exhaustification to account for the scenarios we have considered here would be a radical move. We leave it to future work to determine whether such a move is indeed warranted by the data we have considered.

6   Conclusion

In this paper we presented a scenario where inquisitive semantics for conditionals appears to make the wrong predictions. This scenario does not pose a problem for semantic frameworks with a more fine-grained notion of semantic content, such as alternative semantics and truthmaker semantics. There is, however, an argument against adopting a more fine-grained perspective on semantic content, due to Ciardelli and Roelofsen (2017, Sect. 5.1), who argue that alternative semantics has difficulty implementing an account of Hurford's constraint based on redundancy (proposed, e.g. by Katzir and Singh 2013; Meyer 2013, 2014; Simons 2001). This is an interesting tension, which raises the question whether there is some 'Goldlilocks' notion of semantic content yet to be found; one fine enough to account for our interpretation of conditional antecedents, but not too fine that it runs into problems predicting redundancies.

References

Aloni, M., Ciardelli, I.: A semantics for imperatives. Unpublished manuscript (2011). https://pdfs.semanticscholar.org/9cdd/fb56130329b403ff5240dbeb5ef3e3f2ccaa.pdf

Alonso-Ovalle, L.: Disjunction in alternative semantics. Ph.D. thesis, University of Massachusetts Amherst (2006). http://people.linguistics.mcgill.ca/luis.alonso-ovalle/papers/alonso-ovalle-diss.pdf

Alonso-Ovalle, L.: Counterfactuals, correlatives, and disjunction. Linguist. Philos. **32**(2), 207–244 (2009). https://doi.org/10.1007/s10988-009-9059-0

Briggs, R.: Interventionist counterfactuals. Philos. Stud. **160**(1), 139–166 (2012). https://doi.org/10.1007/s11098-012-9908-5

Chierchia, G.: Scalar implicatures, polarity phenomena and the syntax/pragmatics interface. In: Structures and Beyond, pp. 39–103. Oxford University Press, Oxford (2004)

Ciardelli, I.: Lifting conditionals to inquisitive semantics. Semant. Linguist. Theory **26**, 732–752 (2016). https://doi.org/10.3765/salt.v26i0.3811

Ciardelli, I., Roelofsen, F.: Hurford's constraint, the semantics of disjunction, and the nature of alternatives. Nat. Lang. Semant. **25**(3), 199–222 (2017). https://doi.org/10.1007/s11050-017-9134-y

Ciardelli, I., Roelofsen, F., Theiler, N.: Composing alternatives. Linguist. Philos. **40**(1), 1–36 (2017). https://doi.org/10.1007/s10988-016-9195-2

Ciardelli, I., Groenendijk, J., Roelofsen, F.: Inquisitive Semantics. Oxford University Press, Oxford (2018a)

Ciardelli, I., Zhang, L., Champollion, L.: Two switches in the theory of counterfactuals. Linguist. Philos. (2018). https://doi.org/10.1007/s10988-018-9232-4

Fine, K.: Counterfactuals without possible worlds. J. Philos. **109**(3), 221–246 (2012). https://doi.org/10.5840/jphil201210938

Fine, K.: Truth-maker semantics for intuitionistic logic. J. Philos. Log. **43**(2), 549–577 (2014). https://doi.org/10.1007/s10992-013-9281-7

Fine, K.: Truthmaker semantics. In: A Companion to the Philosophy of Language, chapter 22, pp. 556–577. Wiley, Hoboken (2017). https://doi.org/10.1002/9781118972090.ch22

Güngör, H.: Counterfactuals, hyperintensionality and hurford disjunctions. Linguist. Philos. 1–27 (2022). https://doi.org/10.1007/s10988-022-09360-3

Hamblin, C.L.: Questions in Montague English. In: Montague Grammar, pp. 247–259. Elsevier, Amsterdam (1973). https://doi.org/10.1016/B978-0-12-545850-4.50014-5

Hurford, J.R.: Exclusive or inclusive disjunction. Found. Lang. 11, 409–411 (1974)

Katzir, R., Singh, R.: Hurford disjunctions: embedded exhaustification and structural economy. Proc. Sinn und Bedeutung 18, 201–216 (2013). https://semanticsarchive.net/sub2013/SeparateArticles/Katzir&Singh.pdf

Kratzer, A., Shimoyama, J.: Indeterminate pronouns: the view from Japanese. In: Otsu, Y. (ed.) The Proceedings of the Third Tokyo Conference on Psycholinguistics, pp. 1–25 (2002). https://people.umass.edu/partee/RGGU_2004/Indeterminate%20Pronouns.pdf

Lewis, D.: Counterfactuals. Wiley, Hoboken (1973)

Meyer, M.-C.: Ignorance and grammar. Ph.D. thesis, MIT (2013)

Meyer, M.-C.: Deriving Hurford's constraint. Semant. Linguist. Theory 24, 577–596 (2014)

Partee, B.: Topic, focus and quantification. Semant. Linguist. Theory 1, 159–188 (1991). https://doi.org/10.3765/salt.v1i0.2918

Roelofsen, F., van Gool, S.: Disjunctive questions, intonation, and highlighting. In: Aloni, M., Bastiaanse, H., de Jager, T., Schulz, K. (eds.) Logic, Language and Meaning. LNCS (LNAI), vol. 6042, pp. 384–394. Springer, Heidelberg (2010). https://doi.org/10.1007/978-3-642-14287-1_39

Romoli, J., Santorio, P., Wittenberg, E.: Alternatives in counterfactuals: what is right and what is not. J. Semant. 39(2), 213–260 (2022). https://doi.org/10.1093/jos/ffab023

Santorio, P.: Alternatives and truthmakers in conditional semantics. J. Philos. 115(10), 513–549 (2018). https://doi.org/10.5840/jphil20181151030

Santorio, P.: Interventions in premise semantics. Philosophers' Imprint (2019). http://hdl.handle.net/2027/spo.3521354.0019.001

Schulz, K.: The similarity approach strikes back: negation in counterfactuals. In: Sauerland, U., Solt, S. (eds.) Proceedings of Sinn und Bedeutung 22, volume 2 of ZASPiL, vol. 61, pp. 343–360. Leibniz-Centre General Linguistics, Berlin (2018). https://semanticsarchive.net/sub2018/Schulz.pdf

Simons, M.: Disjunction and alternativeness. Linguist. Philos. 24(5), 597–619 (2001). https://doi.org/10.1023/A:1017597811833

Stalnaker, R.: A theory of conditionals. In: Harper, W.L., Stalnaker, R., Pearce, G. (eds.) Ifs, pp. 41–55. Springer, Heidelberg (1968). https://doi.org/10.1007/978-94-009-9117-0_2

Lambek Calculus with Optional Divisions

Tikhon Pshenitsyn$^{(\boxtimes)}$ (iD)

Department of Mathematical Logic and Theory of Algorithms,
Faculty of Mathematics and Mechanics, Lomonosov Moscow State University,
GSP-1, Leninskie Gory, Moscow 119991, Russian Federation
ptihon@yandex.ru

Abstract. In this paper, we introduce an extension of the Lambek calculus by optional divisions (L_{opt}). Namely, the right optional division $A \angle B$ is defined as $A \wedge (A/B)$, and the left one $B \searrow A$ is defined as $A \wedge (B \backslash A)$. A possible linguistic motivation to consider the new operations is describing verbs with optional arguments, e.g. *reads* in *Tim reads the book*. L_{opt} is a fragment of the multiplicative-additive Lambek calculus, so it would be interesting to compare the two calculi. The main part of the paper is devoted to the following grammar result: finite intersections of context-free languages can be generated by grammars over the calculus L_{opt}. The proof involves introducing a useful normal form for Lambek grammars, namely, the notion of an *interpretable grammar*.

1 Introduction

The Lambek calculus L introduced by Joachim Lambek in [4] is a logical and algebraic formalism designed to model syntax of natural languages. This calculus underlies a class of formal grammars called *Lambek categorial grammars*. Categorial grammars in general are designed as follows: a grammar is a finite correspondence between items of a lexicon (e.g. words of a natural language) and some abstract categories; besides, there is a general mechanism (a "universal grammar") deciding if a given sequence of categories is correct or not. Then, a categorial grammar accepts a string composed of items of the lexicon if and only if each item in the string can be replaced by a corresponding category in such a way that the resulting string of categories is correct from the point of view of the general mechanism. In the case of Lambek categorial grammars, L plays the role of the general mechanism, and categories are those of L (constructed using two divisions \, / and product ·, see Sect. 2). An overview of the Lambek calculus and of its grammars can be found in [6].

It turns out, however, that some features of natural languages cannot be described using the Lambek calculus. This is one of the reasons various extensions and modifications of L have been proposed. For example, in [7], the *displacement calculus* generalizing L is introduced in order to describe language

The study was supported by the Theoretical Physics and Mathematics Advancement Foundation "BASIS"; the Interdisciplinary Scientific and Educational School of Moscow University "Brain, Cognitive Systems, Artificial Intelligence".

phenomena invloving some kind of discontinuity, e.g. discontinuous idioms, or medial extraction etc. Another example is adding modalities to the Lambek calculus, which is done in [5]. On the other hand, there are modifications of the Lambek calculus arising due to non-linguistic purposes. The most important example for us in this study is the *multiplicative-additive Lambek calculus* MALC introduced in [3]: in this calculus, conjunction $\wedge$ and disjunction $\vee$ connectives are added to the Lambek calculus. We draw the reader's attention to the following result concerning grammars based on MALC (from [3]):

Theorem 1. *Any finite intersection of context-free languages without the empty word can be generated by a categorial grammar over MALC such that a correspondence between lexicon and categories is a partial function, i.e. at most one category corresponds to each item of the lexicon.*

This theorem holds even for the Lambek calculus with conjunction $L_\wedge$ (in fact, disjunction is not needed at all in the proof).

Our objective is to consider a fragment of $L_\wedge$, namely, the Lambek calculus enriched with optional divisions denoted as L_{opt}. The latter are defined through conjunction and divisions as follows: $A \angle B := A \wedge (A/B)$, $B \diagdown A := A \wedge (B \backslash A)$. Informally, $A \angle B$ waits for a structure of category B from the right side in order to become a structure of category A; however, it can stop waiting anytime and just become a structure of category A. Linguistically, new operations seemingly suit for describing verbs with optional arguments, e.g. the word *reads* in the sentences *Tim reads* and *Tim reads the book*; a discussion of the topic is in Sect. 3.

The Lambek calculus with optional divisions is a fragment of MALC hence the former is not stronger than the latter. However, is the former weaker than the latter or not? We prove that L_{opt} enjoys several properties at the level of categorial grammars, which show that it is quite powerful. Namely, we prove two theorems similar to Theorem 1.

In Sect. 2, we give all basic definitions regarding the Lambek calculus, MALC, and context-free grammars. In Sect. 3, we give some linguistic motivation for considering optional disivions and formally introduce them; there we also formulate the main theorems (note that they are not related to the linguistic part). In Sect. 4, we prove the theorems, and along the way introduce some important notions, namely, that of an *interpretable Lambek grammar* (it might be useful for other technical reasonings) and that of a *telescopic conjunction*, which is defined trough optional divisions and product. In Sect. 5, we conclude.

2 Preliminaries

In this section, we define the Lambek calculus and some its extensions of interest, introduce formal definitions of a categorial grammar and of a language generated by the one, and also recall the definition of context-free grammars.

2.1   Lambek Calculus and Its Extensions

Firstly, let us define *categories* of the Lambek calculus. We fix a set $Pr = \{p_1, p_2, \dots\}$ of primitive categories. The set Cat of all categories is defined as follows: $Cat := Pr \mid Cat\backslash Cat \mid Cat \cdot Cat \mid Cat/Cat$. E.g. $(p_1\backslash p_2)/p_3$ is a category of the Lambek calculus.

In this paper small letters $p, q, \dots$ and strings composed of them (e.g. np, cp) range over primitive categories. Capital letters $A, B, \dots$ usually range over categories. Capital Greek letters range over finite (possibly empty) sequences of categories. Sequents are of the form $\Gamma \to A$, where Γ is nonempty; Γ is called an antecedent, and A is called a succedent.

In this work we focus on the Lambek calculus in the Gentzen style. There is only one axiom, which is $A \to A$, and rules are the following:

$$\frac{\Pi \to A \quad \Gamma, B, \Delta \to C}{\Gamma, \Pi, A\backslash B, \Delta \to C} \ (\backslash \to) \qquad \frac{A, \Pi \to B}{\Pi \to A\backslash B} \ (\to \backslash) \qquad \frac{\Gamma, A, B, \Delta \to C}{\Gamma, A \cdot B, \Delta \to C} \ (\cdot \to)$$

$$\frac{\Pi \to A \quad \Gamma, B, \Delta \to C}{\Gamma, B/A, \Pi, \Delta \to C} \ (/ \to) \qquad \frac{\Pi, A \to B}{\Pi \to B/A} \ (\to /) \qquad \frac{\Gamma \to A \quad \Delta \to B}{\Gamma, \Delta \to A \cdot B} \ (\to \cdot)$$

It can be proven that the following cut rule is admissible in L:

$$\frac{\Pi \to A \quad \Gamma, A, \Delta \to C}{\Gamma, \Pi, \Delta \to C} \ (cut)$$

A sequent $T_1, \dots, T_n \to T$ is derivable in the Lambek calculus if it can be obtained from axioms using rules. We denote derivability of a sequent in a calculus K as follows: $K \vdash T_1, \dots, T_n \to T$.

The multiplicative-additive Lambek calculus MALC is obtained from L by adding two new binary connectives $\wedge$ and $\vee$ and the following rules for them:

$$\frac{\Gamma, A_i, \Delta \to C}{\Gamma, A_1 \wedge A_2, \Delta \to C} \ (\wedge_i \to), \ i = 1, 2 \qquad \frac{\Pi \to A_1 \quad \Pi \to A_2}{\Pi \to A_1 \wedge A_2} \ (\to \wedge)$$

$$\frac{\Pi \to A_i}{\Pi \to A_1 \vee A_2} \ (\to \vee_i), \ i = 1, 2 \qquad \frac{\Gamma, A_1, \Delta \to C \quad \Gamma, A_2, \Delta \to C}{\Gamma, A_1 \vee A_2, \Delta \to C} \ (\vee \to)$$

Obviously, the definition of categories needs to be extended by encountering new connectives. Note that disjunction will not play a substantial role in this paper while conjunction is important for our investigations. An extension of the Lambek calculus by only $\wedge$ is denoted as $L_\wedge$, and the set of its categories is denoted by $Cat(\wedge)$.

Finally, we would like to define *the Lambek calculus with the unit* L_1^*. For this calculus, we change the definition of a sequent and allow antecedents to be empty. Then we add a constant $\mathbf{1}$ along with the following axiom and rule:

$$\to \mathbf{1}$$

$$\frac{\Gamma, \Delta \to A}{\Gamma, \mathbf{1}, \Delta \to A} \ (\mathbf{1} \to)$$

Notice that one can obtain new calculi by taking different sets of connectives, e.g. $\backslash, \cdot, /, \vee, \mathbf{1}$ or $/, \wedge$.

2.2   Categorial Grammars

In order to describe syntax of a natural language using a categorial grammar one assigns several categories to each English word; besides, a distinguished category T has to be chosen. Then a sequence of English words $w_1 \ldots w_n$ is said to be grammatically correct if one can choose a corresponding category T_i for each w_i such that the sequent $T_1, \ldots, T_n \to T$ is derivable in the Lambek calculus (or in some other considered calculus). This idea is formalized by the notion of categorial grammar:

Definition 1. A K-grammar is a triple $\langle \Sigma, T, \triangleright \rangle$, where Σ is a finite set (alphabet), T is some distinguished category from the set of categories of the calculus K, and $\triangleright$ is a finite binary relation between elements of Σ and types of K.

Given a grammar G, we denote the set of categories T, for which there exists $a \in \Sigma$ such that $a \triangleright T$ by $Cat(G)$. It follows from the definition that $Cat(G)$ is finite.

Definition 2. The language $L(G)$ generated by a K-grammar $G = \langle \Sigma, T, \triangleright \rangle$ consists of strings $a_1 \ldots a_n$ ($n > 0$), for which there exist types $T_1, \ldots, T_n$ such thatt $\forall i = 1, \ldots, n$ $a_i \triangleright T_i$ and $K \vdash T_1, \ldots, T_n \to T$.

If $K = L$, then an L-grammar is called *a Lambek grammar*.

2.3   Context-Free Grammars

One of fundamental notions in the theory of formal grammars is context-free grammar. Despite known insufficiency of this formalism in describing natural languages, it is a basis for a number of other formal systems dealing with languages. In the next section we will study a relation between context-free languages and languages recognized by grammars of L_{opt}, so here we start with required formal definitions of context-free grammars.

Definition 3. A context-free grammar G is a tuple $\langle N, \Sigma, P, S \rangle$, where N and Σ are disjoint finite sets (nonterminal and terminal alphabets resp.), P is a finite set of productions, and $S \in N$ is a start symbol. Each production is of the form $A \to \alpha$ where $A \in N$ and $\alpha \in (\Sigma \cup N)^*$.

Definition 4. If $A \to \alpha$ is a production from P, then $\beta A \gamma$ directly derives $\beta \alpha \gamma$ (this is denoted as $\beta A \gamma \Rightarrow \beta \alpha \gamma$). The reflexive transitive closure of $\Rightarrow$ is denoted as $\overset{*}{\Rightarrow}$. If $\phi \overset{*}{\Rightarrow} \psi$, then we say that ϕ derives ψ.

Definition 5. The language generated by a context-free grammar G is the set of strings $L(G) = \{w \in \Sigma^* \mid S \overset{*}{\Rightarrow} w\}$.

We say that two grammars (possibly based on different formalisms, e.g. a Lambek grammar and a context-free grammar) are equivalent if they generate the same language.

It is proved that any context-free language without the empty word can be generated by a Lambek grammar and vice versa (see [9]), so we shall use any of these formalisms when speaking about context-free languages.

3 Lambek Calculus with Optional Divisions

Let us consider the following simple examples from [4]:

$$\begin{array}{cc} \text{John} & \text{works} \\ np & np\backslash s \end{array} \quad \to s$$

$$\begin{array}{ccc} \text{John} & \text{likes} & \text{Jane} \\ np & (np\backslash s)/np & np \end{array} \quad \to s$$

Here s is a distinguished category, which is interpreted as a marker of declarative sentences. Sentences *John works* and *John likes Jane* are correct in this simple grammar, because corresponding sequents $np, np\backslash s \to s$ and $np, (np\backslash s)/np, np \to s$ are derivable in the Lambek calculus.

One notices that connectives $\backslash$ and $/$ (called left division and right division resp.) in the latter examples represent obligatory arguments of verbs. Current rules imply that in order to obtain a correct sentence a verb must take all its arguments. However, there are such cases when arguments of verbs are (at first glance) optional, i.e. can be omitted. For example:

$$\begin{array}{lcl} \text{Tim helped.} & \& & \text{Tim helped Helen.} \\ \text{Tim reads.} & \& & \text{Tim reads the book.} \end{array}$$

In order to describe such sentences by means of the Lambek calculus it suffices to assign two different categories to verbs, e.g. *reads* ▷ $np\backslash s$, *reads* ▷ $(np\backslash s)/np$. However, these two categories look close so it would be nice to make them one reflecting that the only difference between them is presence or absence of the right division. In order to do this we introduce new operations named optional divisions. There is a left and a right one denoted by $\diagdown$ and $\angle$ resp.

Definition 6. *Optional divisions* are operations defined through conjunction and divisions as follows:

$$B\diagdown A := A \wedge (B\backslash A)$$
$$A\angle B := A \wedge (A/B)$$

The Lambek calculus enriched with optional divisions is denoted as L_{opt}. The set of categories built using operations $\backslash, \cdot, /, \diagdown, \angle$ is denoted as $Cat(\diagdown, \angle)$.

Example 1. Consider the sentence *Tim reads* along with the following type assignment:

$$\begin{array}{cc} \text{Tim} & \text{reads} \\ np & (np\backslash s)\angle np \end{array}$$

The sequent $np, (np\backslash s)\angle np \to s$ is derivable:

$$\frac{\dfrac{s \to s \quad np \to np}{np, np\backslash s \to s} \; (\backslash \to)}{np, (np\backslash s)\angle np \to s} \; (\wedge_1 \to)$$

The sequent $np, (np\backslash s)\angle np, np \to s$ is derivable as well; it corresponds to the sentence *Tim reads the book.*

From the linguistic point of view, adding new connectives may be considered as merely syntactic sugar used in the cases when we want to make the list of types corresponding to a word shorter and clearer. The following example from [2] shows that sometimes this may drastically reduce the number of types:

$$\text{Tim bet (Helen) (five dollars) (that they hired Alex).} \qquad (1)$$

Each of three arguments of *bet* can be omitted in this sentence according to [2], so there can be 8 variants of this sentence. Thus we would have to add 6 types corresponding to *bet*: $np\backslash s$, $(np\backslash s)/np$, $(np\backslash s)/cp$, $(np\backslash s)/cp/np$, $(np\backslash s)/np/np$, $(np\backslash s)/cp/np/np$ (cp denotes a subordinate clause). However, using optional divisions we can assign only one category $(np\backslash s)\angle cp\angle np\angle np$ to the word *bet*, which allows one to generate all 8 possible variants of (1).

From the point of view of programming, if one understands a category A/B as a program that takes an argument of the category B and returns a type-A value, then $A\angle B$ denotes a special case of a polymorphic function, when a program can either take an argument and use it during the computation process or ignore lack of the argument and do whatever A prescribes. This happens in programming: a function may have additional parameters that are not necessary to be present, but if they are, then computing a value for this function takes them into account. Clearly, such a program can also be considered as two different programs with the same name but with different lists of arguments.

Let us return to the mathematical and logical investigations. Nicely, optional divisions can also be defined through disjunction:

$$B\diagdown A := (B \vee 1)\backslash A$$
$$A\angle B := A/(B \vee 1)$$

In order to establish equivalence of the two definitions one needs to derive $A/(B \vee 1) \to A \wedge (A/B)$ and $A \wedge (A/B) \to A/(B \vee 1)$ in the multiplicative-additive Lambek calculus with the unit. Let us show one of the derivations:

$$\cfrac{\cfrac{\to 1}{A \to A \quad \cfrac{\to 1}{\to B \vee 1} (\to \vee_2)}{\cfrac{A \to A \quad \to B \vee 1}{A/(B \vee 1) \to A} (/\to)} \qquad \cfrac{A \to A \quad \cfrac{\cfrac{B \to B}{B \to B \vee 1}(\to \vee_1)}{\cfrac{A/(B \vee 1), B \to A}{\cfrac{A/(B \vee 1) \to A/B}{}}(/\to)}{}(\to /)}{A/(B \vee 1) \to A \wedge (A/B)} (\to \wedge)$$

The definition through disjunction also corresponds to the intuitive understanding of optional divisions: a structure of category $A\angle B$ consumes either a category B or nothing. In the remainder of this work, however, we do not use this representation but stick to the definition through conjunction.

Definition 6 yields that the L_{opt} is a fragment of the Lambek calculus with conjunction $L_\wedge$. It is interesting to investigate recognizing power of the L_{opt} (i.e. the set of languages generated by L_{opt}-grammars) and to compare it with the recognizing power of $L_\wedge$. At first glance L_{opt} is weaker than $L_\wedge$ because conjunction can join any two categories while conjunction in optional divisions joins only categories of a specific form closely related to each other. Nevertheless, below we show that conjunction hidden inside $B \backslash A$ and $A \angle B$ is quite powerful. Namely, we present the following theorems:

Theorem 2. *Any context-free language without the empty word can be generated by an L_{opt}-grammar $\langle \Sigma, T, \triangleright \rangle$ such that for all $a \in \Sigma$ it holds that $|\{T | a \triangleright T\}| \leq 1$ (i.e. at most one type corresponds to each symbol).*

Theorem 3. *Any finite intersection of context-free languages without the empty word can be generated by an L_{opt}-grammar.*

Note that these theorems can be naturally proved for $L_\wedge$; for example, to prove Theorem 2 we just combine all the categories corresponding to a fixed symbol a into a single category via $\wedge$ and assign it to a. This is done in [3].

Both theorems together are similar to Theorem 1 for MALC and $L_\wedge$. Theorem 3 narrows the gap between L_{opt} and $L_\wedge$ and even allows us to raise a question whether L_{opt}-grammars generate the same class of languages as $L_\wedge$-grammars.

4 Proofs of Theorems

Before proving theorems we need to make preparations. In Subsect. 4.1, we define the free group interpretation of types of the Lambek calculus and of $L_\wedge$ (this technique is taken from [9] and extended to categories with conjunction). In Subsect. 4.2, we define *interpretable Lambek grammars* and prove that each Lambek grammar can be turned into an equivalent interpretable one. In Subsect. 4.3, we define *telescopic conjunction* and establish its basic properties. In Subsects. 4.4 and 4.5, we prove Theorem 2 and Theorem 3 resp.

4.1 Free Group Interpretation

We prove both theorems by analysing free group interpretations of categories and sequents. In this section we define the notion of the free group interpretation.

Let FG stand for the free group generated by the set of primitive categories $Pr = \{p_i | i \in \mathbb{N}\}$. The identity element is denoted by ε.

Definition 7. A pair of elements $g_1, g_2 \in FG$ of a free group can be reduced if $g_1 = h_1 P$, $g_2 = P^{-1} h_2$, and P equals either p_i or p_i^{-1} for some i ($p_i \in Pr$). Such a pair is called irreducible if it cannot be reduced.

Definition 8. In [9] the mapping $[\![\,]\!] : Cat \to FG$ is defined as follows:

$$[\![p_i]\!] := p_i \qquad \begin{aligned} [\![A/B]\!] &:= [\![A]\!][\![B]\!]^{-1} & [\![A \cdot B]\!] &:= [\![A]\!][\![B]\!] \\ [\![B \backslash A]\!] &:= [\![B]\!]^{-1}[\![A]\!] & [\![A_1 \ldots A_n]\!] &:= [\![A_1]\!] \ldots [\![A_n]\!] \end{aligned}$$

It is called the free group interpretation.

Now we extend it to categories with conjunction, i.e. to $Cat(\wedge)$. Let the extended interpretation be a finite subset of FG; its definition is also inductive and it inherits Definition 8. The difference is that now $[\![p_i]\!] = \{p_i\}$ and that all operations are understood to be operations on sets (namely, $[\![A \cdot B]\!] = \{uv \mid u \in [\![A]\!], v \in [\![B]\!]\}$ and $[\![A]\!]^{-1} = \{u^{-1} \mid u \in [\![A]\!]\}$). We add the following definition for the conjunction case:

$$[\![A \wedge B]\!] := [\![A]\!] \cup [\![B]\!].$$

Example 2. $[\![(p \wedge q) \cdot (r \wedge s)/t]\!] = \{prt^{-1}, pst^{-1}, qrt^{-1}, qst^{-1}\}.$

For the Lambek calculus the following lemma holds:

Lemma 1. *If* $L \vdash \Gamma \to C$*, then* $[\![\Gamma]\!] = [\![C]\!]$*.*

We also extend it to $L_{\wedge}$. In order to do that we define a set $LimCat(\wedge) \subseteq Cat(\wedge)$ as follows:

Definition 9. $LimCat(\wedge)$ *is the least set satisfying the following requirements:* $Pr \subseteq LimCat(\wedge)$*; if* $A, B \in LimCat(\wedge)$*, then* $A \cdot B, A \wedge B \in LimCat(\wedge)$*; if* $A \in LimCat(\wedge), C \in Cat$*, then* $A/C, C\backslash A \in LimCat(\wedge)$*.*

In other words, we consider categories without conjunction in a denominator.

Lemma 2. *If* $L_{\wedge} \vdash A_1, \ldots, A_n \to B_1 \wedge \ldots \wedge B_k$ *and* $A_i \in LimCat(\wedge), B_j \in Cat$ *then* $[\![A_1, \ldots, A_n]\!] \supseteq [\![B_1 \wedge \ldots \wedge B_k]\!]$*.*

Proof. Induction on the length of a derivation of $A_1, \ldots, A_n \to B_1 \wedge \ldots \wedge B_k$. The base case is when $n = k = 1$, and $A_1 = B_1$, which is trivial. Let us consider some cases of the induction step depending on the last rule applied in the derivation.
    Case 1. $k = 1$, and the last rule applied is $(\to /)$; then $B_1 = C_1/C_2$ and

$$\frac{A_1, \ldots, A_n, C_2 \to C_1}{A_1, \ldots, A_n \to C_1/C_2} \ (\to /)$$

By the induction hypothesis, $[\![A_1 \ldots A_n, C_2]\!] \ni [\![C_1]\!]$ (note that C_1, C_2 are without conjunction). Then $[\![A_1 \ldots A_n]\!] \ni [\![C_1]\!][\![C_2]\!]^{-1}$ (each element of $[\![A_1 \ldots A_n]\!]$ should be multiplied by $[\![C_2]\!]^{-1}$ from the right).   □

    Consequently, if for some j $[\![A_1, \ldots, A_n]\!] \not\supseteq [\![B_j]\!]$, then $L_{\wedge} \not\vdash A_1, \ldots, A_n \to B_1 \wedge \ldots \wedge B_k$.

4.2   Interpretable Lambek Grammars

Now let us present a new normal form for Lambek grammars, which is convenient to work with.

Definition 10. A Lambek grammar $G = \langle \Sigma, t, \triangleright \rangle$ is *interpretable* if $t \in Pr$, and for each sequence of categories $T_1, \ldots, T_k$ where categories are taken from $Cat(G)$ the following requirements are satisfied:

(a) $[\![T_1 \ldots T_k]\!] \neq \varepsilon$;

(b) $[\![T_1 \ldots T_k]\!] = t$ implies $L \vdash T_1, \ldots, T_k \to t$;

(c) t does not appear in denominators of categories in $Cat(G)$.

Theorem 4. *Any context-free grammar without empty word is equivalent to an interpretable Lambek grammar.*

In order to prove this theorem we start from a context-free language L and present an interpretable grammar that generates it.

Definition 11. A context-free grammar $G = \langle \Sigma, N, P, S \rangle$ is said to be in the Rosenkrantz normal form (RNF) if each rule in P is of one of the following forms:

1. $A \to a\alpha d$ $(a, d \in \Sigma, \alpha \in (\Sigma \cup N)^*)$;
2. $A \to a$ $(a \in \Sigma)$.

Theorem 5. (Rozenkrantz). *Any context-free grammar without empty word is equivalent to a context-free grammar in the RNF.*

See the proof in [10].

Proof. (of Theorem 4). Let us consider a context-free grammar $G_1 = \langle \Sigma, N, P, S \rangle$ in the RNF generating L. We introduce $|\Sigma|$ new nonterminal symbols: $T_\Sigma = \{T_a\}_{a \in \Sigma}$. We define $N' := N \cup T_\Sigma$. We also define the function $\widehat{\ }: (N \cup \Sigma)^+ \to (N')^+$ by the following equalities:

$$\widehat{A} = A\ (A \in N); \quad \widehat{a} = T_a\ (a \in \Sigma); \quad \widehat{w_1 w_2} = \widehat{w_1}\widehat{w_2}.$$

At the next step we construct $G_2 = \{\Sigma, N', P', S\}$ where $P' = \{A \to a\widehat{\delta}, A \to a\delta \in P\} \cup \{T_a \to a | a \in \Sigma\}$. Clearly, $L(G_1) = L(G_2)$. One notices that G_2 does not have right recursion (this notion is defined in [1]; it means that there is no derivation of the form $A \overset{*}{\Rightarrow} \alpha A$ for A being nonterminal). Indeed, the rightmost symbol of each production from P' is from T_Σ but if $A = T_a \in T_\Sigma$, then we can only derive a from it.

Let us further assume without loss of generality that N' is a subset of Pr. We construct a Lambek grammar $G_3 = \langle \Sigma, S, \triangleright \rangle$ as follows: $a \triangleright T$ if and only if we have $T = A/B_m/\ldots/B_1$ for such $A, B_1, \ldots, B_m \in N'$ that $A \to aB_1 \ldots B_m \in P', m \geq 0$ (note that every rule in G_2 is of this form).

It is argued that G_3 satisfies properties (a) and (b) from Definition 10. The main observation is that a reduction between interpretations of $Cat(G_3)$ categories corresponds to a composition of rules in the context-free grammar G_2. The formal proof is given below.

We define a new set $CatExt$ as the least set satisfying the following criteria: $CatExt \supseteq Cat(G_3)$; if $A/B_m/\ldots/B_1, B_1/C_k/\ldots/C_1 \in CatExt$ then $A/B_m/\ldots/B_2/C_k/\ldots/C_1 \in CatExt$. Speaking informally, categories in $CatExt$ are composed of categories in $Cat(G_3)$ using the transitivity rule: $A/p, p/C \to A/C$. $\square$

Lemma 3. *For each $T = A/B_n/\ldots/B_1 \in CatExt$ there is a rule of the form $A \to \sigma B_1 \ldots B_n, \sigma \in \Sigma^+$ which is got as a composition of several rules from P'.*

Proof. We shall use induction on the number of applications of the transitivity rule when constructing T. If $T \in Cat(G_3)$ then this follows from the definition of G_3. Let $T = A/B_m/\ldots/B_2/C_k/\ldots/C_1$, and let it be composed of $A/B_m/\ldots/B_1$, $B_1/C_k/\ldots/C_1 \in CatExt$. The induction hypothesis implies that there are rules $A \to \sigma B_1 \ldots B_m$, $B_1 \to \tau C_1 \ldots C_k$ for some $\sigma, \tau \in \Sigma^+$ which are got by a composition of several rules of G_2. Then we can apply the second rule within the first rule and get $A \to \sigma B_1 \ldots B_m \to \sigma \tau C_1 \ldots C_k B_2 \ldots B_m$. This completes the proof. □

Lemma 4. (checking property a). $\forall n \; \forall T_1, \ldots, T_n \in CatExt$ $[\![T_1]\!] \ldots [\![T_n]\!] \neq \varepsilon$.

Proof. Induction on n.

If $n = 1$, then $T_1 = A/B_m/\ldots/B_1$, and there is a composition of rules from P' of the form $A \to \sigma B_1 \ldots B_m, \sigma \in \Sigma^+$. Because there is no right recursion in G_2, $A \neq B_m$. Then $[\![T_1]\!] = A B_m^{-1} \cdots \neq \varepsilon$.

The induction step is proved as follows: if none of two adjacent factors within $[\![T_1]\!] \ldots [\![T_n]\!]$ can be reduced, then the whole product is irreducible, and thus does not equal ε. If $T_i = A/B_m/\ldots/B_1$, $T_{i+1} = C/D_k/\ldots/D_1$ and $[\![T_i]\!][\![T_{i+1}]\!]$ can be reduced, then $C = B_1$ and $A/B_m/\ldots/B_2/D_k/\ldots/D_1 \in CatExt$. The induction hypothesis completes the proof since we can replace the pair T_i, T_{i+1} by T. □

Lemma 5. (checking property b). $\forall n \; \forall T_1, \ldots, T_n \in CatExt$ $[\![T_1]\!] \ldots [\![T_n]\!] = S \Rightarrow L \vdash T_1, \ldots, T_n \to S$.

Proof. Induction on n.

If $n = 1$, then $T_1 = S$ and $L \vdash S \to S$.

The induction step is proved as follows: if there can be no reductions within $[\![T_1]\!] \ldots [\![T_n]\!]$, then there are at least two positive occurences of primitive categories in this product and therefore it cannot be equal to S. Consequently, there is some i such that the pair $[\![T_i]\!]$, $[\![T_{i+1}]\!]$ can be reduced. Let $T_i = A/B_m/\ldots/B_1$ and $T_{i+1} = B_1/D_k/\ldots/D_1$. Then $T = A/B_m/\ldots/B_2/D_k/\ldots/D_1 \in CatExt$. Applying the induction hypothesis, one gets $L \vdash T_1, \ldots, T_{i-1}, T, T_{i+2}, \ldots, T_n \to S$. Finally,

$$\frac{T_i, T_{i+1} \to T \quad T_1, \ldots, T_{i-1}, T, T_{i+2}, \ldots, T_n \to S}{T_1, \ldots, T_n \to S} \; (cut)$$

□

Summing up the above lemmas we conclude that G_3 satisfies properties (a) and (b) of interpretable grammars. Now we present $G_4 = \langle \Sigma, \widetilde{S}, \widetilde{\triangleright} \rangle$, where $\widetilde{S}$ is a new primitive category and $a \widetilde{\triangleright} T$ if either $a \triangleright T$ or $T = \widetilde{S}/S \cdot T'$ for $a \triangleright T'$. If some sequent $T_1, \ldots, T_p \to \widetilde{S}$ is derived where $a_1 \widetilde{\triangleright} T_1, \ldots, a_p \widetilde{\triangleright} T_p$, then there is exactly one category in the antecedent of the form $\widetilde{S}/S \cdot T'$ — and it is the first one. Hence $T_1 = \widetilde{S}/S \cdot T_1', a_1 \triangleright T_1', a_i \triangleright T_i (i \geq 2)$ and $L \vdash T_1', T_2, \ldots, T_p \to S$. This proves $L(G_4) \subseteq L(G_3)$. The reverse inclusion is obvious: if $a_i \triangleright T_i$ $(i \geq 1)$ and $L \vdash T_1, \ldots, T_p \to S$, then one can derive $L \vdash \widetilde{S}/S \cdot T_1, T_2, \ldots, T_p \vdash \widetilde{S}$. Therefore, $L = L(G_1) = L(G_2) = L(G_3) = L(G_4)$.

Finally, we claim that G_4 satisfies all the properties of interpretable grammars:

1. $\widetilde{S}$ is primitive.
2. Let $T_1, \ldots, T_n$ be categories from $Cat(G_4)$. If one of these categories contains $\widetilde{S}$, then $[\![T_1, \ldots, T_n]\!]$ contains it as well (since $\widetilde{S}$ does not appear in denominators) and $[\![T_1, \ldots, T_n]\!] \neq \varepsilon$. Otherwise, all categories are from $Cat(G_3)$; hence, using interpretability of G_3, we obtain $[\![T_1, \ldots, T_n]\!] \neq \varepsilon$.
3. Let $[\![T_1, \ldots, T_n]\!] = \widetilde{S}$. Then there is exactly one index $i \in \{1, \ldots, n\}$ such that T_i contains $\widetilde{S}$ while for $j \neq i$ T_j belongs to $Cat(G_3)$. $[\![T_i, \ldots, T_n]\!] = \widetilde{S}g$ for $g \in FG$, so $[\![T_1, \ldots, T_{i-1}]\!] = \varepsilon$. However, the property (a) for G_3 implies that this cannot be the case; the only possible way is that $i = 1$. Recall that $T_1 = \widetilde{S}/S \cdot T_1'$ for T_1' being from G_3; thus

$$\widetilde{S} = [\![T_1, \ldots, T_n]\!] = \widetilde{S}S^{-1}[\![T_1', \ldots, T_n]\!]$$

Consequently, $S = [\![T_1', \ldots, T_n]\!]$ and, due to the property (b) of G_3 $L \vdash T_1', \ldots, T_n \to S$. Finally, using the rule $(/ \to)$ one can derive $T_1, \ldots, T_n \to \widetilde{S}$.

$\square$

4.3 Telescopic Conjunction

The following construction, as it will be seen further, can substitute for conjunction in some way.

Definition 12. Telescopic conjunction of categories $T_1, \ldots, T_n$ is a category

$$T_1 \times \cdots \times T_n := T_1 \cdot (T_1 \diagdown T_2) \cdot (T_2 \diagdown T_3) \cdot \ldots \cdot (T_{n-1} \diagdown T_n).$$

Telescopic conjunction indeed works like a telescope: we can use each of optional divisions to consume a category standing on the left-hand side of it. Consequently, we can shorten such a category in a way stated in

Lemma 6. If $1 \leq i < n$, then $L_{opt} \vdash T_1 \times \cdots \times T_n \to T_i \cdot T_n$.

The proof is done by induction, it suffices to present a straightforward derivation.

Lemma 7. For categories $T_1, \ldots, T_n$ from Cat it holds that $[\![T_1 \times \cdots \times T_n]\!] = \{[\![T_{i_1}]\!] \ldots [\![T_{i_k}]\!] | k \geq 1, 1 \leq i_1 < \cdots < i_k = n\}$.

Proof. Induction on n. The case $n = 1$ is obvious. The general case is proven by such equalities:

$$[T_1 \cdot T_1 \backslash T_2 \cdot T_2 \backslash T_3 \cdots \cdot T_{n-1} \backslash T_n] = [T_1][T_1 \backslash T_2][T_2 \backslash T_3 \cdots \cdot T_{n-1} \backslash T_n] =$$
$$= [T_1]\{[T_1^{-1}], \varepsilon\}[T_2 \cdot T_2 \backslash T_3 \cdots \cdot T_{n-1} \backslash T_n] = \{\varepsilon, [T_1]\} \ldots \{\varepsilon, [T_{n-1}]\}[T_n].$$

We apply the induction hypothesis to obtain the last equality. □

4.4 Proof of Theorem 2

Proof. Let us consider an interpretable Lambek grammar $G = \langle \Sigma, s, \triangleright \rangle$ which generates a given language. Let us fix a new primitive category $\xi \in Pr$. We construct an L_{opt}-grammar $\widetilde{G} = \langle \Sigma, s, \widetilde{\triangleright} \rangle$ as follows. Given a symbol a, let $T_1^a, \ldots, T_{k_a}^a$ be all categories T for which $a \triangleright T$ holds. Then

$$a \widetilde{\triangleright} P_a : \quad P_a = (T_1^a/\xi) \times \cdots \times (T_{k_a}^a/\xi) \times \xi.$$

The role of ξ is to restrict undesirable variants of using optional divisions, e.g. when we omit all of them in a complex category.

Firstly, using Lemma 6, we obtain $L_{opt} \vdash P_a \to T_i^a/\xi \cdot \xi$. In the Lambek calculus (and consequently in L_{opt}) one can derive $T_i^a/\xi \cdot \xi \to T_i^a$, so $L_{opt} \vdash P_a \to T_i^a$ for all $i = 1, \ldots, k_a$. Therefore if $a_j \triangleright T_j, j = 1, \ldots, l$ and $L \vdash T_1, \ldots, T_l \to s$, then one can derive $P_{a_1}, \ldots, P_{a_l} \to s$ using the cut rule. This means that $L(G) \subseteq L(\widetilde{G})$.

In order to prove that $L(\widetilde{G}) \subseteq L(G)$ we need to show that $L_{opt} \vdash P_{a_1}, \ldots, P_{a_l} \to s$ $(a_j \in \Sigma)$ implies $L \vdash T_{i_1}^{a_1}, \ldots, T_{j_l}^{a_l} \to s$ for some $j_1, \ldots, j_l$. Instead, we will focus on analyzing free group interpretations. If $L_{opt} \vdash P_{a_1}, \ldots, P_{a_l} \to s$, then $s \in [P_{a_1}, \ldots, P_{a_l}]$ (Lemma 2).

By Lemma 7, the interpretation of P_a is the following set:

$$[P_a] = \{\xi\} \cup \{[T_j^a]\}_{j=1}^{k_a} \cup \{[T_{j_1}^a]\xi^{-1}[T_{j_2}^a]\xi^{-1} \ldots \xi^{-1}[T_{j_m}^a] | m \geq 2, j_1 < \cdots < j_m\}.$$

Let $g_i \in [P_{a_i}], i = 1, \ldots, l$ and $\Pi := g_1 \ldots g_l = s$. Note that only ξ, ξ^{-1} and $[T_i^a]$ may appear in Π, and there always is a nonempty sequence of category interpetations $[T_i^a]$ between any two ξ and ξ^{-1} standing nearby each other in Π. Since G is interpretable the sequence of $[T_i^a]$ cannot be reduced to ε (due to the property (a)). This means that, if some primitive category ξ or ξ^{-1} appears within one of g_i, then it cannot be reduced with some other primitive category ξ^{-1}, ξ resp. Hence g_i can be only of the form $[T_{j_i}^{a_i}]$. Recalling that $[T_{j_1}^{a_1}] \ldots [T_{j_l}^{a_l}] = g_1 \ldots g_l = s$ and using the property (b) of interpretable grammars, we obtain

$$L \vdash T_{j_1}^{a_1}, \ldots, T_{j_l}^{a_l} \to s,$$

which completes the proof. □

4.5   Proof of Theorem 3

The main idea of the proof is to combine categories of different grammars using telescopic conjunction again.

The following notation is used:

Definition 13.

$$B^\delta \backslash A = \begin{cases} A & \text{if } \delta = 0, \\ B \backslash A & \text{if } \delta = 1. \end{cases}$$

Proof. Let $L_1, \ldots, L_N$ be N context-free languages without the empty word and let $G_i = \langle \Sigma, s_i, \triangleright_i \rangle, i = 1, \ldots, N$ be interpretable Lambek grammars generating them. Our goal is to construct an L_{opt}-grammar generating $L_1 \cap \ldots \cap L_N$. It can be assumed without loss of generality that, for $i \neq j$, categories in $Cat(G_i) \cup \{s_i\}$ and categories in $Cat(G_j) \cup \{s_j\}$ are built of disjoint sets of primitive categories.

We fix a primitive category $\xi \in Pr$ that does not occur in all the considered grammars and introduce a new grammar

$$G = \langle \Sigma, s_1 \wedge \ldots \wedge s_N, \triangleright \rangle.$$

Given a symbol a let $T_1^{a,i}, \ldots, T_{k_{a,i}}^{a,i}$ be all categories T for which $a \triangleright_i T$ holds. Then

$$a \triangleright T \text{ if } T = (T_{j_1}^{a,1}/\xi) \times \cdots \times (T_{j_N}^{a,N}/\xi) \times \xi, 1 \leq j_l \leq k_{a,l}, 1 \leq l \leq N.$$

Note that $|\{T \mid a \triangleright T\}| = k_{a,1} \cdot \ldots \cdot k_{a,N}$.

The inclusion $\bigcap\limits_{i=1}^{N} L(G_i) \subseteq L(G)$ follows from the fact that for all $l = 1, \ldots, N$

$$L \vdash (T_{j_1}^{a,1}/\xi) \times \cdots \times (T_{j_N}^{a,N}/\xi) \times \xi \rightarrow T_{j_l}^{a,l}.$$

For the other inclusion we need to prove that if $a_i \triangleright T_i$ $(i = 1, \ldots, n)$ and $L_\wedge \vdash T_1, \ldots, T_n \rightarrow s_1 \wedge \ldots \wedge s_N$, then $a_1 \ldots a_n$ belongs to all $L_i, i = 1, \ldots, N$. Assuming the "if" statement, we obtain that $[\![T_1, \ldots, T_n]\!] \supseteq \{s_1, \ldots, s_N\}$. As in the previous proof, one can notice that if $a \triangleright T$, then the following holds for some indices $j_1, \ldots, j_N$ $(1 \leq j_l \leq k_{a,l})$:

$$[\![T]\!] = \{\xi\} \cup \{[\![T_{j_i}^{a,i}]\!]\}_{i=1}^{N} \cup \{[\![T_{j_{i_1}}^{a,i_1}]\!]\xi^{-1}[\![T_{j_{i_2}}^{a,i_2}]\!]\xi^{-1}\cdots\xi^{-1}[\![T_{j_{i_m}}^{a,i_m}]\!]\mid$$
$$m \geq 2, i_1 < \cdots < i_m\}.$$

Let $g_1 \in [\![T_1]\!], \ldots, g_n \in [\![T_n]\!], n \geq 1$ and let

$$\Pi = g_1 \ldots g_n = s_M \tag{2}$$

hold for some fixed M.

Can one of g_i equal ξ or $[\![T_{j_{i_1}}^{a,i_1}]\!]\xi^{-1}[\![T_{j_{i_2}}^{a,i_2}]\!]\xi^{-1}\cdots\xi^{-1}[\![T_{j_{i_m}}^{a,i_m}]\!]$? No, it cannot. Otherwise, if ξ appears, it has to be reduced with some ξ^{-1}. If this happens, let us consider the sequence of category interpretations between them, which has to be reduced to ε. This sequence is composed of several slices, each of which corresponds to some specific grammar:

$$\Pi = \cdots \xi \underbrace{[\![T^{a_1^1,m_1}_{j_1^1}]\!] \cdots [\![T^{a_{M_1}^1,m_1}_{j_{M_1}^1}]\!]}_{\text{slice } 1} \cdots \underbrace{[\![T^{a_1^p,m_p}_{j_1^p}]\!] \cdots [\![T^{a_{M_p}^p,m_p}_{j_{M_p}^p}]\!]}_{\text{slice } p} \xi^{-1} \cdots$$

Here slice 1 consists of interpretations of categories from G_{m_1}, slice 2 consists of interpretations of categories from G_{m_2} and so on. One notices that none of such slices can reduce to ε (because each G_i is interpretable); besides, reductions cannot happen between different slices (since different slices consist of disjoint sets of primitive categories). So the whole sequence of interpretations between ξ and ξ^{-1} cannot be reduced to ε, hence ξ or ξ^{-1} appeared once shall not disappear.

This yields that g_i have to be of the form $[\![T^{a,M}_l]\!]$ for some a, l: otherwise, if $g_t = [\![T^{a,j}_l]\!]$ for some t and $j \neq M$, then the slice containing g_t cannot be completely reduced (because every considered grammar is interpretable) and the whole product $g_1 \ldots g_n$ cannot be equal to s_M. This means that $g_i = [\![T'_i]\!]$, such that $a_i \rhd_M T'_i, i = 1, \ldots, n$, and finally, due to the property (b) of interpretable grammars, which holds for G_M,

$$L \vdash T'_1, \ldots, T'_n \rightarrow s_M.$$

We conclude that $a_1 \ldots a_n \in L_M$. Since the above reasonings hold for each M, this finally proves $\bigcap_{i=1}^{N} L(G_i) = L(G)$.

In order to construct the required L_{opt}-grammar, we have to change a distinguished category (the current category is defined through conjunction, which cannot be done in L_{opt}). Suppose that $N = 2^u, u \in \mathbb{N}$ (proving under this assumption suffices to prove the theorem for each N). Let us encode integers $k = 1, \ldots, N$ by u-tuples $(\epsilon_1(k); \ldots; \epsilon_u(k))$, $\epsilon_i(k) \in \{0, 1\}$, $i = 1, \ldots, u$. Then we present new primitive categories $s, \sigma_1, \ldots, \sigma_u$ and change each of G_i by replacing s_i by $\sigma_u^{\epsilon_u(i)} \backslash \ldots \backslash \sigma_1^{\epsilon_1(i)} \backslash s$ everywhere in $Cat(G_i)$ and in the distinguished category s_i. Let us denote new grammars as $\widetilde{G}_i$. It is not hard to prove that G_i is equivalent to $\widetilde{G}_i$ (this follows from interpetability of G_i).

Now we construct $\widetilde{G}$ from $\widetilde{G}_i$ in the same way as it is done above for G from G_i except for the distinguished category: we shall take $\sigma_u \diagdown \ldots \sigma_1 \diagdown s$ instead of $s_1 \wedge \cdots \wedge s_N$. Again, the more difficult part is to prove that $L(\widetilde{G}) \subseteq \bigcap_{i=1}^{N} L(\widetilde{G}_i)$. It is proved the same way as for G; however, we additionally have to answer why, when considering a sequence of category interpretations between ξ and ξ^{-1}, there cannot be reductions between different slices (note that now there are some common primitive categories contained in categories of different grammars G_i: those are s and $\sigma_1, \ldots, \sigma_u$). Because of the property (c), s_i does not occur in denominators of categories in $Cat(G_i)$. Therefore s^{-1} and σ_i, $i = 1, \ldots, u$ do not appear in interpretations of categories in $Cat(\widetilde{G})$, and there can be no more reductions within Π than before replacing s_i by $\sigma_u^{\epsilon_u(i)} \backslash \ldots \backslash \sigma_1^{\epsilon_1(i)} \backslash s$. $\qquad \square$

Example 3. Consider the grammar $\langle \Sigma, s, \rhd \rangle$:

$$a \rhd q/p, (s/t)/p;$$
$$b \rhd p, q \backslash p;$$
$$c \rhd t, u, u \backslash t, u/t.$$

This grammar generates the language $L_c = \{a^n b^n c^k | n, k \geq 1\}$, and it is already interpretable. Theorem 2 says that we can generate L_c by the following L_{opt}-grammar where only one category is assigned to each symbol:

$a \triangleright (q/p)/\xi \cdot ((q/p)/\xi) \diagdown (((s/t)/p)/\xi) \cdot (((s/t)/p)/\xi) \diagup \xi$
$b \triangleright p/\xi \cdot (p/\xi) \diagdown ((q\backslash p)/\xi) \cdot ((q\backslash p)/\xi) \diagup \xi$
$c \triangleright t/\xi \cdot (t/\xi) \diagdown (u/\xi) \cdot (u/\xi) \diagdown ((u\backslash t)/\xi) \cdot ((u/t)/\xi) \diagdown ((u/t)/\xi) \cdot ((u/t)/\xi) \diagup \xi$

Now let us consider the grammar $\langle \Sigma, s_2, \triangleright' \rangle$:

$a \triangleright' t_2, u_2, u_2 \backslash t_2, u_2/t_2.$
$b \triangleright' (t_2 \backslash s_2)/p_2, q_2/p_2;$
$c \triangleright' p_2, q_2 \backslash p_2;$

This grammar is also interpretable, and it generates $L_a = \{a^k b^n c^n | n, k \geq 1\}$. Theorem 2 allows us to construct an L_{opt}-grammar $\langle \Sigma, \sigma_1 \diagdown s, \widetilde{\triangleright} \rangle$ that generates $L_a \cap L_c = \{a^n b^n c^n | n \geq 1\}$:

$a \widetilde{\triangleright} ((s/t)/p)/\xi \cdot (((s/t)/p)/\xi) \diagdown (t_2/\xi) \cdot (t_2/\xi) \diagup \xi,$
$\quad (q/p)/\xi \cdot ((q/p)/\xi) \diagdown (t_2/\xi) \cdot (t_2/\xi) \diagup \xi,$
$\quad \ldots (2 \times 4 = 8 \text{ categories at all});$
$b \widetilde{\triangleright} p/\xi \cdot (p/\xi) \diagdown (((t_2 \backslash \sigma_1 \backslash s)/p_2)/\xi) \cdot (((t_2 \backslash \sigma_1 \backslash s)/p_2)/\xi) \diagup \xi,$
$\quad p/\xi \cdot (p/\xi) \diagdown ((q_2/p_2)/\xi) \cdot ((q_2/p_2)/\xi) \diagup \xi,$
$\quad (q\backslash p)/\xi \cdot ((q\backslash p)/\xi) \diagdown (((t_2 \backslash \sigma_1 \backslash s)/p_2)/\xi) \cdot (((t_2 \backslash \sigma_1 \backslash s)/p_2)/\xi) \diagup \xi,$
$\quad (q\backslash p)/\xi \cdot ((q\backslash p)/\xi) \diagdown ((q_2/p_2)/\xi) \cdot ((q_2/p_2)/\xi) \diagup \xi;$
$c \widetilde{\triangleright} t/\xi \cdot (t/\xi) \diagdown (p_2/\xi) \cdot (p_2/\xi) \diagup \xi,$
$\quad t/\xi \cdot (t/\xi) \diagdown ((q_2 \backslash p_2)/\xi) \cdot ((q_2 \backslash p_2)/\xi) \diagup \xi,$
$\quad \ldots (4 \times 2 = 8 \text{ categories at all}).$

5   Conclusion and Future Work

L_{opt} is a fragment of the multiplicative-additive Lambek calculus, which, however, preserves several properties of the latter and hence is quite powerful. Note that in the proofs of Theorems 2 and 3 we use only the left optional division; moreover, it does not appear in denominators of categories. Possibly, we can obtain even more expressive power of L_{opt}-grammars when using both divisions and more complex categories. However, our proof of Theorem 3 does not look pretty, and it is hard to generalize it: there are some technical tricks such as a special symbol ξ, or a distinguished category of the form $\sigma_u \diagdown \ldots \diagdown \sigma_1 \diagdown s$. It would be nice to find more elegant constructions involving optional divisions.

There is a series of questions that naturally arise in view of Theorem 3:

1. Is the set of languages generated by L_{opt}-grammars closed under intersection?
2. Does this set contain the set of languages generated by conjunctive grammars (introduced in [8])?
3. Does this set equal the set of languages generated by $L_\wedge$-grammars?

Questions regarding algorithmic complexity are also interesting: are there any benefits in parsing sequents of L_{opt} comparing with those of MALC (the derivability problem for the latter is known to be PSPACE-complete)?

Another direction is to study linguistic motivation deeper. Is describing optional arguments of verbs using optional divisions adequate? Is there natural semantics for optional divisions? Another topic is the following: optional divisions appear only in numerators of categories in given examples in Sect. 3. Is there any example in the English language or in some other natural language where optional divisions appear in a denominator of a category? How else can optional divisions be used?

Acknowledgments. Thanks to my scientific advisor Prof. Mati Pentus for helping me in many ways, thanks to reviewers for valuable advice, and thanks to Aleksey Starchenko for fruitful discussions.

References

1. Aho, A.V., Sethi, R., Ullman, J.D.: Compilers: principles, techniques, and tools. Addison-Wesley Series in Computer Science/World Student Series Edition, Addison-Wesley (1986)
2. De Kuthy, K., Detmar Meurers, W.: Dealing with optional complements in HPSG-Based grammar implementations. In: Proceedings of the HPSG03 Conference, Michigan State University, East Lansing (2003)
3. Kanazawa, M.: The Lambek calculus enriched with additional connectives. J. Logic Lang. Inform. **1**, 141–171 (1992)
4. Lambek, J.: The mathematics of sentence structure. Amer. Math. Monthly **65**(3), 154–170 (1958)
5. Moortgat, M.: Multimodal linguistic inference. J. Logic. Lang. Inf. **5**, 349–385 (1996)
6. Moot, R., Retoré, C.: The Logic of Categorial Grammars. LNCS, vol. 6850. Springer, Heidelberg (2012). https://doi.org/10.1007/978-3-642-31555-8
7. Morrill, G., Valentín, O., Fadda, M.: The displacement calculus. J. Logic Lang. Inform. **20**(1), 1–48 (2011)
8. Okhotin, A.: Conjunctive grammars. J. Logic Lang. Inform. **6**(4), 519–535 (2001)
9. Pentus, M.: Lambek grammars are context free. In: Proceedings of the 8th Annual Symposium on Logic in Computer Science, Montreal, Canada (1993)
10. Rosenkrantz, D.J.: Matrix equations and normal forms for context-free grammars. J. ACM **14**(3), 501–507 (1967)

A Logical Framework for Understanding Why

Yu Wei$^{(\boxtimes)}$

Department of Philosophy, East China Normal University, Shanghai, China
ywei@philo.ecnu.edu.cn

Abstract. Epistemic logic pays barely any attention to the notion of understanding, which stands in total contrast to the current situation in epistemology and in philosophy of science. This paper studies understanding why in an epistemic-logic-style. It is generally acknowledged that understanding why moves beyond knowing why. Inspired by philosophical ideas, we consider whereas knowing why requires knowing horizontal explanations, understanding why additionally requires vertical explanations. Based on justification logic and existing logical work for knowing why, we build up a framework by introducing vertical explanations, and show it could accommodate different philosophical viewpoints via adding conditions to the models. A sound and complete axiomatization for the most general case is given.

Keywords: Understanding why · Knowing why · Epistemic logic · Justification logic

1 Introduction

There has been a resurgence of interest among epistemologists and philosophers of science in the nature of understanding recently. Different uses of 'understanding' seem to mean so many different things. Literature tends to suppose three main types of understanding (cf. [10]):

- Propositional understanding or understanding-that: "I understand that X."
- Atomistic understanding or understanding-wh: "I understand why/when/ where/what X."
- Objectual understanding or holistic understanding: "I understand X."

Among all the types above, plenty of recent work focus on understanding-why, which is also called a narrow conception of understanding.[1]

---

[1] See, for instance [16,20,22,31] etc. All mentions of "understanding" in their work should be read as concerning "understanding why". And the author of [20] refers to understanding why as a narrow conception of understanding.

A. Pavlova et al. (Eds.): ESSLLI 2019/2020/2021, LNCS 14354, pp. 203–220, 2024.
https://doi.org/10.1007/978-3-031-50628-4_13

While a lot of discussions have been taking place among philosophers, there is barely any attention to characterizing understanding in the literature on epistemic logic (an exception being [9], which aims for "understanding a proposition"). Apart from "knowing that", there has been a growing interest in epistemic logic in various knowledge expressions in terms of "knowing what", "knowing how", "knowing why" and so on (see the survey in [30]). It would be interesting to introduce the notion of understanding into the current framework of epistemic logic, to see what would happen between understanding and knowing and what the distinct logical principles for understanding are. This paper focuses on understanding why, and the main motivation is to contribute to the explication of "understanding why" from the perspective of epistemic logic.

As noted in [25], the relation between understanding and knowing has been a prominent theme in the search for a satisfactory account of understanding. Hence we start by considering the logic of knowing why. Xu, Wang and Studer recently take the ideas similar to justification logic together with the standard notions of epistemic logic to capture knowing why in [33]. There is a very general connection between knowledge and wh-questions discovered by Hintikka in the framework of quantified epistemic logic (cf. [15]). The authors thus view knowing why φ as knowing an answer to the question "Why φ?", which intuitively amounts to knowing an explanation of φ. Xu et al. stay neutral to the nature of explanations and focus on their most abstract logical structure. Moreover, the explanatory relation between explanations and propositions is characterized by the format $t : \varphi$, which is a formula from justification logic originally stating that "t is a justification of φ". The analysis of "knowing why φ" is $\exists t \mathsf{K}_i(t : \varphi)$. This is a nice start point because "understanding why" is widely termed as "explanatory understanding",[2] which indicates the close relations between the notions of understanding why and explanation.

According to the philosophical ideas, it is widely assumed that understanding why φ moves beyond knowing why φ, in which knowing why φ is commonly analyzed as identifying the dependencies, say knowing that "φ because ψ". This view, called non-reductionist, is understanding why cannot be reduced to knowing why. Pritchard [23] introduces a scenario where a child knows via testimony that a house burned down because of faulty wiring. The child then could answer a corresponding why-question since she accepts the information, and say, ready to repeat it to her friends. However, while the parent understands why the house burned down because the parent also knows how the faulty wiring caused the fire, the child has no conception of that and thus has no understanding why.

It seems plausible that understanding why requires more than merely knowing an answer to the why-question. This "more" is usually illustrated by more questions in literatures like [24]: if the child were asked the question of why the introduction of faulty wiring caused the fire, she would be unable to respond. Non-reductionists argue that one having understanding-why could in addition answer a kind of "vertical" follow-up why question (see [19]) or a "what-if-things-had-been-different" question (see [12]). We will present both notions in

---

[2] For example, see [3] and the bibliographies therein.

Sect. 2.1. Since providing an explanation amounts to answering a why-question, these philosophical insights inspire us to introduce more (sorts of) explanations into the notion of understanding why, so as to respond to asking for further information. We will combine the idea that understanding why φ requires answers to more questions with the apparatus in [33], and analyze understanding why φ as $\exists t_1 \exists t_2(\mathsf{K}(t_2 : (t_1 : \varphi)))$, where t_1 is an answer to "Why φ?" and t_2 is an answer to the vertical follow-up question "Why t_1 is the answer to 'Why φ?'?", or to the question "What if things in t_1 had been different?".[3]

The paper is organized as follows. Section 2 looks at the philosophical discussions and logical work relevant to our topic in a little more details. Section 3 provides a logical framework for making such analysis of understanding why precise. As we will see, the framework is flexible enough to analyze different assumptions of different philosophical points, by addition with different conditions to the models. Section 4 gives an axiomatization of the general version of understanding why. We conclude in Sect. 5 with discussions on the potentially future work.

2 Preliminary

2.1 Philosophical Views

Before going any further, let us first illustrate the philosophical ideas relevant to the topic. According to the authors of [18,22,28] and [29] etc., views on the nature of understanding why fall into two broad camps: reductionists and non-reductionists, in which the former hold that: one understands why φ iff one knows why φ. Knowing why φ is analyzed as knowledge of causes of φ, or more generally, knowledge of dependencies (cf. [11,13]). By contrast, non-reductionists mainly argue that knowing why is not sufficient for understanding why, and their view can be illustrated with Pritchard's case of the house fire above.

In response to the house-fire-like cases, on one side, Grimm [13] holds that they contain an inadequate idea of what it means to have knowledge of causes. Knowing why amounts to having a sufficient conception of how cause and effect might be related, which is called "modal relationship" in [13], rather than just assenting to the proposition that describe this relationship. The notion of knowing why such understood is a kind of (limited) understanding why.

On the other side, Pritchard [24] famously proposes that while knowing-why requires identifying the cause, understanding-why requires having a sound explanatory story regarding how cause and effect are related, which is a kind of

---

[3] As mentioned by an anonymous review, both the knowing why logic by [33] and the understanding why logic introduced in this paper could be seen as a sub-logic of some kind of justification logic with existential quantifiers and knowledge operators. Some work corresponding to the full logic have been formalized in the literature. For example, the authors of [6] propose an axiomatization of a justification logic with operators $\exists r\varphi$, $B\varphi$, and $r : \varphi$ to capture the notion of reason-based belief.

cognitive achievement.[4] When trying to clarify the "sound explanatory story" proposed by Prichard, Lawer [19] borrows the idea from [27]: whenever you answer a why-question, you create an opportunity for your questioner to immediately ask "why?" about your answer. Recall the experiences with children. There are two importantly different ways to ask "why?" about the answer to a why-question:

1. "horizontal" follow-up why-question: someone says "φ because r" and you ask "why is it the case that r?" Traces this chain of reasons "backward".
2. "vertical" follow-up why-question: we step outside the chain of reasons, and ask what the facts in the chain have done to belong in the chain. We are asking, not which facts are reasons, but why those facts are reasons.

Generally speaking, while the "horizontal" follow-up why-questions seek for lower-level explanations, the "vertical" follow-up why-questions seek higher-order explanations, that is, the explanations why those explanations are explanations. Take the following event (borrowed from [27]). Suzy throws a rock at a window but Billy sticks his mitt out, thereby catching the rock before it hits. Why didn't the window break? Because Billy stuck his mitt out. It is a lower-level explanation. And why is Billy's act the reason why the window didn't break? Because Suzy threw the rock, which is a higher-order explanation. Lawler [19] suggests that the essence of a sound explanatory story regarding how cause and effect are related is an answer to the "vertical" follow-up why-question.

Besides, Hills [14] suggests that the distinction between knowing why and understanding why lies in "grasping" an explanation, which means answering questions of "What if ...?" sort, like "what-if-things-had-been-different" proposed by Woodward [32].

Although these philosophical views are varied, we can find a common thread: understanding why requires at least two explanations of different levels. Bermúdez [4] acknowledges a distinction between *horizontal explanation* and *vertical explanation*, which could be made use of to refer to these different levels. Think of horizontal explanation as the explanation required in ordinary knowing-why, vertical explanations can broadly be characterized as explaining the grounds of horizontal explanations, which is able to accommodate "modal relationship" in the knowledge of causes and answers to vertical follow-up why questions and "what if" questions.

Vertical explanations are not automatically horizontal explanations, i.e. the following conditional is false: necessarily, if s is a vertical explanation of t explains φ, then s is a horizontal explanation of φ. It is obvious due to the above throwing rock example. They are indeed two different levels.

One may wonder why stop at two levels of explanations in accounting for the notion of understanding. We shall not give an extended argument here except to mention two points. First, as stated in [5], the term "understanding" is commonly

---

[4] Note that the notions of knowing why and understanding why in Pritchard's work are particularly to do with causal matters. The paper [19], to be mentioned later, also follows this restriction for simplicity.

used in a seeming binary way: one understands why or one doesn't understand why, even though understanding is a matter of degree. Therefore some threshold is required in the account. Second, understanding why is investigated by studying what sets it apart from knowing-why, and based on the findings from philosophical viewpoints, the distinguishing feature is: whereas understanding why additionally requires a vertical explanation, knowing why does not. Hence two levels suffice, just as only one level of explanation is considered in lots of work about knowing why other than knowing that.

2.2   A Logic of Knowing Why and Fitting Model

For lack of space, we only look at the logic recently introduced in [33], which takes the notion of explanation seriously in the formal work, and thus inspires our techniques. Initially, the analysis of "knowing why φ" is $\exists t K_i(t : \varphi)$. Xu et al. in [33] pack the quantifier and modality together, and introduce a new operator $Ky_i\varphi$ to denote $\exists t K_i(t : \varphi)$ into the language of standard multi-agent epistemic logic.

The semantics is defined in a classical epistemic model with some apparatus similar to Fitting model of justification logic. A knowing why model $\mathfrak{M}$ is defined as a tuple $(W, E, \{R_i \mid i \in I\}, \mathcal{E}, V)$ where $(W, \{R_i \mid i \in I\}, V)$ is an epistemic model, E is a non-empty set of explanations, and $\mathcal{E}$ is an admissible explanation function specifying the set of worlds where $t \in E$ is an explanation of φ.

The truth conditions for the classical operators from epistemic logic are routine, and with: $Ky_i\varphi$ holds at $\mathfrak{M}, w$ iff (1) there exists $t \in E$ such that for all v with $wR_i v$, $v \in \mathcal{E}(t, \varphi)$; and (2) for all v with $wR_i v$, φ holds at v.

A Fitting model $\mathfrak{M}^J$ for justification logic is a tuple $(W^J, R^J, \mathcal{E}^J, V^J)$ based on a single-agent Kripke model (W^J, R^J, V^J), in which $\mathcal{E}^J$ is an evidence function assigning justification terms to formulas on each world. The evaluation of the format $t : \varphi$ follows that: $t : \varphi$ holds at a pointed model $\mathfrak{M}^J, w$ iff (1) $w \in \mathcal{E}^J(t, \varphi)$; and (2) for all v with $wR^J v$, φ holds at v.

As noted in [33], Fitting models typically have a monotonicity condition, i.e. $w \in \mathcal{E}^J(t, \varphi)$ and $wR^J v$ imply $v \in \mathcal{E}^J(t, \varphi)$. When R^J is an equivalence relation, it follows that all indistinguishable worlds have the same justification for the same formula, that is, $w \in \mathcal{E}^J(t, \varphi)$ iff $v \in \mathcal{E}^J(t, \varphi)$ whenever $wR^J v$. Compared with knowing why models, Fitting models only store known explanations (justifications) but all other possible explanations (justifications) are dropped. Therefore Fitting models cannot tell the difference between $\exists t K(t : \varphi)$ and $K \exists t(t : \varphi)$, which is thought of by the authors as essential for the analysis of knowing why. Justification formula $t : \varphi$ accommodates a strict "justificationist" reading in which it means t is accepted by the agent as a justification of φ. However, in [33] the format $t : \varphi$ actually is assigned an externalist and nonjustificationist reading, which could be used to formalize understanding.

Given the vertical explanation idea above, one may be tempted to consider that the semantics for understanding why φ as $\mathsf{KyKy}\varphi$. Unfortunately it is infelicitous. $\mathsf{KyKy}\varphi$ states that some explanation (say t_2) is known as an explanation of that some explanation (say t_1) is known as an explanation of φ, which is indeed a matter of introspection of one's knowing why. As a simple example from [33], the window is broken since someone threw a rock at it, and an agent knows that because she saw it, or someone told her about it. This kind of explanations is certainly not what we have in mind of the vertical explanations, and cannot be accepted as an answer to what-if questions as well. Thus we are ready to build a new logical framework.

3 A Framework for Understanding Why

In this section we introduce formally the language and the semantics. We will be interested in the issue of what it means to ascribe understanding to individual agents, so for the time being we set multi-agent aside for simplicity.

Definition 1 (Epistemic language of understanding-why). *Fix nonempty set P of propositional letters, the language* **ELUy** *is defined as (where $p \in P$):*

$$\varphi ::= p \mid \neg\varphi \mid (\varphi \wedge \varphi) \mid \mathsf{K}\varphi \mid \mathsf{Ky}\varphi \mid \mathsf{Uy}\varphi$$

The explication of understanding why is intended to be done by studying its relations with the notion of knowing why, so a new "packed" modality Uy for understanding why is introduced into the language in [33]. Besides, K is included because we intend to connect the notion of explanation with justification in our logic. That is to say, the explanation packed in $\mathsf{KyK}\varphi$ is considered as a justification for $\mathsf{K}\varphi$.

We accept the view in [33] that although something is a tautology, you may not know why it is a tautology. A special set of "self-evident" tautologies Λ is introduced, which the agent is assumed to know why. For example, we can let all the instances of $\varphi \wedge \psi \rightarrow \varphi$ and $\varphi \wedge \psi \rightarrow \psi$ be Λ. At present, we do not suppose any necessitation rule for Uy.

Definition 2. *An* **ELUy** *model $\mathcal{M}$ is a tuple $(W, E, R, \mathcal{E}, V)$ where:*

- *W is a non-empty set of possible worlds.*
- *E is a non-empty set of explanations equipped with operators $\cdot$, $!$ and c such that:*
  1. *If $t, s \in E$, then $t \cdot s \in E$,*
  2. *If $t \in E$, then $!t \in E$,*
  3. *A special symbol c is in E.*
- *$R \subseteq W \times W$ is an equivalence relation over W.*
- *$\mathcal{E} : E \times (\textbf{ELUy} \cup \langle E \times \textbf{ELUy}\rangle) \rightarrow 2^W$ is an admissible explanation function satisfying the following conditions:*
  1. *Horizontal Application: $\mathcal{E}(t, \varphi \rightarrow \psi) \cap \mathcal{E}(s, \varphi) \subseteq \mathcal{E}(t \cdot s, \psi)$,*
  2. *Constant Specification: If $\varphi \in \Lambda$, then $\mathcal{E}(c, \varphi) = W$,*

3. *Vertical Application:*
    $\mathcal{E}(t_2, \langle t_1, \varphi \to \psi \rangle) \cap \mathcal{E}(s_2, \langle s_1, \varphi \rangle) \subseteq \mathcal{E}(t_2 \cdot s_2, \langle t_1 \cdot s_1, \psi \rangle)$,
4. *Vertical Explanation Factivity:* $\mathcal{E}(t_2, \langle t_1, \varphi \rangle) \subseteq \mathcal{E}(t_1, \varphi)$.
5. *Epistemic Introspection:* $\mathcal{E}(t, \bigcirc\varphi) \subseteq \mathcal{E}(!t, \langle t, \bigcirc\varphi \rangle)$ *for* $\bigcirc = \mathsf{K}, \mathsf{Ky}, \mathsf{Uy}$.
- $V : P \to 2^W$ *is a valuation function.*

Operators $\cdot$, ! and c are read as in justification logic. The set E is closed under the application operator $\cdot$, which combines two explanations into one, and the (positive) introspection operator !. The operator $\cdot$ is not assumed to be commutative or associative, as in standard justification logic in [1]. Moreover, the special element c in E is the self-evident explanation for all formulas in the designated set Λ. The basic sum operator $+$ in justification logic is excluded since otherwise it will meet the following condition $\mathcal{E}(t, \varphi) \cup \mathcal{E}(s, \varphi) \subseteq \mathcal{E}(t + s, \varphi)$, and in situations different worlds have different explanations $(t_1, \ldots, t_n$ respectively) for the same formula φ, $\mathsf{Ky}\varphi$ will possibly hold by virtue of a uniform explanation $t_1 + \ldots + t_n$.

The admissible explanation function $\mathcal{E}$ specifies the set of worlds for both horizontal explanations $(\mathcal{E}(t, \varphi))$ and vertical explanations $(\mathcal{E}(t_2, \langle t_1, \psi \rangle))$. If $w \in \mathcal{E}(t, \varphi)$ then t is a (horizontal) explanation for φ in the world w, and if $v \in \mathcal{E}(t_2, \langle t_1, \psi \rangle)$ then v is a world where t_2 is a vertical explanation for that t_1 is an explanation of ψ. Function $\mathcal{E}$ satisfies several conditions, to which we come in a minute. Again, we have chosen to stop at two levels of explanations in $\mathcal{E}$, which is well motivated from a philosophical viewpoint. More levels than two can certainly be explored technically for finding whether there are interesting results, and we leave it to a future occasion.

Returning to the definition of $\mathcal{E}$ in $\mathcal{M}$. The first two conditions are for horizontal explanations as in the knowing-why case, of which the *horizontal application* condition says that two (horizontal) explanations separately for different claims can be combined to produce a more complex explanation for something else that needs both to explain. Extra conditions for the binary operator "$\cdot$", such as associative, commutative and idempotent might be of much interest, which is left for future work.[5] The special operator c in E is the uniform explanation for all the self-evident tautologies in Λ.

The third is for vertical application. Given $w \in W$, if $w \in \mathcal{E}(t_2, \langle t_1, \varphi \to \psi \rangle) \cap \mathcal{E}(s_2, \langle s_1, \varphi \rangle)$, then $w \in \mathcal{E}(t_1 \cdot s_1, \psi)$ holds with the help of the *horizontal explanation* condition and the *vertical explanation factivity* condition to be elucidated later. Meanwhile $t_2 \cdot s_2$ can be relevant vertical explanation with respect to "$t_1 \cdot s_1$ explaining ψ at w". For example, r is a proof (explanation) for the mathematical proposition p. Intuitively, the vertical explanation of "r explains/proves p" involves spelling out details that are left implicit in the proof, and indicating where in the proof certain of the theorem's hypotheses are needed, or, perhaps, providing counterexamples that show what goes wrong when various hypotheses are omitted, and so forth (see [2] for more details). While t_2 could explain why the step φ to ψ are natural or to be expected in $t_1 \cdot s_1$ explaining ψ, s_2 could

---

[5] In actual fact it is a question in justification logics for justification application as well, as remarked in [8].

explain why the hypothesis φ is indispensable. Thus $t_2 \cdot s_2$ should be classified as vertical explanation. Obviously understanding comes in degrees, and since the fundamental idea for the threshold of understanding why is that both horizontal and vertical explanations are required, this condition amounts to the later axiom $\mathsf{Uy}(\varphi \to \psi) \to (\mathsf{Uy}\varphi \to \mathsf{Uy}\psi)$.

The fourth condition says vertical explanations yield horizontal explanations, that is, $w \in \mathcal{E}(t_2, \langle t_1, \varphi \rangle)$ implies w is a world where t_1 explains φ. We do not specify any more conditions on the case that $w \in \mathcal{E}(t_2, \langle t_1, \varphi \rangle)$ solely holds. That is why we call it *a general framework*. Further conditions corresponding to philosophical views discussed in Sect. 2.1 will be referred to later.

This is the reason the *epistemic introspection* condition of $\mathcal{E}$ is introduced. As mentioned before, $\mathsf{KyK}\varphi$ corresponds to a why-question: why one knows φ. Typically, the inquirer of this why-question does not expect the agent to give reasons for why she is not being Gettiered in her belief that φ; rather, she should simply provide her reasons for believing that φ, that is, her justification for φ (some relevant arguments could be found in [21]). That is to say, justification takes on the role as explanation in this sort of cases. If $w \in \mathcal{E}(t, \mathsf{K}\varphi)$ then w is also a world where t is a justification of φ. Hence there is a bridge between "t explains $\mathsf{K}\varphi$" in this work and "t is a justification for φ" in mainstream justification logics, in the sense that explanations can be justifications.

Justification logics on the market have the following logical principle:

$$t : \varphi \to !t : (t : \varphi).$$

Fitting argues in [8] that we are generally able to substantiate the reasons we have for our knowledge in everyday life, and indeed a purported piece of reason is of no value without some justification for its being reason. So this principle is required in justification logic, which says that $!t$ is always a justification for $t : \varphi$, or $!t$ is an introspective act confirming that $t : \varphi$. Then it immediate to obtain a parallel logical principle here: if $w \in \mathcal{E}(t, \mathsf{K}\varphi)$ then $w \in \mathcal{E}(!t, \langle t, \mathsf{K}\varphi \rangle)$, and without obstacle to include the two other epistemic modalities Ky and Uy for the same reason as that of Fitting.

It is interesting to note that the *epistemic introspection* condition will give rise to the following nontrivial axioms about understanding:

- $\mathsf{KyK}\varphi \to \mathsf{UyK}\varphi$
- $\mathsf{KyKy}\varphi \to \mathsf{UyKy}\varphi$
- $\mathsf{KyUy}\varphi \to \mathsf{UyUy}\varphi$

If there is an explanation t for epistemic claims, then there always exists an introspective vertical explanation $!t$ of t so as to bring about understanding why. Otherwise, t being an explanation for the non-epistemic claim φ, in which case t is not a justification, does not entail t can be transformed into a vertical explanation for that t explains φ.

Note that by the *vertical explanation factivity* and the *epistemic introspection* conditions, we will have:

- $\mathcal{E}(t, \bigcirc\varphi) = \mathcal{E}(!t, \langle t, \bigcirc\varphi \rangle)$ for $\bigcirc = \mathsf{K}, \mathsf{Ky}, \mathsf{Uy}$.

Below are the truth clauses, which we are already familiar with:

Definition 3.

$\mathcal{M}, w \vDash p$	$\Leftrightarrow w \in V(p)$
$\mathcal{M}, w \vDash \neg\varphi$	$\Leftrightarrow \mathcal{M}, w \nvDash \varphi$
$\mathcal{M}, w \vDash \varphi \wedge \psi$	$\Leftrightarrow \mathcal{M}, w \vDash \varphi$ and $\mathcal{M}, w \vDash \psi$
$\mathcal{M}, w \vDash \mathsf{K}\varphi$	$\Leftrightarrow \mathcal{M}, v \vDash \varphi$ for all v such that wRv
$\mathcal{M}, w \vDash \mathsf{Ky}\varphi \Leftrightarrow$	*(1) there exists $t \in E$ such that for all $v \in W$ with $wRv, v \in \mathcal{E}(t, \varphi)$* *(2) for all $v \in W$ with wRv, $\mathcal{M}, v \vDash \varphi$*
$\mathcal{M}, w \vDash \mathsf{Uy}\varphi \Leftrightarrow$	*(1) there exist $t_1, t_2 \in E$ such that for all $v \in W$ with wRv, $v \in \mathcal{E}(t_2, \langle t_1, \varphi \rangle)$;* *(2) for all $v \in W$ with wRv, $\mathcal{M}, v \vDash \varphi$*

While the formula $\mathsf{Ky}\varphi$ is roughly $\exists t \mathsf{K}(t : \varphi) \wedge \mathsf{K}\varphi$, the structure of our $\mathsf{Uy}\varphi$ could be displayed as $\exists t_1 \exists t_2 \mathsf{K}(t_2 : (t_1 : \varphi)) \wedge \mathsf{K}\varphi$. It is natural to consider the underlying structure $\exists t_1 \mathsf{K} \exists t_2(t_2 : (t_1 : \varphi)) \wedge \mathsf{K}\varphi$ in the current models. Relevant discussions will come shortly, and we will see that it expresses another non-trivial notion of knowing why.

We have got the *vertical explanation factivity* condition in the models. Now we show that the *horizontal explanation factivity* defined in the following is not assumed.

Definition 4. *An* **ELUy** *model* $\mathcal{M}$ *has the property of horizontal explanation factivity, if whenever* $w \in \mathcal{E}(t, \varphi)$*, then* $\mathcal{M}, w \vDash \varphi$*.*

Given an **ELUy** model $\mathcal{M} = (W, E, R, \mathcal{E}, V)$, its horizontal factive companion $\mathcal{M}^F = (W, E, R, \mathcal{E}^F, V)$ can be constructed, where

$$\begin{cases} \mathcal{E}^F(t, \varphi) = \mathcal{E}(t, \varphi) - \{w \mid \mathcal{M}, w \nvDash \varphi\} \\ \mathcal{E}^F(t_2, \langle t_1, \varphi \rangle) = \mathcal{E}(t_2, \langle t_1, \varphi \rangle) - \{w \mid \mathcal{M}, w \nvDash \varphi\} \end{cases}$$

It is easy to check that the $\mathcal{M}^F$ constructed is indeed an **ELUy** model. Obviously, $\mathcal{M}$ and $\mathcal{M}^F$ coincide for each horizontal factive model $\mathcal{M}$. The proposition below asserts that the **ELUy**-formulas are neutral in respect to the horizontal facitvity.

Proposition 1. *For any* **ELUy** *formula* φ *and any* $w \in W$*,* $\mathcal{M}, w \vDash \varphi$ *iff* $\mathcal{M}^F, w \vDash \varphi$*.*

Proof. We do induction on the structure of the **ELUy**-formula. Boolean cases and the case of $\mathsf{K}\varphi$ are trivial.

– For $\mathsf{Ky}\varphi$,
  • $\Longrightarrow$ Suppose $\mathcal{M}, w \vDash \mathsf{Ky}\varphi$, then there is a $t \in E$ such that for all v with wRv, we have $\mathcal{M}, v \vDash \varphi$ and $v \in \mathcal{E}(t, \varphi)$. The by definition we have $v \in \mathcal{E}^F(t, \varphi)$. Hence by IH we conclude $\mathcal{M}^F, w \vDash \mathsf{Ky}\varphi$.
  • $\Longleftarrow$ The proof is similar as above.

– For the case of $\mathsf{U}y\varphi$,
- $\Longleftarrow$ Suppose $\mathcal{M}^F, w \vDash \mathsf{U}y\varphi$, then there exist $t_1, t_2 \in E$ such that for all v with wRv, we have $\mathcal{M}^F, v \vDash \varphi$ and $v \in \mathcal{E}^F(t_2, \langle t_1, \varphi \rangle)$. The by definition we get $v \in \mathcal{E}(t_2, \langle t_1, \varphi \rangle)$. Therefore by IH $\mathcal{M}, w \vDash \mathsf{U}y\varphi$.
- $\Longrightarrow$ Similarly.

Based on this general framework, many shades of assumptions mentioned in Sect. 2.1 could be reflected in distinct conditions for $\mathcal{E}$ in some sense:

Grimm's Limited Understanding: If $w \in \mathcal{E}(t_1, \varphi)$, then there exists a $t_2 \in E$ such that $w \in \mathcal{E}(t_2, \langle t_1, \varphi \rangle)$.

In accord with Grimm [13], if, in Pritchard's case, we credit the child with knowing-why, then she truly has some conception of "the why". Thus properly understood knowing why (adequate knowing why) or limited understanding why in fact equals to $\exists t_1 \mathsf{K} \exists t_2 (t_2 : (t_1 : \varphi)) \wedge \mathsf{K}\varphi$.

Note that the distinction between adequate and inadequate knowing why in [13], which are also termed shallow and non-shallow knowing why by Lawer [19], cannot be clarified in the logic of [33]. It is clear the notion of knowing why has been enriched under the present framework incidentally. So we might introduce a new adequate knowing why modality Ky^A that equals to $\exists t_1 \mathsf{K} \exists t_2 (t_2 : (t_1 : \varphi)) \wedge \mathsf{K}\varphi$ into the language, and clearly in Grimm's context, see that $\mathsf{Ky}\varphi$ is identified with $\mathsf{Ky}^A\varphi$. Grimm suggests that the epistemic state Ky^A is indeed a kind of (limited) understanding state.

Answering Vertical Follow Up Question: $\mathcal{E}(t_2, \langle t_1, \varphi \rangle) \subseteq \mathcal{E}(t_1, \varphi) \cap \mathcal{E}(t_2, \mathsf{Ky}\varphi)$.

We might think an explanation for why φ could also constitute a propositional justification for why φ is known. Literature on epistemology beginning with [7] makes a distinction between propositional and doxastic justification.[6] The most obvious difference between these two notions is that propositional justification does not require belief: one can have propositional justification without actually believing it. Hence we could assume $\mathsf{KyKy}\varphi$ does not only say that the agent knows why she "knows" why φ, but also she knows why she knows "why" φ, that is, she can seek a convincing propositional justification for her knowing why, so as to answer a relevant vertical why-question. This condition for $\mathcal{E}$ will give rise to a valid formula $\mathsf{U}y\varphi \to \mathsf{Ky}\varphi \wedge \mathsf{KyKy}\varphi$ under these **ELUy** models containing it.

Answering What If Question: If $w \in \mathcal{E}(t_2, \langle t_1, \varphi \rangle)$, then $w \in \mathcal{E}(t_1, \varphi)$ and $v \in \mathcal{E}(t_2, \neg\varphi)$ whenever $v \nvDash \varphi$.

An example from [17] is adapted: a firm hires Jones (φ) because he had extensive prior experience (t_1). Moreover, his other credentials were fairly non-descript such that he would not have been hired had he lacked this experience

---

[6] For more details about these two notions the reader is referred to [26] and the bibliographies therein.

(t_2). Agent a knowing that Jones is hired because of his superior experience knows why Jones is hired ($Ky_a\varphi$). Agent b understanding why knows in addition that if other hiring criteria (e.g. education) had been the deciding factor, Jones would not have been hired ($Uy_b\varphi$). That is to say, agent b has horizontal explanation t_2 of $\neg\varphi$ in a different world v, where the hiring criteria are different.

4   An Axiomatization

More conditions on $\mathcal{E}$ may invoke more debates. In this section we provide a sound and complete axiomatization for the most general case.

System SUY

(TAUT) Classical Propositional Axioms
(K) $K(\varphi \to \psi) \to (K\varphi \to K\psi)$
(T) $K\varphi \to \varphi$
(4) $K\varphi \to KK\varphi$
(5) $\neg K\varphi \to K\neg K\varphi$
(KYK) $Ky(\varphi \to \psi) \to (Ky\varphi \to Ky\psi)$
(IMP) $Ky\varphi \to K\varphi$
(UYK) $Uy(\varphi \to \psi) \to (Uy\varphi \to Uy\psi)$
(UK) $Uy\varphi \to Ky\varphi$
(4*) $\bigcirc\varphi \to K\bigcirc\varphi$ \qquad for $\bigcirc = Ky, Uy$
(KYU) $Ky\bigcirc\varphi \to Uy\bigcirc\varphi$ \qquad for $\bigcirc = K, Ky, Uy$

Rules
(MP) Modus Ponens
(N) $\vdash \varphi \Rightarrow \vdash K\varphi$
(NE) If $\varphi \in \Lambda$, then $\vdash Ky\varphi$

It is worth noting that the axiom (KYU) expresses that "understanding why" is necessary for "knowing why" in epistemic situations, which corresponds to *epistemic introspection* condition in the model. $KyUy\varphi \to UyUy\varphi$, as an instantiation of (KYU), suggests that the introspection of Uy (i.e. $Uy\varphi \to UyUy\varphi$) will be obtained once we accept $Uy\varphi \to KyUy\varphi$ as a reasonable new axiom. However both are not valid without further conditions on **ELUy** models.

Theorem 1. SUY *is sound over* **ELUy** *models.*

Proof. We omit the cases of standard axioms and rules, as well most other cases without special tricks.

KYU: For each **ELUy** model $\mathcal{M}$, suppose $\mathcal{M}, w \vDash Ky\bigcirc\varphi$ where $\bigcirc$ can be K, Ky, or Uy. Then there is a $t \in E$ such that for all v with wRv, we have $\mathcal{M}, v \vDash \bigcirc\varphi$ and $v \in \mathcal{E}(t, \bigcirc\varphi)$. By the *epistemic introspection* condition of $\mathcal{E}$, we get $v \in \mathcal{E}(!t, \langle t, \bigcirc\varphi\rangle)$, which means that we have $t, !t \in E$ such that for all v with wRv, $\mathcal{M}, v \vDash \varphi$ and $v \in \mathcal{E}(!t, \langle t, \varphi\rangle)$ hold. Therefore $\mathcal{M}, w \vDash Uy\bigcirc\varphi$. $\square$

Let Ω denote the set of all maximal SUY-consistent sets of formulas.

Definition 5 (Canonical Model). *The canonical model* $\mathcal{M}^c$ *for* SUY *is a tuple* $(W^c, E^c, \mathcal{F}^c, R^c, \mathcal{E}^c, V^c)$ *where:*

- E^c *is defined in BNF:* $t ::= c \mid \varphi \mid (t \cdot t) \mid !t$ *where* $\varphi \in \mathbf{ELUy}$.
- $W^c := \{\langle \Gamma, F, G, f, g, h \rangle \mid \langle \Gamma, F, G \rangle \in \Omega \times \mathcal{P}(E^c \times \mathbf{ELUy}) \times \mathcal{P}(E^c \times (E^c \times \mathbf{ELUy})), f : \{\varphi \mid \mathsf{Ky}\varphi \in \Gamma\} \to E^c, g : \{\varphi \mid \mathsf{Uy}\varphi \in \Gamma\} \to E^c, h : \{\varphi \mid \mathsf{Uy}\varphi \in \Gamma\} \to E^c$ *such that* f *and* g *satisfy the following conditions*}
  1. *If* $\langle t, \varphi \to \psi \rangle, \langle s, \varphi \rangle \in F$, *then* $\langle t \cdot s, \psi \rangle \in F$.
  2. *If* $\varphi \in \Lambda$, *then* $\langle c, \varphi \rangle \in F$.
  3. *If* $\langle t_2, \langle t_1, \varphi \to \psi \rangle \rangle, \langle s_2, \langle s_1, \varphi \rangle \rangle \in G$ *then* $\langle t_2 \cdot s_2, \langle t_1 \cdot s_1, \psi \rangle \rangle \in G$.
  4. $\langle t_2, \langle t_1, \varphi \rangle \rangle \in G$ *implies* $\langle t_1, \varphi \rangle \in F$.
  5. $\langle t, \bigcirc\varphi \rangle \in F$ *implies* $\langle !t, \langle t, \bigcirc\varphi \rangle \rangle \in G$ *for* $\bigcirc = \mathsf{K}, \mathsf{Ky}, \mathsf{Uy}$.
  6. $\mathsf{Ky}\varphi \in \Gamma$ *implies* $\langle f(\varphi), \varphi \rangle \in F$.
  7. $\mathsf{Uy}\varphi \in \Gamma$ *implies* $\langle h(\varphi), \langle g(\varphi), \varphi \rangle \rangle \in G$.
- $\langle \Gamma, F, G, f, g, h \rangle R^c \langle \Delta, F', G', f', g', h' \rangle$ *iff* (1) $\{\varphi \mid \mathsf{K}\varphi \in \Gamma\} \subseteq \Delta$, *and* (2) $f = f', g = g', h = h'$.
- $\mathcal{E}^c : E^c \times (\mathbf{ELUy} \cup \langle E^c \times \mathbf{ELUy} \rangle) \to 2^{W^c}$ *is defined by*

$$\begin{cases} \mathcal{E}^c(t, \varphi) = \{\langle \Gamma, F, G, f, g, h \rangle \mid \langle t, \varphi \rangle \in F\} \\ \mathcal{E}^c(t_2, \langle t_1, \varphi \rangle) = \{\langle \Gamma, F, G, f, g, h \rangle \mid \langle t_2, \langle t_1, \varphi \rangle \rangle \in G\} \end{cases}$$

- $V^c(p) = \{\langle \Gamma, F, G, f, g, h \rangle \mid p \in \Gamma\}$.

In the construction, the definition of E^c and W^c are based on those in [33]. Since the nested explanations are needed here, we introduce $!t$ in E^c. For each world in W^c, it contains information about the horizontal and/or vertical explanations for all Ky and Uy formulas belonging to it.

More specifically, f is a witness function picking one horizontal t for each formula in $\{\varphi \mid \mathsf{Ky}\varphi \in \Gamma\}$, while g picking one horizontal t_1 for every $\varphi \in \{\varphi \mid \mathsf{Uy}\varphi \in \Gamma\}$. h is a witness function picking one vertical explanation t_2 for each pair $\varphi \in \{\varphi \mid \mathsf{Uy}\varphi \in \Gamma\}$. Note that the cases of $\mathsf{Ky}\varphi$ and $\mathsf{Uy}\varphi$ can have different horizontal explanations for φ, i.e. we can have $\langle f(\varphi), \varphi \rangle \in F$ & $\langle g(\varphi), \varphi \rangle \in F$ & $f(\varphi) \neq g(\varphi)$. The following shows that W^c is indeed nonempty.

Definition 6. *Given any* $\Gamma \in \Omega$, *construct* $F^\Gamma, G^\Gamma, f^\Gamma, g^\Gamma, h^\Gamma$ *as follows:*

- $F_0^\Gamma = \{\langle \varphi, \varphi \rangle \mid \mathsf{Ky}\varphi \in \Gamma\} \cup \{\langle c, \varphi \rangle \mid \varphi \in \Lambda\}$, $G_0^\Gamma = \{\langle \varphi \cdot \varphi, \langle !\varphi, \varphi \rangle \rangle \mid \mathsf{Uy}\varphi \in \Gamma\}$
- $F_{n+1}^\Gamma = F_n^\Gamma \cup \{\langle t \cdot s, \psi \rangle \mid \langle t, \varphi \to \psi \rangle, \langle s, \varphi \rangle \in F_n^\Gamma$ *for some* $\varphi\} \cup \{\langle t_1, \varphi \rangle \mid \langle t_2, \langle t_1, \varphi \rangle \rangle \in G_n^\Gamma\}$
- $G_{n+1}^\Gamma = G_n^\Gamma \cup \{\langle t_2 \cdot s_2, \langle t_1 \cdot s_1, \psi \rangle \rangle \mid \langle t_2, \langle t_1, \varphi \to \psi \rangle \rangle, \langle s_2, \langle s_1, \varphi \rangle \rangle \in G_n^\Gamma$ *for some* $\varphi\}$
  $\cup \{\langle !t, \langle t, \bigcirc\varphi \rangle \rangle \mid \langle t, \bigcirc\varphi \rangle \in F_n^\Gamma$ *for* $\bigcirc = \mathsf{K}, \mathsf{Ky}, \mathsf{Uy}\}$
- $F^\Gamma = \bigcup_{n \in \mathbb{N}} F_n^\Gamma$
- $G^\Gamma = \bigcup_{n \in \mathbb{N}} G_n^\Gamma$
- $f^\Gamma : \{\varphi \mid \mathsf{Ky}\varphi \in \Gamma\} \to E^c, f^\Gamma(\varphi) = \varphi$.
- $g^\Gamma : \{\varphi \mid \mathsf{Uy}\varphi \in \Gamma\} \to E^c, g^\Gamma(\varphi) = !\varphi$.

$- h^\Gamma : \{\varphi \mid \mathsf{U}\mathsf{y}\varphi \in \Gamma\} \to E^c, h^\Gamma(\varphi) = \varphi \cdot \varphi.$

In the base case of G_0^Γ, we choose $\langle \varphi \cdot \varphi, \langle !\varphi, \varphi \rangle \rangle$ instead of, e.g., $\langle \varphi, \langle \varphi, \varphi \rangle \rangle$ for no technical reason. It is evident from the above account that $\mathsf{U}\mathsf{y}\varphi$ can have a different horizontal explanation for φ from that of $\mathsf{K}\mathsf{y}\varphi$, with a distinct vertical explanation.

Proposition 2. *For any* $\Gamma \in \Omega$, $\langle \Gamma, F^\Gamma, G^\Gamma, f^\Gamma, g^\Gamma, h^\Gamma \rangle \in W^c$.

Proof. We show that the conditions $1 - 7$ in the definition of W^c are all satisfied. Merely selected conditions are discussed below:

- For the condition 1, suppose $\langle t, \varphi \to \psi \rangle, \langle s, \varphi \rangle \in F^\Gamma$. Since $F_n^\Gamma \subseteq F_{n+1}^\Gamma$ for each n, then there exists $k \in \mathbb{N}$ such that both $\langle t, \varphi \to \psi \rangle$ and $\langle s, \varphi \rangle$ are in F_k^Γ. Thus we have $\langle t \cdot s, \psi \rangle \in F_{k+1}^\Gamma$, and so $\langle t \cdot s, \psi \rangle \in F^\Gamma$ by the construction of F^Γ.
- For the condition 3, suppose $\langle t_2, \langle t_1, \varphi \to \psi \rangle \rangle, \langle s_2, \langle s_1, \varphi \rangle \rangle \in G^\Gamma$. Then there exist $k, l \in \mathbb{N}$ such that $\langle t_2, \langle t_1, \varphi \to \psi \rangle \rangle \in G_k^\Gamma, \langle s_2, \langle s_1, \varphi \rangle \rangle \in G_l^\Gamma$. Assume without loss of generality that $k > l$. Then we get $\langle t_2 \cdot s_2, \langle t_1 \cdot s_1, \psi \rangle \rangle \in G_{k+1}^\Gamma$ by the construction. Therefore $\langle t_2 \cdot s_2, \langle t_1 \cdot s_1, \psi \rangle \rangle \in G^\Gamma$.
- For the condition 5, suppose $\langle t, \bigcirc \varphi \rangle \in F^\Gamma$. Then we have $\langle t, \bigcirc \varphi \rangle \in F_k^\Gamma$ for some k, which implies $\langle !t, \langle t, \bigcirc \varphi \rangle \rangle \in G_{k+1}^\Gamma$ by the construction of G^Γ.
- For the condition 6, suppose $\mathsf{K}\mathsf{y}\varphi \in \Gamma$. Then $\langle \varphi, \varphi \rangle \in F^\Gamma$ holds following the constructions of F_0^Γ and F^Γ, which implies $\langle f^\Gamma(\varphi), \varphi \rangle \in F^\Gamma$ by f^Γ construction.
- For the condition 7, suppose $\mathsf{U}\mathsf{y}\varphi \in \Gamma$. Then we get $\langle \varphi \cdot \varphi, \langle !\varphi, \varphi \rangle \rangle \in G^\Gamma$ by the constructions of G_0^Γ and G^Γ. Moreover, we have $\langle h^\Gamma(\varphi), \langle g(\varphi), \varphi \rangle \rangle \in G^\Gamma$ by the constructions of g^Γ and h^Γ. □

For the construction of R^c in the canonical model in Definition 5, we claim:

Proposition 3. R^c *is an equivalence relation.*

Proof. It is trivial by the construction of R^c and axioms (T), (4) and (5). □

As for the construction of $\mathcal{E}^c$ in canonical models, we can check the following:

Proposition 4. $\mathcal{E}^c$ *satisfies all the conditions in* **ELUy** *model definition.*

Proof. We only check some of these cases:

Horizontal application: Suppose $\langle \Gamma, F, G, f, g, h \rangle \in \mathcal{E}^c(t, \varphi \to \psi) \cap \mathcal{E}^c(s, \varphi)$. By the construction of $\mathcal{E}^c$, we have both $\langle t, \varphi \to \psi \rangle$ and $\langle s, \varphi \rangle$ are in F. Then by condition 1 of W^c, we have $\langle t \cdot s, \psi \rangle \in F$, which means $\langle \Gamma, F, G, f, g, h \rangle \in \mathcal{E}^c(t \cdot s, \psi)$.

Constant specification: Suppose $\varphi \in \Lambda$. For every $\langle \Gamma, F, G, f, g, h \rangle \in W^c$, by condition 2 of W^c, we have $\langle c, \varphi \rangle \in F$, which means $\mathcal{E}^c(c, \varphi) = W^c$.

Vertical application: Suppose $\langle \Gamma, F, G, f, g, h \rangle \in \mathcal{E}^c(t_2, \langle t_1, \varphi \to \psi \rangle) \cap \mathcal{E}^c(s_2, \langle s_1, \varphi \rangle)$. By definition of $\mathcal{E}^c$, we have $\langle t_2, \langle t_1, \varphi \to \psi \rangle \rangle, \langle s_2, \langle s_1, \varphi \rangle \rangle \in G$. Then by condition 3 of W^c, we have $\langle t_2 \cdot s_2, \langle t_1 \cdot s_1, \psi \rangle \rangle \in G$, which means $\langle \Gamma, F, G, f, g, h \rangle \in \mathcal{E}^c(t_2 \cdot s_2, \langle t_1 \cdot s_1, \psi \rangle)$.

Vertical explanation factivity: Suppose $\langle \Gamma, F, G, f, g, h \rangle \in \mathcal{E}^c(t_2, \langle t_1, \varphi \rangle)$, which implies $\langle t_2, \langle t_1, \varphi \rangle \rangle \in G$. Then by condition 4, we have $\langle t_1, \varphi \rangle \in F$, which imply $\langle \Gamma, F, G, f, g, h \rangle \in \mathcal{E}^c(t_1, \varphi)$.

Epistemic introspection: It is clear by condition 5.   □

Hence the canonical model is well-defined, based on Proposition 2, 3 and 4.

Proposition 5. *The canonical model $\mathcal{M}^c$ is well-defined.*

Now we prove the existence lemmas for K, Ky and Uy respectively.

Lemma 1 (K Existence Lemma). *For any $\langle \Gamma, F, G, f, g, h \rangle \in W^c$, if $\widehat{\mathsf{K}}\varphi \in \Gamma$, then there exists a $\langle \Delta, F', G', f', g', h' \rangle \in W^c$ such that $\langle \Gamma, F, G, f, g, h \rangle R^c \langle \Delta, F', G', f', g', h' \rangle$, and $\varphi \in \Delta$.*

Proof. (Sketch) Suppose $\widehat{\mathsf{K}}\varphi \in \Gamma$. Let $\Delta^- = \{\psi \mid \mathsf{K}\psi \in \Gamma\} \cup \{\varphi\}$. First, Δ^- is consistent. The proof is routine by (K) and (N). Next we extend Δ^- into a MCS Δ. Finally, we construct F', G', f', g' and h' to form a world in W^c. We can simply let $F' = F, G' = G$, and $f' = f, g' = g, h' = h$.   □

In order to refute $\mathsf{Ky}\psi$ while keeping $\mathsf{K}\psi$ semantically, we could construct an accessible world where the horizontal explanation for ψ is not identical to that at the current world. In [33], all original horizontal explanations for ψ are replaced by something different in the construction. But we will simplify the demonstration by deleting all those explanations for ψ when construct a canonical world refuting $\mathsf{Ky}\psi$.

Lemma 2 (Ky Existence Lemma). *For any $\langle \Gamma, F, G, f, g, h \rangle \in W^c$ where $\mathsf{K}\psi \in \Gamma$, if $\mathsf{Ky}\psi \notin \Gamma$, then for any $\langle t, \psi \rangle \in F$, there exists a $\langle \Delta, F', G', f', g', h' \rangle \in W^c$ such that $\langle t, \psi \rangle \notin F'$ and $\langle \Gamma, F, G, f, g, h \rangle R^c \langle \Delta, F', G', f', g', h' \rangle$.*

Proof. Suppose $\mathsf{Ky}\psi \notin \Gamma$, we construct $\langle \Delta, F', G', f', g', h' \rangle$ as follows.

- $\Delta = \Gamma$
- $F' = \{\langle s, \varphi \rangle \mid \langle s, \varphi \rangle \in F \text{ and } \mathsf{Ky}\varphi \in \Gamma\}$
- $G' = \{\langle s', \langle s, \varphi \rangle \rangle \mid \langle s', \langle s, \varphi \rangle \rangle \in G \text{ and } \mathsf{Ky}\varphi \in \Gamma\}$
- $f' : \{\varphi \mid \mathsf{Ky}\varphi \in \Delta\} \to E^c$ is defined as: $f'(\varphi) = f(\varphi)$
- $g' : \{\varphi \mid \mathsf{Uy}\varphi \in \Delta\} \to E^c$ is defined as: $g'(\varphi) = g(\varphi)$
- $h' : \{\varphi \mid \mathsf{Uy}\varphi \in \Delta\} \to E^c$ is defined as: $h'(\varphi) = h(\varphi)$

Note that $F' \subseteq F, G' \subseteq G$. The main idea behind the constructions of F' and G' is to "carefully" delete all horizontal explanations for $\{\psi \mid \mathsf{Ky}\psi \notin \Gamma\}$. Clearly $\langle t, \psi \rangle \notin F'$ for any $\langle t, \psi \rangle \in F$ by the construction, given $\mathsf{Ky}\psi \notin \Gamma$. In order to complete this proof, firstly, we show that $\langle \Delta, F', G', f', g', h' \rangle \in W^c$ by checking the conditions 1–7 in the definition of W^c. Only four cases are written below:

- For the condition 1, suppose $\langle t, \varphi \rightarrow \psi \rangle, \langle s, \varphi \rangle \in F' \subseteq F$. Obviously $\langle t \cdot s, \psi \rangle \in F$. Moreover due to axiom (KYK) and the fact that $\mathsf{Ky}(\varphi \rightarrow \psi), \mathsf{Ky}\varphi \in \Gamma$, we have $\mathsf{Ky}\psi \in \Gamma$, hence $\langle t \cdot s, \psi \rangle \in F'$.
- For the condition 3, Suppose $\langle t_2, \langle t_1, \varphi \rightarrow \psi \rangle \rangle, \langle s_2, \langle s_1, \varphi \rangle \rangle \in G' \subseteq G$, then $\langle t_2 \cdot s_2, \langle t_1 \cdot s_1, \varphi \rangle \rangle \in G$. Moreover due to the axiom (KYK) and the fact that $\mathsf{Ky}(\varphi \rightarrow \psi), \mathsf{Ky}\varphi \in \Gamma$, we have $\mathsf{Ky}\psi \in \Gamma$. Hence $\langle t_2 \cdot s_2, \langle t_1 \cdot s_1, \psi \rangle \rangle \in G'$.
- For condition 5, suppose $\langle t, \bigcirc \varphi \rangle \in F' \subseteq F$. Then we get $\langle !t, \langle t, \bigcirc \varphi \rangle \rangle \in G$ and $\mathsf{Ky} \bigcirc \varphi \in \Gamma$, which implies $\langle !t, \langle t, \bigcirc \varphi \rangle \rangle \in G'$.
- For condition 7, suppose $\mathsf{Uy}\varphi \in \Delta$. Then we get $\mathsf{Uy}\varphi \in \Gamma$ by $\Gamma = \Delta$, thus $\langle h(\varphi), \langle g(\varphi), \varphi \rangle \rangle \in G$. By (UK) and the property of MCS, we have $\mathsf{Ky}\varphi \in \Delta$, so $\langle h'(\varphi), \langle g'(\varphi), \varphi \rangle \rangle = \langle h(\varphi), \langle g(\varphi), \varphi \rangle \rangle \in G'$.

Secondly, $\langle \Gamma, F, G, f, g, h \rangle R^c \langle \Delta, F', G', f', g', h' \rangle$ holds. We just need to check the following two conditions:

- Since $\Delta = \Gamma$, obviously we have $\{\varphi \mid \mathsf{K}\varphi \in \Gamma\} \subseteq \Delta$.
- Since $\Delta = \Gamma$, it is clear that $dom(f) = dom(f')$, and $dom(g) = dom(g')$. Then for any $\varphi \in \{\varphi \mid \mathsf{Ky}\varphi \in \Delta\}$, by definition of f', we have $f(\varphi) = f'(\varphi)$. Similarly, for any $\varphi \in \{\varphi \mid \mathsf{Uy}\varphi \in \Delta\}$, we have $dom(h) = dom(h')$. Then by definition of h', we have $h'(\varphi) = h(\varphi)$. Hence $f = f'$, $g = g'$ and $h = h'$. □

Similarly, to refute $\mathsf{Uy}\chi$ while keeping $\mathsf{Ky}\chi$, we construct an accessible world where the vertical explanation for χ is not identical to that at the current world.

Lemma 3 (Uy Existence Lemma). *For any $\langle \Gamma, F, G, f, g, h \rangle \in W^c$ where $\mathsf{Ky}\chi \in \Gamma$, if $\mathsf{Uy}\chi \notin \Gamma$, then for any $\langle s, \langle t, \chi \rangle \rangle \in G$, there exists a $\langle \Delta, F', G', f', g', h' \rangle \in W^c$ such that $\langle s, \langle t, \chi \rangle \rangle \notin G'$ and $\langle \Gamma, F, G, f, g, h \rangle R^c \langle \Delta, F', G', f', g', h' \rangle$.*

Proof. Suppose $\mathsf{Uy}\chi \notin \Gamma$, note that $\chi \neq \bigcirc \varphi$ for any φ since $\mathsf{Ky}\chi \in \Gamma$. We construct $\langle \Delta, F', G', f', g', h' \rangle$ by deleting all current vertical explanations for χ:

- $\Delta = \Gamma$
- $F' = \{\langle s, \varphi \rangle \mid \langle s, \varphi \rangle \in F \text{ and } \mathsf{Ky}\varphi \in \Gamma\}$
- $G' = \{\langle s', \langle s, \varphi \rangle \rangle \mid \langle s', \langle s, \varphi \rangle \rangle \in G \text{ and } \mathsf{Uy}\varphi \in \Gamma\}$
- $f' : \{\varphi \mid \mathsf{Ky}\varphi \in \Delta\} \rightarrow E^c$ is defined as: $f'(\varphi) = f(\varphi)$
- $g' : \{\varphi \mid \mathsf{Uy}\varphi \in \Delta\} \rightarrow E^c$ is defined as: $g'(\varphi) = g(\varphi)$
- $h' : \{\varphi \mid \mathsf{Uy}\varphi \in \Delta\} \rightarrow E^c$ is defined as: $h'(\varphi) = h(\varphi)$

Given $\mathsf{Uy}\chi \notin \Gamma$, we have $\langle s, \langle t, \chi \rangle \rangle \notin G'$ for each $\langle s, \langle t, \chi \rangle \rangle \in G$ by the construction clearly. In order to complete remaining proof, firstly, we show that $\langle \Delta, F', G', f', g', h' \rangle \in W^c$, i.e. this tuple satisfies the conditions $1 - 7$ in the definition of W^c. We omit some cases due to limited space:

- For the condition 3, suppose $\langle t_2, \langle t_1, \varphi \rightarrow \psi \rangle \rangle, \langle s_2, \langle s_1, \varphi \rangle \rangle \in G' \subseteq G$, then $\langle t_2 \cdot s_2, \langle t_1 \cdot s_1, \psi \rangle \rangle \in G$ and $\mathsf{Uy}(\varphi \rightarrow \psi), \mathsf{Uy}\varphi \in \Gamma$. We have $\mathsf{Uy}\psi \in \Gamma$ due to the axiom (UYK) and the property of MCS, hence $\langle t_2 \cdot s_2, \langle t_1 \cdot s_1, \psi \rangle \rangle \in G'$.
- For the condition 4, suppose $\langle t_2, \langle t_1, \varphi \rangle \rangle \in G' \subseteq G$. Then we have $\langle t_1, \varphi \rangle \in F$ and $\mathsf{Uy}\varphi \in \Gamma$. So $\mathsf{Ky}\varphi \in \Gamma$ by (UK), which means $\langle t_1, \varphi \rangle \in F'$.

- For condition 7, suppose $\mathsf{U}y\varphi \in \Delta$. Then we get $\mathsf{U}y\varphi \in \Gamma$ and $\langle h(\varphi), \langle g(\varphi), \varphi\rangle\rangle \in G$. Thus $\langle h'(\varphi), \langle g'(\varphi), \varphi\rangle\rangle = \langle h(\varphi), \langle g(\varphi), \varphi\rangle\rangle \in G'$.

Secondly, we can show $\langle \Gamma, F, G, f, g, h\rangle R^c \langle \Delta, F', G', f', g', h'\rangle$ as above.   □

Lemma 4 (Truth Lemma). *For all φ, $\langle \Gamma, F, G, f, g, h\rangle \vDash \varphi$ iff $\varphi \in \Gamma$.*

Proof. The proof is by induction on the structure of φ. The atomic case and boolean cases are routine. For the case of $\varphi = \mathsf{K}\psi$, it is clear by Lemma 1. For the case of $\varphi = \mathsf{K}y\psi$, the proof is not hard with the help of Lemma 1 and 2.

For the case of $\mathsf{U}y\psi$,

- $\Longleftarrow$: Suppose $\mathsf{U}y\psi \in \Gamma$. Then for any $\langle \Delta, F', G', f', g', h'\rangle$ such that $\langle \Gamma, F, G, f, g, h\rangle R^c \langle \Delta, F', G', f', g', h'\rangle$, we get $\mathsf{U}y\psi \in \Delta$, which implies $\psi \in \Delta$ by (4*), (UK), (IMP), (T), and the property of MCS. Thus $\langle \Delta, F', G', f', g', h'\rangle \vDash \psi$ by IH. Furthermore, we have $\langle \langle h(\psi), \langle g(\psi), \psi\rangle\rangle \in G$, $\langle \langle h'(\psi), \langle g'(\psi), \psi\rangle\rangle \in G'$ and $g = g', h = h'$, which means there exist $g(\psi) = g'(\psi) \in E^c$ and $h(\psi) = h'(\psi) \in E^c$, as well as $\langle \Delta, F', G', f', g', h'\rangle \in \mathcal{E}^c(h(\psi), \langle g(\psi), \psi\rangle)$. Hence $\langle \Gamma, F, G, f, g, h\rangle \vDash \mathsf{U}y\psi$.
- $\Longrightarrow$: Suppose $\mathsf{U}y\psi \notin \Gamma$. Then we have the following three cases:
  - $\mathsf{K}\psi \notin \Gamma$. By Lemma 1, we have $\langle \Gamma, F, G, f, g, h\rangle \nVdash \mathsf{K}\psi$, thus $\langle \Gamma, F, G, f, g, h\rangle \nVdash \mathsf{U}y\psi$.
  - $\mathsf{K}\psi \in \Gamma$ and $\mathsf{K}y\psi \notin \Gamma$. By Lemma 2, we have $\langle \Gamma, F, G, f, g, h\rangle \nVdash \mathsf{K}y\psi$, thus $\langle \Gamma, F, G, f, g, h\rangle \nVdash \mathsf{U}y\psi$.
  - $\mathsf{K}\psi \in \Gamma$, and $\mathsf{K}y\psi \in \Gamma$. If $\langle t_2, \langle t_1, \psi\rangle\rangle \notin G$ for any $t_1, t_2 \in E^c$, then by the semantics, $\langle \Gamma, F, G, f, g, h\rangle \nVdash \mathsf{U}y\psi$. If there exist t_1 and t_2 with $\langle t_2, \langle t_1, \psi\rangle\rangle \in G$, then we complete the proof by Lemma 3.   □

Theorem 2. *The system* SUY *is strongly complete over* **ELUy** *models.*

Proof. Given a SUY-consistent set Σ^-, it can be extended to a MCS $\Sigma \in \Omega$. Then there exist $F^\Sigma, G^\Sigma, f^\Sigma, g^\Sigma, h^\Sigma$ such that $\langle \Sigma, F^\Sigma, G^\Sigma, f^\Sigma, g^\Sigma, h^\Sigma\rangle \in W^c$ by Proposition 2. By the Truth Lemma 4, we have a canonical model $\mathcal{M}^c$ satisfying Σ and hence Σ^-.   □

5   Conclusions and Future Work

Understanding why is considered requiring more than knowing why. But philosophers differ on the nature of this "more". Inspired by non-reductionists, we think of this "more" as providing more explanations to more questions. We build up a general framework by introducing vertical explanations, and show that it could accommodate different points on the nature of understanding why via adding different conditions in the models. Furthermore, the notion of knowing why seems to have interesting different variants, which can also be captured in the present framework. We study understanding why on the base of knowing why, and the logical framework for understanding then, in turn, enriches the notion of knowing why. Only one axiomatization for models without these extra conditions is provided. Hence one of the future directions is to develop axiomatizations with more reasonable conditions on $\mathcal{E}$ in the models. Besides, understanding why can be studied on basis of knowing how as well. It should not be overlooked that philosophical literatures are glutted with expressions such as "understanding why requires *knowing how* cause and effect are related".

Acknowledgements. The author wishes to thank Fernando Velazquez Quesada, Sonja Smets and Yanjing Wang for their patient guidance and helpful suggestions on this project. The research was also supported by CSC, which made my visit to ILLC possible. I'm grateful to the anonymous reviewers for their careful work and thoughtful suggestions that have helped improve this paper substantially. Many thanks to Qiang Wang for her inspired comments and careful inspection. Last but not least, the support from Shanghai Pujiang Program (Grant No. 22PJC034) is acknowledged.

References

1. Artemov, S., Fitting, M.: Justification Logic: Reasoning with Reasons, vol. 216. Cambridge University Press, Cambridge (2019)
2. Avigad, J.: Understanding proofs. In: The Philosophy of Mathematical Practice, pp. 317–353 (2008)
3. Baumberger, C., Beisbart, C., Brun, G.: What is understanding? an overview of recent debates in epistemology and philosophy of science. In: Baumberger, S.G.C., Ammon, S. (eds.) Explaining Understanding: New Perspectives from Epistemolgy and Philosophy of Science, pp. 1–34. Routledge (2017)
4. Bermúdez, J.L.: Philosophy of Psychology: A Contemporary Introduction. Routledge, Abingdon (2004)
5. Dellsén, F.: Beyond explanation: understanding as dependency modeling (2018)
6. Égré, P., Marty, P., Renne, B.: Knowledge, justification, and adequate reasons. Rev. Symb. Logic **14**(3), 687–727 (2021)
7. Firth, R.: Are epistemic concepts reducible to ethical concepts? In: Values and Morals, pp. 215–229. Springer, Heidelberg (1978). https://doi.org/10.1007/978-94-015-7634-5_12
8. Fitting, M.: A logic of explicit knowledge. In: Logica Yearbook, pp. 11–22 (2004)
9. Gattinger, M., Wang, Y.: How to agree without understanding each other: public announcement logic with Boolean definitions. Electron. Proc. Theor. Comput. Sci. **297**, 206–220 (2019)
10. Gordon, E.C.: Is there propositional understanding? Logos Episteme **3**(2), 181–192 (2012)
11. Greco, J.: Episteme: knowledge and understanding. In: Virtues and their Vices, pp. 285–302 (2014)
12. Grimm, S.R.: Is understanding a species of knowledge? Br. J. Phil. Sci. **57**(3), 515–535 (2006)
13. Grimm, S.R.: Understanding as knowledge of causes. In: Fairweather, A. (ed.) Virtue Epistemology Naturalized. SL, vol. 366, pp. 329–345. Springer, Cham (2014). https://doi.org/10.1007/978-3-319-04672-3_19
14. Hills, A.: Understanding why. Noûs **49**(2), 661–688 (2015)
15. Hintikka, J.: New foundations for a theory of questions and answers. In: Questions and Answers, pp. 159–190. Springer, Heidelberg (1983). https://doi.org/10.1007/978-94-009-7016-8

16. Khalifa, K.: The role of explanation in understanding. Br. J. Phil. Sci. **64**(1), 161–187 (2013)
17. Khalifa, K.: Understanding, Explanation, and Scientific Knowledge. Cambridge University Press, Cambridge (2017)
18. Lawler, I.: Reductionism about understanding why. In: Proceedings of the Aristotelian Society, vol. 116, pp. 229–236. Oxford University Press (2016)
19. Lawler, I.: Understanding why, knowing why, and cognitive achievements. Synthese **196**(11), 4583–4603 (2019)
20. Lipton, P.: Understanding without explanation. In: Scientific Understanding: Philosophical Perspectives, pp. 43–63 (2009)
21. McKinnon, R.: How do you know that 'how do you know?' challenges a speaker's knowledge? Pac. Phil. Q. **93**(1), 65–83 (2012)
22. Palmira, M.: Defending nonreductionism about understanding. Thought J. Phil. **8**(3), 222–231 (2019)
23. Pritchard, D.: Knowing the answer, understanding and epistemic value. Grazer Philosophische Studien **77**(1), 325–339 (2008)
24. Pritchard, D.: Knowledge and understanding. In: Fairweather, A. (ed.) Virtue Epistemology Naturalized. SL, vol. 366, pp. 315–327. Springer, Cham (2014). https://doi.org/10.1007/978-3-319-04672-3_18
25. Ross, L.D.: Is understanding reducible? Inquiry **63**(2), 117–135 (2020)
26. Silva, P., Oliveira, L.R.G.: Propositional justification and doxastic justification. In: Lasonen-Aarnio, M., Littlejohn, C.M. (eds.) Routledge Handbook of the Philosophy Evidence. Routledge (2020)
27. Skow, B.: Reasons Why. Oxford University Press, Oxford (2016)
28. Sliwa, P.: Iv-understanding and knowing. In: Proceedings of the Aristotelian Society, vol. 115, pp. 57–74. Oxford University Press, Oxford (2015)
29. Sullivan, E.: Understanding: not know-how. Phil. Stud. **175**(1), 221–240 (2018)
30. Wang, Y.: Beyond knowing that: a new generation of epistemic logics. In: van Ditmarsch, H., Sandu, G. (eds.) Jaakko Hintikka on Knowledge and Game-Theoretical Semantics. OCL, vol. 12, pp. 499–533. Springer, Cham (2018). https://doi.org/10.1007/978-3-319-62864-6_21
31. Whiting, D.: Epistemic value and achievement. Ratio **25**(2), 216–230 (2012)
32. Woodward, J.: Making Things Happen: A Theory of Causal Explanation. Oxford University Press, Oxford (2005)
33. Xu, C., Wang, Y., Studer, T.: A logic of knowing why. Synthese **198**(2), 1259–1285 (2021)

Author Index

Printed in the United States
by Baker & Taylor Publisher Services

Printed in the United States
by Baker & Taylor Publisher Services